Unreal Engine 5 VFX Cookbook

Production-ready recipes for Niagara, Niagara Fluids, Chaos, and cinematic rendering

Hussin Khan

‹packt›

Unreal Engine 5 VFX Cookbook

Portfolio Director: Rohit Rajkumar
Relationship Lead: Neha Pande
Program Manager: Sandip Tadge
Content Engineer: Shreya Sarkar
Technical Editor: Irfa Ansari
Indexer: Hemangini Bari
Proofreader: Shreya Sarkar
Production Designer: Ganesh Bhadwalkar
Growth Lead: Namita Velgekar

First published: July 2026

Production reference: 1220726

Published by Packt Publishing Ltd.
Grosvenor House
11 St Paul's Square
Birmingham
B3 1RB, UK.

ISBN 978-1-83620-905-8
`www.packtpub.com`

I would like to dedicate this book to my wife, whose love, patience, and support continue to be my greatest source of strength, and to my beloved cats, Donny, Junior, Fifi, Dottie, and Precious, who have kept me company through many long writing days and nights.

– Hussin Khan

Foreword

What up, what up, Winbush here! When Hussin Khan reached out and asked if I would write the foreword for the *Unreal Engine 5 VFX Cookbook*, I didn't hesitate. Anyone who has spent time in real-time production knows how valuable clear, practical guidance can be, especially when it comes to building visual effects inside Unreal Engine.

I personally started working in Unreal Engine with version 4, and since then, I've seen it evolve far beyond its origins as a game engine. Today, it's a creative hub for filmmakers, motion designers, VFX artists, game developers, educators, and storytellers who want to craft high-quality visuals in real time. Whether you're creating smoke, fire, electricity, destruction, cloth simulations, or atmospheric cinematic moments, the real challenge isn't just finding the right button, but understanding how all the systems inside Unreal work together, which can sometimes be intimidating.

That's exactly why this book stands out. Hussin approaches VFX from the perspective of both an artist and an educator. The recipes in this book are built to be hands-on, visual, and production-ready. Instead of burying readers in theory, he walks you through effects you can actually build, iterate on, and reuse in your own Unreal Engine projects.

One thing I appreciate about a resource like this is the structure. There's no shortage of tutorials online, but having a curated collection of focused VFX recipes in one place that is tangible and offline is a huge advantage. It saves time, reduces confusion, and gives artists a clear path forward. More importantly, it encourages experimentation, which is where real growth happens.

If you're exploring Unreal Engine for cinematic VFX, real-time filmmaking, virtual production, or game visuals, this cookbook is a powerful companion. It gives you the foundation to start creating effects immediately, while also giving you the creative direction to push those effects further and make them your own.

I'm excited to see what artists build with it.

Jonathan Winbush

Multi-Award-Winning Motion Graphics Artist

Contributors

About the author

Hussin Khan is an Unreal Authorized Instructor (UAI) and real-time production educator with over a decade of experience in professional training. He previously served as the Head of Education at Rhythm & Hues, the Academy Award-winning visual effects studio behind *Life of Pi* (2012), and has contributed to productions such as *2036 Origin Unknown* (2018) and *RIFT* by HaZimation, an animated film created entirely in Unreal Engine.

Hussin leads EFXCO Academy in Malaysia, where he delivers professional training and certification programs in graphics and motion design, virtual production, virtual reality, visual effects, and real-time production workflows. He is also a certified instructor for Foundry Nuke and Unity.

Unreal Engine 5 VFX Cookbook is Hussin's second book with Packt. His first book, *Virtual Filmmaking with Unreal Engine 5,* is also available and focuses on using Unreal Engine for real-time cinematic storytelling and virtual filmmaking.

With a background that bridges education, visual effects, animation, and real-time technology, Hussin is passionate about helping artists, educators, and studios adopt Unreal Engine as part of modern media and entertainment pipelines.

I would like to extend my heartfelt thanks to my family for accepting that I needed to work long hours on this book, often during family time. I would also like to thank Neha Pande for giving me the opportunity to write this book, which has been a deeply enriching experience.

Special thanks to Shreya Sarkar, Sandip Tadge, Ts Nadhirah Ishak, Zaid Hakimi, and Abang Khadafi for their valuable input, support, and time during the writing of this book. I would also like to thank the entire EFXCO Academy and Packt team for their guidance and support throughout the process.

About the reviewer

Nadhirah Ishak is the Head of Training and an Instructor at EFXCO in Malaysia, where she leads technical training programs in creative technology. She was selected as one of the creators for the Epic Games Women Creators Program, focusing on Unreal Editor for Fortnite (UEFN) workflows. Her core technical expertise lies in Unreal Engine 3D environment design, cinematic pipelines, and creative design tools. She applies her hands-on experience in technical education and multimedia design to evaluate structured learning content, ensuring practical design and production-ready visual standards.

Table of Contents

Preface

Unreal Engine has changed how artists, filmmakers, designers, and studios create visual effects. What was once seen mainly as a game engine has become a powerful real-time production platform for film, animation, virtual production, motion design, broadcast, and game cinematics. Effects that once required long offline simulation and rendering times can now be created, adjusted, previewed, timed, and rendered inside the same real-time environment.

The *Unreal Engine 5 VFX Cookbook* is written for artists who want to create practical, art-directable visual effects for cinematic shots. The focus is not on covering every setting in Unreal Engine, but on building useful recipes that can be understood, controlled, adjusted, and reused. Throughout the book, you will create effects such as smoke, dust, rain, snow, lightning, electrical arcs, Niagara Fluids, fog, fire, explosions, Chaos destruction, and Chaos Cloth.

This book assumes that you already have some basic experience with Unreal Engine and Niagara. You should be comfortable navigating the editor, creating Levels, placing Actors, and working with simple Niagara systems. From there, the recipes guide you into more cinematic workflows, including **User Parameters**, **Sequencer** timing, **Niagara Life Cycle** tracks, **Movie Render Queue**, Niagara Fluids, Chaos caching, and cloth simulation.

A key idea throughout the book is that VFX should support the shot. Smoke should add atmosphere, dust should sell impact, lightning should hit at the right frame, rain and snow should shape the mood, and destruction should feel controlled rather than random. For cinematic work, the effect is not only about looking impressive; it must also be readable, timed properly, and useful to the story or visual moment.

You are encouraged to experiment with the recipes as you work through them. Adjust the colors, timing, density, velocity, camera angle, lighting, and scale. The values used in the book are *starting points,* not *fixed rules*. Many of the best results come from small adjustments made while looking through the final camera.

By the end of this book, you will have built a practical collection of Unreal Engine VFX recipes using Niagara, Niagara Fluids, Chaos Destruction, and Chaos Cloth. More importantly, you will understand how to create real-time effects that are controllable, reusable, and ready for cinematic production.

Who this book is for

This book is for intermediate cinematic VFX artists, technical artists, motion designers, real-time filmmakers, and Unreal Engine users who want to create practical, art-directable visual effects for cinematic shots. It is especially useful for virtual production, animation, game cinematics, and motion design teams that need Niagara effects to be timed in **Sequencer** and rendered reliably using **Movie Render Queue (MRQ)**.

Readers should already be comfortable with the Unreal Engine editor and have a basic understanding of Niagara. Rather than covering beginner fundamentals, this book focuses on hands-on, production-ready recipes for building smoke, dust, rain, snow, lightning, electrical effects, Niagara Fluids, Chaos destruction, and Chaos Cloth setups in Unreal Engine 5.6.

By following the recipes, artists will learn how to create, control, refine, art-direct, and render real-time VFX that can be used in cinematic shots, trailers, previs, virtual production, and animation workflows.

What this book covers

Chapter 1, Cinematic Niagara Workflow for Sequencer and Movie Render Queue, sets up a stable cinematic VFX workflow using Niagara, **Sequencer** timing, repeatable playback, and **Movie Render Queue**.

Chapter 2, Niagara Smoke Effects for Cinematics, covers soft smoke wisps, thick smoke plumes, impact smoke puffs, and ground fog for cinematic atmosphere.

Chapter 3, Niagara Dust and Debris Atmosphere for Cinematics, explores impact dust, footstep dust, dust trails, and dust motes to add weight, motion, and depth.

Chapter 4, Niagara Rain for Cinematics, teaches rain streaks, splashes, ripples, and wet-surface details for creating believable rainy cinematic environments.

Chapter 5, Niagara Snow for Cinematics, covers soft snowfall, blizzard layers, snow swirls, and snow kick-up effects for winter and action scenes.

Chapter 6, Niagara Lightning and Electrical Effects for Cinematics, explores lightning bolts, electrical arcs, and character sparks using Niagara ribbons and cinematic timing control.

Chapter 7, Niagara Fluids for Cinematic Volume Effects, introduces volumetric fog, explosions, storm clouds, and fire-on-mesh effects using Niagara Fluids and Grid3D Gas.

Chapter 8, Chaos Destruction and Cloth for Cinematics, combines Chaos wall destruction, Niagara Fluids smoke, cached cinematic playback, and Chaos Cloth flag simulation.

To get the most out of this book

You will need Unreal Engine installed, preferably version 5.6. At the time of writing, the recipes in this book were created using **Unreal Engine 5.6.1**. Although newer versions of Unreal Engine, such as 5.8, may be available, the workflows covered in this book are designed for Unreal Engine 5.6 and should be applicable across the 5.6 release series.

Software/hardware covered in the book	Operating system requirements
Unreal Engine 5.6.1	Windows 11
A ray tracing-capable graphics card	
Optional – image editing software (Photoshop, GIMP)	

Note that the author acknowledges the use of AI tools, such as ChatGPT, with the sole aim of enhancing the language and clarity within the book, thereby ensuring a smooth reading experience for readers. All technical workflows, settings, screenshots, examples, testing, and final content decisions were created, reviewed, and validated by the author. It's important to note that the content itself has been crafted by the author and edited by a professional publishing team. Packt does not accept AI-generated content that replaces the author's subject-matter expertise.

Download the example code/resource files

This book includes a complete downloadable code/resource bundle containing all the example projects and files used throughout the chapters. We recommend downloading the bundle so you can follow along smoothly and experiment with the examples.

Use the bundle as a practical starting point. Modify it, extend it, and apply what you learn by creating your own variations as you progress through the chapters.

Get the code/resource bundle

If you bought the book directly from Packt:

1. Go to `packtpub.com`.
2. Click your profile picture and select **Your Orders**.
3. Find this book and click **Download Code**.

If you bought this book from Amazon or any other channel partner:

1. Go to `packtpub.com/unlock` or scan the following QR code:
2. Search for this book.
3. Sign up or log in to your free Packt account.
4. Upload your proof of purchase and download the code/resource bundle locally.

Usage note: You're free to use and modify this code/resource for personal learning and non-commercial projects. The GitHub repository contains the project file and a `README` with project setup instructions. A short introductory video is also available at `https://packt.link/pdbaH`. Before working through the recipes, it is recommended that you review both the `README` and the video to set up the project.

Download the color images

Your purchase includes a color, DRM-free PDF copy of this book, ideal for viewing color images, screenshots, and diagrams. Refer to the *Free benefits with your book section* at the end of the *Preface* to unlock your PDF copy.

Conventions used

There are a number of text conventions used throughout this book.

`CodeInText`: Indicates code words in text, database table names, folder names, filenames, file extensions, pathnames, dummy URLs, user input, and X (formerly Twitter) handles. For example: "In the **Content Browser**, go to your `Niagara_Systems` folder, right-click, and create a new Niagara System."

Bold: Indicates a new term, an important word, or words that you see on the screen. For instance, words in menus or dialog boxes appear in the text like this. For example: "In the **Particle Update** section, add a **Wind Force** node."

> **Note**
>
> Warnings or important notes appear like this.

> **Tip**
>
> Tips and tricks appear like this.

Sections

In this book, you will find several headings that appear frequently (*Getting ready*, *How to do it...*, *How it works...*, *There's more...*, and *See also*).

To give clear instructions on how to complete a recipe, use these sections as follows:

Getting ready

This section tells you what to expect in the recipe and describes how to set up any software or any preliminary settings required for the recipe.

How to do it...

This section contains the steps required to follow the recipe.

How it works...

This section usually consists of a detailed explanation of what happened in the previous section.

There's more...

This section consists of additional information about the recipe in order to make you more knowledgeable about the recipe.

See also

This section provides helpful links to other useful information for the recipe.

Get in touch

Feedback from our readers is always welcome.

General feedback: If you have questions about any aspect of this book or have any general feedback, please email us at `customercare@packt.com` and mention the book's title in the subject of your message.

Errata: Although we have taken every care to ensure the accuracy of our content, mistakes do happen. If you have found a mistake in this book, we would be grateful if you reported this to us. Please visit `http://www.packt.com/submit-errata`, click **Submit Errata**, and fill in the form.

Piracy: If you come across any illegal copies of our works in any form on the internet, we would be grateful if you would provide us with the location address or website name. Please contact us at `copyright@packt.com` with a link to the material.

If you are interested in becoming an author: If there is a topic that you have expertise in and you are interested in either writing or contributing to a book, please visit `http://authors.packt.com/`.

Free benefits with your book

This book includes free benefits designed to support your learning and help you apply what you learn effectively. Activate them now for instant access (see the *How to unlock* section for instructions).

Here's a quick overview of what you can instantly unlock with your purchase:

Complete Code Bundle

Download the full source code for this book's examples and projects.

DRM-Free PDF Version

Download DRM-free PDF and ePub copies of this book.

7-Day Packt Library Access

Get 7-day unlimited access to 8,000+ books and videos. No credit card required.

Available for first-time Packt+ trial users only.

Next-Gen Reader Access

Read this book on Packt Reader with progress sync, dark mode and note-taking.

How to unlock

Scan the QR code (or go to `packtpub.com/unlock`). Search for this book by name, confirm the edition, and then follow the steps on the page.

UNLOCK NOW

Note: Have your invoice handy. Purchases made directly from the Packt website don't require an invoice.

Share your thoughts

Once you've read *Unreal Engine 5 VFX Cookbook*, we'd love to hear your thoughts! Scan the QR code below to go straight to the Amazon review page for this book and share your feedback.

https://packt.link/r/1836209053

Your review is important to us and the tech community and will help us make sure we're delivering excellent quality content.

1

Cinematic Niagara Workflow for Sequencer and Movie Render Queue

Unreal Engine has made cinematic VFX faster to iterate than ever, but speed only helps when effects behave predictably across shots, timelines, and final renders. The *Unreal Engine 5 VFX Cookbook* focuses on production-minded workflows and reusable "recipes" for real-time VFX in Unreal Engine 5.6, so you can art-direct confidently, troubleshoot quickly, and deliver consistent results. We will prioritize practical setups, repeatable control, and render correctness, especially for Niagara-driven effects in shot-based pipelines.

You will also cover shot timing using the **Niagara Life Cycle Track** and basic **Movie Render Queue** (**MRQ**) checks, so your effects render correctly from frame 1. The goal is to reduce surprises in production: predictable timing, repeatable behavior, and controls that make it easy to art-direct the same effect across different shots.

The following recipes are grouped together because they form one complete **shot-ready Niagara workflow**. You start with a reusable sandbox for consistent lookdev (look development), then add a "Shot Control" layer (**User Parameters**) so the same controls can drive multiple systems reliably. From there, the chapter focuses on production stability: repeatable playback and scrubbing, precise triggering via **Sequencer Life Cycle Tracks**, and essential **MRQ** checks (warmup/first frame) so effects render correctly.

In this chapter, we'll cover the following recipes:

- Setting up a reusable VFX "Sandbox" level for cinematic lookdev
- Building a Niagara "Shot Control" system with User Parameters
- Making Niagara effects stable for scrubbing and repeatable playback (repeatable takes)
- Preparing Niagara Effects for Movie Render Queue

Figure 1.1 - Final look for Setting up a reusable VFX "Sandbox" level for cinematic lookdev recipe

> **Note**
>
> **Download the code/resource bundle and the PDF version of this book**
>
> Your purchase includes a DRM-free PDF copy of this book, the code/resource bundle, and a range of exclusive benefits. To unlock everything, follow the *Free benefits with your book* section in the *Preface*.

Technical requirements

To complete the recipes in this chapter, you will need **Unreal Engine 5.6** (`https://www.unrealengine.com/en-US/download`). This can be installed by following these steps:

1. Download the **Epic Games Launcher** using the link above and follow the installation procedure.

2. Once installed, you'll need to get the **Unreal Engine 5.6** version. You can do so by navigating to the **Unreal Engine** section of the launcher, then to the **Library** tab.
3. In the **Library** tab, you'll see the **plus** (+) icon, which will let you download the Unreal version to be used throughout this book. This is demonstrated as follows:

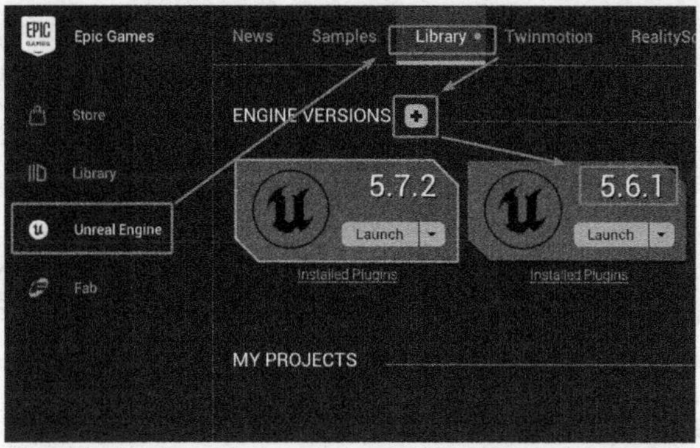

Figure 1.2 - Installing Unreal Engine 5.6

As for the hardware aspects, the following setup is recommended:

- **CPU**: 8–16 cores (16–32 threads). Example tier: Intel Core i7/i9 / AMD Ryzen 7/9
- **RAM**: 32–64 GB
- **GPU**: 12–24 GB VRAM (especially for heavy Niagara, high-res textures, and MRQ). Example tier: NVIDIA RTX 4070 Ti / 4080 / 4090, or AMD RX 7900 series
- **Storage**: NVMe SSD with 300 GB+ free, plus a secondary SSD/HDD for archiving renders

You can download the example project for this book by following the instructions in the *Download the example code/resource files* section in the *Preface* of this book.

The complete example project is included in the downloadable code/resource bundle.

And don't worry – I'll make sure to remind you in the relevant *Getting ready* sections of the recipes if there is an already-created file that you can use to follow along with.

> **Note**
>
> Several recipes throughout this book use Unreal Engine's **Starter Content** assets. If you're using Unreal Engine 5.7 or later and your project does not include **Starter Content**, follow the instructions in the *Appendix* before proceeding.

Setting up a reusable VFX "Sandbox" level for cinematic lookdev

When you build VFX in a blank level, it is easy to fall into a trap: the effect looks great in isolation, then breaks the moment you drop it into a real shot. Lighting changes, exposure shifts, background contrast fight your values, and scale feels *off*, so you end up tweaking the same effect repeatedly just to make it readable.

This recipe solves this problem by creating a dedicated, reusable sandbox scene that behaves like a neutral testing stage for cinematic work. You will set up a simple lookdev level with consistent lighting, camera framing, and scene context. This ensures every effect you create later can be evaluated in the same conditions and iterated faster with fewer surprises when it moves into production shots.

Getting ready

First, we need to download **Unreal Engine 5.6** before we can start creating the basic studio scene. At the time of writing, I'm using **version 5.6.1**. If you are using a different version of Unreal Engine, some settings, interface options, or results may vary. Refer to the *Technical requirements* section on how to download and install Unreal Engine 5.6.

For this first recipe, you'll just need Unreal Engine 5.6 installed and ready to go.

How to do it...

Follow these steps to set up a simple sandbox level that we can reuse for all our VFX lookdev work:

1. Launch **Unreal Engine 5.6** using the **Epic Games Launcher** application by clicking on the **Launch** button.
2. Go to **Film / Video & Live Events** category in the Unreal Project Browser and select the **Motion Design** option, as shown in *Figure 1.3*.
3. Select a location for your project, give it a name (I'm using `VFX_COOKBOOK`). Then, click **Create**.

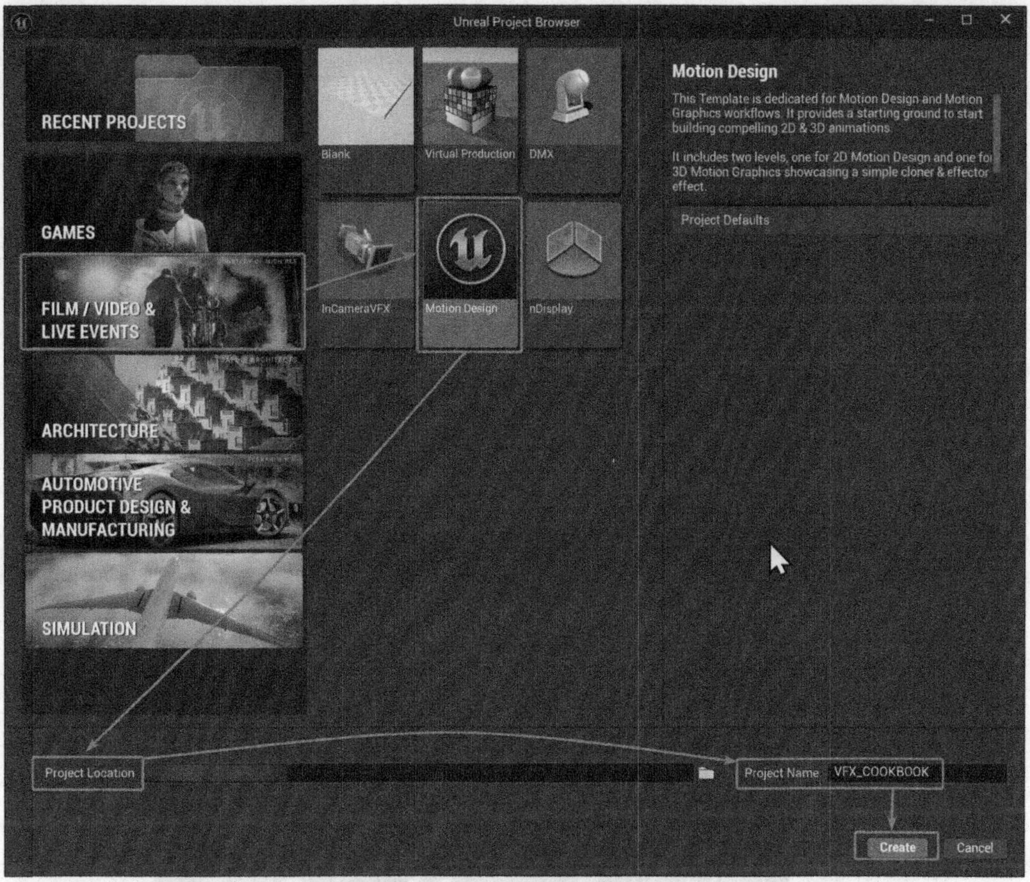

Figure 1.3 - Setting up the project

4. Once the editor loads, click on **File** | **New Level...** option and select **3D Motion Graphics** map, and click **Create**.
5. To save this level, click on **File** | **Save Current Level As...**, rename it as `LV_VFX_Sandbox`, and click **Save**.

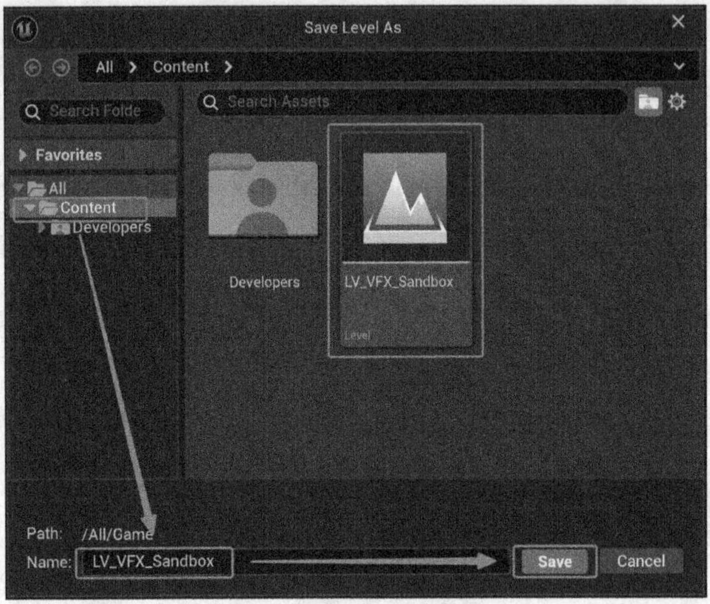

Figure 1.4 - Setting up the project

6. In the **Outliner**, select the **ClonerSystem** asset, delete it, and confirm deletion.
7. Next, delete the **Pedestal** and **Ring** assets.

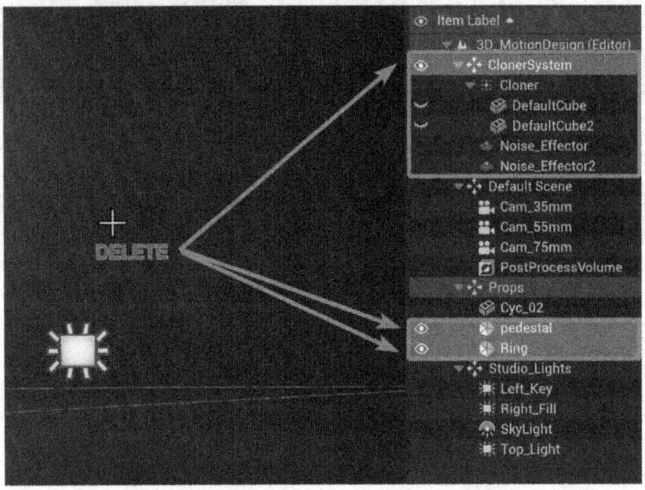

Figure 1.5 - Deleting unnecessary assets

8. Press *Ctrl* + *Shift* + *S* to save the level.

We now have a perfect stage to create our VFX recipes using Niagara.

How it works...

The reason I chose the **Motion Design** template at the start is simple: it saves time. Instead of building a test stage from scratch, the template already provides a solid starting setup, including a backdrop, lighting, and cameras. I kept what was useful and deleted anything that was not needed for this chapter, so the final sandbox stays clean and focused.

Having a fixed camera setup, with quick close, mid, and wide framings, is important because VFX must be judged at real shot distances. An effect that looks perfect in a close-up can become too small, too noisy, or even disappear in a wide shot, so checking different framings early prevents rework later.

The staging area is kept simple and mostly empty on purpose. Working in the same sandbox every time also builds good habits: your eye becomes trained to what "too dense" or "too fast" looks like under consistent lighting and camera conditions.

In short, this sandbox acts like a controlled lab. It helps you solve VFX problems early, keep your work repeatable, and avoid surprises when you move into **Sequencer** and final renders.

There's more...

Upon re-launching or reopening your project, the Unreal Engine editor will revert to a default project that was pre-defined in the **Project Settings**. To have the Unreal Editor always load the `LV_VFX_Sandbox` level we just created, here are a few steps you can take:

1. Click **Edit** | **Project Settings**.
2. In the **Project Settings** window, select the **Maps & Modes** section, and change **Editor Startup Map** and **Game Default Map** to **LV_VFX_Sandbox**.
3. Close the **Project Settings** tab and save the project.

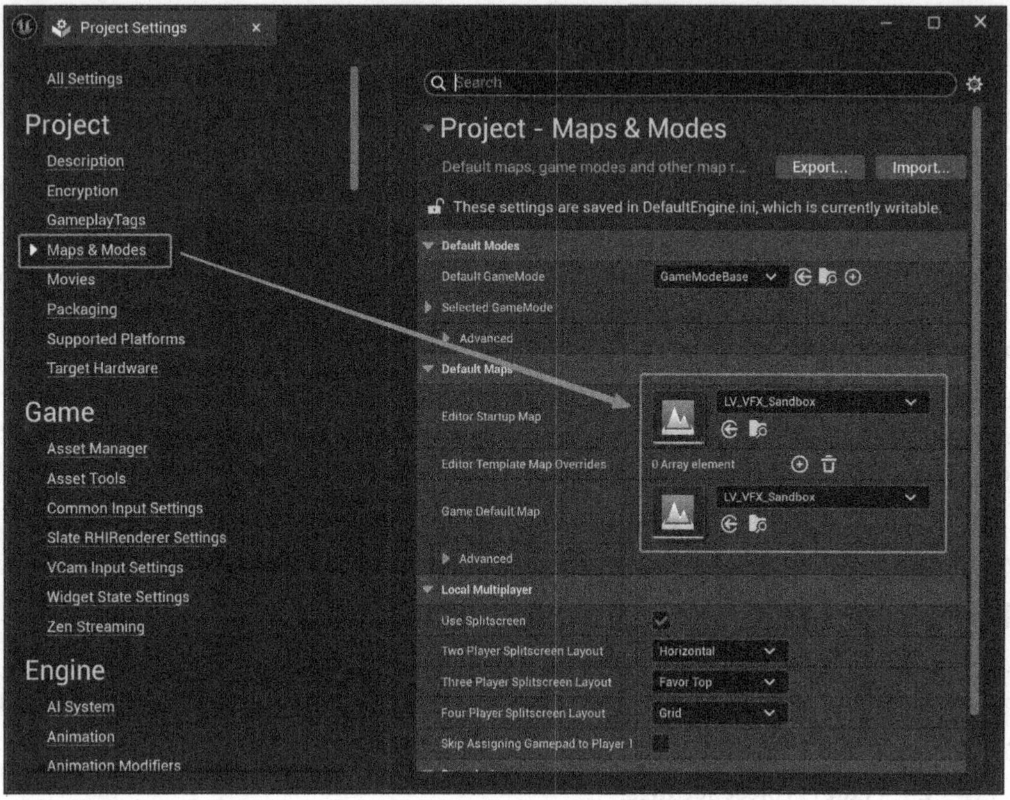

Figure 1.6 - Setting Maps & Modes in Project Settings

See also

In this recipe, we created and saved a new level within Unreal's **Content Browser**. If you care about organization, there are many different styles that you can follow to keep things tidy. One thing I would like to refer to is **Allar's UE5 style guide**, which you can find out more about here: `https://github.com/Allar/ue5-style-guide/tree/main`.

Building a Niagara "Shot Control" system with User Parameters

This recipe shows you how to build a reusable "Shot Control" layer using Niagara **User Parameters**. Niagara Systems can quickly become complicated, with many modules and settings spread across the stack, and it's easy to lose time hunting for the right value to change. **User Parameters** solves this problem by giving you a small set of clear controls that are exposed to the Level itself. Instead of re-tweaking the effect every time a shot needs a change, you adjust a few predictable knobs, such as intensity, scale, speed, wind, color, and variation. These controls can also be keyed in **Sequencer** later, which makes shot timing and art direction much easier, but they are still useful even without **Sequencer** because they keep your adjustments consistent and organized.

By the end of this recipe, you will have a clean parameter set that can drive almost every effect in this book (smoke, dust, rain, snow, leaves, and lightning). Just as importantly, you will be able to hand the system to another artist, and they can make shot changes quickly without digging through the Niagara stack or accidentally breaking the effect.

Getting ready

We will create a simple Niagara System, and we will decide on the standard parameter names in the *How to do it...* section:

1. Launch the **Epic Games launcher**.
2. Double-click on the `VFX_COOKBOOK` project.
3. If you have followed the instructions in the *There's more...* section in the previous recipe, the `LS_VFX_Sandbox` level is now open and ready for us to proceed.

How to do it...

Let's start by making our very first simple Niagara System:

1. Press the *1* key across the keyboard to reset the Viewport, then right-click anywhere in the **Content Browser** and select **Niagara System**.
2. In the **Create Niagara System** pop-up window, search for `Fountain` and click **Create**. Since a Niagara System can be made using multiple emitters, we are going to start with the **Fountain** emitter template.
3. You'll have an opportunity to name the Niagara System; let's use `NS_VFX_Basic` for now. You can change it later if needed.
4. Drag `NS_VFX_Basic` into the scene, then double-click to open the `NS_VFX_Basic` Niagara System.

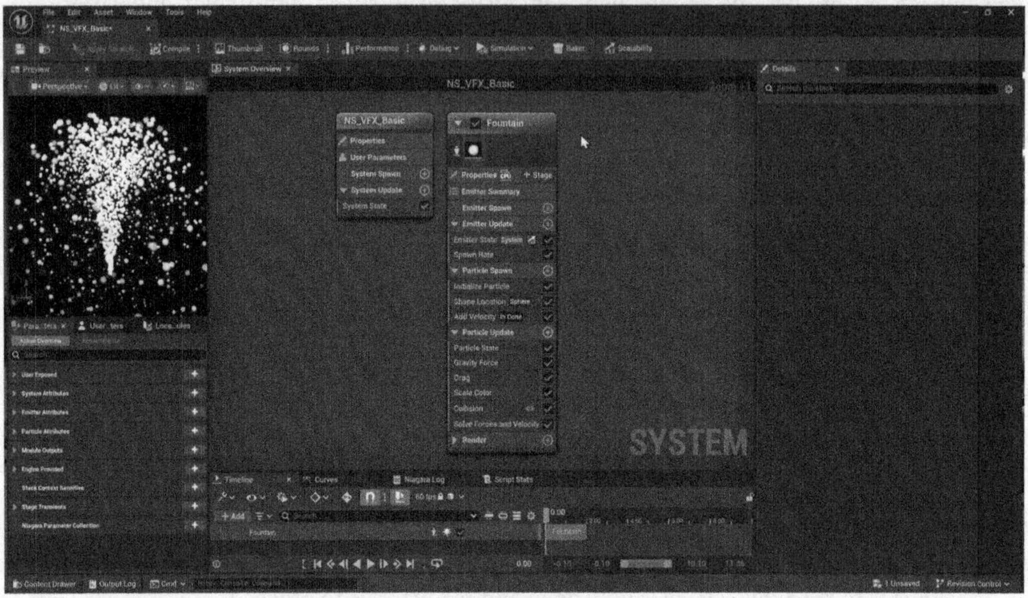

Figure 1.7 - The Niagara System Editor

To make this Niagara effect look interesting, let's first add a **Collision** module so the particles will bounce when hitting the ground.

1. Click the *green* + sign of the **Particle Update** section and search for and add the **Collision** module. It will appear as part of the sub-module of the **Particle Update** module, which can be confirmed by checking the Preview window.

Figure 1.8 - Particles colliding with the floor

2. Back in the main level, at this point, your particles should bounce when they hit the ground, which gives us a simple but visible behavior to work with.

Now let's build the "Shot Control" setup mentioned earlier. We'll use Niagara **User Parameters** so we can drive the main look controls from a small, consistent set of values.

1. When creating the **User Parameters**, we will use these default values:
   - **Parameter name**: `FX_Color`, Type: **Linear Color**, set color to `white`
   - **Parameter name**: `FX_Intensity`, Type: **float**, set value to `5000`
   - **Parameter name**: `FX_Size`, Type: **float**, set value to `5`
   - **Parameter name**: `FX_Speed`, Type: **float**, set value to `1000`
2. On the bottom left of the Niagara Editor, select the **User Parameters** tab.
3. Click the + sign and use the parameter names and values as suggested above.

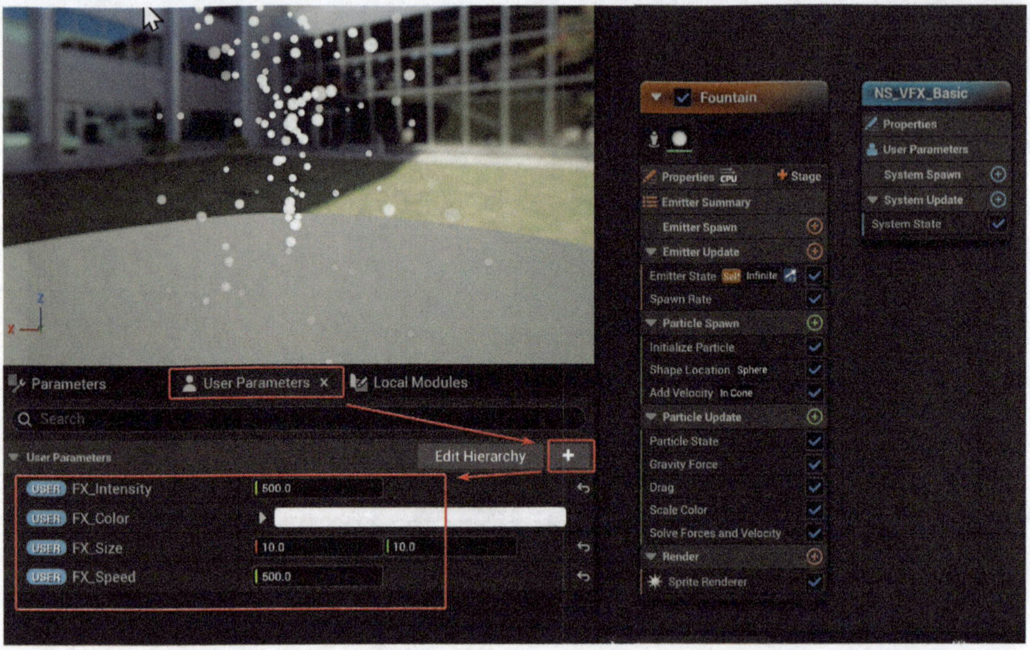

Figure 1.9 - Accessing the User Parameters Tab

4. To create each parameter, click the + sign and search for the parameter type. For instance, in the case of `FX_Intensity`, it is a **float**. Keep adding the parameters as shown in *Figure 1.10*.

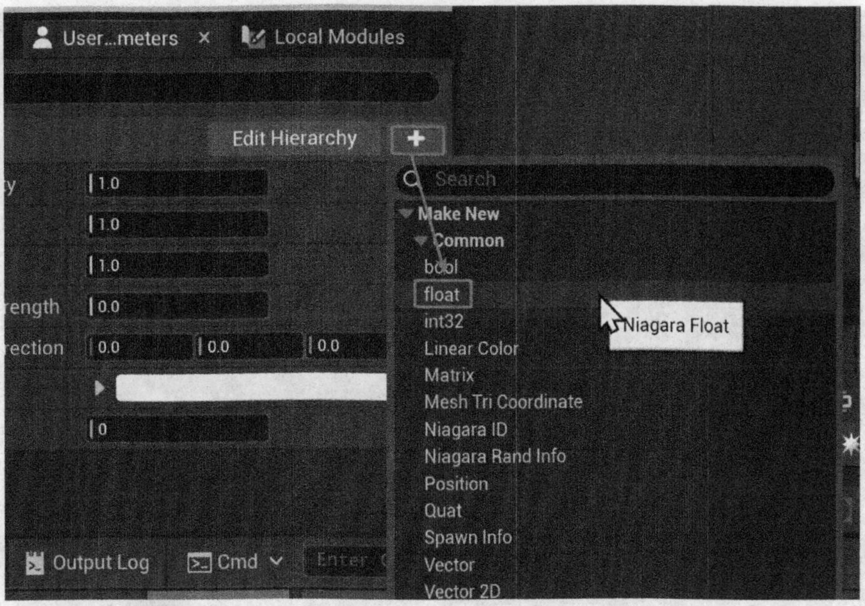

Figure 1.10 - Creating the User Parameters

5. For `FX_Size`, in the **Initialize Particle** module, change the **Sprite Size Mode** to **Uniform** first. In the case of the **Sprite Size Mode**, **Uniform** will allow you to change the size of the sprite uniformly.
6. Once completed, click the **Save** button on the top left of the editor and close it.
7. Jump back to the main Level to see what you've created so far.
8. Select `NS_VFX_Basic` in the **Outliner**. You'll now be able to access the **User Parameters** section in the **Details** panel, as shown in *Figure 1.11*:

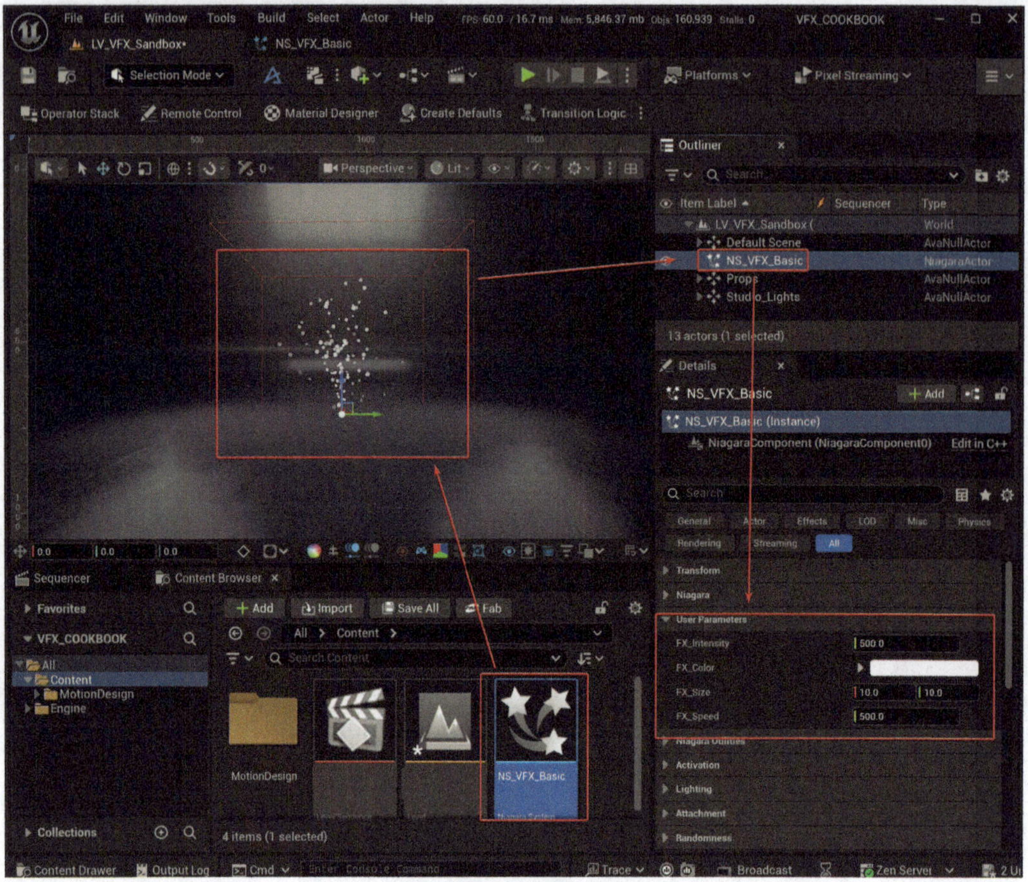

Figure 1.11 - Adding the Niagara System to the Level

Although non-functional at the moment, you have succeeded in creating the "exposed" parameter at the main level – Congratulations!

Now let's pipe the **User Parameters** to the Niagara System modules so we can control the properties within the Level itself, starting with `FX_Intensity`:

1. Back in the Niagara Editor for `NS_VFX_Basic`, in the **Fountain** emitter node, select the **Spawn Rate** module.
2. In its **Details** panel, click on the down-pointing arrow, then select **Link Inputs** | **User** | **FX_Intensity**, which will add the User Parameter you created, `FX_Intensity`.

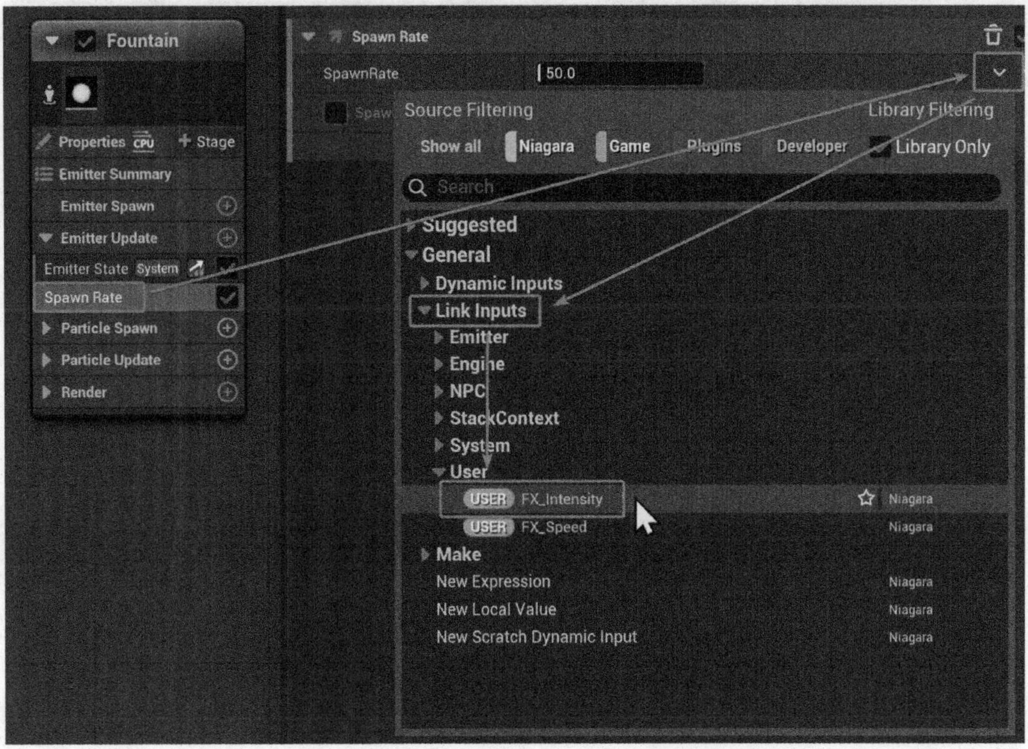

Figure 1.12 - Piping the FX_Intensity User Parameter

3. For `FX_Color`, select the **Initialize Particle** module.
4. In its **Details** panel, select the **Color** property, click the down-pointing arrow, and choose **Link Inputs** | **User** and select **FX_Color**.

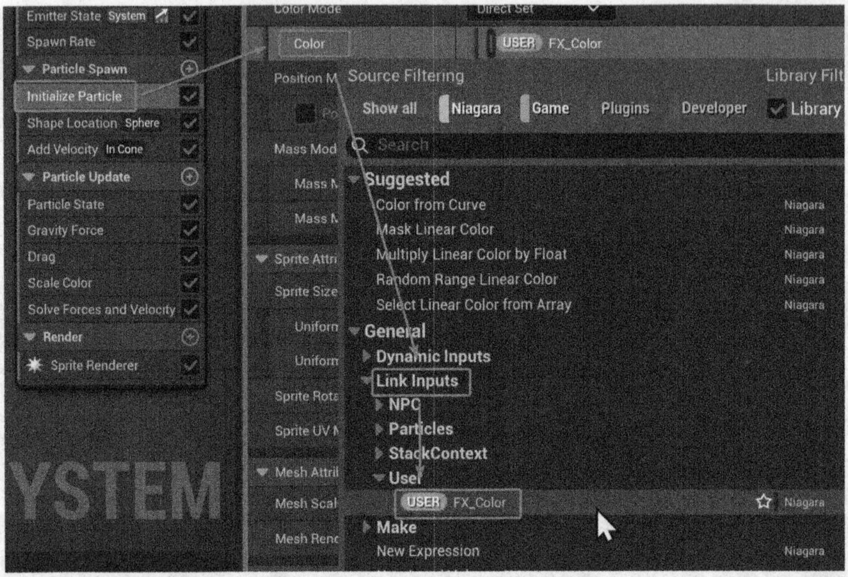

Figure 1.13 - Piping the FX_Color User Parameter

5. For `FX_Size`, do the same process using the **Sprite Size** module.
6. For the `FX_Speed`, select the **Add Velocity** module and use the **Cone Velocity** property.
7. Once you've completed the piping process, click the **Compile** button and jump back to the main Level, access the **User Parameters** in the **Details** panel, and change the values to test the system.

Now that you understand how to add these controls, go ahead and add a few extra controls by yourself.

How it works...

In this recipe, you built a simple Niagara System and then turned it into a controllable "shot-ready" effect. You started by creating a Niagara System from the **Fountain** template, which gives you a working emitter right away without building everything from scratch. You then added a **Collision** module, so the particles visibly bounce on the ground, making it easy to confirm the system is updating and behaving correctly.

After that, you created four **User Parameters** (color, intensity, size, and speed). At first, these parameters are only "exposed controls," which is why you could see them in the Level's **Details** panel after dragging the system into the scene, but they didn't change the effect yet.

The key step is the *piping process*: you linked each User Parameter into real Niagara modules (**Spawn Rate**, particle **Color**, **Sprite Size**, and **Velocity**). Once compiled, the system reads those values from the Level, so you can adjust the look directly from the **Details** panel without reopening the Niagara stack every time.

A good habit is to keep your **User Parameters** small and meaningful, like simple knobs an artist would use on a shot. Use clear names, sensible defaults, and link each parameter to the one place where it has the biggest impact, so changes feel predictable. If a parameter doesn't seem to work, the first things to check are whether you linked to the correct property, whether the system compiled successfully, and whether you are adjusting the parameter on the correct Niagara Actor in the Level.

As you build more effects, reusing the same control set across systems will save time and make shot work easier, because you'll already know which control changes intensity, which one changes size, and which one changes motion.

There's more...

Now that you know how to set up **User Parameters,** I'll show you how easy it is to go back and change or add new user parameters. Let's use Particle Size as an example. We will add an additional User Parameter to randomize between two different sizes of the particles:

1. Reopen `NS_VFX_Basic` Niagara System.
2. Access the **Initialize Particle** module.
3. Change the **Sprite Size Mode** to **Random Uniform**. You'll now have access to two values, the **Uniform Sprite Size Min** and **Uniform Sprite Size Max**. We will add a User Parameter to these two values.

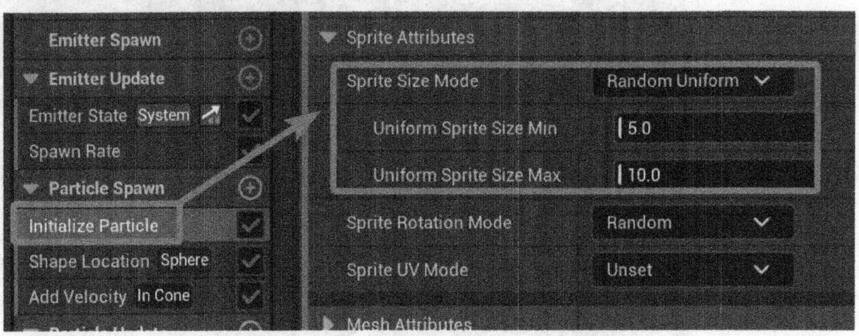

Figure 1.14 - Changing the Sprite Size Mode

4. In the **User Parameters** tab, right-click on `FX_Size` and duplicate it. Rename as `FX_Size_Max`. Rename `FX_Size` to `FX_Size_Min`. Change the `FX_Size_Max` value to `20`.

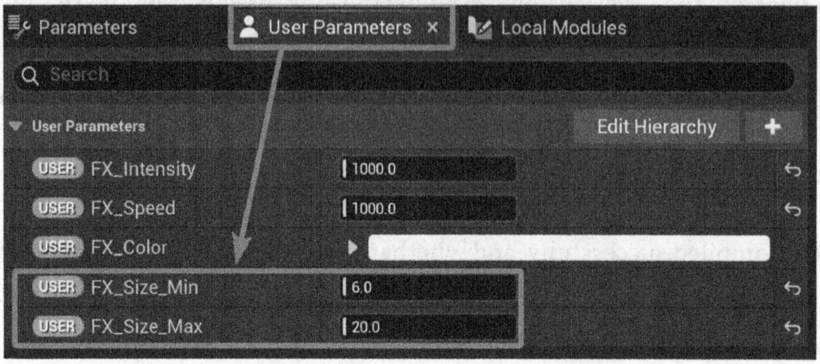

Figure 1.15 - Duplicating and renaming FX_Size

5. Now let's assign these two parameters to the Sprite Size in the **Initialize Particle** module. Click the **Uniform Sprite Size Min** down-pointing arrow and search and select `FX_Size_Min`. Do the same for `FX_Size_Max`.

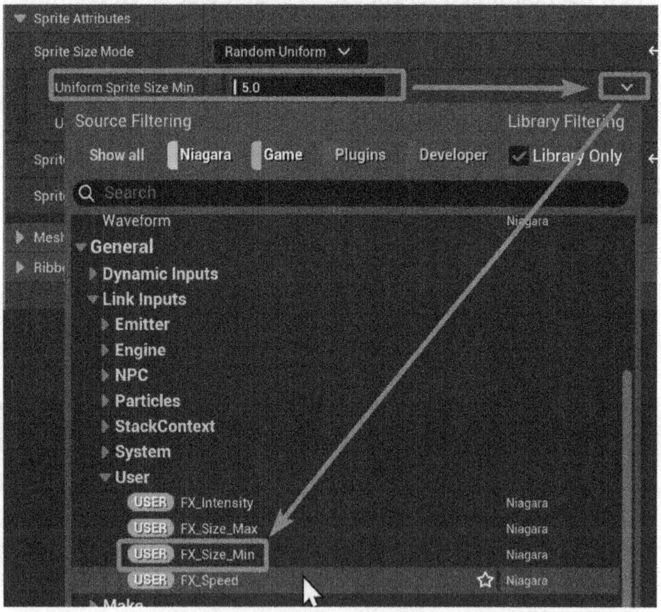

Figure 1.16 - Assigning the User Parameters

6. Compile and save. Now, at the main level, you'll see that the Niagara System emits two sizes of particles randomly.

See also

Check out the **Niagara Editor interface** official documentation: `https://dev.epicgames.com/documentation/en-us/unreal-engine/editor-ui-reference-for-niagara-effects-in-unreal-engine`.

Making Niagara effects stable for scrubbing and repeatable playback (repeatable takes)

In cinematic work, an effect is not useful if it only looks good once. Niagara Systems can behave differently when you scrub the timeline, play back in **Sequencer**, or render through **Movie Render Queue**. This recipe focuses on making your effects predictable and repeatable, so you can review a shot confidently and render multiple takes without unwanted changes.

Getting ready

Before starting, set up a simple test environment for this recipe:

1. Use the `NS_VFX_Basic` Niagara System we created in the *Building a Niagara "Shot Control" system with User Parameters* recipe as your test subject.
2. In the `VFX_Sandbox` level, from the *Setting up a reusable VFX "Sandbox" level for cinematic lookdev* recipe, create a **Level Sequence** that is 5 seconds long.
3. Place the Niagara System in the level and make sure it is visible in a close shot and a wide shot.
4. If you completed the *Setting up a reusable VFX "Sandbox" level for cinematic lookdev* recipe, make sure the following parameters are available:
   - **FX_Intensity**
   - **FX_Color**
   - **FX_Size**
   - **FX_Speed**
5. Finally, decide what "stable" means for this recipe:
   - The effect should look consistent when you scrub back and forth in **Sequencer.**
   - The effect should look the same across two renders of the same shot, within reason.

Have a simple test plan ready:

- **Scrub test**: Jump between Frame 0, middle, and end repeatedly

- **Play test**: Press **Play** in **Sequencer** and watch for pops
- **Render test**: Render twice (same settings) and compare

How to do it...

Let's start by creating our first Level Sequence:

1. In the **Content Browser**, right-click and select **Level Sequence**. Rename it to `LS_VFX_Test` (*LS* is an acronym for Level Sequence).
2. Double-click to open the sequence and, from the **Outliner**, drag the **Cam_35mm** into the **Sequencer**. This operation will also create a **Camera Cuts** track and give us a sequence of 150 frames, which is perfect for the test.

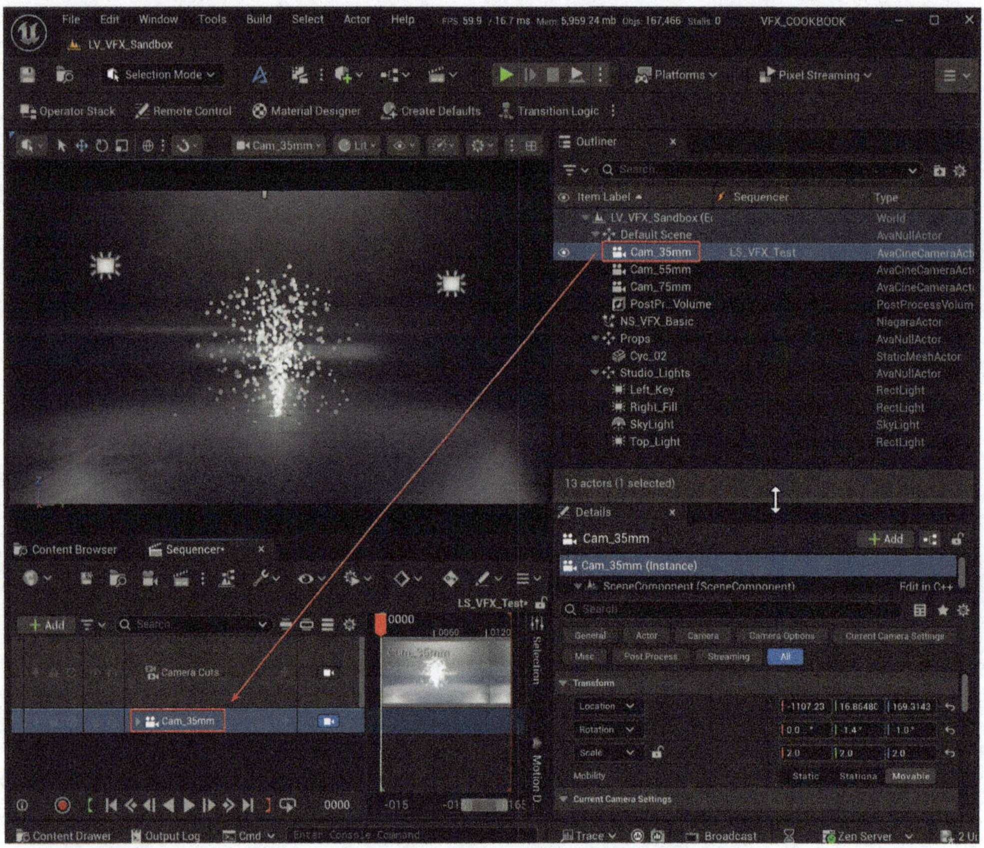

Figure 1.17 - Adding the 35mm camera

3. Click the **camera** icon in the **Camera Cuts** track to lock the camera in place. To unlock, you can either click the **camera** icon or use the *Shift + C* keyboard shortcut.

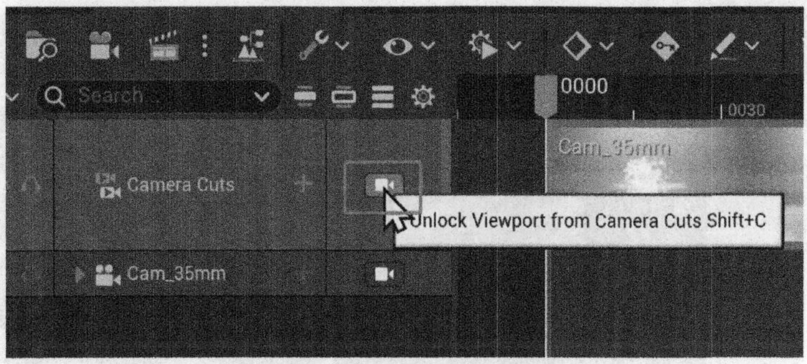

Figure 1.18 - Locking the camera

4. Next, drag the **NS_VFX_Basic** asset into the **Sequencer**, then click the + sign next to the **NS_VFX_Basic** track and select **NiagaraComponent0**. We will use this to access the User Parameter we made earlier in the chapter.

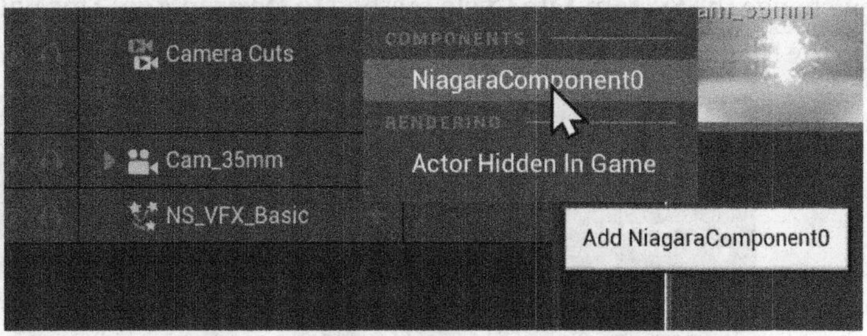

Figure 1.19 - Adding the NiagaraComponent0

5. Next, click the + sign beside the **NiagaraComponent0** track and from the selection, choose **Niagara System Life Cycle Track**.

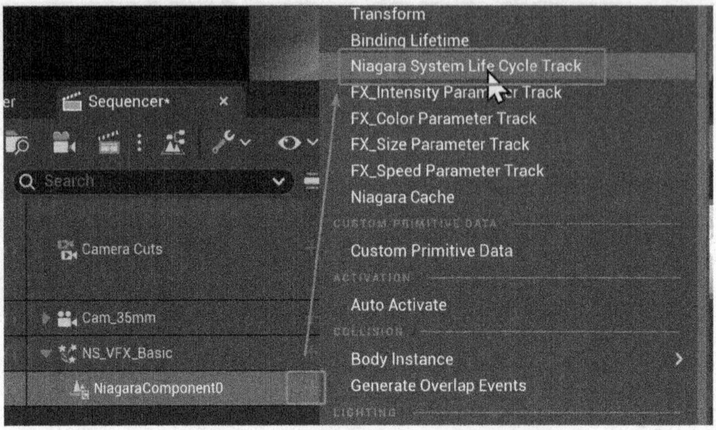

Figure 1.20 - Niagara System Life Cycle Track

6. Then change the **System Life Cycle** method to **Desired Age**. This will allow you to scrub the Niagara effect along the timeline as if you're playing back a video.

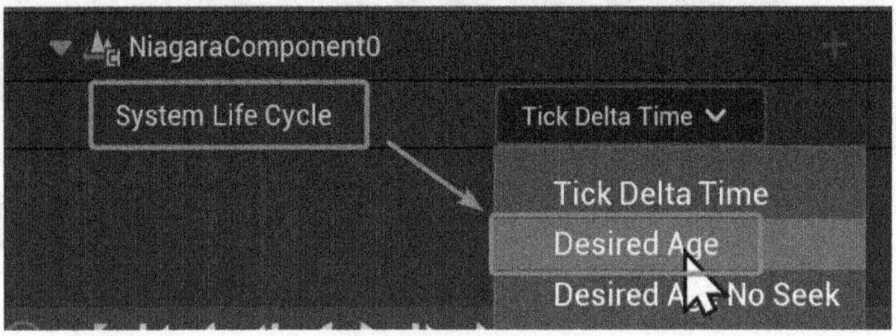

Figure 1.21 - Selecting the Desired Age mode

7. Go ahead and scrub the Playhead backward or forward, or click the **Play** icon at the bottom of the **Sequencer** to test the Niagara effect.

Now that you have set up the scrubbing and repeatable Playback, let's add the **User Parameters** we created earlier. It is a very straightforward process:

1. With the **Sequencer** still open, click the + sign beside the **NiagaraComponent0** and add the **FX_Color** Parameter Track, **FX_Intensity** Parameter Track, **FX_Size** Parameters Track and **FX_Speed** Parameter Track.

> **Note**
>
> If you followed the *Building a Niagara "Shot Control" system with User Parameters* recipe and created two values for the particle size, you'll need to add both parameters to the sequence.

2. Drag the Playhead to **Frame 0** and add a keyframe for all the above Parameter tracks by clicking on the **diamond shape** icon.

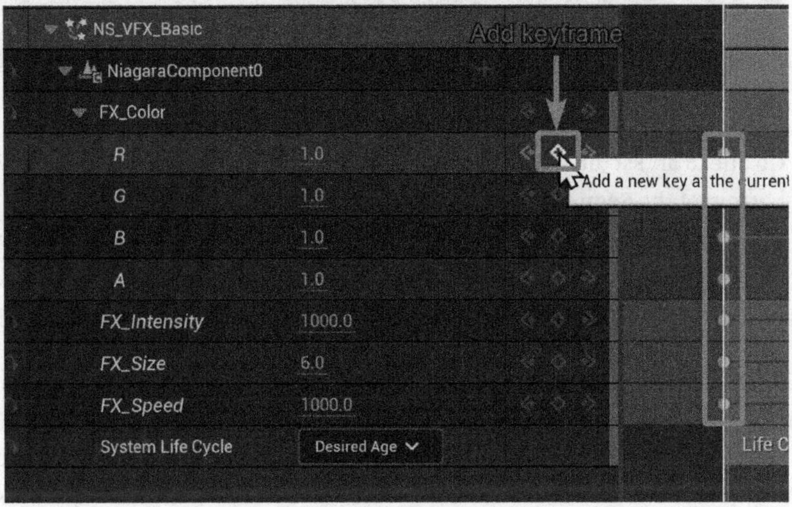

Figure 1.22 - Adding keyframes at Frame 0

Now we will add additional keyframes to each track. Use the following settings:

1. At **Frame 0075**: For **FX_Color**, adjust the following:
    - Keep **R** as **1.0**
    - Change **G** and **B** to `0` (remember to press *Enter* each time to add the keyframe)

   Do not create keyframes for **FX_Intensity**, **FX_Size**, and **FX_Speed**, as we do not want to change their values just yet.

2. At **Frame 0149**: Change **FX_Intensity** to `0`, **FX_Size** to `10` and **FX_Speed** to `0`. Leave **FX_Color** at the same values.
   The timeline should look like *Figure 1.23*:

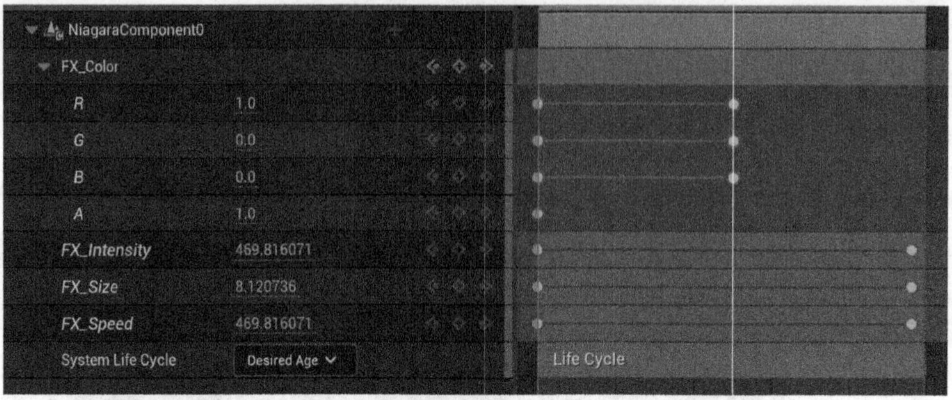

Figure 1.23 - The completed timeline

3. Go ahead and scrub the Playhead backward and forward or click the **Play** icon at the bottom of the **Sequencer** to test the Niagara effect.

You should now have a Fountain FX that changes color, with **Intensity**, **Size**, and **Speed** for 150 frames. Simple, but we have achieved our goal in creating a scrubbable Niagara FX timeline. Spend some time changing the parameters to see if you can come up with something cool.

How it works...

In this recipe, you turned a Niagara effect into something you can control like a normal shot element in **Sequencer**. You first created a **Level Sequence** and added a camera, then locked it, so it renders correctly. This matters because if the camera is not selected and locked, there is a high chance of you accidentally moving the camera.

Next, you added the Niagara System into **Sequencer** and selected the **NiagaraComponent0**, which is the component that exposes the **User Parameters** you created earlier. Once the Niagara System **Life Cycle Track** was added, you switched its method to **Desired Age**. This is the key step that makes scrubbing possible, because **Sequencer** can now evaluate the Niagara System at a specific time on the timeline, instead of relying only on real-time playback.

After the effect became scrubbable, you added your **User Parameters** as tracks and set keyframes. The first keyframe at **Frame 0** locks in the starting values, so the system has a clear baseline. The new keyframes later in the timeline show how the effect can be art-directed over time, just like any other animated element. In our recipe, the color changes at **Frame 0075**, and at the end of the shot, the intensity and speed drop to zero while the size increases, which makes the effect feel like it is fading out or "settling" before the cut.

The main idea is that once the system is controlled by a **Life Cycle Track** and driven by parameter keyframes (`FX_Color`, `FX_Intensity`, `FX_Size`, `FX_Speed`), you can repeat the same result every time you scrub, play, or render the shot, and you can adjust the look without opening the Niagara stack.

See also

If you need an in-depth explanation of the **System Life Cycle** settings, check out this Unreal Engine documentation: `https://dev.epicgames.com/documentation/en-us/unreal-engine/controlling-your-niagara-systems`.

Preparing Niagara Effects for Movie Render Queue

In production, an effect can look fine in the Viewport and still fail in the final render, especially if it needs time to settle before the shot begins. That is why this recipe focuses on a practical **Movie Render Queue (MRQ),** Unreal Engine's high-quality rendering tool, using short test renders and early result checks.

Before sending any Niagara effect to the **Movie Render Queue**, it is important to make sure the system is already working in a stable and predictable way. The goal of this recipe is not to rebuild the effect or retime it, but to prepare it for rendering and make sure it appears correctly from the first frame.

Getting ready

Before starting, set up your test environment as follows:

1. Open the `LS_VFX_Test` sequence if it is not already open.
2. Use the Niagara System (`NS_VFX_Basic`) from the *Making Niagara effects stable for scrubbing and repeatable playback (repeatable takes)* recipe as your working effect.

How to do it...

Let's now prepare the shot for rendering and run a quick test using **Movie Render Queue** (**MRQ**) to make sure everything is working as expected:

1. Confirm the shot is ready to render by first clicking on the camera switch in the **Camera Cuts** track. This is important to ensure the render will be from the selected camera.

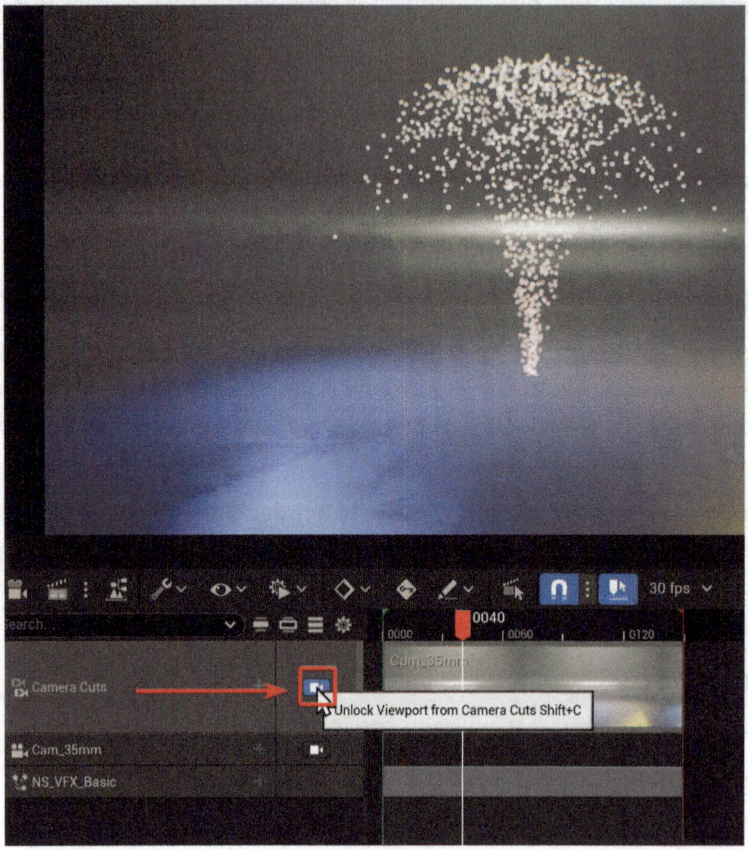

Figure 1.24 - Enabling the Camera Cuts camera switch

2. Click the **clapper board** icon in the **Sequencer** panel to open the **Movie Render Queue** (**MRQ**) floating panel. The `LS_VFX_Test` level will be listed and ready to render.

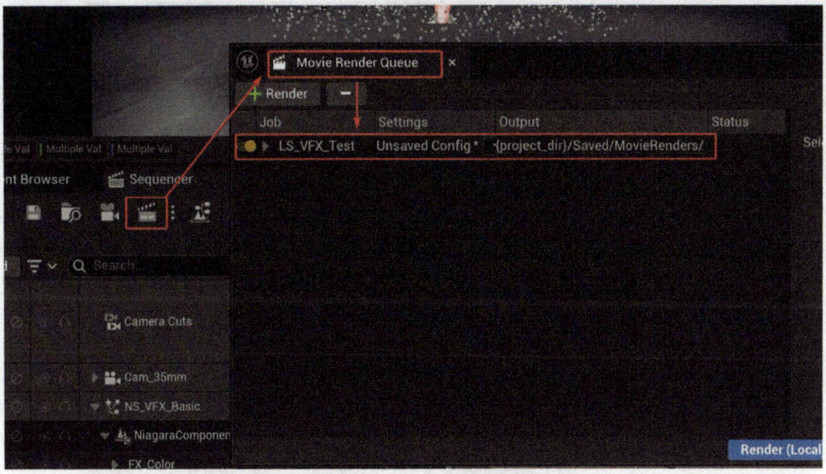

Figure 1.25 - Opening the Movie Render Queue panel

Before we hit the **Render** button, we will need to configure the file format and output path. Follow these steps:

1. In the **Movie Render Queue** panel, click the **Unsaved Config** settings to reveal yet another panel.
2. In that panel, select the **.jpg Sequence [8bit]** module and disable it by clicking the *yellow* button.
3. Next, click the **Settings** button with the *green* + (plus) sign and choose the **H.264 MP4 [8bit]** encoder.

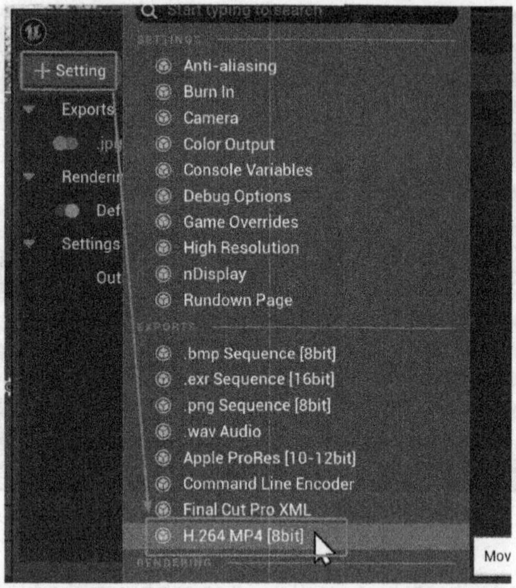

Figure 1.26 - The MRQ settings panel

4. In the **Output** directory section, click the **... (ellipses)** sign and locate and create a folder to save the video.

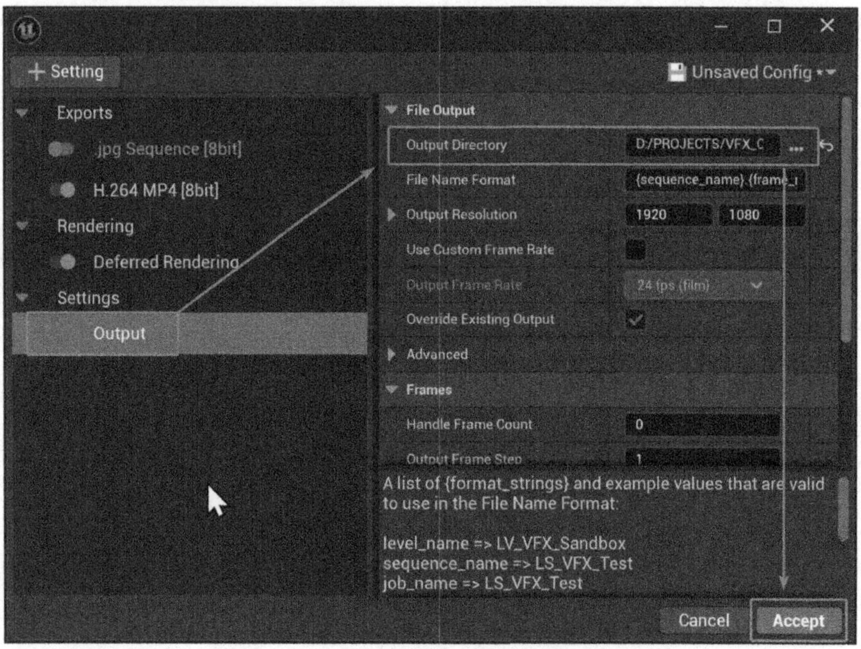

Figure 1.27 - Setting the save location

Before jumping back to the **Movie Render Queue** panel, let's save this config for future use. Now, follow these steps:

1. Click the **Unsaved Config** dropdown in the top right corner of the panel.
2. Select **Save As Preset** – rename as `MRQ_MP4` and click **Accept**.

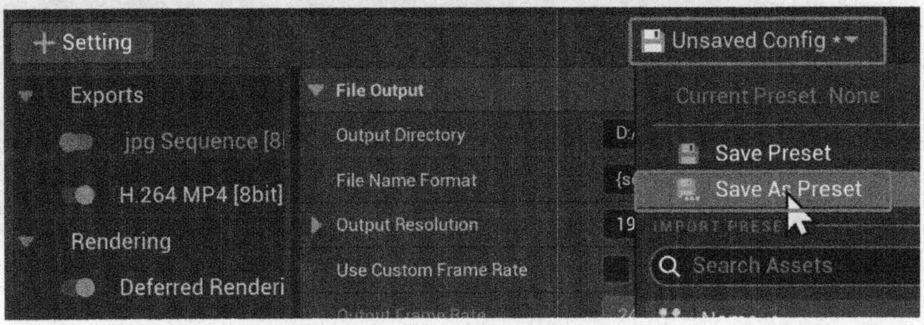

Figure 1.28 - Saving the preset

3. Back in the **Movie Render Queue** panel, click the **Render (Local)** button to start the rendering process. Depending on your PC specifications, this process should take less than a minute.

Once the MP4 is ready, you can use any video editing application, such as Adobe Premiere Pro or **Blackmagic DaVinci Resolve**, to view it. I personally use **DJV** (`https://sourceforge.net/projects/djv/`), a review software with scrubbable capabilities.

When scrubbing backward, you'll notice that the Niagara particles aren't as smooth as we would like them to be. This is because it must reset from the beginning of the **Life Cycle Track** and run up to the current frame. Each reset gives a random value.

To overcome this problem, you'll need to enable the **Determinism** switch in the **Emitter**. Follow these steps:

1. Open the `NS_VFX_Basic` Niagara System and select the **Fountain** emitter.
2. In its **Details** panel, in the **Emitter** section, enable the **Determinism** check box.
3. Click compile and save.

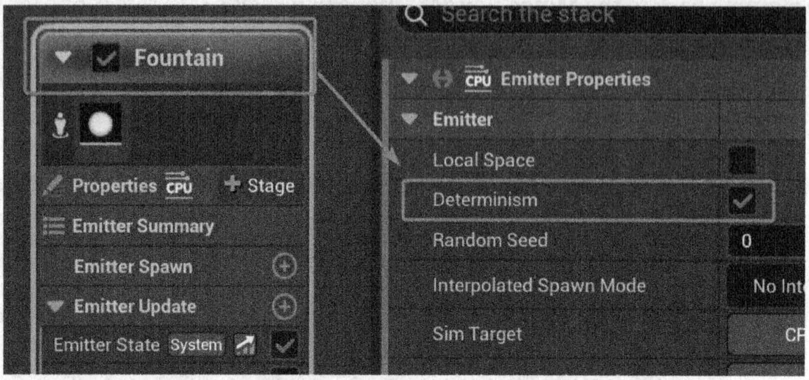

Figure 1.29 - Enabling Determinism

You'll now have much smoother playback.

How it works...

This recipe works because it tests your Niagara shot the same way it will be delivered: through **Movie Render Queue**, not just the Viewport. Even if a shot looks correct in **Sequencer**, the final render can still give unexpected results if the wrong camera is used or if the output settings are not configured properly. That is why the first step is to enable the camera switch in the **Camera Cuts** track, so **MRQ** renders the correct view.

You then open **MRQ** from **Sequencer**, choose a clear output format, and set up a save location. Switching from a JPG image sequence to an H.264 MP4 is a practical choice for a quick test because it creates a single file that is easy to review and share. Saving the settings as a preset also matters, because it gives you a repeatable "test render" setup you can reuse for every effect in the book.

After rendering, the main check is whether the animation plays back smoothly when you scrub. If you notice the particles changing or looking uneven when scrubbing backward, it is usually because the system is being re-evaluated from the start of the **Life Cycle Track** each time, and any random values can change on each reset.

Enabling **Determinism** on the emitter reduces that problem by making the simulation use predictable random values, so the result becomes more consistent from take to take.

In short, this recipe is less about making the effect prettier and more about proving that the shot can be rendered, reviewed, and scrubbed reliably, which is exactly what you need before moving on to more complex cinematic effects.

See also

This online **Unreal Engine documentation** gives an in-depth explanation with videos: `https://dev.epicgames.com/documentation/en-us/unreal-engine/niagara-for-linear-content`.

2

Niagara Smoke Effects for Cinematics

Smoke is one of the most used visual effects in cinematic scenes. From subtle drifting wisps to dense plumes and atmospheric haze, smoke helps add motion, depth, and mood to an environment.

In this chapter's recipes, we'll create several practical smoke effects using Niagara in Unreal Engine 5.6, focusing on techniques suitable for cinematic work. Using GPU sprite particles, layered emitters, and controlled motion forces, these recipes demonstrate how to build smoke that looks natural while remaining efficient and easy to reuse across different scenes.

By the end of this chapter, you will have learned the following recipes:

- Creating soft smoke wisps (hero-friendly GPU sprites)
- Creating a rolling smoke/steam plume loop
- Creating an impact smoke puff (burst + linger layers)
- Building ground fog/low haze for depth and mood

Technical requirements

Before starting this recipe, ensure the following:

- Make sure **Unreal Engine 5.6** is installed (see the *Technical requirements* section in *Chapter 1* for details).
- A project with the **Niagara** plugin enabled.

- A test environment or sandbox level where the effect can be previewed – you may use the sandbox environment we created in the *Setting up a reusable VFX "Sandbox" level for cinematic lookdev* recipe in *Chapter 1*.
- Practice creating a folder structure, such as the following, to keep the assets organized throughout the chapters:
  - `Content`
    - `Niagara_Systems`
    - `Sequences`
    - `Textures`
    - `Materials`
    - `MRQ`

You can download the example project for this book by following the instructions in the *Download the example code/resource* files section in the *Preface* of this book.

The complete example project is included in the downloadable code/resource bundle.

Creating soft smoke wisps (hero-friendly GPU sprites)

Soft smoke wisps are commonly used in cinematic scenes to add subtle motion and atmosphere without distracting from the main subject.

In this recipe, we will create a lightweight smoke wisp effect using Niagara GPU sprites, combining soft smoke textures, gentle upward motion, and turbulence forces to produce natural drifting smoke suitable for close-up cinematic shots. This setup is designed to be art-directable and reusable, making it a reliable building block for more complex smoke effects later in the chapter.

Figure 2.1 - The final Smoke Wisps

Getting ready

To kick off this recipe, we'll be using the LV_VFX_Sandbox level we created in the *Setting up a reusable VFX "Sandbox" level for cinematic lookdev* recipe, in *Chapter 1*, but we'll start off by organizing our content folder:

1. Make five new folders: Niagara_Systems, Sequences, Textures, Materials, and MRQ.
2. Move the NS_VFX_Basic to the Niagara_Systems folder, LS_VFX_Test to the Sequences folder, and the MRQ_MP4 preset to the MRQ folder.
3. The VFX_Sandbox level should already be opened by default. Delete the NS_VFX_Basic from the **Outliner** so we can start working on our Smoke VFX (if you get a warning message, just click **Delete**).

How to do it...

Unreal Engine 5.6 comes with a free **Content Pack** containing the smoke material we'll be using for this recipe. Let's begin the recipe by adding that to our project:

1. In the **Content Browser**, select the **Content** folder, then click the **+ Add** button and select **Add Feature or Content Pack.**

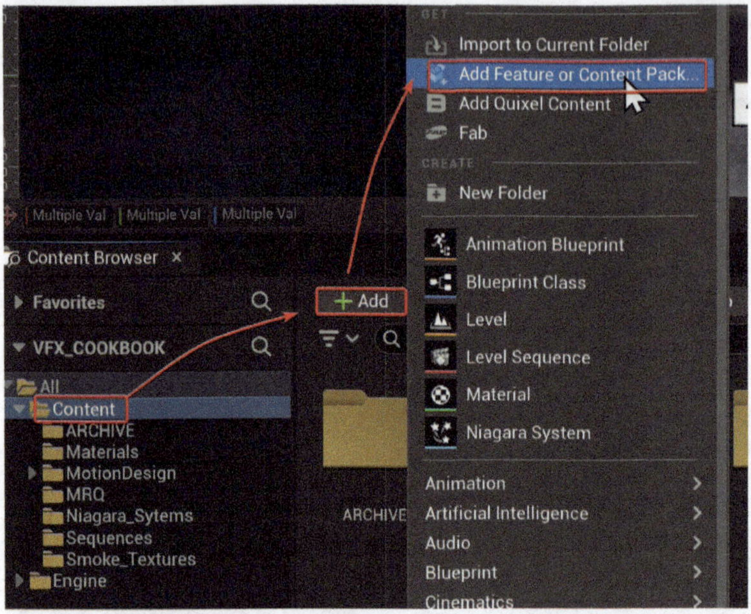

Figure 2.2 - Adding the Content Pack

2. In the pop-up window, select the **Content** tab, select **Starter Content**, and click **Add to Project**.

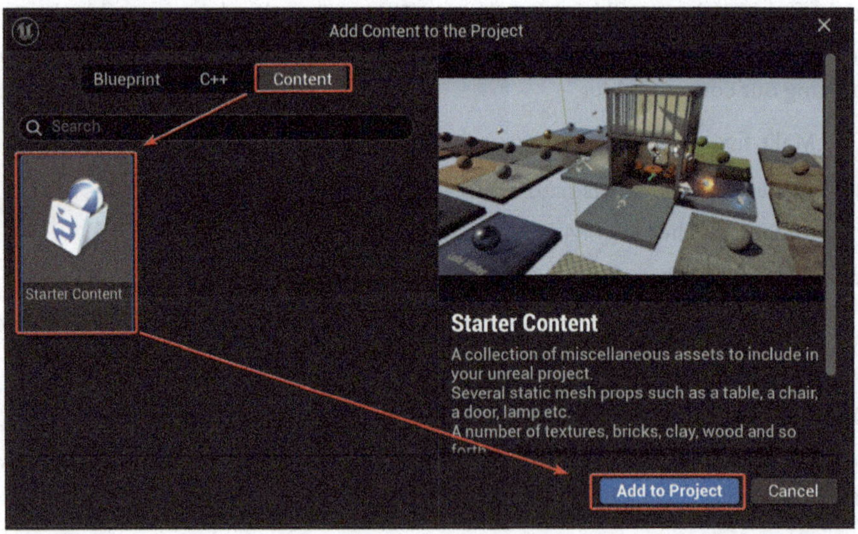

Figure 2.3 - Adding the Content Pack

> **Note**
>
> As of Unreal Engine 5.7, the **Content Pack** has been excluded. If you'd like to access it for UE5.7 and beyond, you'll need to migrate it from a previously installed Unreal Engine 5.6. See *Appendix* for details.

3. Open the `Niagara_Systems` folder, right-click, and select **Niagara System**. From the pop-up window, choose **SimpleSpriteBurst** Niagara emitter, rename it as `NS_Smoke_Wisps`.
4. Drag `NS_Smoke_Wisps` Niagara System into the level, then double-click to open the Niagara Editor.
5. There isn't much going on yet. Select the **SimpleSpriteBurst** emitter, then in the **Emitter** section, change **Sim Target** to **GPUCompute Sim** (see *Figure 2.4*). This will allow the Niagara System to use the GPU to create the particles instead of the CPU, which will handle a large number of particles efficiently and produce smoother motion.
6. You'll get a warning requesting that you change the **Emitter**'s bounds mode. In the **Calculate Bounds Mode**, change from **Dynamic** to **Fixed**, as shown in *Figure 2.4*. This should make the warning go away.

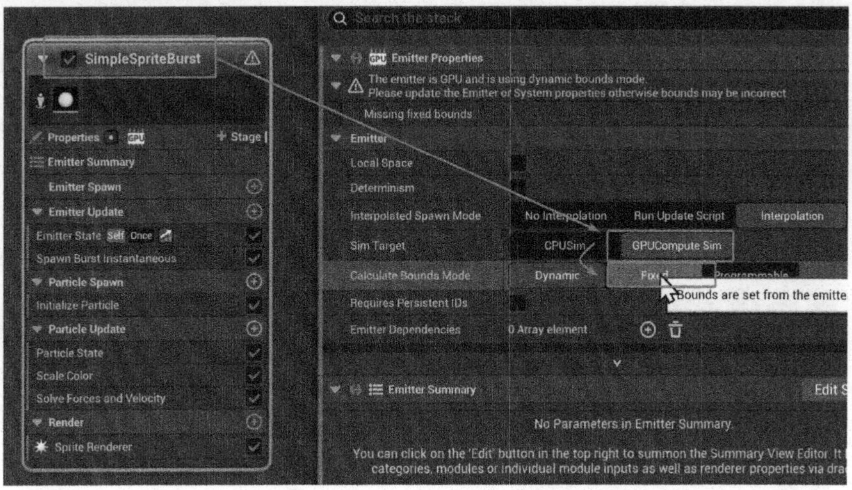

Figure 2.4 - Changing from CPU to GPU and fixing the error

7. Since this is a continuous smoke effect, change the **Emitter State** (in the **Emitter Update** module) to **Infinite**, and leave **Loop Duration** for **2** seconds. The **Infinite**

setting will allow the smoke to be generated continuously, but the **Loop Duration** establishes the duration of the emitter's lifecycle.

8. Delete the **Spawn Burst Instantaneous** module and, using the **+** button in **Emitter Update**, add **Spawn Rate**. Change the **Spawn Rate** to `50`.

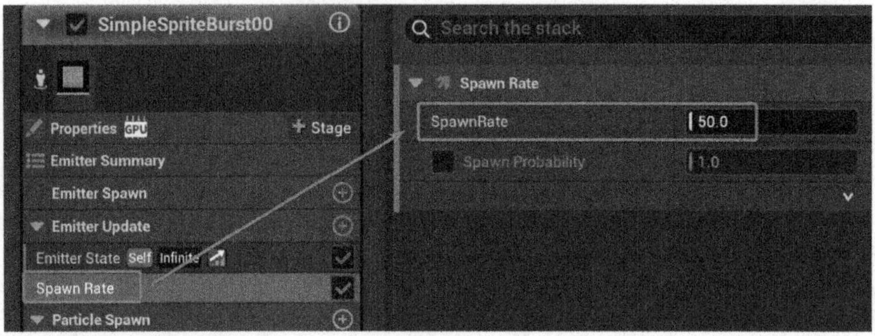

Figure 2.5 - Adding Spawn Rate

9. In the **Particle Spawn** section, select **Initialize Particle.** In the **Point Attributes**, change **Lifetime Mode** to **Random** and **Lifetime Min** set to `2` and **Lifetime Max** to `3`**.** These are calculated in seconds.

10. In the **Sprite Attributes**, change **Sprite Size Mode** to **Random Uniform.** Change **Uniform Sprite Size Min** to `10` and **Uniform Sprite Size Max** to `50`.

11. In **Sprite Rotation Mode,** change to **Direct Normalized Angle (0-1)**. Use the pointing down arrow to change the **Sprite Rotation Mode** to **Random Range Float.** Change **Minimum** to `0.25` and **Maximum** to `0.5`.

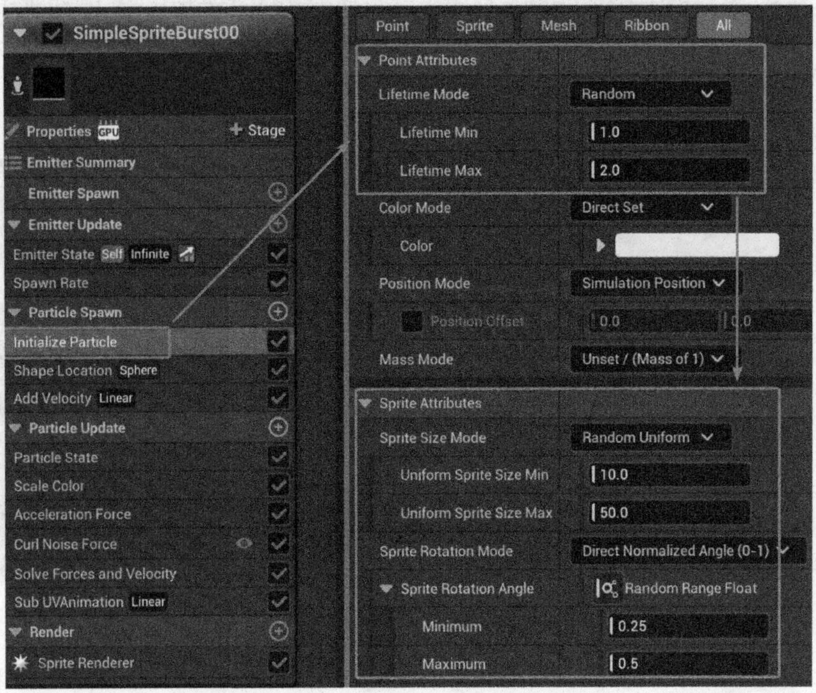

Figure 2.6 - Initialize Particle settings

12. Select the **Particle Spawn** section once more, click on the + sign, and search for the **Shape Location** module. Change **Sphere Radius** to `1.0`.

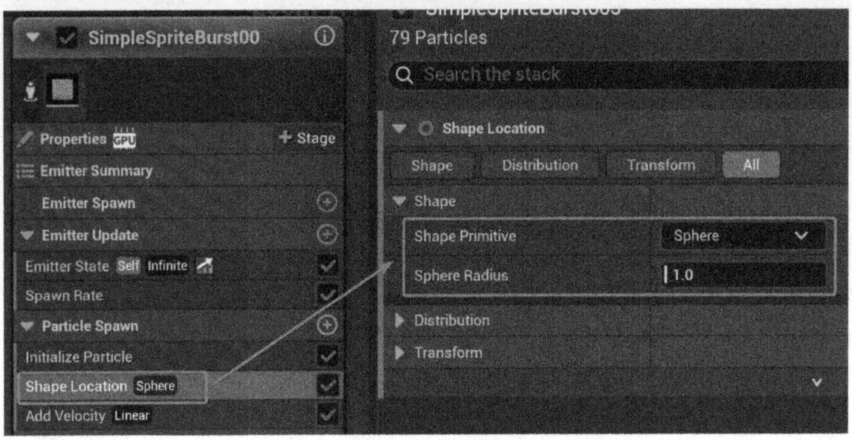

Figure 2.7 - Shape Location settings

13. Back in the **Particle Spawn** section, add the **Add Velocity** module, click the **Velocity** down-pointing arrow, choose **Random Range Vector**, and change the **Minimum** *Z* value (*blue*) to **10** and the **Maximum** *X* value to `20`. The Preview window should now show some subtle upwards movement of the sprite particle.

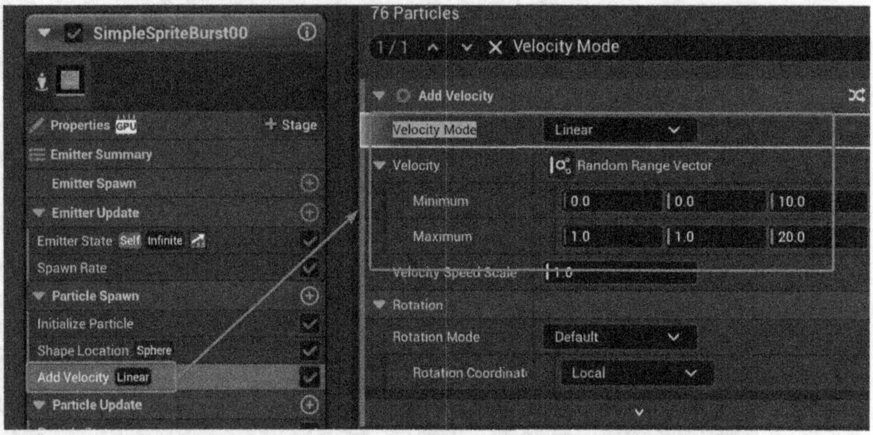

Figure 2.8 - Add Velocity settings

14. Down in the **Render** section, click the **Sprite Renderer**. Click the **Material** down-pointing arrow and search for `M_smoke_subUV` material. This is the smoke material that was made using the smoke texture that is available in the **Content Pack** you installed earlier.

Now let's animate the smoke texture and add motion to bring the effect to life.

1. Still in the **Sprite Renderer** module, change the **Sub Image Size** (under the **Sub UV** section) to `8 x 8`. Slowly but surely, our smoke is taking shape.

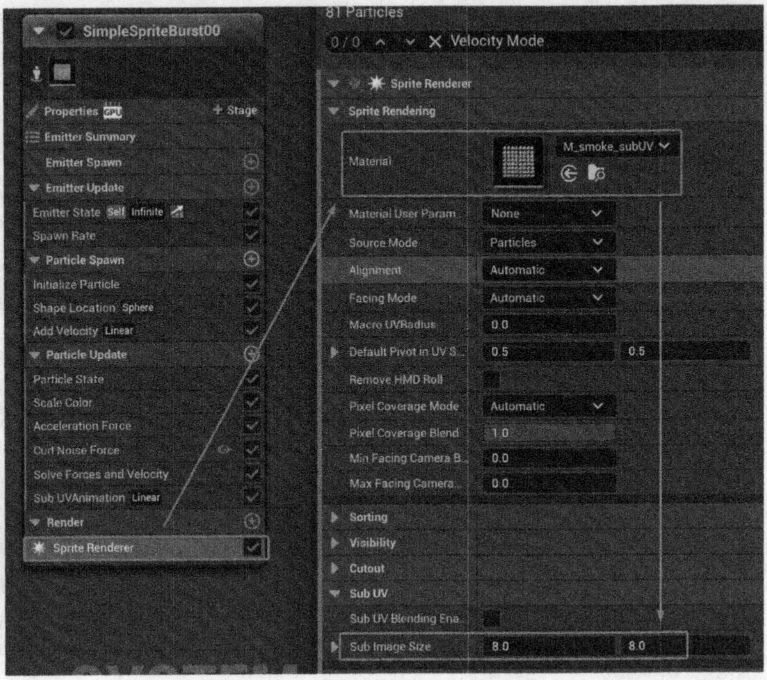

Figure 2.9 - Adding the Smoke material

2. Back to the **Particle Update** section, click the green + sign and search for the `Sub UV Animation` module.

3. Change **Sprite Renderer** to **Sprite Renderer** and in the **Output** section, enable the checkboxes for the **Start** and **End Frame Range Override**. Ensure the start is set to `0`, and the end is set to `63`.

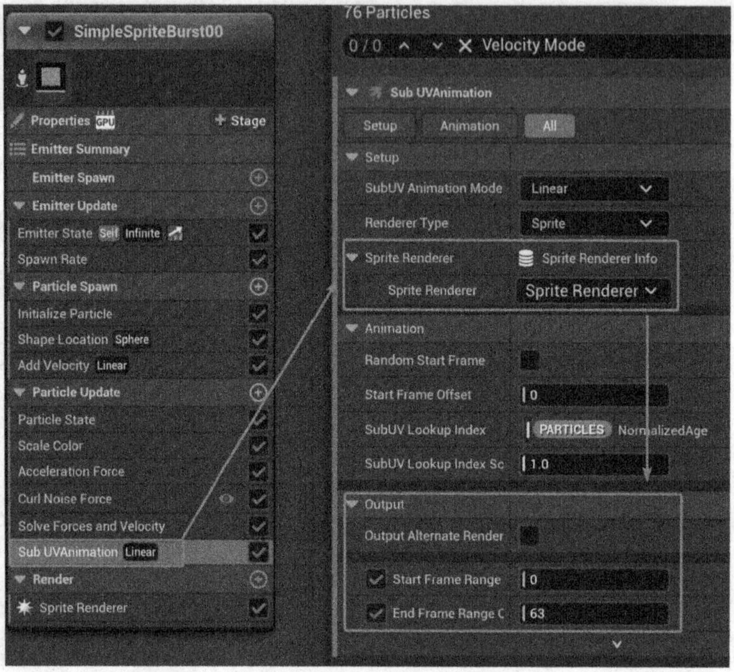

Figure 2.10 - Adding and setting the Sub UVAnimation module

4. Using the same method, add the **Acceleration Force** module and change the **Z** (*blue*) value to `50`.
5. Finally, add **Curl Noise Force**, change **Noise Strength** to `100`, and **Noise Frequency** to `150`.

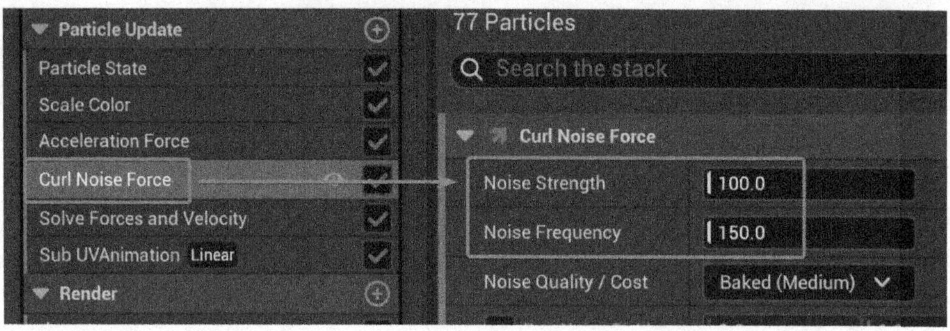

Figure 2.11 - Adding Curl Noise Force effect

6. Compile and save. Your smoke effect is now ready to be admired, as shown in *Figure 2.1*.

How it works...

This effect is created by combining a continuous particle system with controlled motion and animated textures to simulate drifting smoke. By switching the emitter to GPU Compute Simulation, the system can handle a larger number of particles efficiently, which results in smoother motion and allows the smoke to appear soft and detailed.

Using a **Spawn Rate** module instead of a **Spawn Burst Instantaneous** module ensures that particles are generated continuously, forming an ongoing stream of smoke rather than a one-time effect.

The natural look of the smoke comes from the variation introduced during particle initialization and motion. Randomized lifetime, sprite size, and rotation prevent the particles from appearing uniform, while the sphere-based spawn location keeps them clustered around the source. The randomized upward velocity and acceleration force drive the smoke upward, mimicking the buoyant movement of real smoke.

The evolving appearance of the smoke is achieved using an animated **SubUV** texture, which cycles through multiple frames to simulate changing smoke shapes over time. Additional motion detail is introduced through the **Curl Noise Force** module, which creates subtle swirling and breaks up linear movement. Together, these elements produce a soft, drifting smoke effect that feels natural, remains lightweight, and works well for close-up cinematic shots.

There's more...

Our Smoke material looks amazing from every angle, even when zoomed in, but it needs a system that will allow us to tweak the settings directly in the Level itself. This is where our knowledge in setting up **User Parameters** (discussed in *Chapter 1*) comes in handy. Let's set this up:

1. Double-click on `NS_Smoke_Wisps` to open the editor.
2. In the **User Parameters** tab, start creating the parameters as listed below:
    - For **Noise Strength** and **Noise Frequency** (in the **Curl Noise Force** module), choose **Float** to be named as `Noise Strength` and `Noise Frequency`, respectively, with the values of `100` and `150`.
    - For **Acceleration** (in the **Acceleration Force** module), choose **Vector** to be named as `Smoke Speed` with the value of `0,0,50`.

- For **Scale RGB** (in the **Scale Color** module), choose **Vector**, to be named `Smoke Color` with the value of `1,1,1`.
- For **Spawn Rate** (in the **Emitter Update** module), choose **Float**, to be named `Smoke Intensity` with a value of `50`.

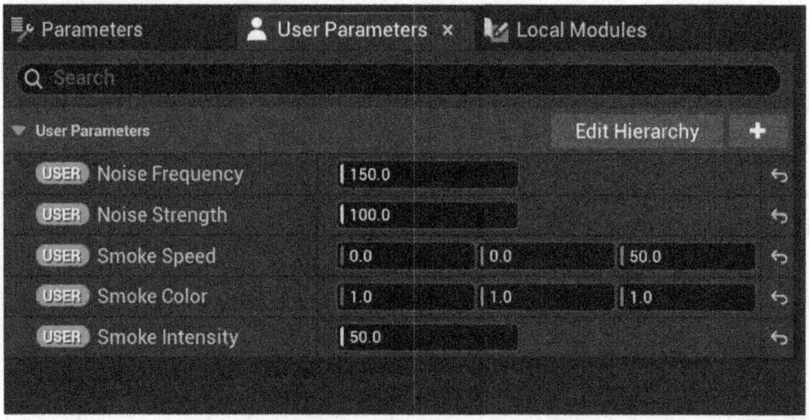

Figure 2.12 - The completed User Parameters settings

3. Back in the main Level, these parameters are now available for you to tweak. The `Smoke Color` parameter only works with values from 0 to 1, so to make red smoke, you set the *RGB* value as `1.0`, `0.0`, `0.0`.

4. As we discovered in *Chapter 1*, these parameters are keyframeable using the **Sequencer**. Go ahead and add it to a Sequence and start keyframing the parameters. If you aren't familiar with the concept of keyframing in the **Sequencer**, the topic is covered in-depth in the *Making Niagara effects stable for scrubbing and repeatable playback (repeatable takes)* recipe in *Chapter 1*.

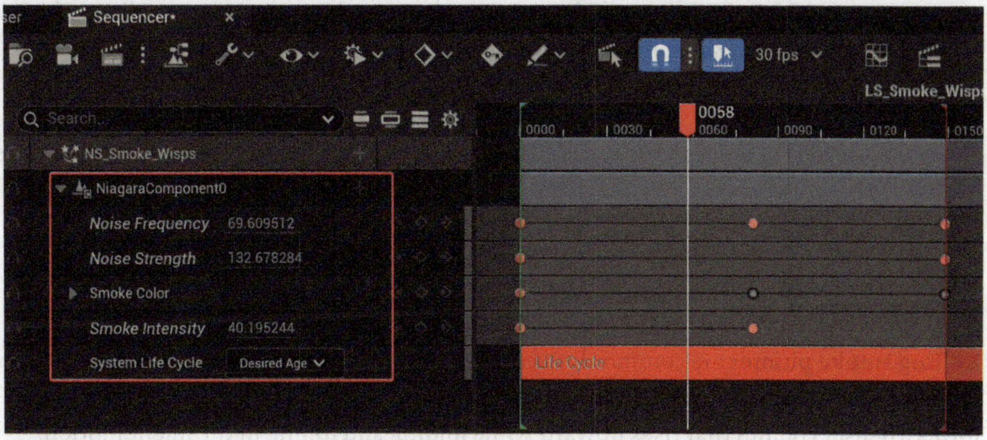

Figure 2.13 - Keyframing the Smoke effect in Sequencer

Finally, to better understand how the smoke effect is constructed, you can explore the material used in the emitter:

1. In the **Content Browser**, navigate to **Starter Content | Particles | Materials**.
2. Here you'll find the `M_smoke_subUV` material. Double-click to open it.
3. In the Material Editor, you'll see how the nodes were put together to achieve the smoke texture animation, as shown in *Figure 2.14*:

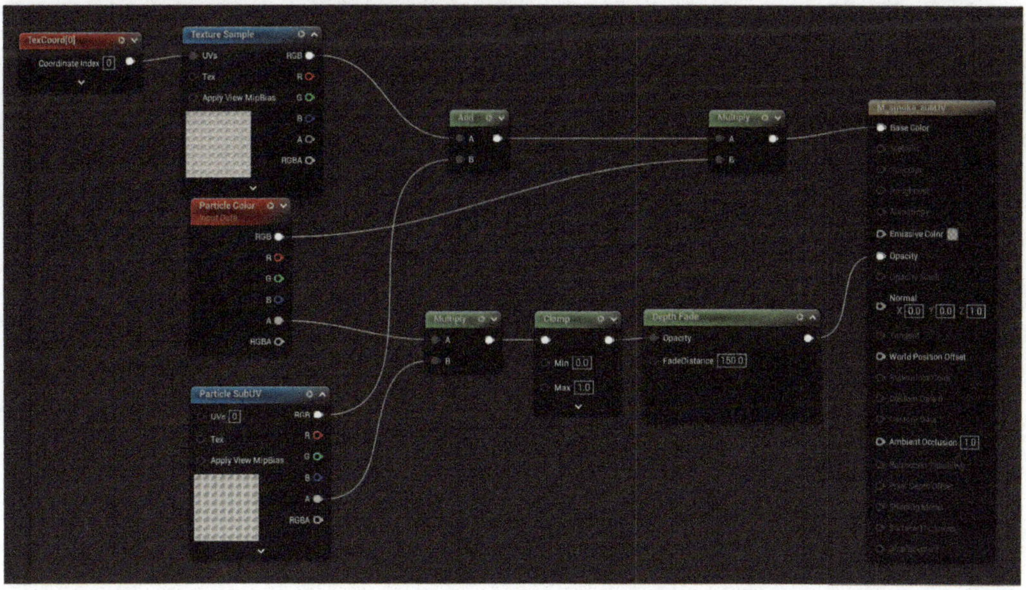

Figure 2.14 - The M_smoke_subUV material nodes

I suggest you reconstruct the material on your own, so you have an understanding of how it was created. In the next section, we will be creating a similar material from scratch.

See also

Explore these best practices from Epic Games when creating **Niagara Effects** in Unreal Engine: `https://dev.epicgames.com/community/learning/tutorials/L7aY/unreal-engine-niagara-example-pack-best-practices`.

Creating a rolling smoke/steam plume loop

Rolling smoke plumes are commonly used to represent continuous sources, such as steam vents, exhaust pipes, or industrial emissions. Unlike soft drifting wisps, this type of smoke forms a denser column that rises upward while folding and rolling in turbulent motion.

In this recipe, we will create a looping smoke plume effect using Niagara GPU sprites, combining upward velocity, turbulence, and animated smoke textures to produce a continuous plume that can run indefinitely without visible repetition in cinematic scenes.

Getting ready

We will be building the Rolling Smoke effect from scratch. We will be revisiting the same steps as before, but adding new modules to achieve the effect we are after.

How to do it...

Let's start by creating a new Niagara System from scratch:

1. In the `Niagara_Systems` folder, right-click to create a new Niagara System, select the **Create Empty Niagara System** button on the bottom left of the dialog box:

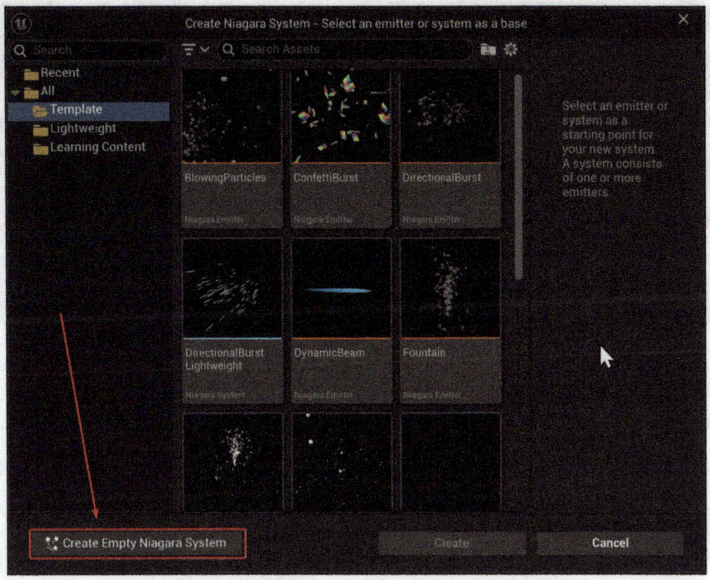

Figure 2.15 - Creating an empty Niagara System

2. Rename it to `NS_Rolling_Smoke`. Double-click to open it.
3. Unlike in the last section, there isn't any emitter here. Right-click anywhere in the editor and choose **Add Emitter**, then choose the **Minimal** emitter. The Preview window will confirm that there aren't any particles yet.
4. Rename the emitter to `Rolling Smoke`, and just like in the last recipe, change the following:
    - Enable **Determinism** – do the same for the **System** node (the *blue* node)
    - Change **Sim Target** to **GPUCompute Sim**
    - Change **Calculate Bounds Mode** to **Fixed**

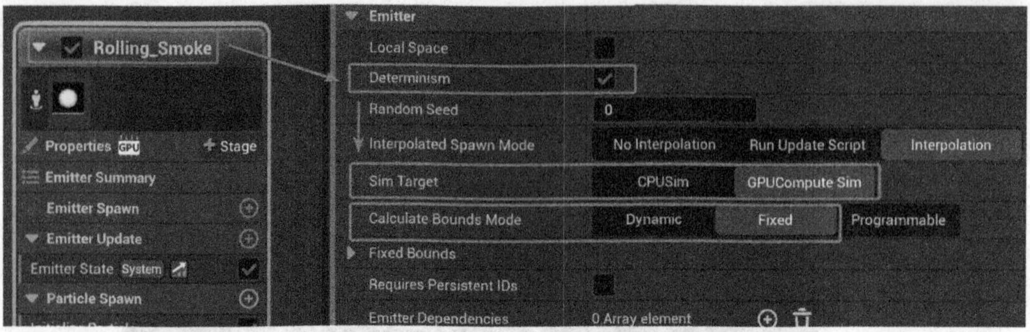

Figure 2.16 - Setting Determinism and Sim Target

5. Next, in the **Emitter Spawn** section, add a **Spawn Rate** module.
6. Click **Fix issue** to let Niagara automatically move the **Spawn Rate** module beneath the **Emitter State** module. Set **Spawn Rate** to `10`.
7. In the Preview panel, now there are particles being born on top of each other. Select the **Initialize Particle** module and make the following changes:
   - Change **Lifetime Mode** to **Random**
   - Change **Lifetime Min** to `3.0` and **Lifetime Max** to `5.0`
   - Change **Color Mode** to **Direct set** and leave **Color** at *white*
   - Under the **Sprite Attributes** section, change **Sprite Size Mode** to **Random Uniform** and set **Uniform Sprite Size Min** to `380` and **Uniform Sprite Size Max** to `500`

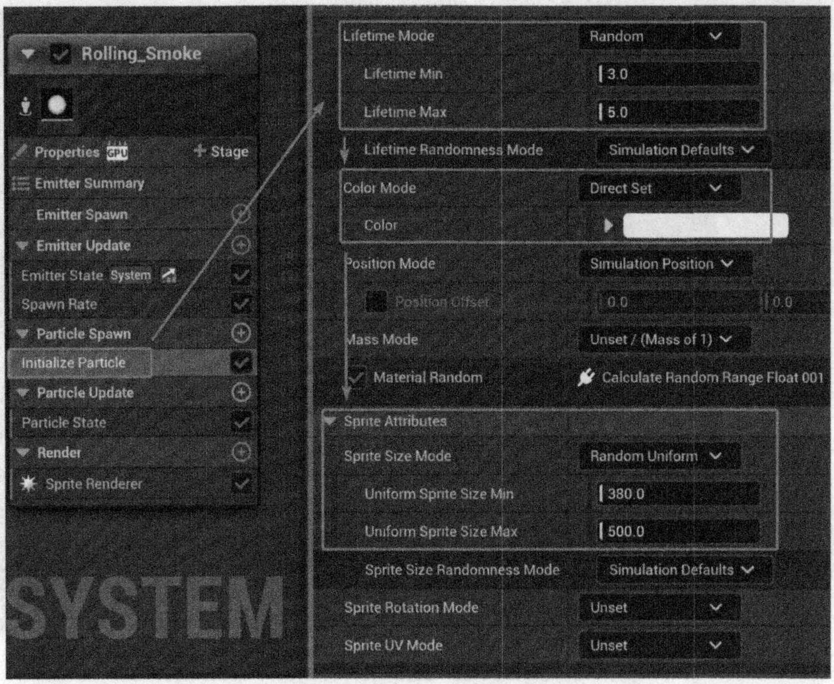

Figure 2.17 - Settings for Initialize Particle section

8. Next, we are going to create a location where the particles are going to spawn. In the **Particle Spawn** section, add a **Shape Location** module. Leave the settings as they are.
9. Let's make the particles move. In the **Particle Spawn** section, add the **Add Velocity** module—if you get an error, click **Fix issue** and change the following:
    - Change **Velocity Mode** to **In Cone**.
    - Using the down-pointing arrow, change the **Velocity Speed** to **Random Range Float** and set **Minimum** to `500` and **Maximum** to `1500`. Observe the Preview panel; you will see the particles moving.

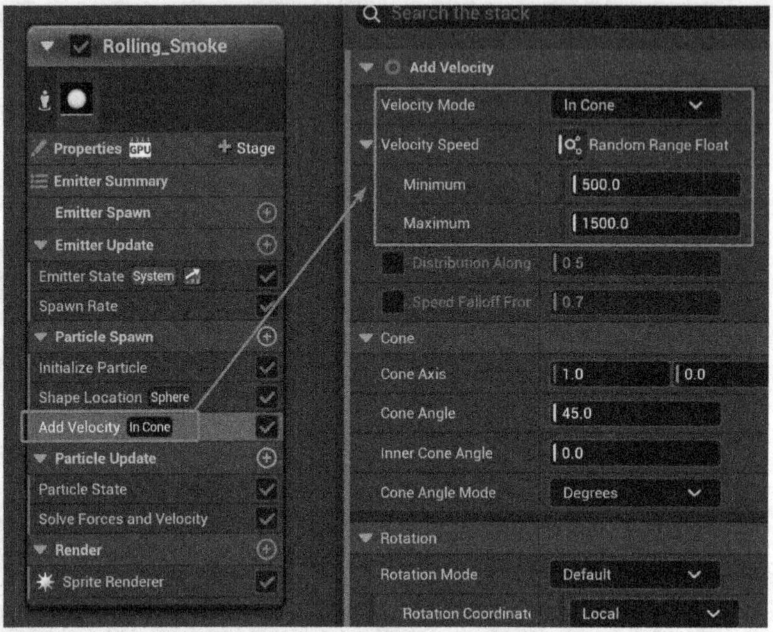

Figure 2.18 - Settings for Particle Spawn section

Now, to give our particles some texture, which will make them look like real smoke, we will create a SubUV material from scratch.

Creating and applying a custom SubUV smoke material

Follow these steps:

1. In the `Materials` folder, right-click and choose **Materials**, and rename it to `M_Smoke_Rolling`.
2. Double-click the material to open the Material Editor. Refer to *Figure 2.19* on how this material was set up. For the textures, use the `T_smoke_sprite_sheet` and `T_smoke_sprite_sheet_N` textures found in the `Textures` | `Chapter 2` folder (to access the project file in the GitHub repository, refer to the instructions in the *Download the example code/resource files* section in the *Preface* of this book).

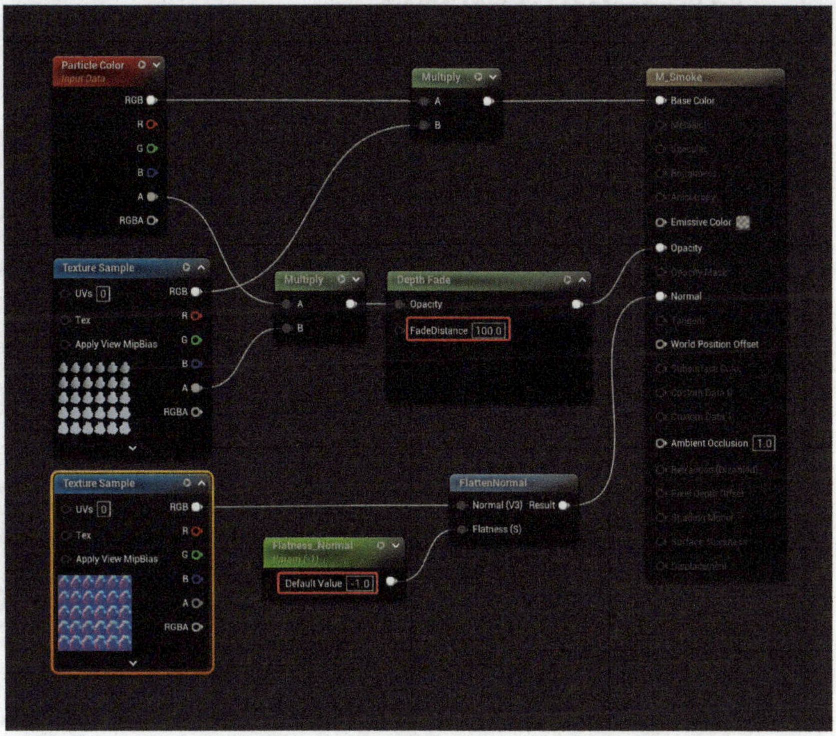

Figure 2.19 - The M_Smoke_Rolling material setup

3. You'll need to make the following changes to the **Result** node before adding the nodes. Here are the settings:
    - Set **Blend Mode** to **Translucent**
    - Enable **Two Sided**
    - Under the **Translucency** section, change **Lighting** mode to **Volumetric Directional**
    - Under the **Usage** section, check the **Used with Niagara Sprites**
4. To add the material to the emitter, under the **Render** section, select the **Sprite Renderer** module, in the **Material** drop-down, search for the `M_Smoke_Rolling` material.
5. If you get a **Missing Cutout Texture** warning, click **Dismiss.** Change the following:
    - Change **Alignment** to **Unaligned**

- Set **Facing Mode** to **Face Camera**
- Under the **Sub UV** section, enable **Sub UV Blending** and set **Sub Image Size** to 6 and 5, respectively.

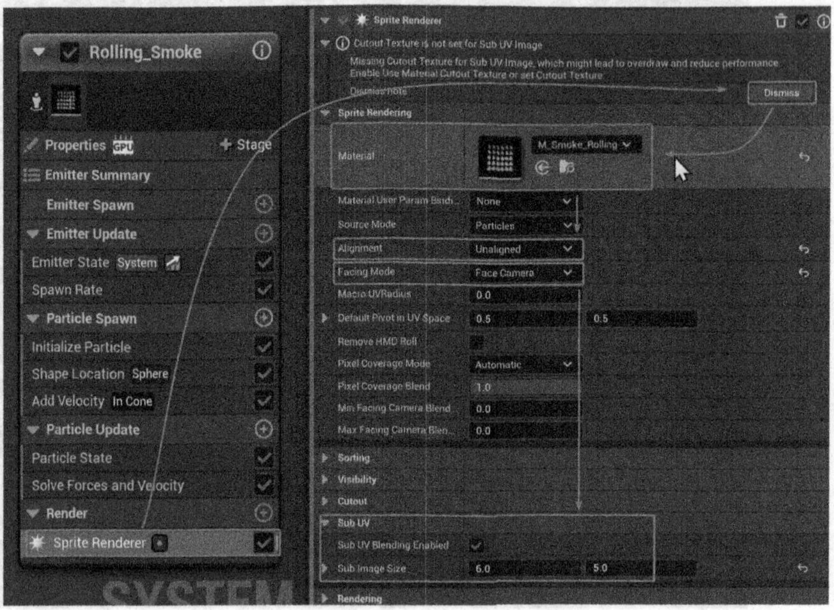

Figure 2.20 - The Sprite Renderer module settings

Our Rolling Smoke is now taking shape; we will need a few more nodes to make it look more realistic.

Refining motion and adding realism to smoke

Let's continue with these steps:

1. In the **Particle Spawn** section, add a **Sub UVAnimation** module, and set the parameters as follows:
    - **SubUV Animation Mode** to **Linear**
    - **Renderer Type** to **Sprite**
    - **Sprite Renderer** to **Sprite Renderer**
    - Enable **Start and End Frame Range Override** and change values to 1 and 30, respectively.

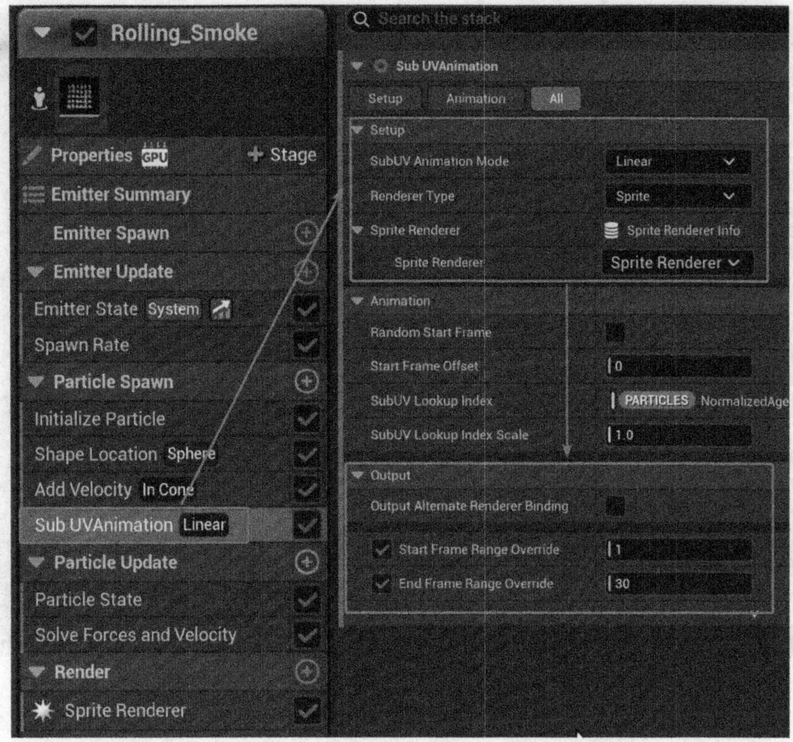

Figure 2.21 - The Sub UVAnimation module settings

2. In the **Particle Update** section, add the **Scale Color** module and change the following:
    - For **Scale RGB**, click the down-pointing arrow and search for `Make Vector from Linear Color RGB`, set **Red** = `1.0`, **Green** = `1.0`, **Blue** = `1.0`, and **Alpha** to `0.1`
    - For **Scale Alpha**, click the down-pointing arrow and search for `Float from Curve`. Make the curve as shown in *Figure 2.22*:

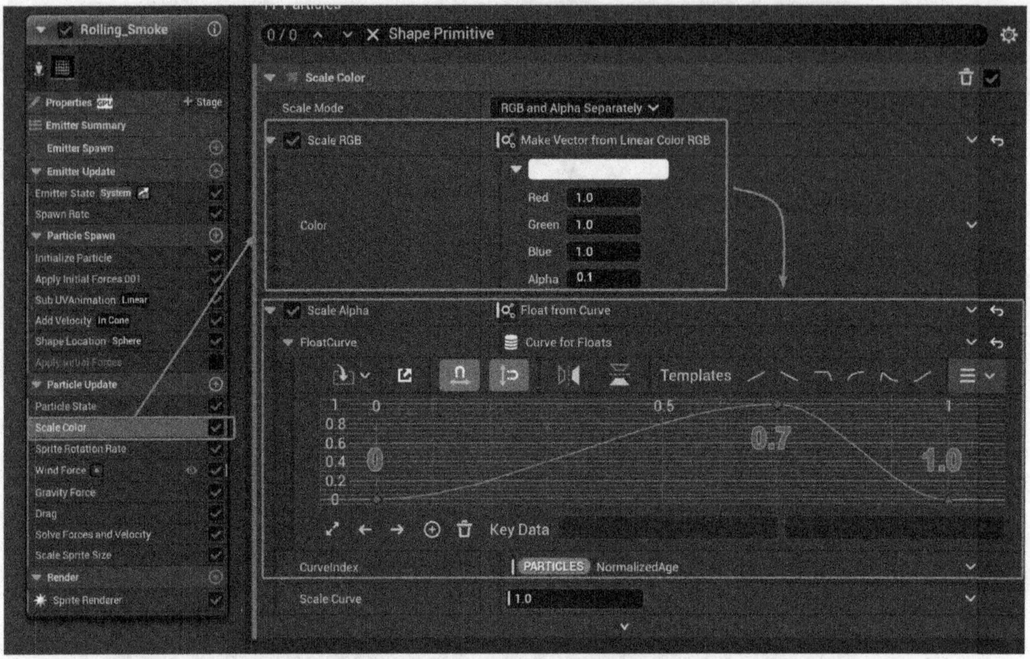

Figure 2.22 - The Scale Color module settings

3. To add some rotation to the smoke particles, add a **Sprite Rotation Rate** module and change the **Rotation Rate** to 15.
4. Add the **Wind Force** module, click **Fix issue**, and set the *X* (*Red*) value to `15`, as well as both *Y* and *Z* to `0`. Set `20` for **Wind Speed Scale**.
5. Add the **Gravity Force** module and set the *Z* (*Blue*) value to `200`. This will make the smoke move upwards.
6. Lastly, if not available yet, add a **Drag** module and set **Drag** to `0.5` and **Rotational Drag** to `1.0`.

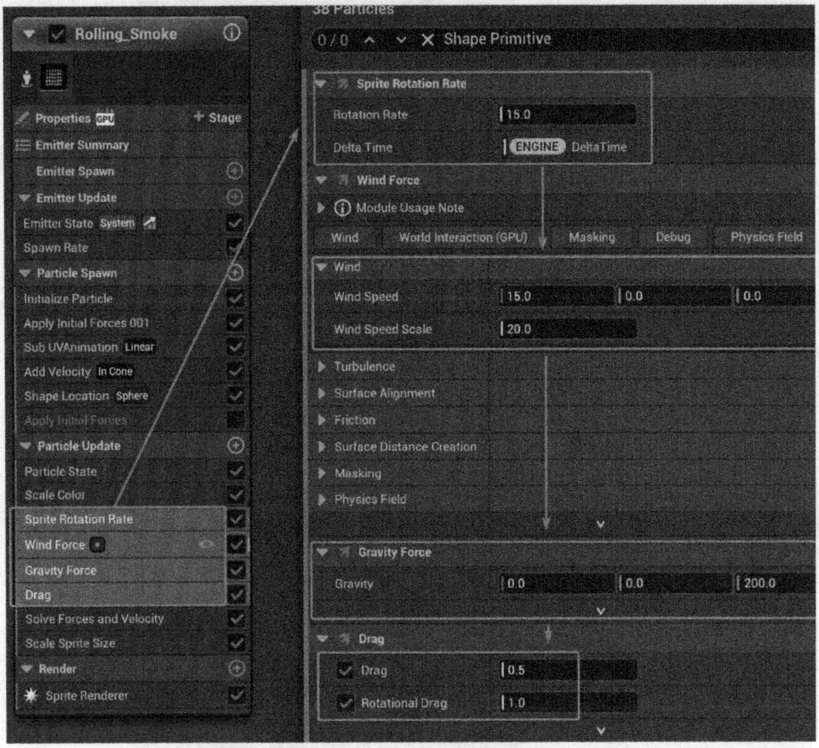

Figure 2.23 - Adding Sprite Rotation, Wind Force, Gravity, and Drag modules

7. Rearrange the modules so they look exactly like the emitter shown in *Figure 2.24*. The placement of the modules is important to get the look we are after. Compile and save.

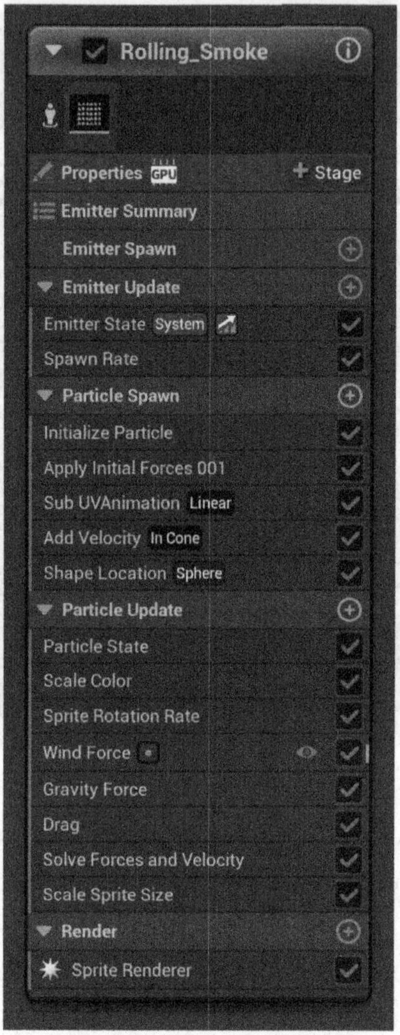

Figure 2.24 - The final emitter

If the scene is dark, in the main level, add a **Directional Light**. You can now manually tweak the parameters like the **Spawn Rate**, **Scale Color**, **Wind Force**, **Gravity Force**, **Drag**, and **Scale Sprite Size** to achieve a different look and feel of the rolling smoke. Alternatively, you can convert them to **User Parameters** to keyframe in **Sequencer**. Creating and keyframing **User Parameters** is covered in the *Building a Niagara "Shot Control" system with User Parameters* recipe in *Chapter 1*.

How it works...

This rolling smoke plume is created using a continuous Niagara emitter that spawns particles at a steady rate and drives them upward using directional forces. By building the system from an empty emitter and enabling GPU Compute Simulation, the effect can handle larger particle counts efficiently while maintaining smooth motion. The use of a **Spawn Rate** module ensures a constant flow of particles, forming a continuous column of smoke rather than a one-time burst.

The structure of the plume comes from how particles are initialized and directed. Randomized lifetime and sprite size introduce variation, so the smoke does not appear uniform, while the cone-based velocity pushes particles upward with slight directional spread. This creates the expanding column shape typically seen in steam or exhaust. The relatively large sprite sizes help fill out the volume of the plume, making it appear dense and cohesive.

The rolling motion of the smoke is driven by a combination of animated textures and motion forces. The **SubUV** animation cycles through frames of a smoke texture, giving the particles an evolving appearance over time. During the update stage, the **Wind Force** module introduces sideways drift, gravity force drives the upward movement to simulate buoyancy, and the **Drag** module slows the particles to create a heavier, more natural motion.

Additionally, the **Sprite Rotation Rate** module and tweaking of the **alpha** channel in the **Scale Color** module further add to the realism of the smoke. Together, these elements create a continuous plume that rises, rolls, and dissipates in a believable way for cinematic scenes.

Figure 2.25 shows the final look of the rolling smoke/steam plume:

Figure 2.25 - The final look of Rolling Smoke/Steam plume

There's more...

One way to make the rolling smoke plume appear thicker and more visually interesting is to add a secondary emitter layer by duplicating the emitter. While the main emitter forms the dense core of the plume, a second emitter can be used to create larger, softer particles that linger around the outer edges of the smoke. These particles should have a longer **Lifetime**, slightly larger **Sprite Size**, and lower **Velocity**, allowing them to drift more slowly and remain visible for longer. This additional layer helps fill out the silhouette of the plume and gives the smoke a fuller, more volumetric appearance.

You can also introduce subtle color variation to enhance the realism of the effect. For example, slightly darkening the core emitter while giving the outer emitter a lighter gray or slightly tinted color can simulate the natural variation often seen in steam or industrial smoke. Small color differences combined with longer-lasting particles help break up uniformity and make the plume feel denser and more dynamic in cinematic shots.

See also

Studying real-world smoke behavior is an excellent way to improve the realism of particle effects. Observing how smoke rises, curls, expands, and dissipates can help you better understand the motion patterns needed to recreate believable smoke in Niagara.

The following royalty-free video libraries contain many examples of rising smoke, steam plumes, and atmospheric haze that you can use as visual references when designing your effects:

- **Pixabay**: Pixabay hosts thousands of royalty-free smoke clips that can be downloaded and used for reference without attribution.
    - **Rising smoke reference footage**: `https://pixabay.com/videos/search/rising%20smoke/`
    - **Smoke plume reference clips**: `https://pixabay.com/videos/search/smoke%20plume/`

  These clips show examples of chimney smoke, industrial plumes, and drifting smoke columns useful for studying rolling smoke behavior.
- **Vecteezy**: Vecteezy hosts hundreds of smoke plume videos contributed by creators and available for royalty-free download. Check out the smoke footage library here: `https://www.vecteezy.com/free-videos/smoke-plume`

When studying these references, pay attention to how smoke:

- Expands as it rises
- Curls and folds in turbulent motion
- Changes density from the source to the outer edges
- Dissipates gradually over time

Analyzing these behaviors frame by frame can help you better replicate natural smoke motion when building Niagara effects.

Creating an impact smoke puff (burst + linger layers)

Impact smoke effects are commonly used to represent sudden events such as debris hits, explosions, collapsing objects, or objects striking the ground. Unlike continuous smoke plumes, impact smoke occurs very quickly, beginning with a short burst of dense particles followed by a slower, dissipating cloud.

In this recipe, we will create an impact smoke puff effect using Niagara GPU sprites. By combining a short burst emitter with a secondary lingering smoke layer, we can produce a convincing impact effect that expands rapidly and then gradually fades away. This technique is commonly used in cinematic scenes to emphasize impacts and add visual weight to fast-moving events.

Getting ready

Before starting this recipe, ensure the following:

1. Make sure **Unreal Engine 5.6** is installed.
2. Check that the **Niagara** plugin is enabled.
3. The `LV_VFX_Sandbox` level created in the *Setting up a reusable VFX "Sandbox" level for cinematic lookdev* recipe *Chapter 1*.

We will be creating a new Niagara System specifically for the impact of smoke.

How to do it...

Creating the Impact Smoke Puff is relatively straightforward; in fact, we'll be using the same effect we made in the *Creating soft smoke wisps (hero-friendly GPU sprites)* recipe, and change a few parameters and add a few new modules to achieve the result we are after. Let's get started:

1. Open the `Niagara_Systems` folder and duplicate `NS_Smoke_Wisps` by selecting it and pressing *Ctrl* + *D*. Rename it to `NS_Smoke_Impact`, double-click to open it.
2. Rename the emitter to `Impact_Smoke`. Then select the **Emitter Start** module to make the effect loop shorter and change **Loop Duration** to `1.0`.

3. Click the + for the **Emitter Update** section and add the **Spawn Burst Instantaneous** module.
4. Change **Spawn Count** to `10` and **Spawn Time** to `0`.
5. Delete the **Spawn Rate** module.
6. Delete the **Shape Location** module and in the **Initialize Particle** module, change the following:
   - Change **Lifetime Min** to `0.2` and **Lifetime Max** to `1.0`
   - Set **Color**: **Red** `1.0`, **Green** `1.0`, Blue `1.0`, and **Alpha** `0.08`
   - Change **Uniform Sprite Size Min** to `10` and **Uniform Sprite Size Max** to `40`

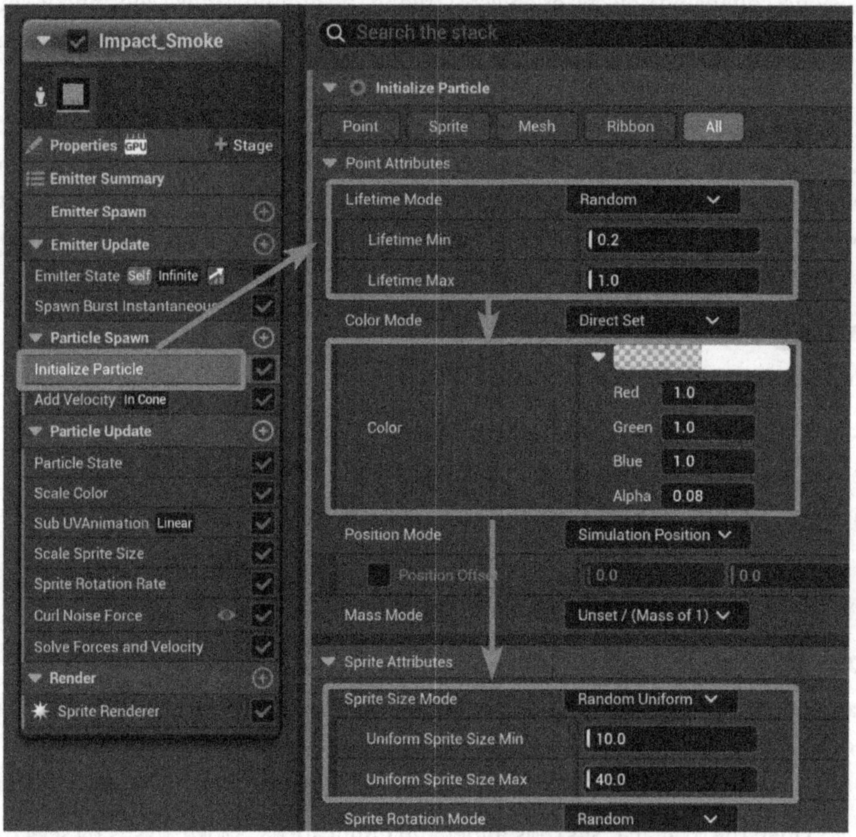

Figure 2.26 - The Initialize Particle module

7. Select the **Add Velocity** module and change the following:
   - **Velocity Mode** to **In Cone**
   - Click the down-pointing arrow for **Velocity Speed** and select **Random Range Float**. Set **Minimum** to `20` and **Maximum** to `250`

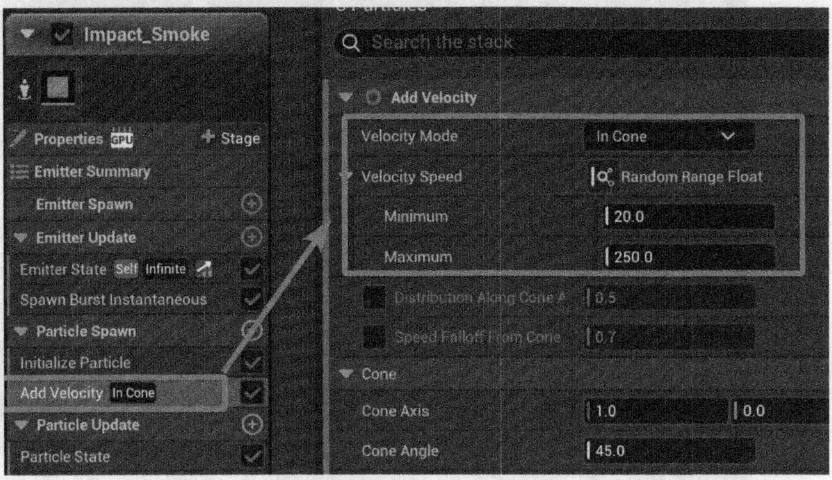

Figure 2.27 - The Add Velocity module

8. In the **Particle Update** section, delete the **Acceleration Force** module and add the **Scale Sprite Size**.
9. For **Scale Sprite Size**, change the **Key Data** value for the second key to `1.0` and `10.0`, and press the *F* key to fit the graph view.
10. Add the **Sprite Rotation Rate** module and change the **Rotation Rate** to `20`.
11. Finally, in the **Curl Noise Force**, change **Noise Strength** to `150` and **Noise Frequency** to `50`.

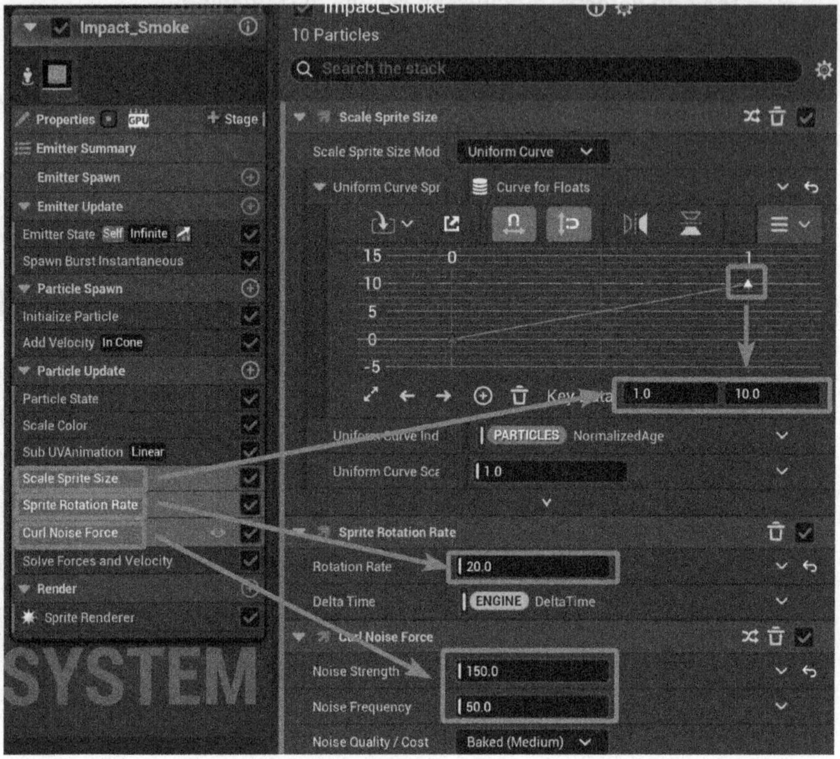

Figure 2.28 - The Scale Sprite Size, Sprite Rotation, and Curl Noise Force modules

12. Rearrange the modules so they look exactly like the emitter in *Figure 2.29*. The placement of the modules is important to get the look we are after. Compile and save.

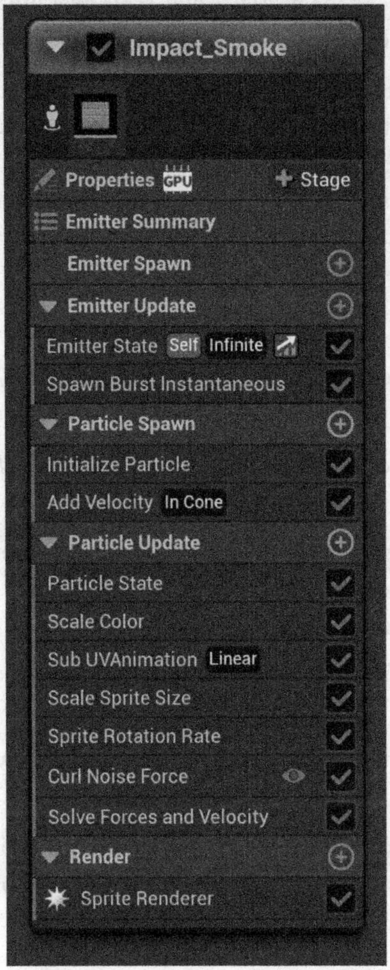

Figure 2.29 - The final Impact_Smoke emitter

How it works...

This impact smoke effect is created by converting a continuous particle system into a short, controlled burst. Instead of using a **Spawn Rate**, the system relies on a **Spawn Burst Instantaneous** module, which releases a fixed number of particles at a single moment. This produces the sharp, sudden appearance typical of impact events. Reducing the particle lifetime ensures the smoke appears quickly and dissipates just as fast, while smaller sprite sizes and low opacity keep the effect lightweight and suitable for fast-moving cinematic shots.

The outward expansion of the smoke is driven by cone-based velocity, which pushes particles away from the impact point with randomized speeds. This creates a natural spread rather than a perfectly uniform shape. As the particles age, scale over life increases their size, giving the impression that the smoke is expanding after the initial burst.

Additional motion detail comes from the update stage. Sprite **Rotation Rate** introduces subtle variation in particle orientation, while **Curl Noise Force** adds turbulence that breaks up uniform movement. Combined with the animated **SubUV** smoke texture, which provides evolving visual detail, these elements create a dynamic smoke puff that expands rapidly, softens over time, and fades naturally, making it suitable for impacts, debris hits, and collision effects in cinematic scenes.

There's more...

It's hard to imagine smoke impacts without some debris or flying particles. In this section, we will add a second emitter that will do exactly that, as an enhancement:

1. If you still have the `NS_Smoke_Impact` open, press the *E* key and choose the **Omnidirectional Burst Emitter,** and click **Add.**
2. In the **Emitter Properties** module, change **Sim Target** to **GPUCompute Sim** and **Calculate Bounds Mode** to **Fixed.** We will be adding a Static Mesh to this effect, so it's best to utilize the GPU processing power.
3. In the **Emitter State** module, for **Loop Behavior**, select the **Infinite** mode and ensure **Loop Duration** is set to `1.0`.
4. In the **Spawn Burst Instantaneous** module, set **Spawn Count** to `100`. This will produce 100 particles on every burst.
5. You should see sprite particles bursting in omnidirectional, but they are not bouncing off the ground. For that, in the **Particle Update section**, add the **Collision** module – that's much better.

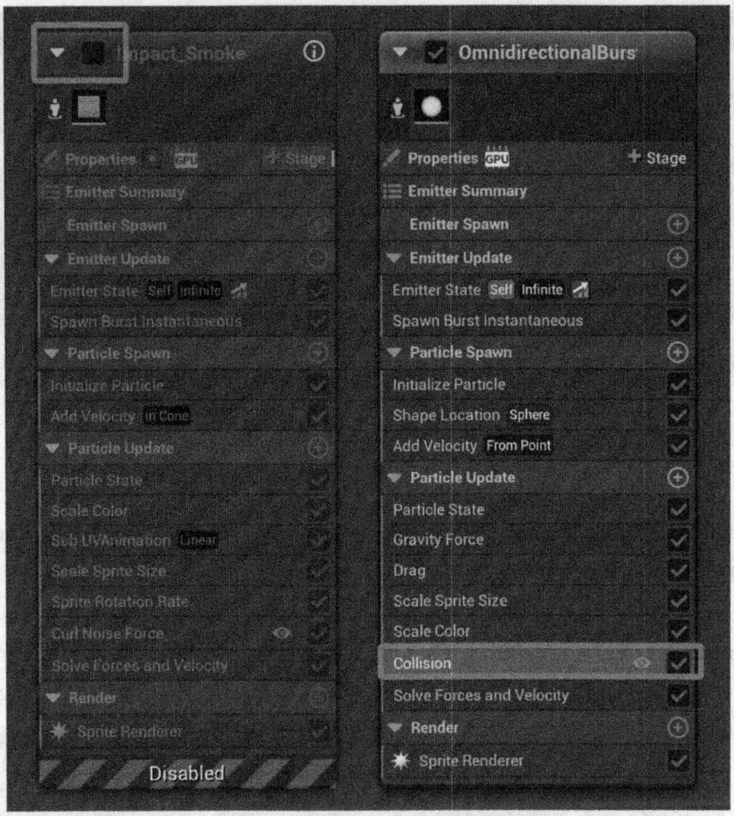

Figure 2.30 - Adding the Collision module

6. To view just the flying particles, you can disable the **Impact_Smoke** emitter by unchecking the top-left box.

Now that we have particles bouncing off the ground, let's add real geometry for realism. Follow these steps:

1. Disable the **Sprite Renderer** module, add a **Mesh Renderer**, and click **Fix issue**.
2. In the **Mesh Renderer** module, click the **triangle** next to **Meshes**, click the down-pointing arrow, and search for `rock`.
3. Select `SM_Rock`. The Rocks are huge!

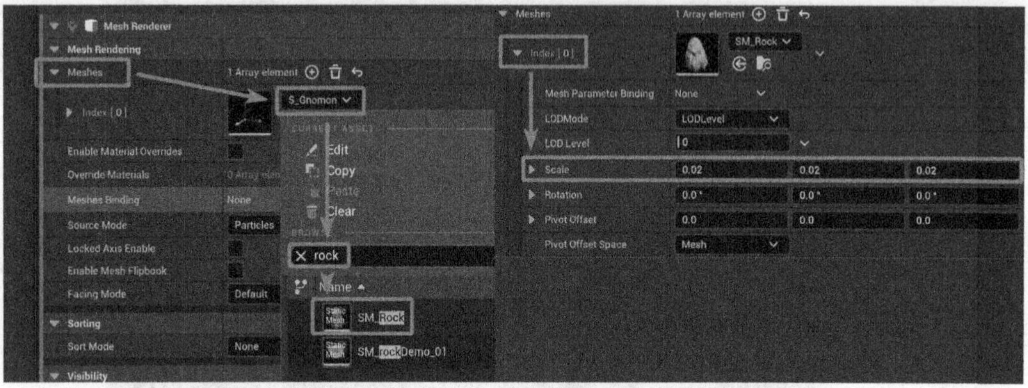

Figure 2.31 - Adding the Mesh Renderer and setting its scale

4. Click the triangle next to **Index [0]** and change **Scale** to `0.02` for *X*, *Y*, and *Z*.
5. To make the Rocks rotate as they hit the ground, in the **Particle Update** section, add an **Update Mesh Rotation** module.
6. Change **Orientation Method** to **Flight Orientation** and set **Up Vector Coordinate Space** to **Local**. I found these settings to be best to make the rock debris behave when hitting the ground, but feel free to tweak the parameters to your liking.

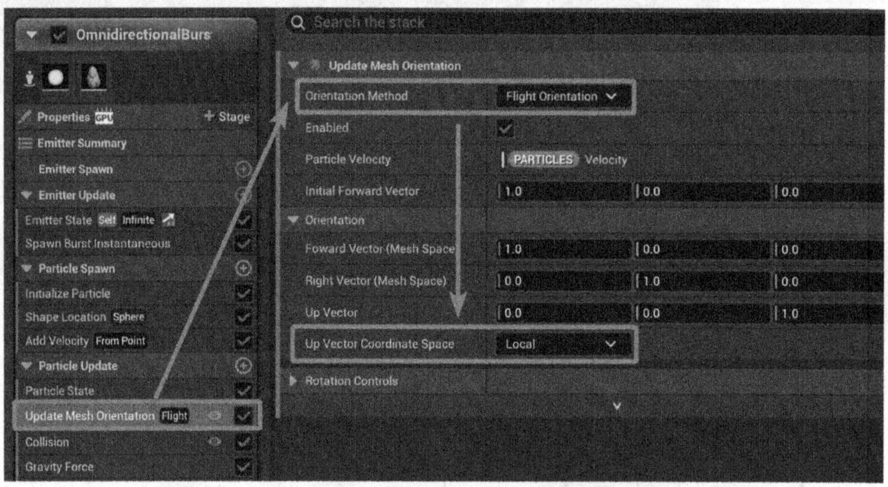

Figure 2.32 - Adding the Update Mesh Orientation module

7. **Delete** or **Disable Scale Sprite Size**, **Scale Color**, and **Sprite Renderer**. We won't be needing these modules as they are the Sprite modules and not the Mesh modules.
8. Reactivate the **Impact Smoke** emitter and adjust the parameters to suit your outcome. You can always create **User Parameters** and add the effect to the **Sequencer** to create a trail of cinematic explosions as you did in earlier recipes.

See also

Studying real-world dust and smoke impacts can help you better understand how these effects behave in motion. The following royalty-free video libraries provide useful visual references for studying the behavior of an impact smoke:

- **Pixabay**: For dust impact/burst reference footage: `https://pixabay.com/videos/search/dust%20explosion/`
- **Vecteezy**: For smoke and debris reference clips: `https://www.vecteezy.com/free-videos/dust-explosion`

Analyzing these behaviors frame-by-frame can help you reproduce a more convincing impact smoke effect in Niagara.

Building ground fog/low haze for depth and mood

Ground fog and **low-lying haze** are commonly used in cinematic scenes to add depth, atmosphere, and a sense of scale. Unlike smoke plumes or bursts, this type of effect remains subtle and spreads across the environment, helping to soften the scene and enhance lighting. It is especially useful for separating foreground and background elements, making compositions feel more layered and immersive.

In this recipe, we will create a ground fog effect using Niagara GPU sprites. By combining slow-moving particles, soft smoke textures, and minimal turbulence, we can build a low-lying haze that gently drifts across the ground. This effect is ideal for cinematic environments where mood and depth are important.

Getting ready

Before starting this recipe, ensure the following:

1. Make sure **Unreal Engine 5.6** is installed.
2. The **Niagara** plugin is enabled.

3. The `LV_VFX_Sandbox` level that was created in the *Setting up a reusable VFX "Sandbox" level for cinematic lookdev* recipe from *Chapter 1*.
4. Smoke materials and textures from previous recipes should already be available in the project from previous recipes. If not, refer to the *Technical requirements* section.

How to do it...

For this recipe, instead of starting from scratch, we'll be using a template that already has the modules we require, which need some tweaking. We will add additional modules if needed. Let's get started:

1. Create a new Niagara System. From the list of selections, choose the **Hanging Particulates** template.
2. Name it `NS_Ground_Fog` and drag it into the Level.
3. In the Preview window, you'll see dust-like particles moving slowly. Double-click to open the editor.
4. For the **Hanging Particulate** emitter, select the **Properties** module and enable **Local Space** and **Determinism** by clicking on the check boxes. By enabling **Local Space**, you'll be able to move the particles as one unit.
5. In the **Emitter State** module, change **Loop Duration** to `5.0`.
6. In the **Initialize Particle** module, change the following:
   - **Lifetime Min** to `2.0` and **Lifetime Max** to `8.0`
   - **Uniform Sprite Size Min** to `30` and **Uniform Sprite Size Max** to `100`
   - **Sprite UV Mode** to **Unset**
7. Select the **Shape Location** module and change the following:
   - Change **Box Size** to `500`, `500`, `1.0`
   - **Reset the Box Midpoint** by clicking the **Reset** button
8. In the **Particle Spawn** section, add the **Add** Velocity module, using the down-pointing arrow, and change **Velocity** to **Random Range Vector**. Change the **Velocity Minimum** to `10`, `0.0`, `0.0`, and **Maximum** to `35`, `1.0`, `1.0`.

Figure 2.33 - Shape Location and Add Velocity settings

9. In the **Particle Update** section, delete **Wind Force**, **Aerodynamic Drag**, and **Scale Sprite Size** modules and add **Sub UVAnimation**, **Curl Noise Force**, and **Drag** modules.
10. In the **Render** section, select the **Sprite Renderer** module and change the **Material** to `M_smoke_subUV`. This is the same material we used earlier in the *Creating soft smoke wisps (hero-friendly GPU sprites)* recipe. Change the **Sub Image Size** to `8.0`, `8.0`.

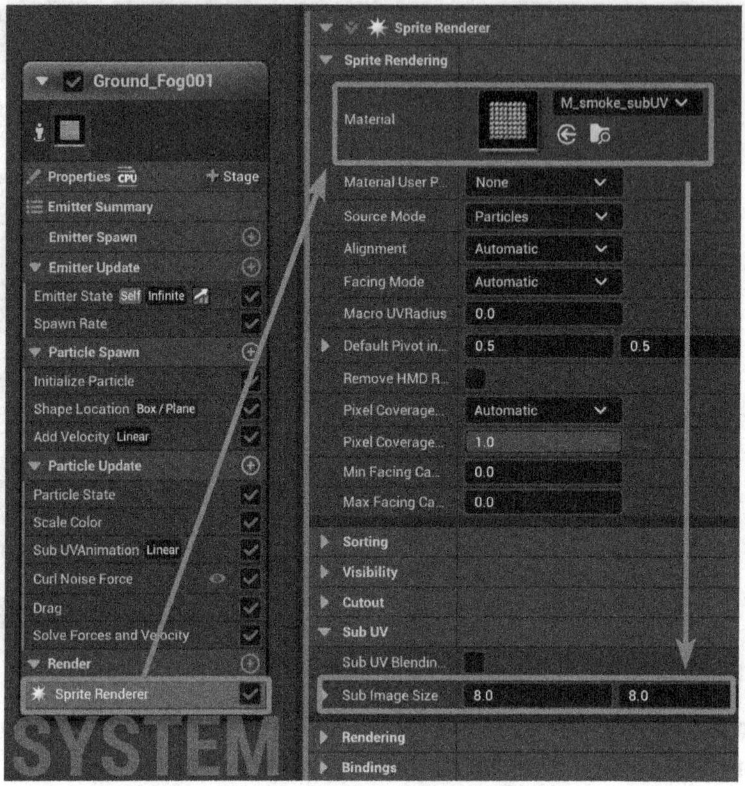

Figure 2.34 - The Sprite Renderer settings

11. If you get a **Cutout Texture** warning, click **Dismiss**.
12. Select the **Sub UVAnimation** module, dismiss the warnings by changing the **Sprite Renderer** to **Sprite Renderer**.

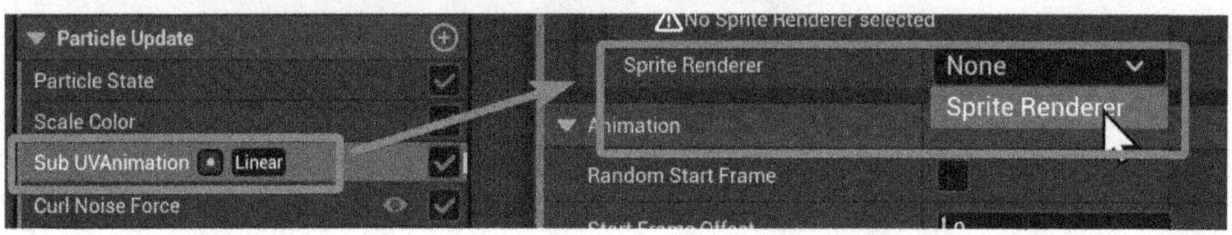

Figure 2.35 - The SubUV Animation settings

13. For the **Curl Noise Force** module, change **Noise Strength** to 25 and leave **Noise Frequency** as 50.

14. For the **Drag** module, change the **Rotational Drag** to `0.0`.
15. You should now have an effect that resembles ground fog or haze. To make the fog less visible, change the **Alpha** value in the **Initialize Particle** module, under the **Color** properties. You can even change the fog color here.

Figure 2.36 - The final Ground Fog/Low Haze

How it works...

This ground fog effect is created using a Niagara System based on the **Hanging Particulates** template, which provides a starting point for slow-moving atmospheric particles. By enabling **Local Space** and **Determinism**, the particles behave as a cohesive unit and remain stable when repositioned in the level. Increasing the particles' lifetime and using larger sprite sizes allows the particles to persist longer and overlap, forming a continuous layer of haze instead of isolated particles.

The wide coverage of the fog comes from the *box-shaped* spawn region, which distributes particles evenly across a flat area. Instead of strong upward motion, the effect uses low horizontal velocity, keeping the particles close to the ground while allowing them to drift gently across the scene. Removing stronger forces, such as wind and aerodynamic drag, helps maintain a calm, grounded look that is appropriate for low-lying fog.

The softness and evolving appearance of the fog are achieved using an animated **SubUV** smoke texture, which cycles through frames to simulate changing shapes over time. Subtle motion is added through **Curl Noise** and **Drag**, preventing the fog from appearing static while keeping movement slow and natural. By carefully balancing particle density, opacity, and motion, the system produces a low haze that enhances depth and atmosphere without overpowering the scene.

There's more...

We have a good-looking Ground Smoke/Fog effect now, but to be able to control the smoke **Opacity** and its **Emissive** (glow) properties will allow us to art-direct the effect further. Let's add that now:

1. Browse to the `Materials` folder, select the `M_smoke_subUV` material and duplicate using *Ctrl* + *D*. Rename to `M_Fog_subUV`**,** then double-click to open it.
2. Rewire the current nodes to look exactly like *Figure 2.37***.** You'll need to add two **ScalarParameter** nodes (highlighted) by holding the *S* key and left-clicking anywhere in the graph editor.
3. Rename the nodes as **Emissive** and **Opacity.** *Alt-click* on the pins to disconnect them.

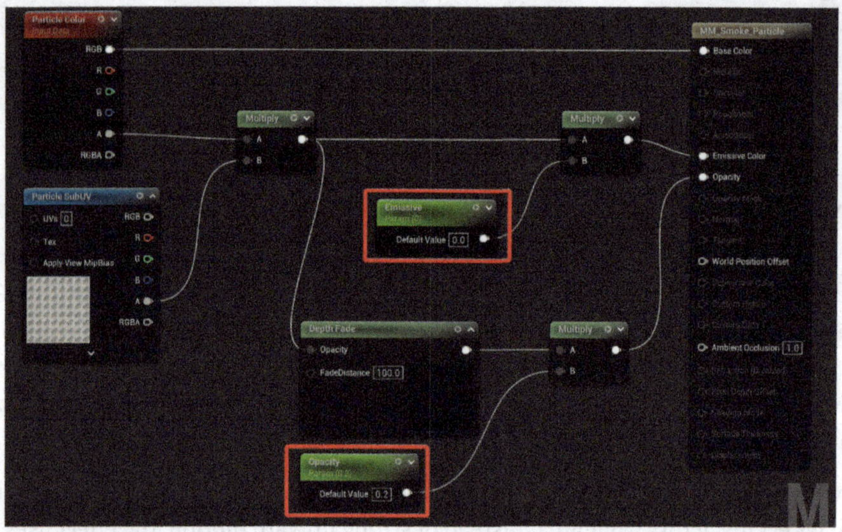

Figure 2.37 - Rewiring the M_Fog_subUV material

4. Set **Emissive** default value to `0.0` and **Opacity** to `0.2`. Apply and **Save**.
5. Back in the browser, right-click on the material you just created and choose **Create Material Instance**, rename it as `MI_Fog_subUV`**,** and double-click to open it.
6. Under the **Global Scalar Parameter Values** section, enable **Emissive** and **Opacity**.

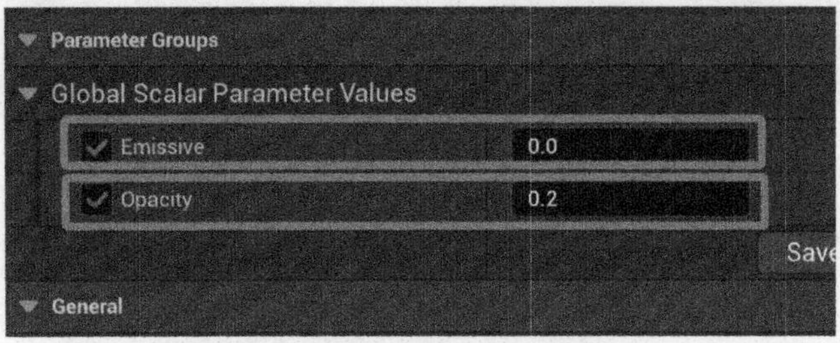

Figure 2.38 - Enabling Emissive and Opacity

7. Lastly, in the `NS_Ground_Fog` Niagara System, change the **Sprite Renderer** material to **MI_Fog_subUV.** You can now keyframe both the **Emissive** and **Opacity** values in a Level Sequence if you wish.

As you can see, you've built a robust and flexible Niagara System that can be adjusted on the fly and adapted to a wide range of cinematic scenarios.

See also

Studying real-world fog and atmospheric haze is essential for creating believable environmental effects. The following royalty-free video libraries provide useful references for ground fog and low haze:

- **Pixabay**: See reference footage for ground fog and mist here: `https://pixabay.com/videos/search/fog/`
- **Vecteezy**: See library for fog and atmospheric effects: `https://www.vecteezy.com/free-videos/fog`

When studying these references, observe how:

- Fog remains close to the ground and spreads horizontally
- Density varies across different areas
- Movement is slow and subtle rather than turbulent
- Lighting interacts with fog to create depth and mood

Pause footage frame by frame to study how fog evolves over time. Replicating these behaviors in Niagara will help you achieve more convincing atmospheric effects in your scenes.

3

Niagara Dust and Debris Atmosphere for Cinematics

Dust is one of the simplest effects you can add to a shot, but it makes a huge difference because it sells scale, weight, and atmosphere. In *Chapter 1*, you set up the foundation for cinematic Niagara work by creating a test environment, building reusable shot controls, timing effects in **Sequencer**, and checking the result in **Movie Render Queue**. In *Chapter 2*, you used those ideas to create smoke effects with soft motion, layered density, and cinematic timing. This chapter builds on both by applying the same workflow to dust, where the focus shifts from drifting smoke to impact, contact, trails, and subtle atmosphere that help ground a shot and make movement feel more believable.

You'll start with a post-impact dust layer (aftershock) that helps hits and destruction feel grounded, then quick bursts for footsteps or landings timed in **Sequencer**. After that, you'll create a dust trail that follows moving objects. Lastly, you'll add subtle cinematic dust motes for "room tone" in light beams.

Each recipe focuses on clean timing, believable motion, and art-directable controls you can reuse across different shots. These are important skills in a VFX production workflow because dust effects often need to match animation, destruction, camera movement, and lighting very closely. A dust burst that appears a few frames too early, or a trail that feels too heavy, can make the shot look disconnected.

In this chapter, we will cover the following recipes:

- Creating a post-impact debris dust layer for aftershock effects
- Creating landing/footstep dust timed in Sequencer
- Designing smoke/dust trails behind a moving object
- Building dust motes in a light beam for cinematic room tone

By learning how to build, time, adjust, and render these dust effects properly, you'll create VFX elements that support the scene instead of distracting from it.

> **Note**
>
> **Download the code/resource bundle and the PDF version of this book**
>
> Your purchase includes a DRM-free PDF copy of this book, the code/resource bundle, and a range of exclusive benefits. To unlock everything, follow the *Free benefits with your book* section in the *Preface*.

Technical requirements

Before starting this recipe, ensure you have the following set up:

- Make sure that **Unreal Engine 5.6** is installed.
- A project with **Niagara** and the **Niagara Sim Caching** plugin enabled.
- A test environment or sandbox level where the effect can be previewed — you can use the sandbox environment we created in *Chapter 1*.
- Be sure to maintain the following folder structure to keep the assets organized:
    - `Content`
        - `Niagara_Systems`
        - `Sequences`
        - `Textures`
        - `Materials`
        - `MRQ`

You can download the example project for this book by following the instructions in the *Download the example code/resource files* section in the *Preface* of this book.

The complete example project is included in the downloadable code/resource bundle.

Creating a post-impact debris dust layer for aftershock effects

In this recipe, you'll build a simple dust "aftershock" effect that appears right after an impact, break, or heavy landing. It has two parts: a quick burst that sells the hit, and a softer lingering haze that hangs in the air and fades out. This is one of the most useful dust setups because you can reuse it for many situations later in the chapter.

We'll use the same approach you set up earlier: a clean Niagara System with a few shot-friendly controls (intensity, size, speed, color) so you can adjust the dust per shot without digging through the stack. You'll also time it in **Sequencer** and do a quick render check, so the result behaves well when scrubbing and stays consistent for repeat takes.

Getting ready

Before starting, set up your test environment as follows:

1. Open the `VFX_COOKBOOK` Unreal Engine project file (see the *Technical Requirements* for details). To access the GitHub repository link, follow the steps in the *Download the example code/resource files* section in the *Preface*.
2. In the **Content Browser**, open the `LV_VFX_Sandbox` level, if it is not already open.
3. Browse to the `Sequences` folder and double-click to open `Ch3_LS_FallingBox`.

How to do it...

The current open sequence (`Ch3_LS_FallingBox`) consists of a 35 mm camera and a simple cube being keyframed to "drop" to the floor. We will keep things basic for now and move on to something more cinematic later in the chapter. Follow these steps:

1. In the **Content Browser** | `Niagara_Systems` folder, right-click to create a new Niagara System. From the pop-up window, choose the **Minimal** Niagara emitter.
2. We can rename it to `NS_PostImpact_Dust` and press *Enter*. Double-click to open in the Niagara Editor.
3. Select the **Properties** module and enable the **Local Space** and **Determinism** check boxes.
4. Change **Sim Target** to **GPUCompute Sim** and for **Calculate Bounds Mode**, select **Fixed**. As I mentioned in *Chapter 2*, **Local Space** will allow you to freely move the Niagara System within the level, **Determinism** will enable smoother playback in the **Sequencer**, and **GPUCompute Sim** will leverage your GPU to create the effect.

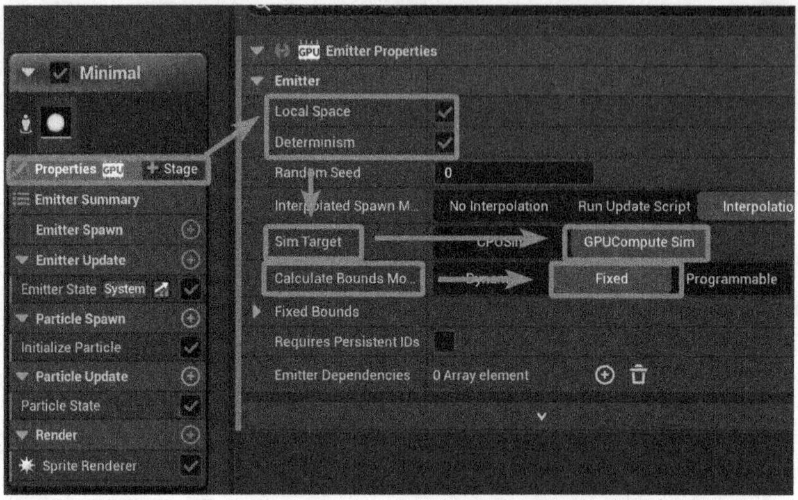

Figure 3.1 - Properties Module settings

5. Select **Emitter State**, change **Life Cycle Mode** to **Self**.
6. Change **Loop Behavior** to **Infinite** and set **Loop Duration** to `2.0`.

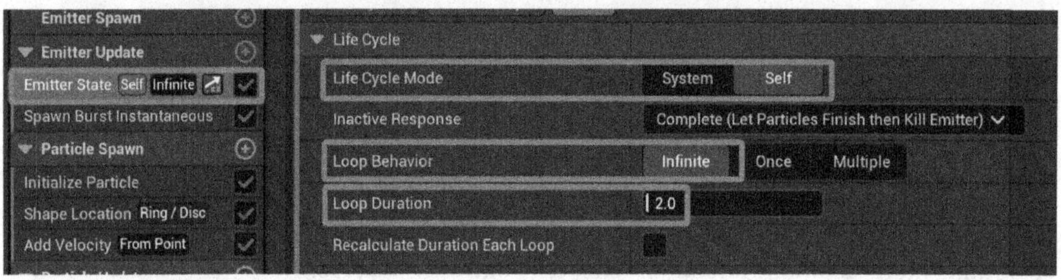

Figure 3.2 - Emitter State Module settings

> **Note**
>
> We are setting the **Loop Behavior** to **Infinite** for testing and preview purposes. This effect only happens once or whenever there is a need for impact dust. Once you've completed the creation of the effects, you'll need to change it to **Once**.

7. In the **Emitter Update** section, click the *orange* + (**plus**) sign and add a **Spawn Burst Instantaneous** module. Change **Spawn Count** to `100`.
8. In the **Render** section, select **Sprite Renderer**. In the **Material** drop-down, search for and select `M_Dust_Particle`.

Figure 3.3 - Sprite Renderer settings

9. In the **Particle Spawn** section, select the **Initialize Particle** module. Change the following:
   - Set **Lifetime Mode** to **Random** and set **Lifetime Max** to `2.5`
   - Change **Color Mode** to **Direct Set,** leave the color as *white* for now; we will change it later
   - Under the **Sprite Attributes**, change **Sprite Size Mode** to **Random Non-Uniform**
   - Change **Sprite Size Min** to `25` for X and Y
   - Change **Sprite Size Max** to `50` for X and Y

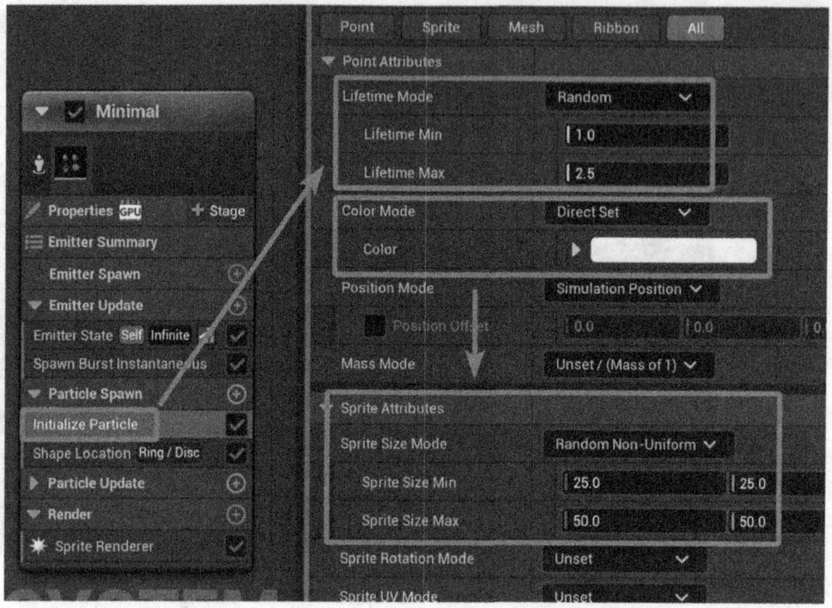

Figure 3.4 - Initialize Particle Module settings

10. In the **Particle Spawn** section, click the *green* + sign to add a **Shape Location** module. We need the impact dust to disperse in all directions, so change the **Shape Primitive** to **Ring/Disc** and **Ring Radius** to `0.1`.
11. In the same section, add the **Add Velocity** module. Change the **Velocity Mode** to **From Point**. For **Velocity Speed**, click the down-pointing arrow and select **Random Range Float**. Change **Minimum** to `150` and **Maximum** to `151`.

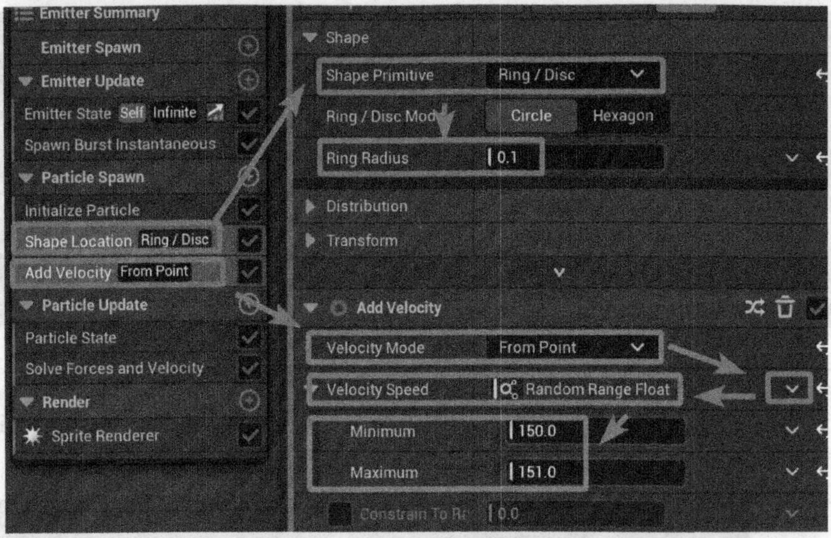

Figure 3.5 - Shape Location and Add Velocity module settings

12. In the **Particle Update** section, search and add the **Scale Sprite Size** module. Select the first **Key Data** (*red* triangle), change the first value to `0.3`, and leave the second value at **0**.
13. Select the next **Key Data**, leave the first value at **1**, and change the second value to `10`. Press the *F* (Fit) key to fit the graph. This setting will make the dust scale over 1 frame.

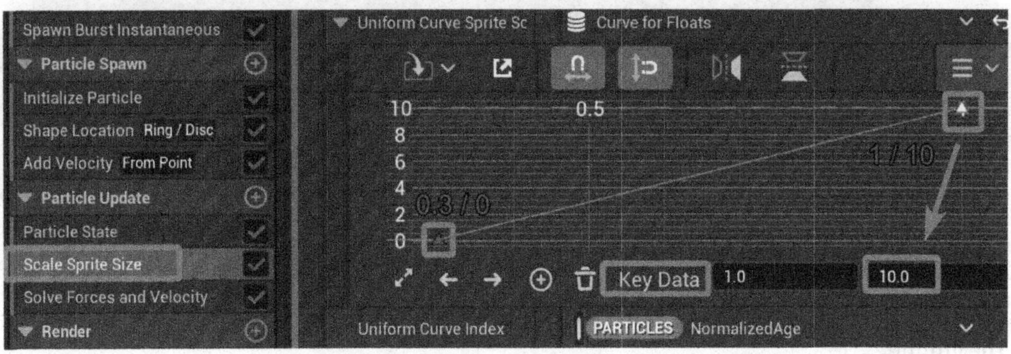

Figure 3.6 - Shape Location and Add Velocity module settings

14. In the same section, add the **Scale Color** module and click the down-pointing arrow of the **Scale Alpha** setting and select **Float from Curve**.
15. From the **Templates** selection, choose the **Smooth Ramp Down** curve to make the dust fade smoothly.

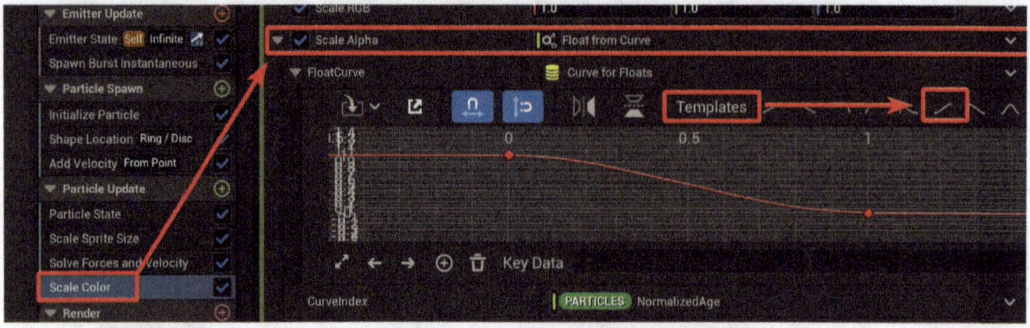

Figure 3.7 - Scale Color module settings

16. You now have a complete Impact Dust effect! Compile and save. In the main level, drag the `NS_PostImpact_Dust` into the level and reset its location to `0,0,0`.

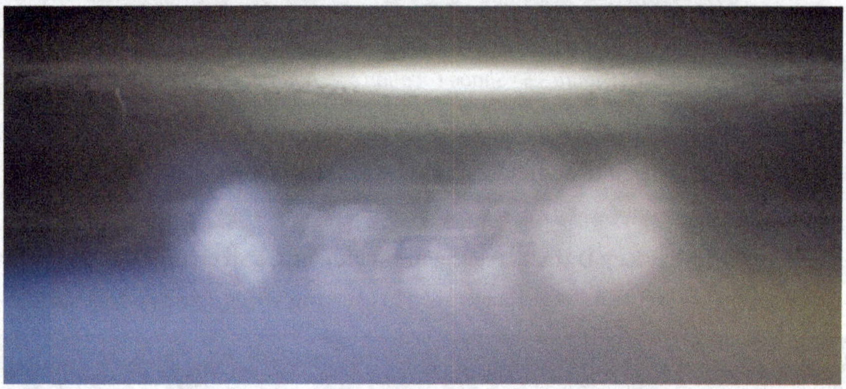

Figure 3.8 - The completed Impact Dust effect

17. The Impact Dust effect will play continuously since we set the **Emitter State** as **Infinite.** This is a good way to visualize and tweak the settings to achieve the effect you are going for. Once you're happy with your result, change the **Emitter State** to **Once** and save the project.

In the next recipe, we are going to art-direct the impact dust in the **Sequencer** as the cube hits the ground.

How it works...

In this recipe, you built a clean "impact dust" system by starting with the **Minimal** Niagara emitter, so you only add what the effect actually needs. You then switched on **Local Space** so the dust stays easy to move and reposition in the level, and enabled **Determinism** so the playback is more predictable when you scrub in **Sequencer**. You also moved the sim to

GPUCompute for better particle throughput and set **Calculate Bounds Mode** to **Fixed** to reduce the chance of the effect popping or disappearing when the camera view changes.

The burst is created using **Spawn Burst Instantaneous**, which gives a single "hit" moment, and the look is handled by a dust sprite material. Inside the **Initialize Particle**, you kept the color simple (white) and used random lifetime and random sprite size values so the burst feels more natural. The **Ring/Disc** setting in the **Shape Location** module makes the dust spread outward along the ground plane, while **Velocity from Point** pushes the particles away from the impact center.

Finally, the **Scale Sprite Size** curve makes the dust expand quickly, while the **Scale Alpha** curve fades it out smoothly, so the effect reads like dust dispersing rather than smoke drifting.

You also set the emitter's **Loop Behavior** to **Infinite** during testing because it's much easier to judge the look when the effect keeps replaying while you tweak values. Once you are happy with the results, switch **Loop Behavior** back to **Once** so the effect behaves like a real impact.

A good habit is to keep dust readable and grounded: if it floats upward too much or lasts too long, it starts to look like smoke. When adjusting the effect, change one thing at a time, usually in this order:

1. Spawn count (overall strength)
2. Size range (shape/readability)
3. Velocity (how far it spreads)
4. Fade (how long it hangs in the air)

There's more...

In *Chapter 1*, in the *Building a Niagara "Shot Control" system with User Parameters* recipe, you learned how to create **User Parameters** manually. In this section, I'll show you a second, faster method: creating a User Parameter directly from the setting you want to control. This is useful in cinematic production because shot changes often happen quickly.

Ensure you have `NS_PostImpact_Dust` opened in the Niagara Editor to follow along with these steps:

1. Identify which parameter you'd like to convert to a User Parameter by selecting it in the **Details** panel. Let's use **Dust Color** as an example.
2. In the **Initialize Particle** module, click the down-pointing arrow for the **Color** parameter and select **Make | Read from new User parameter**.

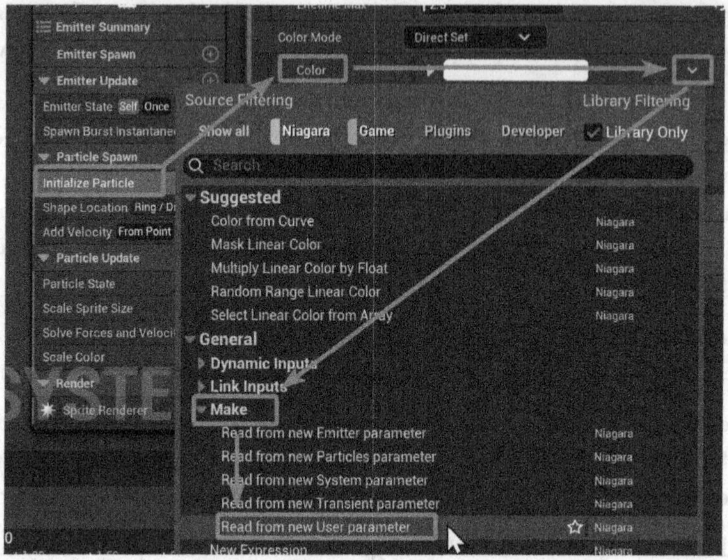

Figure 3.9 - Creating the Dust Color User Parameter

3. You'll now have a new User Parameter labeled **Color** in the **User Parameters** tab. Let's right-click on it to rename it to `Dust Color`.

I found this to be a much faster way to create User Parameters without worrying about the type of parameter you are required to create. Using the same method, create a User Parameter for the **Spawn Count** in the **Spawn Burst Instantaneous** module as shown in *Figure 3.10*:

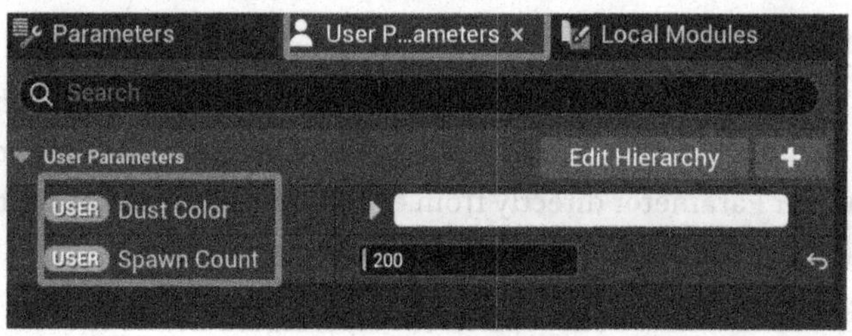

Figure 3.10 - The Dust Color and Spawn Count User Parameters

Compile and save the effect, and you should now have these two parameters exposed in the main level **Details** panel, ready to be tweaked and keyframed in the **Sequencer**. Go ahead and add more parameters as needed.

See also

The *Building a Niagara "Shot Control" system with User Parameters* recipe in *Chapter 1*

Creating landing/footstep dust timed in Sequencer

In the previous recipe, you built a post-impact dust effect from scratch and added User Parameters for further customization. In this recipe, we will focus on art direction. Instead of leaving the dust as a "one-size-fits-all" effect, you will learn how to shape it per shot using **Sequencer**. You will key the dust controls over time, adjust the burst and fade, and make the dust hit feel timed and intentional rather than random.

The goal here is to create a clean and readable impact moment that makes it easier to study timing, synchronization, and dust behavior in **Sequencer**.

By the end of the recipe, you will have a dust effect that you can time, tweak, and repeat reliably for different shots.

Getting ready

Before starting, set up your test environment as follows:

1. Open the `LV_VFX_Sandbox level` (our sandbox level from *Chapter 1*), if it is not already open.
2. Browse to the `Sequences` folder and double-click to open `Ch3_LS_FallingBox`, if it is not already open.
3. From the `Niagara_Systems` folder, drag `NS_PostImpact_Dust` into the level if you have not done so yet

How to do it...

This sequence consists of a 35 mm camera and an animated cube dropping to the floor. Our aim is to time the post-impact dust so that the effect will happen as soon as the cube hits the floor. We will use the techniques we learned in the *Making Niagara effects stable for scrubbing and repeatable playback (repeatable takes)* recipe in *Chapter 1*, where we utilized the **Niagara LifeCycle Track** and **Niagara Cache** to bake the dust effect before rendering it. Now follow the steps in the subsequent sections.

Preparing the impact timing in Sequencer

Let's begin by syncing the dust effect to the exact frame where the cube hits the ground:

1. In the opened sequence, lock the camera view by clicking on the **Camera Cuts** camera icon (**1**), change the timeline to show frames instead of seconds (**2**), and scrub the Playhead to where the cube hits the floor for the first time, which is Frame **0050** (**3**).

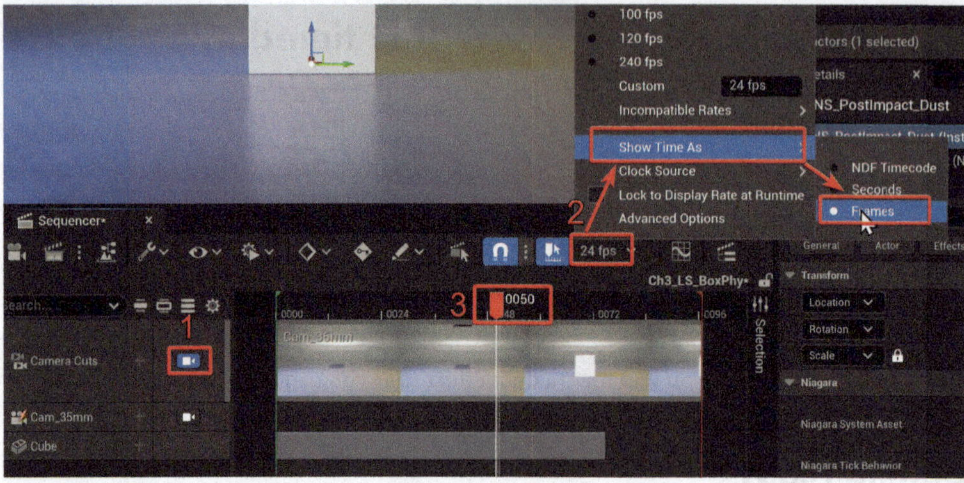

Figure 3.11 - Pre-planning the Post-Impact Dust timing

2. Drag `NS_PostImpact_Dust` from the **Outliner** into the **Sequencer**.
3. To art-direct in the **Sequencer**, here's what you need to do. Click the + icon on the `NS_PostImpact_Dust` and select **NiagaraComponent0.** Then click the + sign on that track and choose **System Life Cycle Track**, and change from **Tick Delta Time** to **Desired Age**.

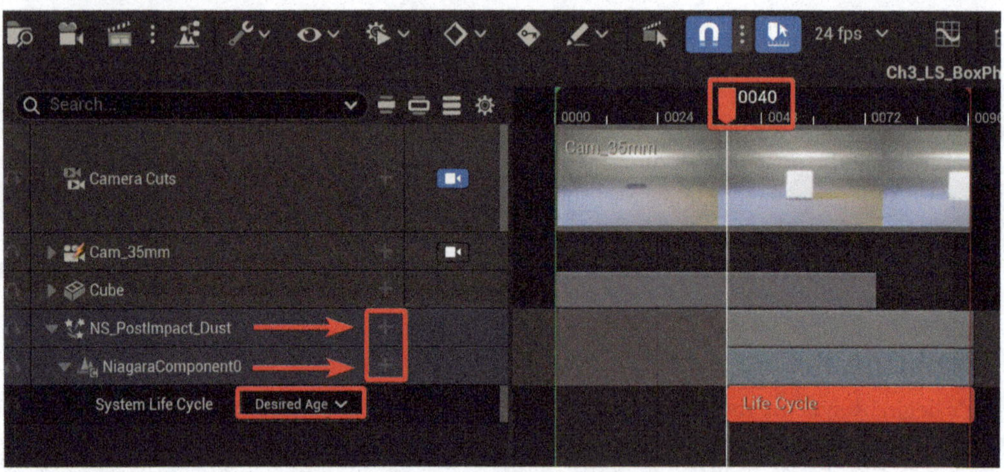

Figure 3.12 - Adding the System Life Cycle track

I find that if you drag the **Life Cycle** (*red*) track to begin at Frame **0040,** the impact of the cube and the dispersion of the dust will sync perfectly. I encourage you to experiment with the timing and the look of the dust using the **User Parameters** in the **Details** panel you created in the previous recipe.

Caching the dust simulation for stable playback

In this stage of the workflow, we will bake the effect before rendering the scene:

1. To bake the Post-Impact Dust effect, click the + sign (**1**) on the **NiagaraComponent0** track and select **Niagara Cache**.
2. Click the *red* record button to start caching the effect (**2**). **Disable** the **System Life Cycle** track (**3**) to confirm that the effect has been baked.

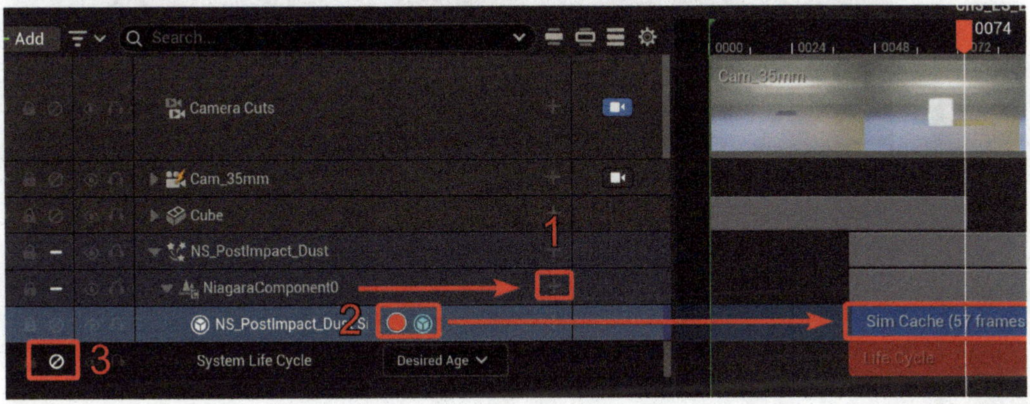

Figure 3.13 - Baking the Post Impact Dust effect

Note

If the **Niagara Cache** option is not available when adding it to the **Sequencer**, you might have missed the step in the *Technical Requirements* section to have the **Niagara** and **Niagara Sim Cache** plugins enabled.

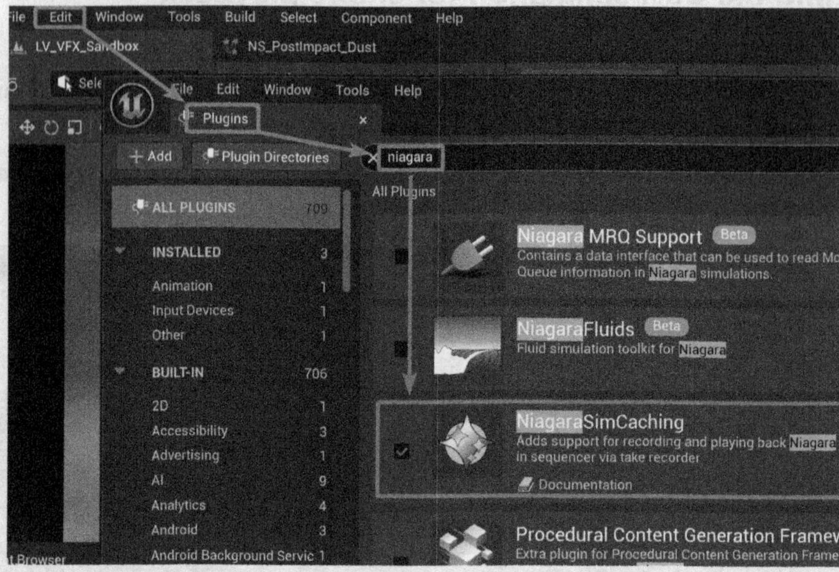

Figure 3.14: Enabling the Niagara SimCaching plugin

Validating the dust effect in Movie Render Queue

Next, to truly check that the Post-Impact Dust effect will render correctly, let's render the scene using the **Movie Render Queue**.

1. In the **Sequencer**, click the **clapperboard** icon (**1**). In the pop-up window, click on the **MRQ_MP4** preset (**2**). Select the **Output** section (**3**).

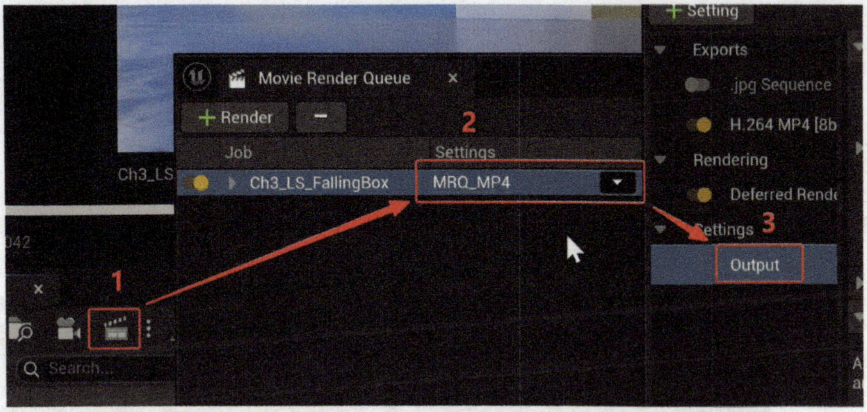

Figure 3.15 - Rendering the scene with Movie Render Queue

2. In the **Output Directory**, browse to a folder where you'd like to save the video file (**4**). Click **Accept** (**5**) and lastly click **Render (Local)** (**6**).

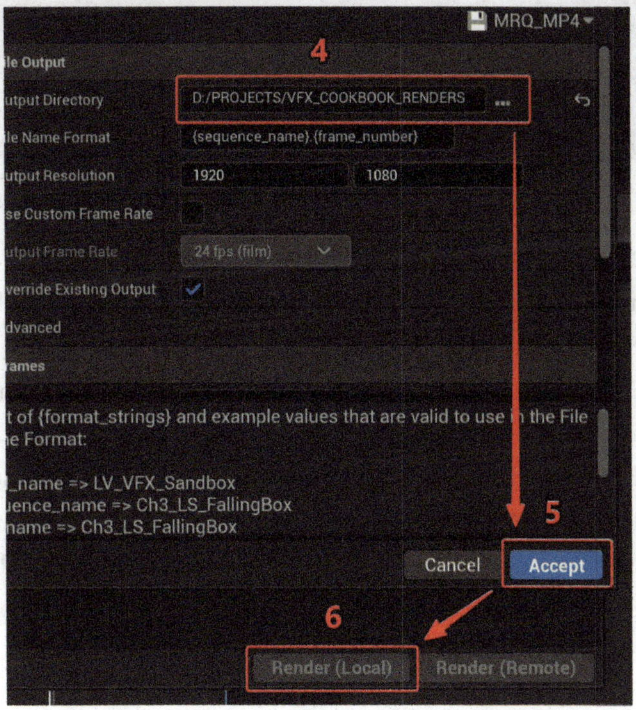

Figure 3.16 - Rendering the scene with Movie Render Queue (continued)

> **Note**
>
> If the `MRQ_MP4` preset is not available, please refer to the *Preparing Niagara Effects for Movie Render Queue* recipe in *Chapter 1*.

3. Open the file you just rendered to check if you achieved the desired effect; otherwise, tweak the settings and re-render.

Figure 3.17 - The final falling cube and post-impact dust scene

Applying the dust effect to a character landing

Knowing what you know now, let's move on to something more practical. Let's add an animated character and the post-impact dust effect we just created:

1. From the `Sequences` folder, double-click to open the pre-made `Ch3_LS_Vanguard` sequence.
2. Lock the camera by selecting the **Camera Cuts** camera icon and scrubbing the Playhead. You have an animated character landing on his feet.
3. Take note of the frame when both feet touch the ground: Frame **0013**.

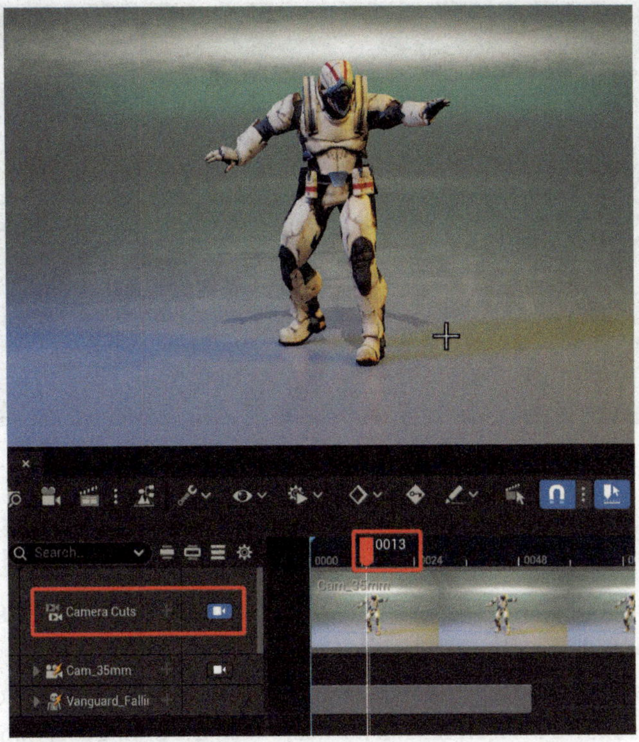

Figure 3.18 - Opening the Ch3_LS_Vanguard sequence

4. Although his feet are touching the ground at the same time, we will create two post-impact dust effects, one for his left foot and another for the right. We will offset the timing in the **Sequencer**.
5. In the `Niagara_Systems` folder, select `NS_PostImpact_Dust` and press *Ctrl* + *D* to duplicate then rename as `NS_PostImpact_Feet.` Save the project.
6. For timing and testing purposes, change its **Loop Behavior** to **Infinite** as we did in the previous recipe. Compile and save.
7. From the `Niagara_Systems` folder, drag `NS_PostImpact_Feet` into the level. You'll notice that the effect is rather large. This is where the use of User Parameters comes in handy. Go ahead and create User Parameters and settings, as shown in *Figure 3.19*:

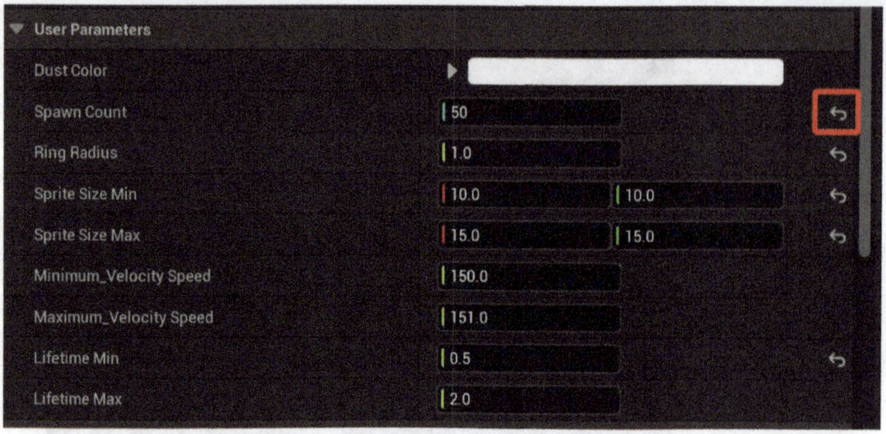

Figure 3.19 - User Parameters settings for NS_PostImpact_Feet

8. Click the **bent arrow** icon if you need to reset the values to the default. Position the first effect under the left foot and scale it down to `0.1` for *X*, *Y*, and *Z*.
9. Now drag `NS_PostImpact_Feet` into the **Sequencer**. Add the **NiagaraComponent0** track and change the **System Life Cycle** to **Desired Age**.
10. Drag the **System Life Cycle Track** to Frame **0007**, which will sync nicely with the left foot, as shown in *Figure 3.20*. If needed, tweak the timing accordingly.

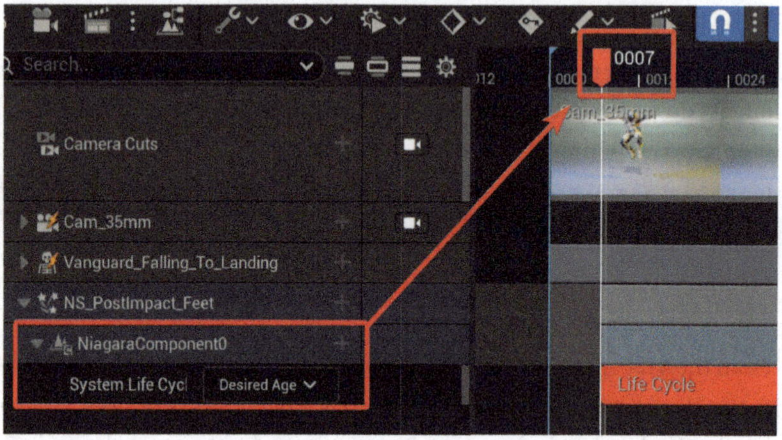

Figure 3.20 - Dragging the System Life Cycle to Frame 0007

11. For the right foot, in the **Sequencer**, select the `NS_PostImpact_Feet` track, right-click, and select **Duplicate.** Click **Yes** to the pop-up message. The Unreal editor wants to make sure that you're duplicating on purpose.

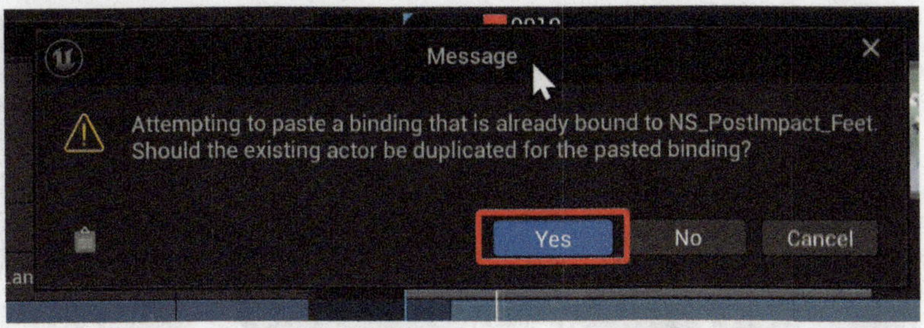

Figure 3.21 - Confirming the duplicate process

12. Drag the second instance to Frame **0009**, which again will sync perfectly with the right foot, as shown in *Figure 3.22*:

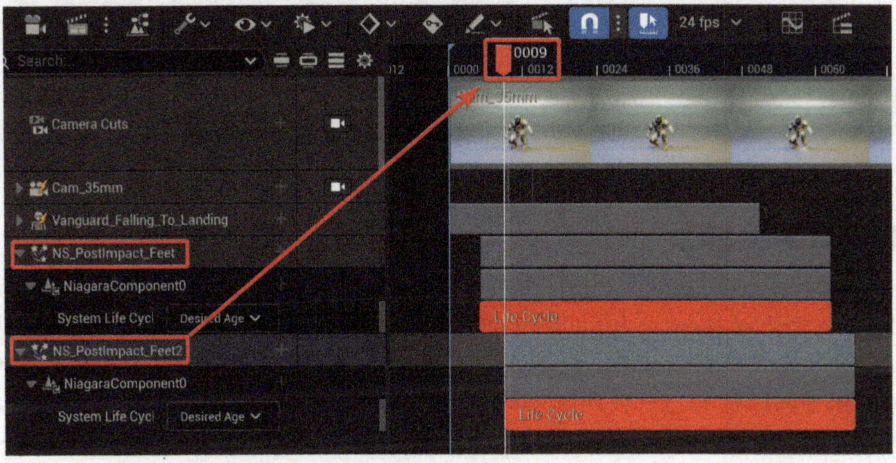

Figure 3.22 - Adding and syncing the second effect

That's it! The process of adding post-impact dust to the character is complete. For further confirmation, you may render the scene using the **Movie Render Queue** as you learned in the previous section. *Figure 3.23* shows the final scene:

Figure 3.23 - The final scene with the Post-Impact Dust

I've changed the **Dust Color** and **Spawn Count** for illustration purposes.

How it works...

In this recipe, you reused the post-impact dust effect from the *Creating a post-impact debris dust layer for aftershock effects* recipe and adapted it for a character landing shot. Instead of building a new effect from scratch, you duplicated `NS_PostImpact_Dust` and created a smaller version called `NS_PostImpact_Feet`. This makes sense because footstep dust uses the same basic idea as an impact dust effect: a short burst that appears at the moment something touches the ground.

The main difference is scale. A full impact dust effect is larger and heavier, while footstep dust must be smaller, quicker, and more controlled, so it supports the animation without overpowering it. By using the **User Parameters**, you could reduce the spawn count, ring radius, sprite size, velocity, and lifetime to create a dust effect that fits under the character's feet.

The **Sequencer** timing is the most important part of this recipe because dust is not just a visual decoration; it is part of the performance. In a cinematic shot, the dust needs to support the character's weight and timing. You first identify the exact frame where the character's feet touch the ground, then place the dust effect slightly earlier, so the particles have enough time to appear and expand at the moment the audience sees the impact. If the dust starts too late, the landing feels weak or disconnected. If it starts too early, it feels like the dust is happening before the character makes contact.

Creating two separate dust instances, one for each foot, gives better control than using one larger effect to cover both feet. Even if the feet land close together, each foot has its own contact point, weight, and timing. Offsetting the System Life Cycle tracks by a few frames makes the landing feel less mechanical and more natural. The cinematic habit here is to always find the contact frame first, then adjust the dust timing around it. A good dust effect should feel physically connected to the action, helping the audience believe the character has real weight in the scene.

There's more...

If you are interested in trying the post-impact dust effects with another animation for practice, I'll show you how to grab some from **Mixamo** (`https://www.mixamo.com/`):

1. Go to `www.mixamo.com`, log in using your Adobe ID. If you do not have one, you can create one for free.

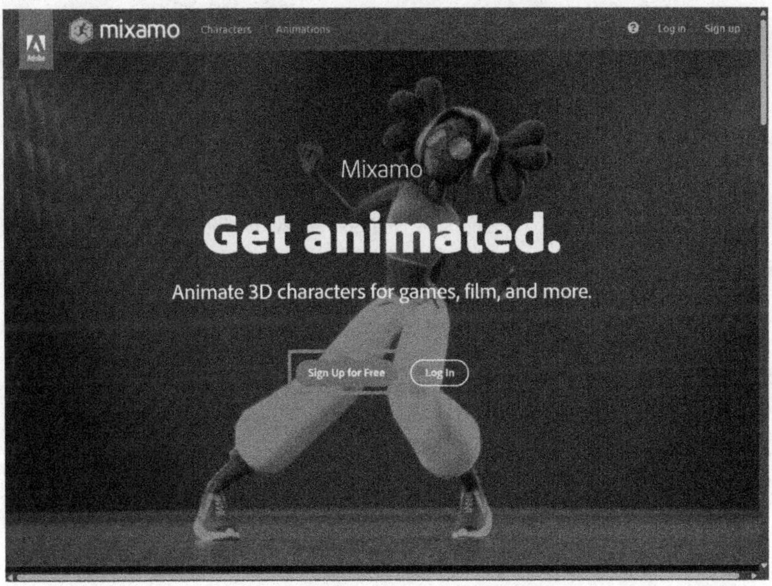

Figure 3.24 - Logging into Mixamo

2. Once logged in, click the **Character** tab and choose any character from the list. Then click the **Animation** tab, where you'll find a list of animations you can use in Unreal Engine.

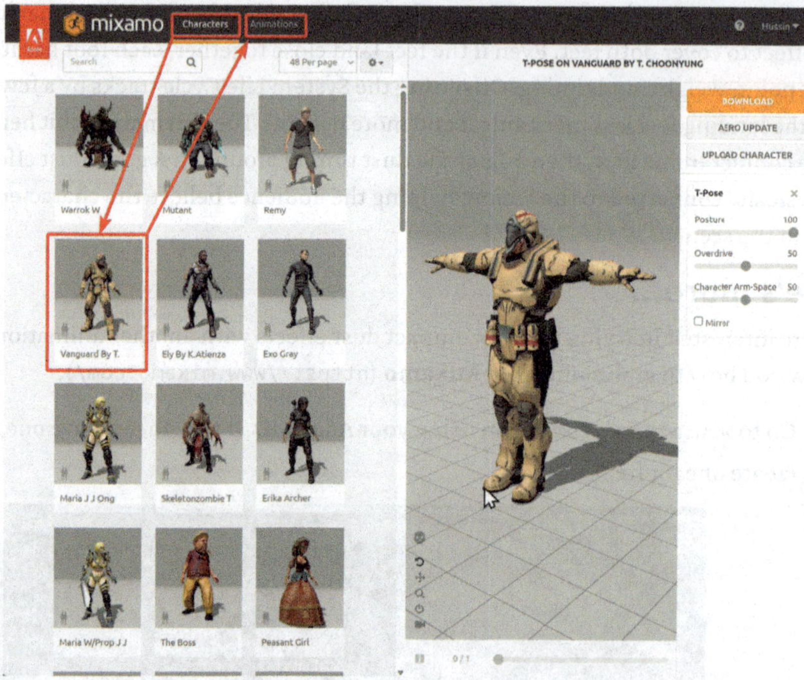

Figure 3.25 - Choosing your Mixamo character

3. Use the **Search** function for a specific animation, then click the **Download** button.

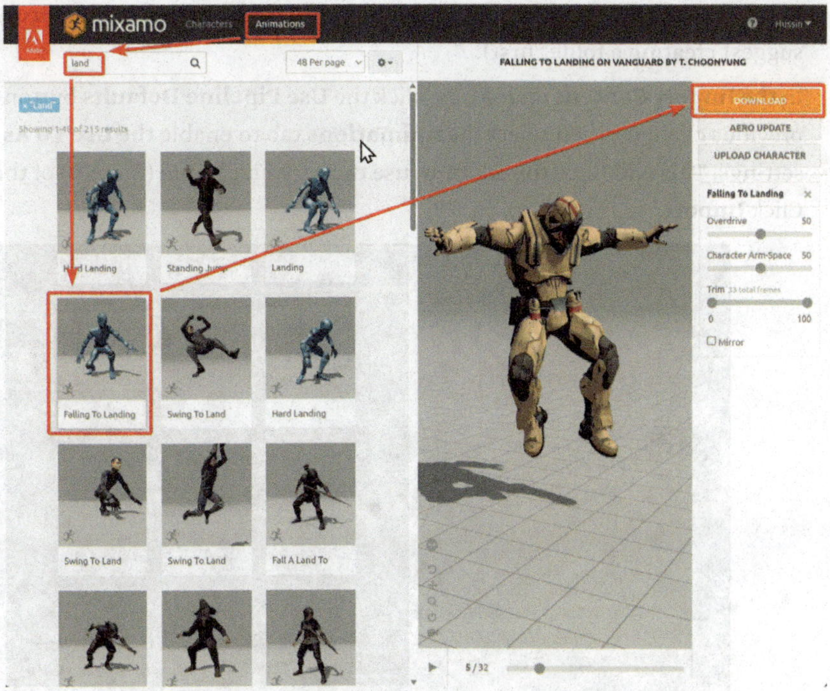

Figure 3.26 - Choosing your Mixamo Animation

4. Since we intend to create cinematics, in the pop-up window, change **Frames per Second** to 24**,** leave the other settings as default, and click **Download**.

   The downloaded animation file has an `.FBX` extension. This is a standard animation file that can be used in almost all 3D applications on the market.

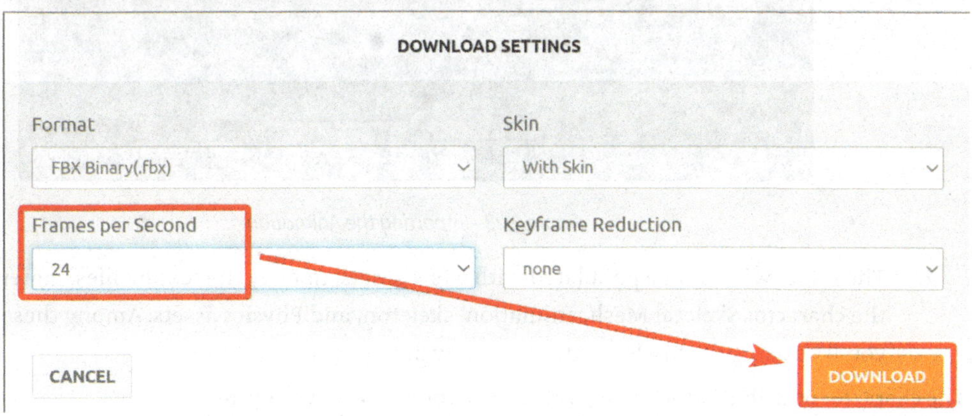

Figure 3.27 - Downloading the Animation

5. In the Unreal Engine editor, drag the animation file into the **Content Browser** (I suggest creating a folder first).
6. In the **Import Content** dialog box, click the **Use Pipeline Defaults** button to reset any previous changes, then select the **Animations** tab to enable the **Use TO As Ref Pose** settings. This will force the editor to use the very first frame (Time **0**) of the animation. Click **Import.**

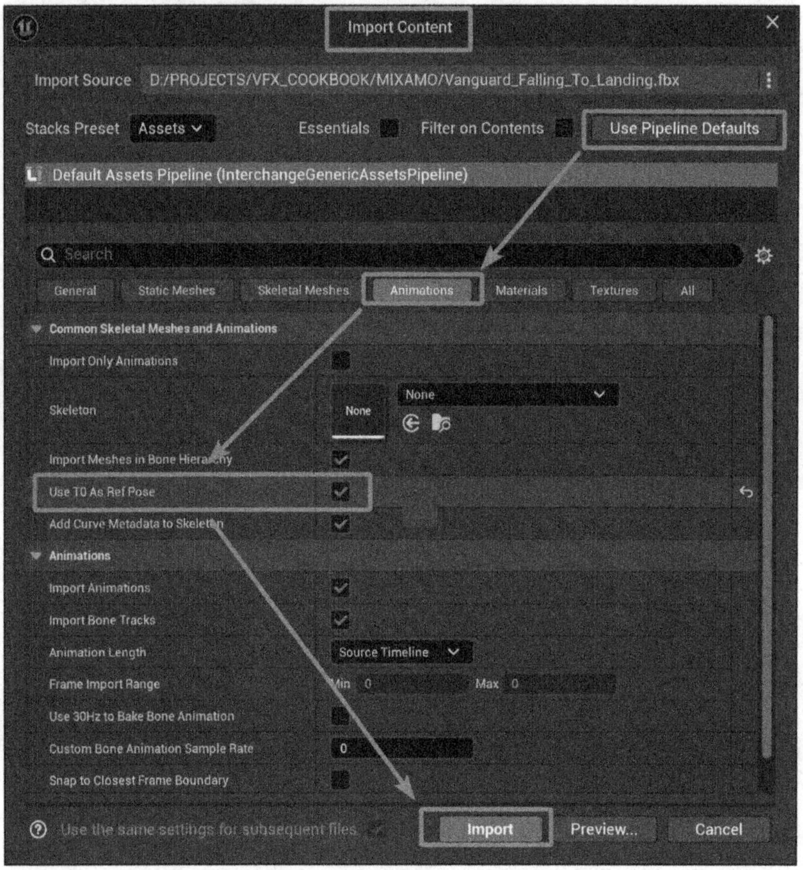

Figure 3.28 - Importing the Animation

7. The folder will now be populated with a few assets, namely the texture files, materials, the character Skeletal Mesh, animation, skeleton, and Physics assets. Among these, you'll be using the **Skeletal Mesh** asset by dragging it into your level.

The character and animation are now ready for you to use in your project.

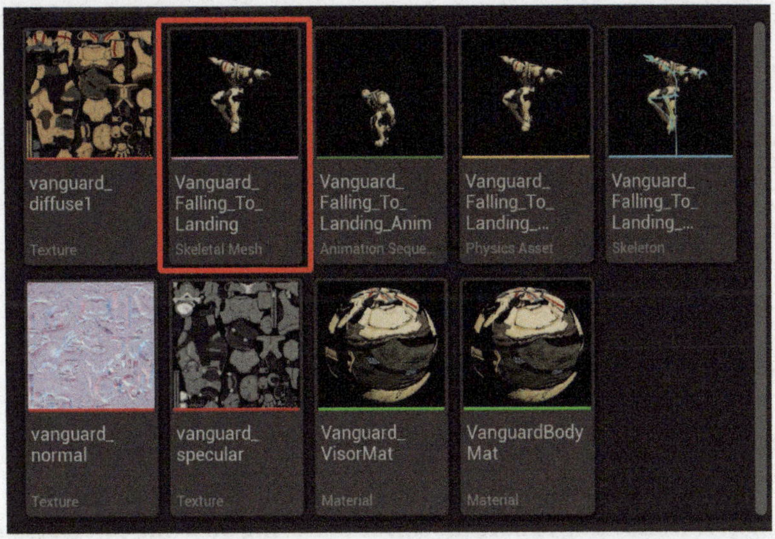

Figure 3.29 - The imported character assets

See also

Here is a comprehensive Epic Games documentation on how to successfully import **FBX animations** into Unreal Engine: `https://dev.epicgames.com/documentation/unreal-engine/importing-animations-using-fbx-in-unreal-engine`.

Designing smoke/dust trails behind a moving object

In this recipe, you will create a smoke/dust trail that follows a moving object and stays readable during camera moves. Instead of building a new Niagara System from scratch, we will reuse the smoke wisp system you created in the *Creating soft smoke wisps (hero-friendly GPU sprites)* recipe in *Chapter 2*, to modify it into a smoke/dust trail. The goal is to show how one base setup can be adapted for different effects by changing spawn behavior, motion, and fade controls.

To keep the recipe simple and easy to scrub in **Sequencer**, we will use a rotating sphere as the moving object. By the end of the recipe, you will have a lightweight dust trail that can be adjusted per shot and reused for vehicles, props, or any object moving close to the ground.

Getting ready

Before starting, set up your test environment as follows:

1. Open `LV_VFX_Sandbox` level (our sandbox sequence from *Chapter 1*) if it is not already open.
2. Browse to the `Sequences` folder and double-click to open `Ch3_LS_SmokeTrail`, where you'll find a rotating sphere ready to go.

How to do it...

We will start by duplicating the smoke wisps you created earlier. Let's begin:

1. In the `Niagara_Systems` folder, locate and duplicate (*Ctrl* + *D*) the `NS_Smoke_Wisps` Niagara System. Rename it as `NS_Smoke_Trail`, then double-click to open it in the editor.
2. The most crucial setting to have the smoke trail along a moving object is by *disabling* the checkbox for **Local Space**, which is in the emitter's **Properties** module. For a dust or smoke trail, we turn **Local Space** off so the particles are left behind as the object moves. This makes the trail look natural instead of sticking to the moving object.
3. Ensure that the **Determinism** checkbox is enabled.

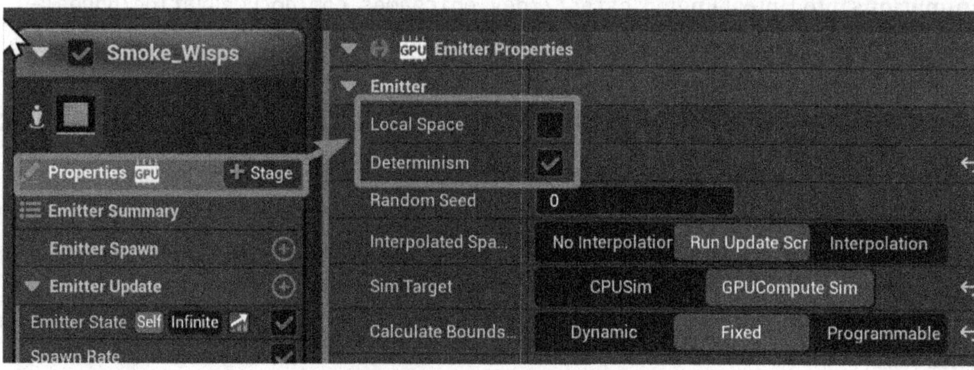

Figure 3.30 - Disabling the Local Space checkbox

4. Next, to change the emitter settings in the main level, create a set of **User Parameters** as shown in *Figure 3.31*. In the case of the **Particle Color**, I made the User Parameter using the **Color** setting in the **Initialize Particle** module.

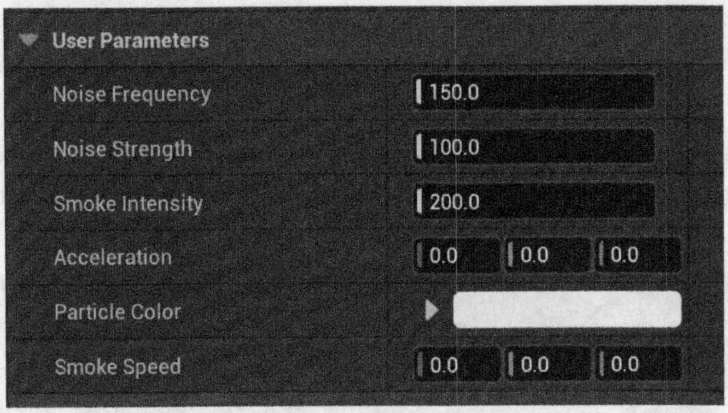

Figure 3.31 - User Parameters for the Smoke/Dust trail effect

5. Now let's attach the effect to the rotating sphere. Drag the `NS_Smoke_Trail` into the level and reset its location to `0,0,0`.
6. Then, in the **Outliner**, drag it onto the **Sphere** to make `NS_Smoke_Trail` the child of the **Sphere**, as shown in *Figure 3.32*. The *green* checkmark denotes you're on the right track.

Figure 3.32 - Parenting the effect to the Sphere

7. To complete the process, select NS_Smoke_Trail and reset its location to 0,0,0. This will re-position the smoke effect to the same location as the **Sphere** while attached to it.
8. In the **Sequencer**, click the **Play** button, and you now have a smoke trail following the sphere. You can now tweak or keyframe the **User Parameters** created earlier to achieve more of a dust look rather than smoke. You have control!

Figure 3.33 - The completed smoke/dust trail effect

How it works...

In this recipe, you reused the smoke wisps system from the earlier chapter and turned it into a smoke/dust trail. This is a useful workflow because many Niagara effects can be adapted from an existing system instead of being rebuilt from nothing.

The most important change was disabling **Local Space**. When **Local Space** is enabled, particles stay relative to the emitter, which is useful for some effects, but not for a trail. For a moving object, the particles need to be left behind in world space, so they form a visible path. By attaching NS_Smoke_Trail to the rotating sphere but allowing the particles to remain in world space, the system follows the sphere as an emitter, while the emitted smoke/dust remains behind as a trail.

The **User Parameters** give you quick control over the look without reopening the Niagara stack every time. Parameters such as noise frequency and noise strength help break up the trail, so it does not look too straight or artificial, while smoke intensity, acceleration, particle color, and smoke speed allow you to push the effect toward smoke, dust, or something more stylized.

The main idea is to understand that a trail is not just a moving particle system. It is a system that emits from a moving source and then leaves particles behind in the shot. If the trail looks too much like a solid tube, reduce density, add more variation, or shorten the lifetime. If it disappears too quickly, increase the lifetime or intensity carefully. Small changes usually work better than big ones here.

There's more...

Since making the smoke/dust trail is a straightforward process, let's convert the smoke/dust into a **fireball** by just tweaking a few settings:

1. In the `Niagara_Systems` folder, duplicate `NS_Smoke_Trail` and rename to `NS_Fire_Trail`.
2. Double-click `NS_Fire_Trail` to open it in the Niagara Editor. Select the emitter and hit *F2* to rename it to `Fire_Trail`**.**
3. In the **Initialize Particle** module, change the **Lifetime Max** to `3`. The larger this number, the longer the fire trail.
4. For **Color Mode**, set to **Unset.** We will be using another module to set the color.
5. Change **Uniform Sprite Size Min** to `50` and **Uniform Sprite Size Max** to `100`. This setting will enlarge the fire particles: the larger the number, the larger the particles.

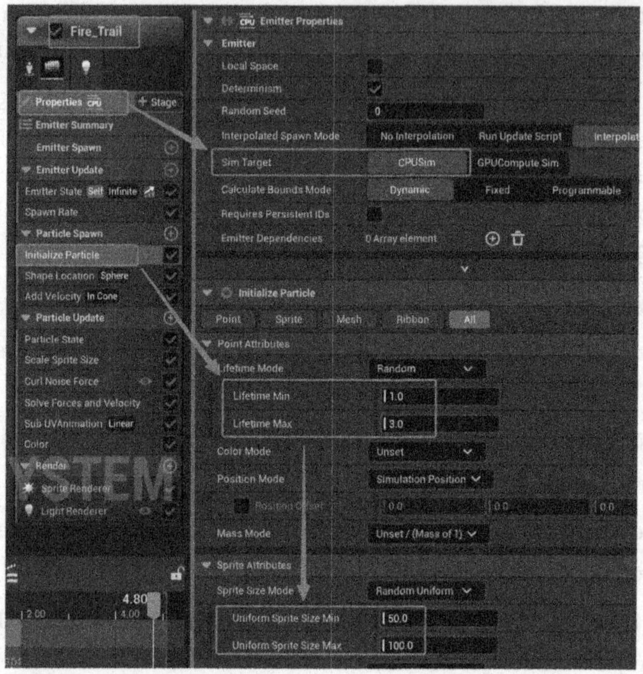

Figure 3.34 - Tweaking the Initialize Particle module

6. In the **Shape Location** module, change the **Sphere Radius** to `20`. This will enlarge the start of the fire to fit the size of the rotating sphere.
7. In the **Sprite Renderer** module, search for and change the **Material** to `M_explosion_subUV`. If this material is not available, please refer to the *Creating soft smoke wisps (hero-friendly GPU sprites)* recipe in *Chapter 2*, where we added the **Starter Content** to the project.
8. Because the fire sprite image is made up of a 6-by-6 image texture, change the **Sub Image Size** to `6.0` for both *X* and *Y* and enable the **Sub UV Blending Enabled** checkbox.

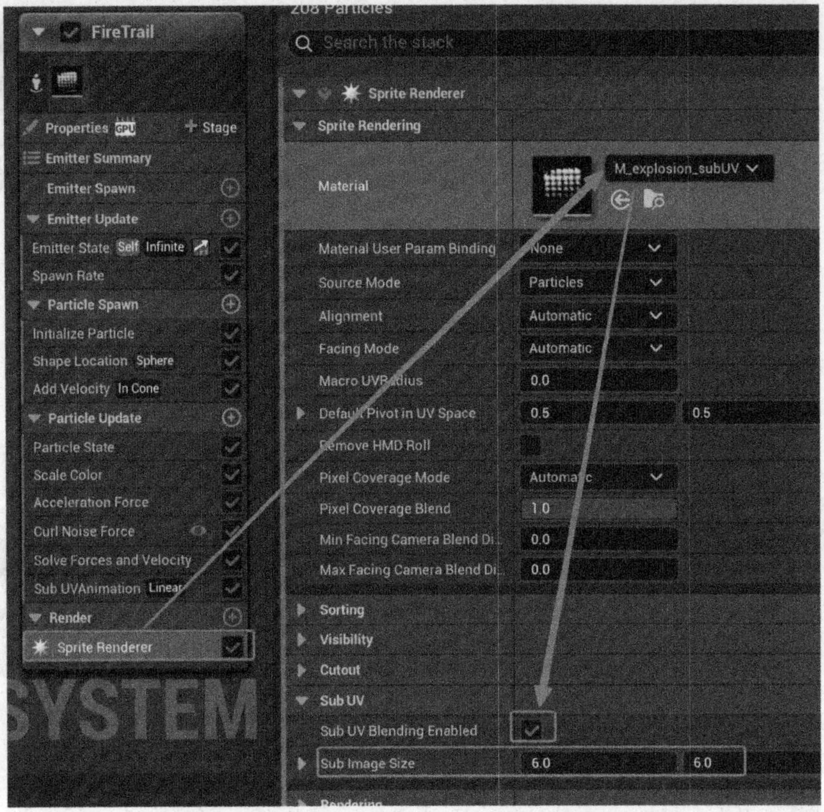

Figure 3.35 - Changing the Smoke to Fire material

9. Click the + sign of the **Render** section and add a **Light Renderer** module. Click the **Fix issue** button to allow the **Light Renderer** to switch to CPU Sim instead of GPU Sim. If the Preview window goes blank, click the **Compile** button.

> **Note**
>
> If you do not see the particles even after hitting the **Compile** button, in the **Emitter Properties** module, under the **Interpolated Spawn** mode, change to **Interpolation,** then back to **Run Update Script**.

10. Uncheck the **Use Inverse Squared Falloff** checkmark for the **Light Renderer** to cast a light reflection on the floor.

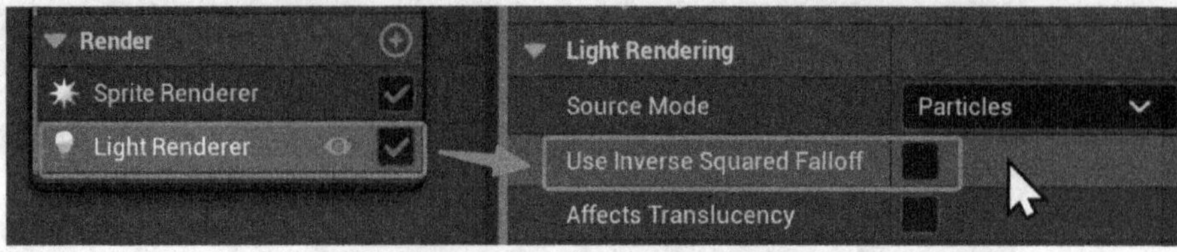

Figure 3.36 - Adding the Light Renderer module

11. In the **Particle Update** section, delete the **Scale Color** and **Acceleration Force** modules and add a **Scale Sprite Size** and **Color** module.
12. Change the **Scale Sprite Size** curve to look like *Figure 3.37* by selecting the **Ease In** template. Adjust the last key if you want a narrower end of the fire trail.

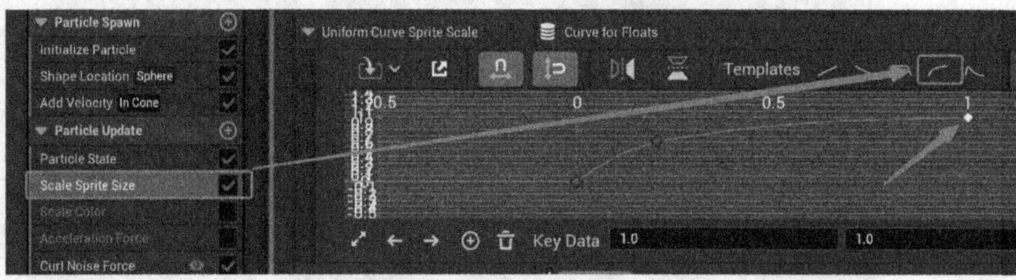

Figure 3.37 - Setting the Scale Sprite Size curve

> **Tip**
>
> If, for any reason, the particles disappear in the Preview window, simply disable and then enable the module using their *blue* checkmarks.

13. Select the **Color** module, click the down-pointing arrow, and choose **Color from Curve**.

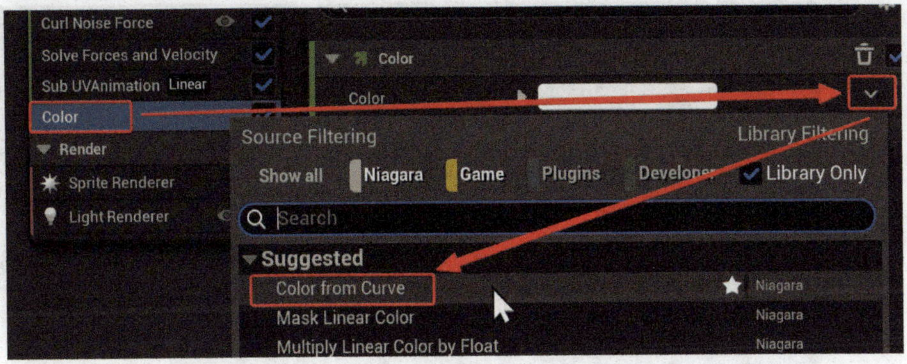

Figure 3.38 - Setting the Color module

14. Add **Color** stops by clicking at the top of the gradient, double-clicking, and changing the color, as shown in *Figure 3.39*, to go for the "fire look." I've added three color stops, from *orange* to *red* to *black*. Try clicking the icon labeled **1** to have a completely different-looking fire.

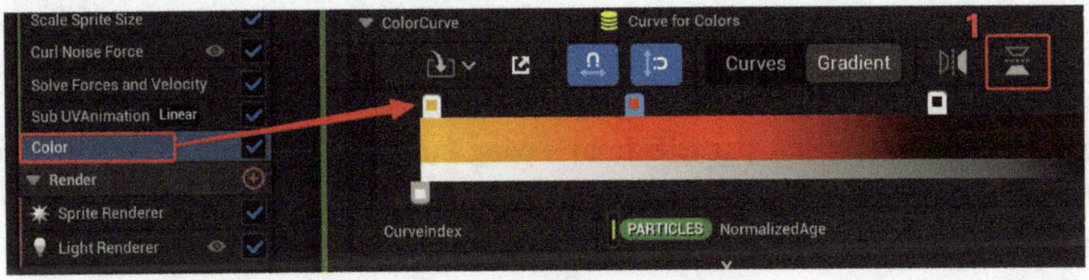

Figure 3.39 - Editing the Color curve

15. Compile and save. You now have an amazing cinematic fire trail effect, complete with light reflection and ready to be keyframed in the **Sequencer**.

Figure 3.40 - The fire trail's final look

See also

In Unreal Engine's Niagara VFX system, **Local Space** is a setting that ties a particle system's coordinate system directly to its owning component rather than the global world. When enabled, the entire particle effect and its particles move, rotate, and scale with the emitter object itself, preventing the particles from leaving a trail as the object moves. More details can be checked out here: `https://dev.epicgames.com/documentation/unreal-engine/emitter-settings-reference-for-niagara-effects-in-unreal-engine`.

Building dust motes in a light beam for cinematic room tone

In this recipe, you will create subtle dust motes that float slowly through a light beam. Unlike impact dust or trails, this effect is not meant to draw attention to itself. It works as a background atmosphere layer, adding gentle movement and depth to the shot.

These particles are usually only visible when light hits them, which is exactly why they feel cinematic. In real life, tiny dust particles are often invisible until they pass through sunlight, a projector beam, or a strong spotlight.

By adding this effect, you can make an empty space feel more alive, give the lighting more presence, and add a quiet sense of mood without making the scene look busy.

Getting ready

Before starting, let's set up the test environment. From the **Content Browser | Levels** folder, open `LV_VFX_DustMotes` level. This level is specially made for this recipe, as I have added fog, a single spotlight, and a ready-to-go **Dust Motes** Niagara System.

How to do it...

Let's begin by building a simple dust mote effect using a Niagara template, then shape it into a subtle cinematic atmosphere layer. Follow these steps:

1. Once in the level, press the *G* key to hide the **overlay** icons.
2. In the **Outliner**, select the `NS_DustMotes_Start` Niagara asset. In its **Details**, double-click the thumbnail to open it in the Niagara Editor. This is a much faster way to open a particular asset in Unreal Engine.

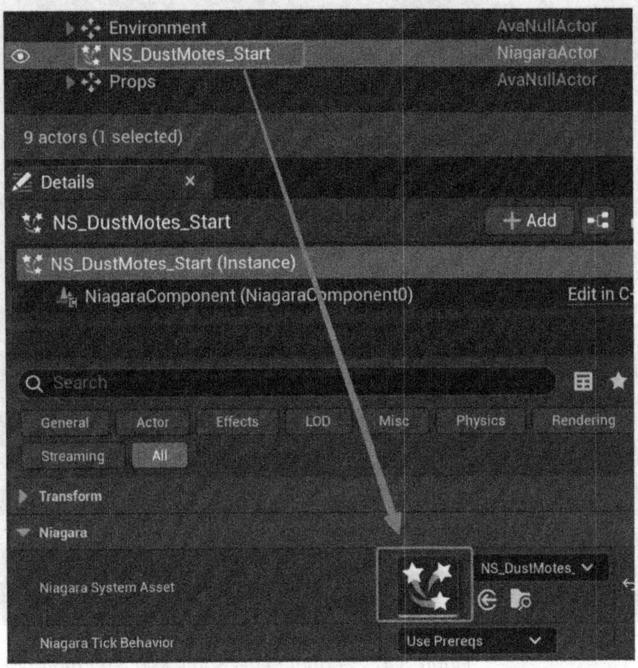

Figure 3.41 - Editing the Dust Mote effect

3. We are going to use a template for this effect and add a few modules to achieve the look we're after. In the editor, right-click and select **Add Emitter**. Choose the **Hanging Particulates** template, click **Add**.

4. Rename the emitter to `Dust Motes` by selecting the emitter and pressing the *F2* key. Compile and save.
5. Back in the Level, you'll notice there are already dust-like particles that we're going for. That's it, we're done! ~ Kidding!

In the introduction, I mentioned that the particles will only be visible if they pass through sunlight, a projector beam, or a strong spotlight. Let's work on that now:

1. Select the **Sprite Renderer** module and in the **Material** settings, search for and change to `M_Dust_Particle`. Change the **Sub Image Size** to `2.0` for *X* and *Y*, and enable the **Sub UV Blending**, so that the particles blend to avoid any hard seams.

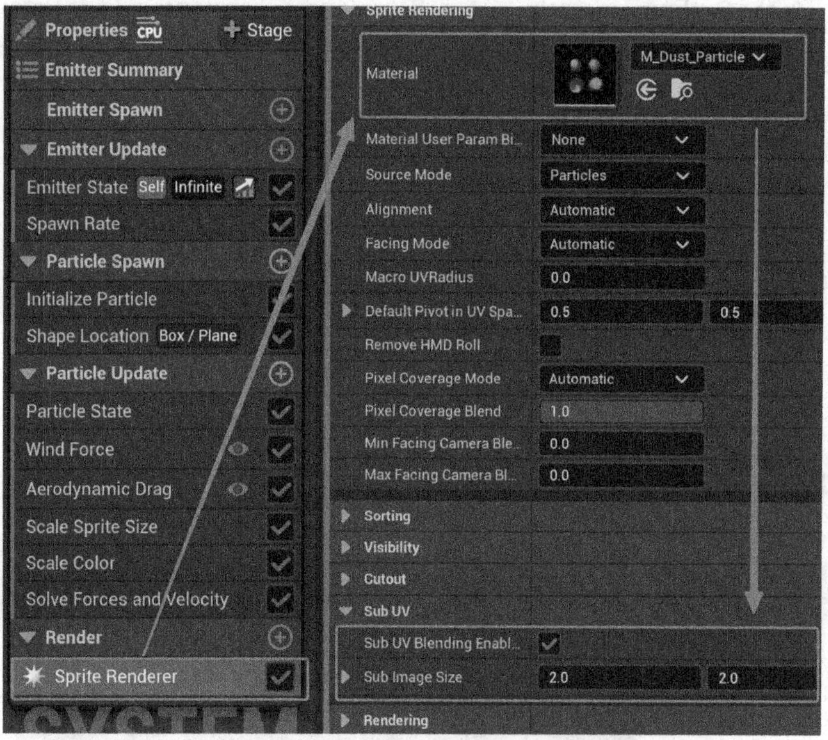

Figure 3.42 - Changing the Sprite Renderer material

2. In the **Properties** module, change to **GPUCompute Sim** to utilize the GPU to create the particles. If you receive a warning, click **Fix issue**.
3. In the **Spawn Rate** module, increase the **Spawn Rate** to `500` – we need more dust!

4. To make the dust swirl around, in the **Particle Update** section, add **Curl Noise Force.** Change the **Noise Frequency** to `100`. You are encouraged to experiment with this number to achieve your desired result.
5. If there is a need to change the size of the dust, increase or decrease the **Uniform Sprite Size Min** and **Uniform Sprite Size Max** in the **Initialize Particle** module.
6. If you need the dust particle to encompass a larger area, increase the **Box Size** in the **Shape Location** module.

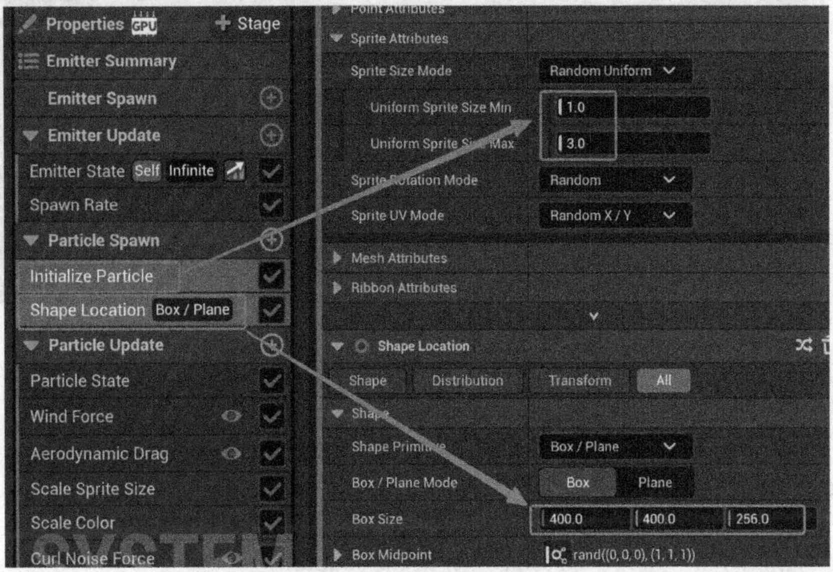

Figure 3.43 - Adjusting particle size and spread

That's it. Dust Motes are ready to go!

Figure 3.44 - The final Dust Motes look

How it works...

In this recipe, you created a subtle atmosphere effect rather than a dramatic impact effect. The **Hanging Particulates** template gives you a quick starting point because it already behaves like slow-floating particles. From there, you changed the sprite material to `M_Dust_Particle` so the particles match the dust style used earlier in the chapter.

You also changed the emitter's **Sim Target** to **GPUCompute Sim**, which is useful because dust motes often need many small particles spread across an area. Increasing the **Spawn Rate** adds more visible particles, while the **Curl Noise Force** gives them a gentle, drifting motion instead of making them look frozen. Adjusting the sprite size in the **Initialize Particle** module and modifying the **Box Size** in the **Shape Location** module controls how visible the dust is and how much space it fills.

The reason this effect feels cinematic is that dust motes are not meant to call attention to themselves. They are usually only visible when light hits them, which is why they work so well with a spotlight, fog, or a strong beam of light. In a shot, this kind of effect adds depth, movement, and mood without becoming the main subject.

The important mindset is to keep it *subtle*. If the particles are too big, too bright, or too fast, they stop feeling like room tone and start looking like snow, ash, or insects. Start with a soft, barely visible result, then increase the spawn rate, size, or light response only if the particles cannot be seen in the camera view.

There's more...

Perhaps you're wondering what makes the particles only visible under a light beam. The answer lies in the materials. Let's find out and make some improvements:

> **Note**
>
> **Warning:** Only proceed with these steps if your computer has the recommended GPU and CPU, as these settings are compute-intensive.

1. In the Emitter, select the **Sprite Renderer** module, then double-click on the `M_Dust_Particle` thumbnail to open the material in the Material Editor.

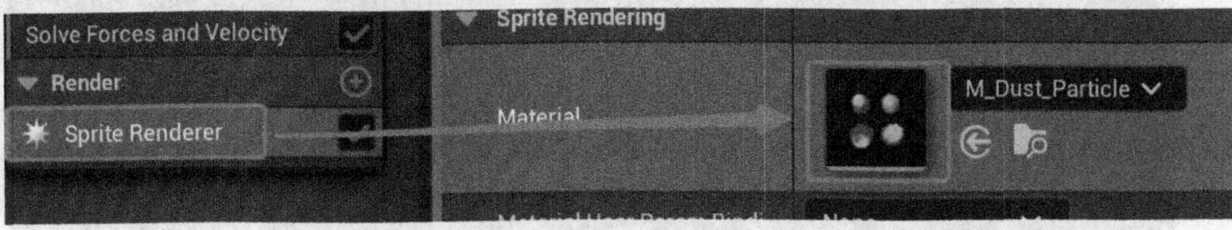

Figure 3.45 - Editing the material

2. The main reason the particles are only visible under a certain lighting environment is the omission of the **Emissive Color** setting. If this is enabled, the particles will tend to glow.

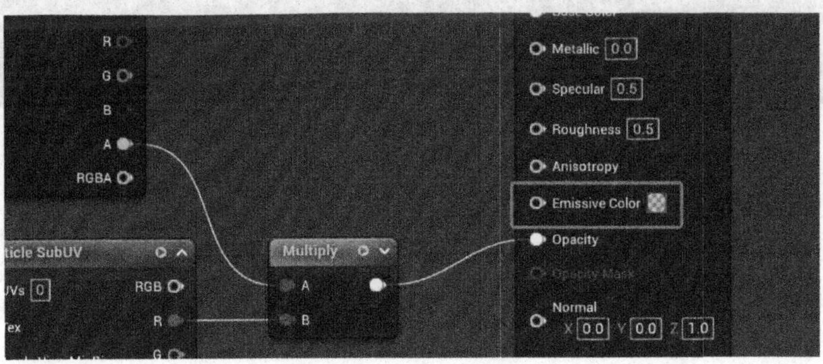

Figure 3.46 - The Emissive shader is inactive

3. Select the **M_Dust_Particle** node and in the **Details** panel, take note of the **Material Domain**, **Blend Mode**, and **Shading Model**.
4. To enhance the dust particle further, change the **Shading Model** to **Subsurface** and the **Lighting Mode** to **Surface ForwardShading**.

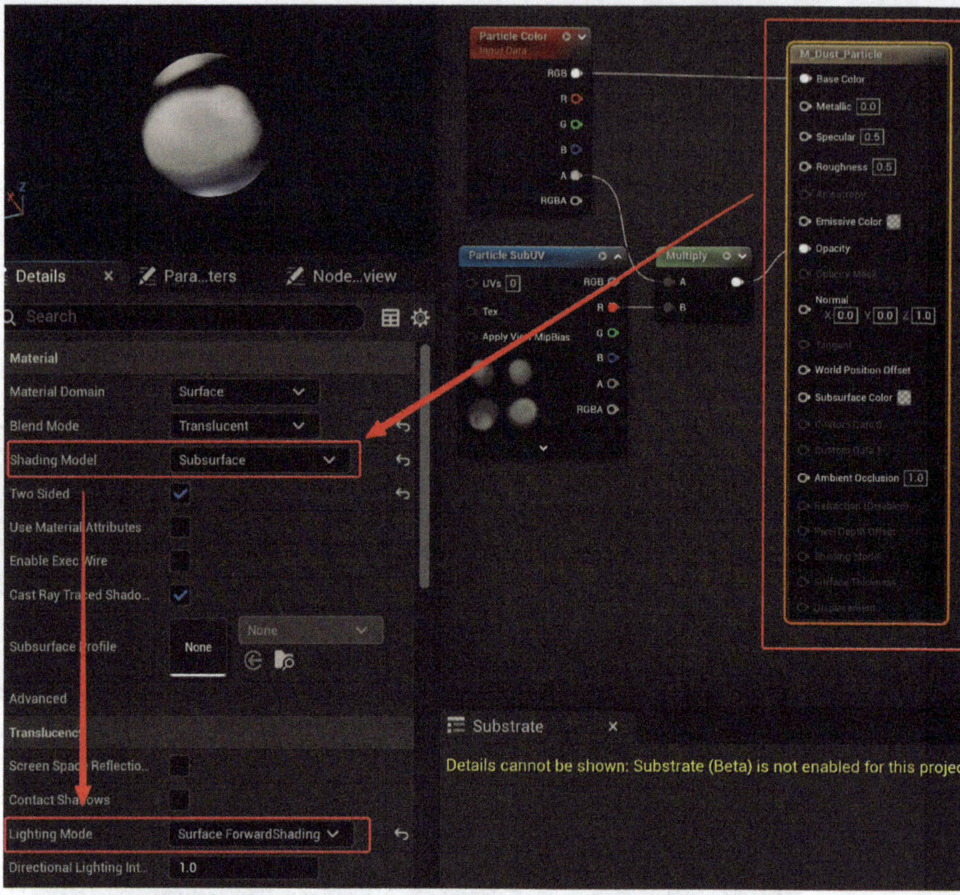

Figure 3.47 - Changing the Shading Model and Lighting Mode

5. Click **Apply** and **Save**.

If you jump back to the Level, you'll notice the particles are much more prominent and visually appealing.

Figure 3.48 - The final look after editing the material shading properties

See also

This Epic Games documentation is useful for understanding the main material settings, including how **Blend Mode** and **Shading Model** affect the final look of a material: `https://dev.epicgames.com/documentation/unreal-engine/unreal-engine-material-properties`.

4

Niagara Rain for Cinematics

In this chapter, we will build a complete cinematic rain setup in stages. **Rain** is a powerful visual effect because it adds mood, movement, reflection, and atmosphere to a shot. It can make a scene feel more dramatic, emotional, or tense, while also helping lights, surfaces, and silhouettes look more cinematic.

We will start with a basic **rain streak effect**, creating falling rain with controlled speed, length, and camera readability. From there, we will add **rain splashes**, so the rain feels like it is actually hitting the ground and surrounding surfaces. Next, we will create **rain ripples** to show how water reacts after impact, adding another layer of realism to wet surfaces. Finally, we will build **puddles** to complete the rain scene, giving the environment a stronger sense of moisture, reflection, and atmosphere.

A believable rain setup is usually built in layers: distant rainfall for atmosphere, foreground streaks for camera readability, and surface reactions such as splashes and puddles to connect the weather to the environment. In production, the challenge is to make rain look realistic as well as controllable, stable in **Sequencer**, and reliable when rendered through **Movie Render Queue**.

In this chapter, we'll cover the following recipes:

- Creating cinematic rain streaks
- Creating a rain splash effect
- Creating a rain ripple effect
- Creating a cinematic rain puddle effect

Technical requirements

Before starting this recipe, ensure the following are set up:

- Make sure **Unreal Engine 5.6** is installed (see *Chapter 1* for details).
- A project with **Niagara** and the **Niagara Sim Caching** plugin enabled.
- A test environment or sandbox level where the effect can be previewed—you may use the sandbox environment we created in the *Setting up a reusable VFX "Sandbox" level for cinematic lookdev* recipe in *Chapter 1*.
- Maintain the folder structure to keep the assets organized, as shown below:
  - `Content`
    - `Niagara_Systems`
    - `Sequences`
    - `Textures`
    - `Materials`
    - `MRQ`

You can download the example project for this book by following the instructions in the *Download the example code/resource files* section in the *Preface* of this book.

The complete example project is included in the downloadable code/resource bundle.

Creating cinematic rain streaks

In this recipe, you will create a simple rain streak effect using Niagara. This will be the main falling rain layer for the chapter and the foundation for the splash, ripple, and puddle effect recipes that will come later in the chapter.

The goal of this recipe is to create rain that is readable in a cinematic shot without making the scene too busy or noisy. You will control the rain speed, length, density, and direction, so it feels natural on camera. We will keep the setup straightforward by focusing only on the falling rain first, before adding surface interaction in the next recipes.

Getting ready

Before starting, open the `LV_VFX_Sandbox` level to use as your test environment for previewing the rain effect.

How to do it...

Let's begin by creating the main falling rain layer. We will keep the setup focused on the rain streaks first, making sure they are readable through the camera before adding splashes, ripples, and puddles in the following recipes:

1. In the **Content Browser,** go to your `Niagara_Systems` folder, right-click, and create a new Niagara System.
2. In the **Niagara System** creation window, select **Minimal** Niagara emitter. When prompted, rename the system to `NS_Rain`**.** A **Minimal emitter** is a basic emitter with essential modules already enabled, so you do not have to create a blank emitter which will take up unnecessary time.
3. Double-click `NS_Rain` to open it in the Niagara Editor.
4. Select the **Properties** module. Enable **Determinism,** change **Sim Target** to **GPUCompute Sim**, and set **Calculate Bounds Mode** to **Fixed.** Rain usually needs many particles, so using the GPU helps keep the effect efficient.
5. In the **Emitter State** module, change **Life Cycle Mode** to **Self**, then ensure the **Loop Behavior** is set to **Infinite.** This allows the rain to keep falling continuously while you preview and adjust the effect.

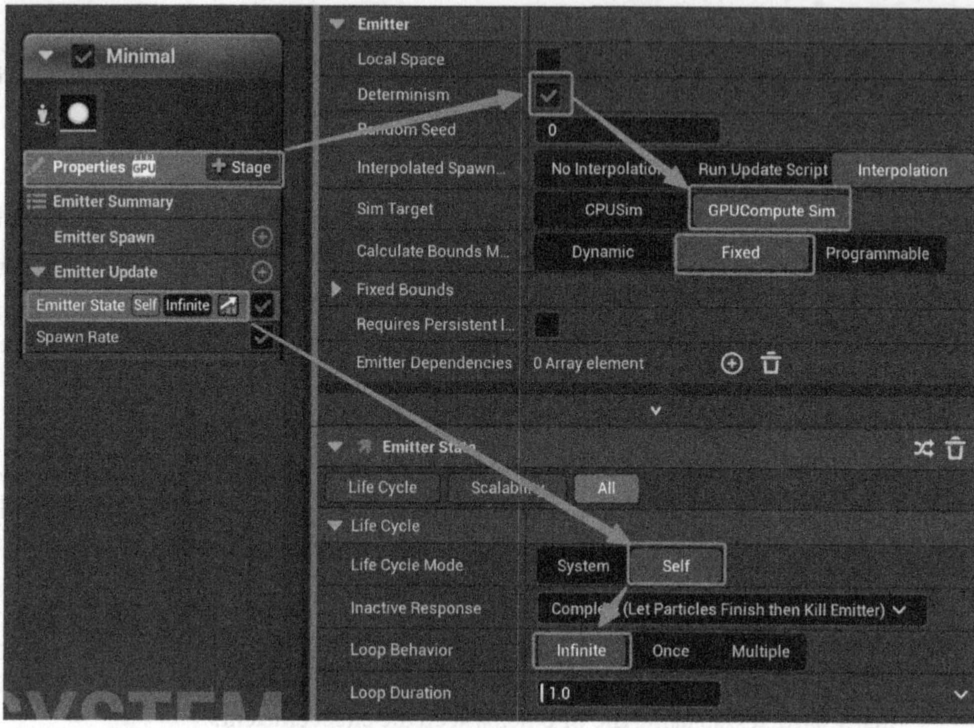

Figure 4.1 - Setting Properties and Emitter State

6. In the **Emitter Update** section, add a **Spawn Rate** module if it is not already there. Start with a value around `1500` to `3000`**.** You can increase or decrease this later, depending on how heavy you want the rain to look.
7. In the **Particle Spawn** section, select **Initialize Particle**. Set the **Lifetime Mode** to **Random** and use a short lifetime, such as `0.8` to `1.2` seconds. Rain particles move fast, so they do not need to stay alive for long.
8. Change **Color Mode** to **Direct Set** and set to a light *gray* or slightly *blue-gray*. Avoid pure white unless the scene is very dark, as bright rain can quickly look too noisy. Set **Alpha** to `0.2`. Press **OK.**
9. Still in **Initialize Particle,** change the **Sprite Size Mode** to **Random Non-Uniform**. Set the rain streaks to be thin and tall, for example:
   - **Sprite Size Min**: **X** = 2, **Y** = `80`
   - **Sprite Size Max**: **X** = 4, **Y** = `150`

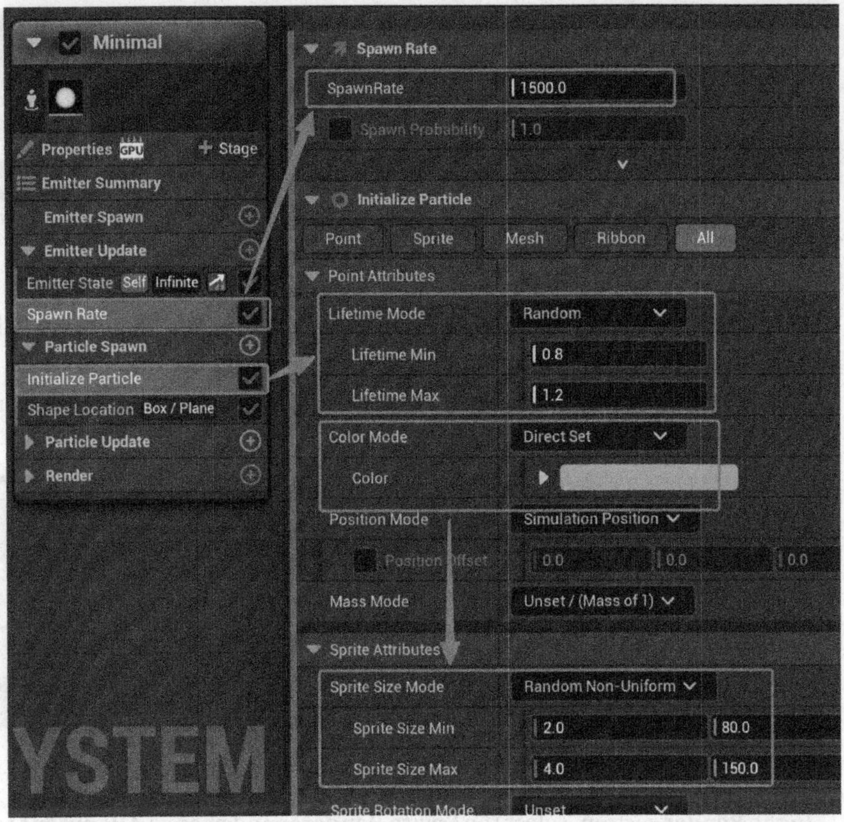

Figure 4.2 - Setting Spawn Rate and Initialize Particle module

10. In the **Particle Spawn** section, add a **Shape Location** module. Change the **Shape** to **Box**. This box will act as the rain spawn area above the scene. A good starting value is **X** = `2000`, **Y** = `2000`, **Z** = `2000`.

    I suggest turning the box size into a User Parameter, because the amount of rain you need depends heavily on the camera's view. A close-up shot may only need a smaller rain area, while a wider shot may need a larger volume to cover the frame properly. By exposing this setting, you can adjust the rain coverage directly from the level or in **Sequencer** without reopening the Niagara System each time.

11. Add an **Add Velocity** module. Click the top **Fix issue** when prompted. Using the down-pointing arrow on the **Velocity** property, choose **Random Range Vector**. Set **Minimum** to **X** = `0.0`, **Y** = `200`, **Z** = `-800` and **Maximum** to **X** = `1.0`, **Y** = `400`, **Z** = `-1500`. This will add some random movement to the falling rain streaks.

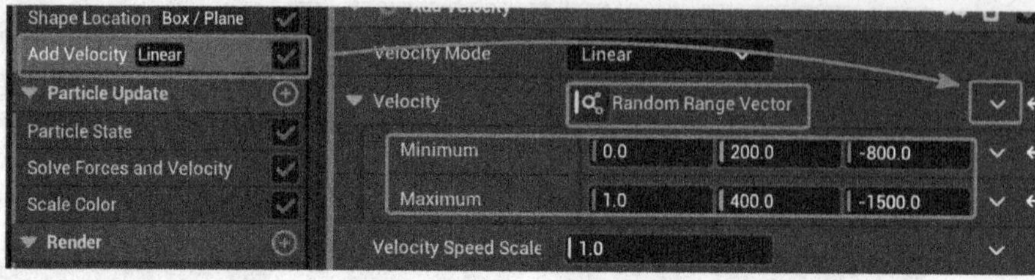

Figure 4.3 - Adding random velocity

12. In the **Particle Update** section, add a **Scale Color** module. For the alpha, click the down-pointing arrow and select **Float from Curve.** Choose the curve from the **Templates** as shown in *Figure 4.4*. This helps the rain appear and disappear more softly instead of popping.

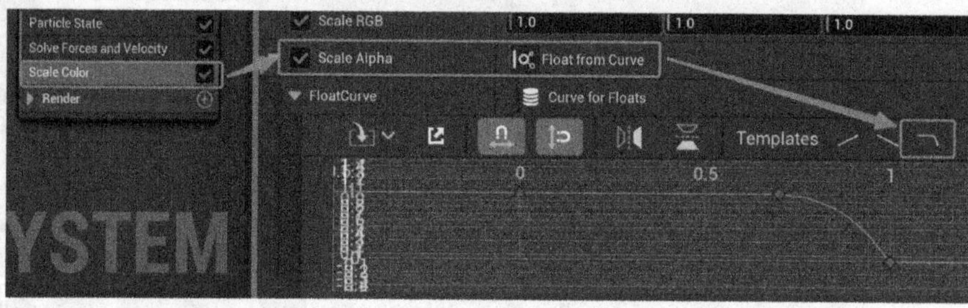

Figure 4.4 - Setting Shape Location and Scale Color modules

13. In the **Render** section, select the **Sprite Renderer** and change **Alignment** to **Velocity Aligned**. This will align the rain streaks with the direction of the falling rain. Compile and save.
14. Now, for faster iteration of the particles, go ahead and create **User Parameters** for the parameters shown in *Figure 4.5*:

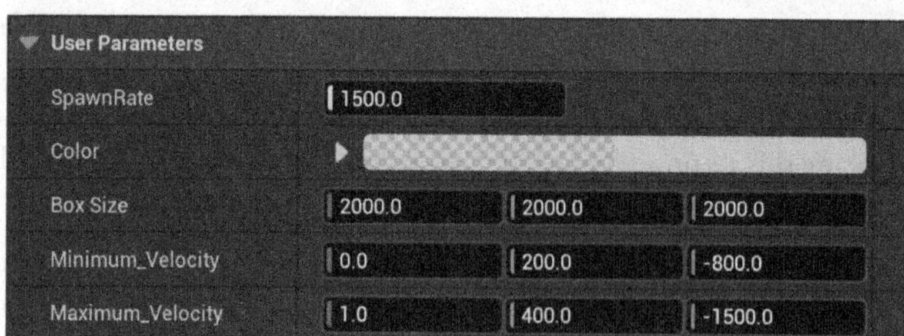

Figure 4.5 - Rain streaks user parameters

> **Note**
>
> **User Parameters** allow you to expose important Niagara settings so they can be adjusted outside the Niagara Editor. This is useful when you want to control values such as color, intensity, size, speed, or timing directly from the Level or keyframe them in **Sequencer**.
>
> If you skipped the earlier chapters, think of **User Parameters** as artist-friendly controls that make an effect easier to tweak for a specific shot. Please refer to the *Building a Niagara "Shot Control" system with User Parameters* recipe in *Chapter 1* for details.

15. Drag the `NS_Rain` into the level. You should now have a rain streak effect, as shown in *Figure 4.6*:

Figure 4.6 - The final rain streaks

How it works...

In this recipe, you created the main falling rain layer for the chapter. Starting with a **Minimal** Niagara emitter keeps the setup simple, so you only add the modules needed for falling rain. Enabling **Determinism** helps keep playback more predictable, while **GPUCompute Sim** is useful because rain usually needs many particles to feel full.

The emitter is set to loop infinitely because rain is a continuous effect, not a one-time burst. The short particle lifetime keeps the rain moving quickly through the frame, while the tall, narrow non-uniform sprite size creates the stretched streak shape we normally see in cinematic rain. The **Shape Location** box acts as the rain volume, and **Add Velocity** pushes the particles downward with some variation, so the rain does not look too mechanical.

The important idea in this recipe is that rain must be judged through the camera. A rain setup that looks good in the Viewport can become too bright, too dense, or too distracting in the final frame. This is why the color is kept slightly gray or blue-gray instead of pure white, and why the **alpha** is kept low.

The **Sprite Renderer** is set to **Velocity Aligned**, so the streaks follow the direction of the falling rain, which makes the motion feel more natural. The **User Parameters** also make the system easier to adjust later, because you can change spawn rate, color, box size, and velocity without digging through the Niagara stack each time. This rain layer is the foundation for the rest of the chapter, so it should look clean, readable, and controllable before you add splashes, ripples, or puddles.

There's more...

Once the basic rain streaks are working, you can improve the cinematic look by adjusting how the rain reads through the camera.

If the rain looks too sharp or noisy, lower the opacity and reduce the particle size. If it disappears too much, increase the **Spawn Rate** slightly, or make the streaks longer, especially in darker shots. Rain should be visible enough to add atmosphere, but not so strong that it distracts from the subject.

You can also create two versions (by duplicating the Niagara System in the **Outliner**) of the same rain system: a *foreground rain layer* and a *background rain layer*. The foreground layer can use larger, brighter streaks with fewer particles, while the background layer can use smaller, softer streaks with more coverage. This layered approach gives more depth and is often more cinematic than trying to make one rain emitter do everything, as shown in *Figure 4.7*:

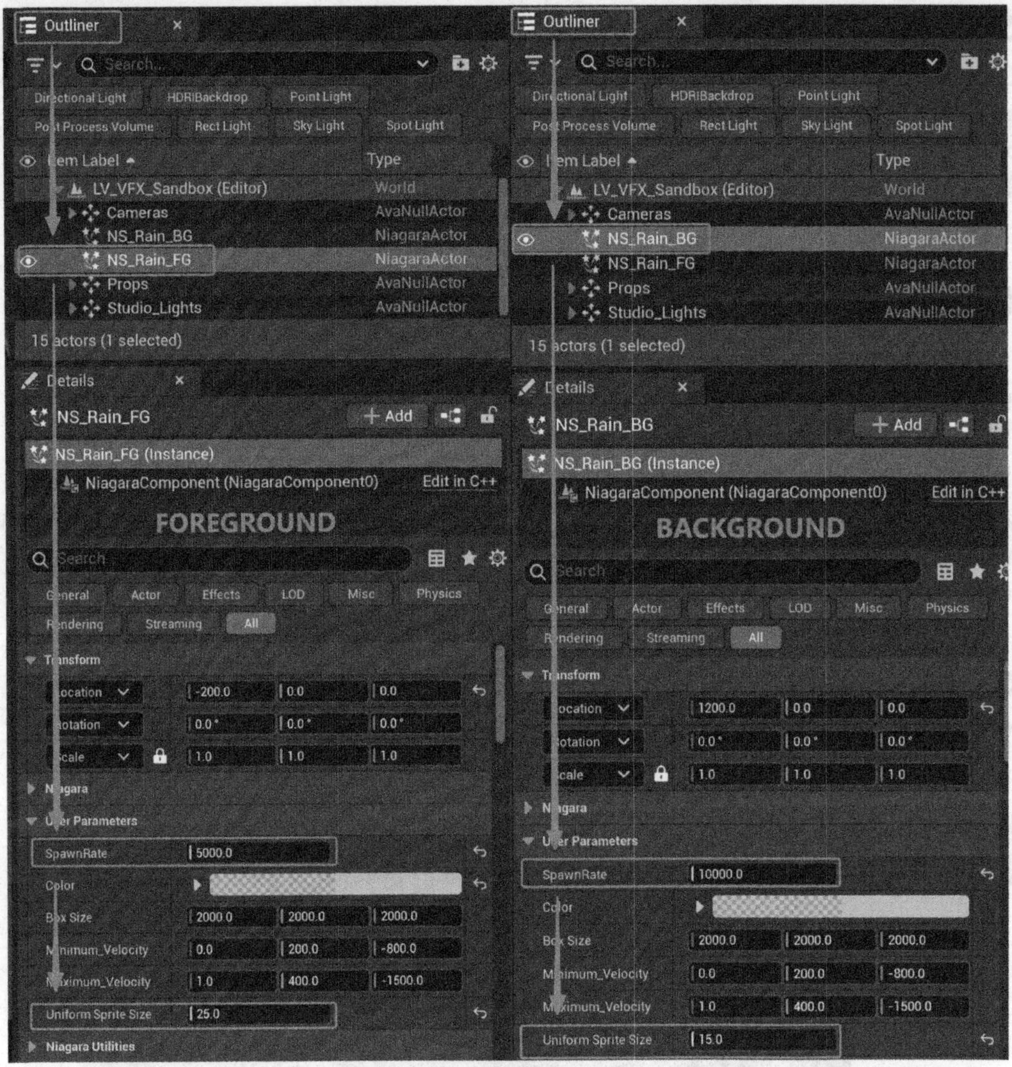

Figure 4.7 - Setting User Parameters for Foreground and Background rain effect

Tip

A simple extra tip: *always judge rain through the camera, not only in the Viewport.* Rain that looks good in the editor may become too dense, too bright, or too noisy once it is rendered.

See also

Use real rain footage as a visual reference before finalizing your Niagara settings. Look closely at how rain streaks behave in front of the camera, how visible they are against dark and bright backgrounds, and how quickly they disappear in motion. **Pexels** (`https://www.pexels.com/search/videos/rain/?utm_source`) has free rain video references, including close-up rainfall, heavy rain, night rain, and rain on surfaces.

Creating a rain splash effect

In the previous recipe, you created lightweight main falling rain streaks. In this recipe, we will add **rain splashes** to show that the rain is hitting the ground or nearby surfaces. This small detail makes a big difference because rain can feel disconnected if there is no reaction where it lands.

We will keep the setup simple by creating a lightweight Niagara splash effect utilizing a **SubUV Animation** texture. The goal is not to simulate every raindrop, but to add enough surface impact to make the shot feel wet, active, and more believable. Later in this chapter, we will build on this effect by adding ripples and puddles.

Getting ready

As we will be expanding upon the *Creating cinematic rain streaks* recipe, please have `NS_Rain` open and ready to go.

How to do it...

Since we will be creating a second emitter, let's first start by renaming the first emitter:

1. Using the *F2* key, rename the **Minimal** emitter to `Rain_Streaks`.
2. Right-click in the empty Niagara Editor and choose **Add minimal emitter.** Rename to `Splashes`.

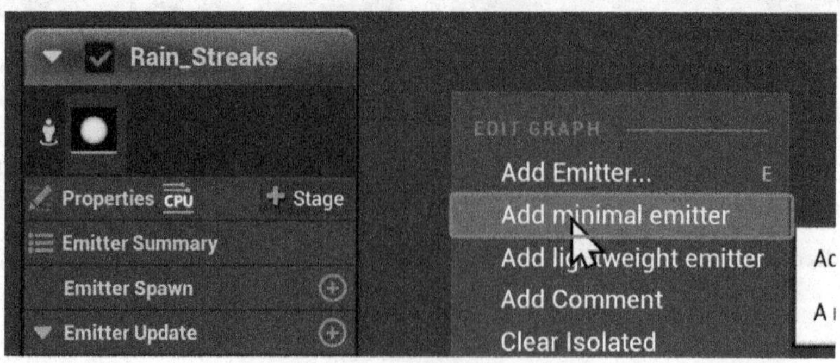

Figure 4.8 - Making the Splashes emitter

3. Select the **Properties** module. Enable **Determinism,** then enable the **Requires Persistent IDs** checkbox. This setting will allow multiple emitters to track the same particles over time.

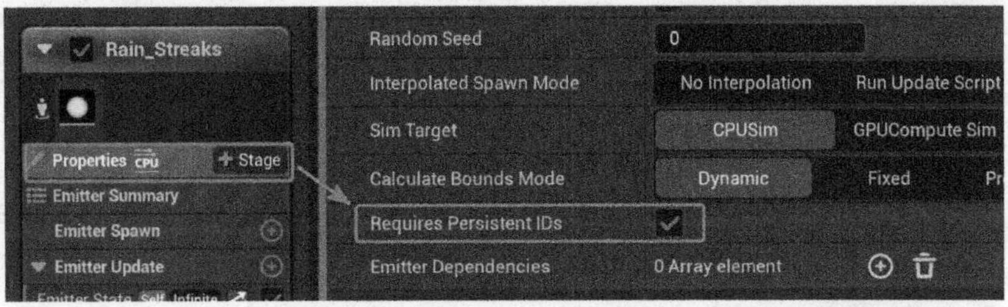

Figure 4.9 - Enabling Requires Persistent IDs

4. Like in the *Creating cinematic rain streaks* recipe, in the **Emitter State** module, change **Life Cycle Mode** to **Self**, then ensure the **Loop Behavior** is set to **Infinite.**

5. In the **Initialize Particle** module, change **Lifetime** to `0.25` to have the splashes only appear for a split second. Change **Sprite Size Mode** to **Uniform** and set **Uniform Sprite Size** to `8`. The larger this number, the larger the splashes will appear.

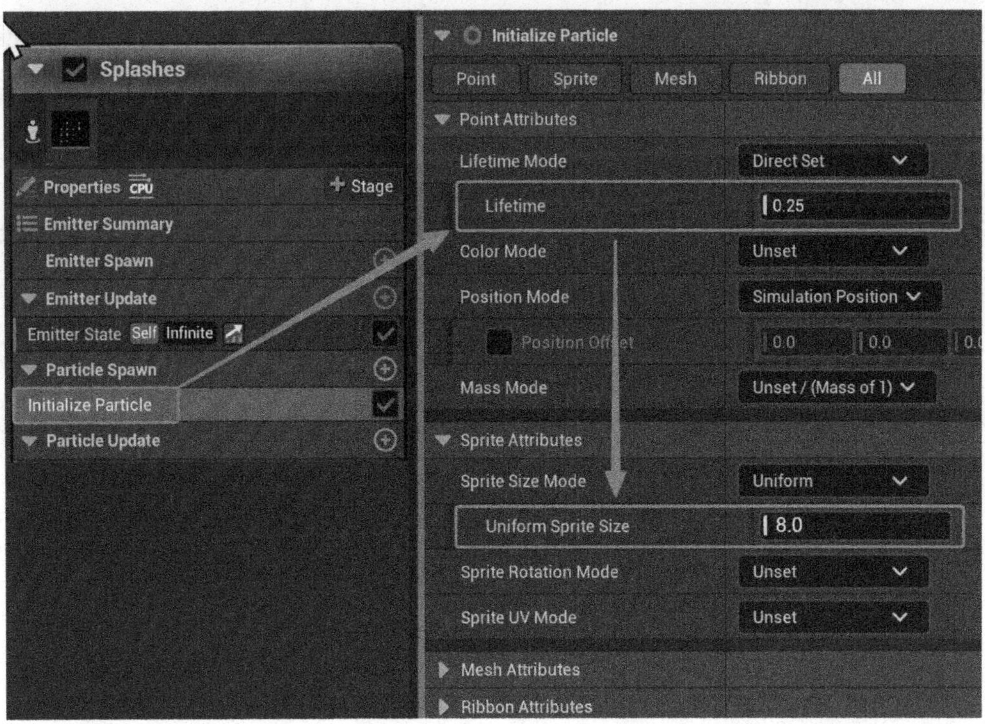

Figure 4.10 - Lifetime and Uniform Sprite Size settings

To have the rain streaks generate the splashes exactly where they hit the surface, there needs to be a connection between the **Rain_Streaks** emitter and the **Splashes** emitter, which we will achieve in the next few steps:

1. In the **Particle Update** section of the **Rain_Streaks** emitter, add a **Generate Collision Event** module. Click the **Fix issue** button to have the emitter automatically add a **Collision** module.
2. The **Rain_Streaks** emitter will flag errors. This can be resolved by enabling **Requires Persistent IDs** and changing **Sim Target** back to **CPUSim** and **Calculate Bounds Mode** to **Dynamic.**

> **Note**
>
> Some Niagara effects cannot always run as GPU simulations, depending on the modules and settings used in the emitter. When a setup includes features that are not supported by GPU simulation, Unreal Engine may switch the emitter back to CPU Sim. This is what happens with the **Rain_Streaks** emitter in this recipe, so we will keep it as CPU Sim for now.

3. While still at the **Rain_Streaks** emitter, in the **Particle Update** section, add a **Kill Particles** module. Then, using the down-pointing arrow, search for `Has Collided`**.** This will remove all unnecessary bouncing particles.

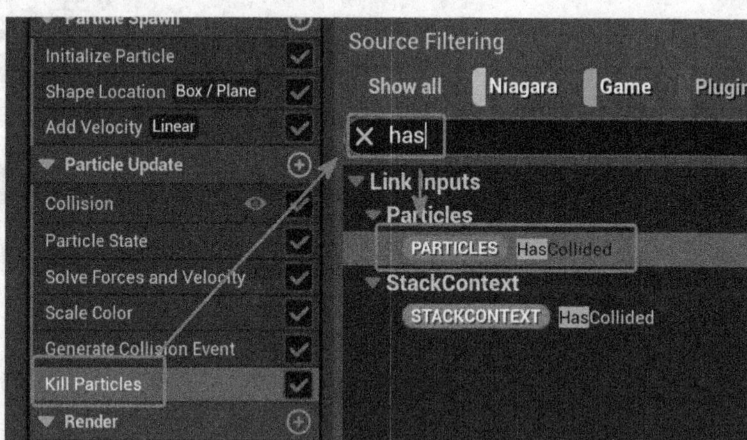

Figure 4.11 - Adding the Kill Particles module

4. Back to the **Splashes** emitter, select the **Properties** module and click the **Stage** button, and add the **Event Handler** module. This module determines how it responds to incoming events—collisions in this case.

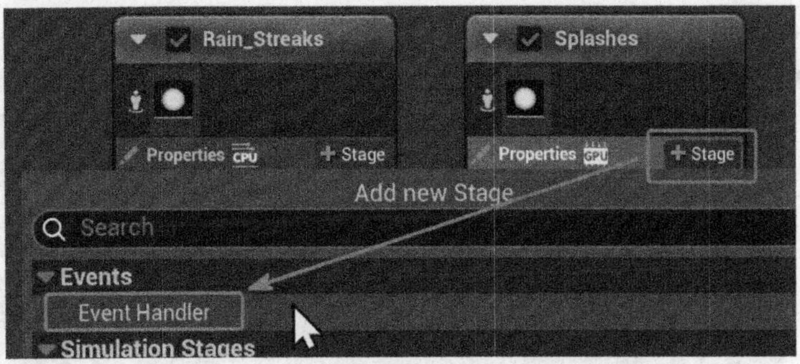

Figure 4.12 - Adding Event Handler module

5. In the **Event Handler** module properties, change **Source** to **Collision Event**. Change **Execution** mode to **Spawned Particles**. Change **Spawn Number** to 1. This allows the **Event Handler** to only affect the spawned particles.

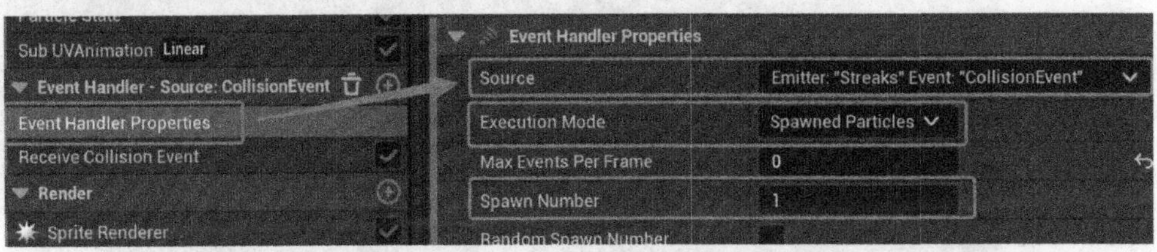

Figure 4.13 - Setting the Event Handler Properties

6. Still in the **Event Handler** section, add a **Receive Collision Event** module.

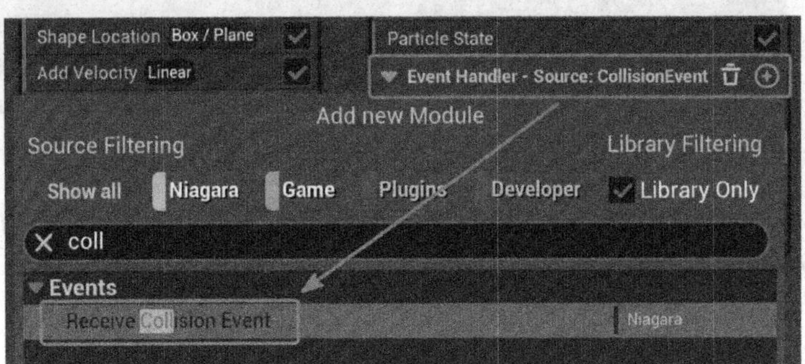

Figure 4.14 - Adding the Receive Collision Event module

7. To make the splash look like an actual water splash, in the Sprite **Renderer module**, change the **Material** to **MI_Splash.** This is a pre-made splash material found in the `Materials` folder. Feel free to inspect it to find out how it was constructed.

8. Change **Sub Image Size** to `4.0` on both **X** and **Y**. Enable **Sub UV Blending** and the **Use Material Cutout Texture**.

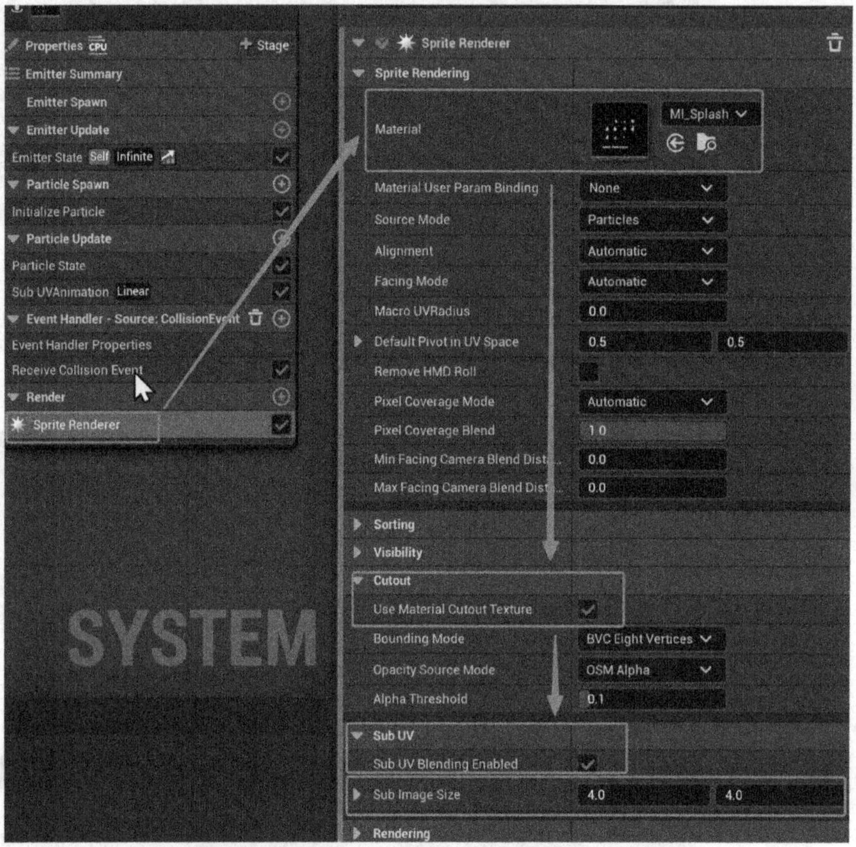

Figure 4.15 - Setting the Event Handler Properties

9. Lastly, in the **Splashes** emitter's **Particle Update** section, add a **Sub UVAnimation** module and change the **Sprite Renderer** setting to **Sprite Renderer.**

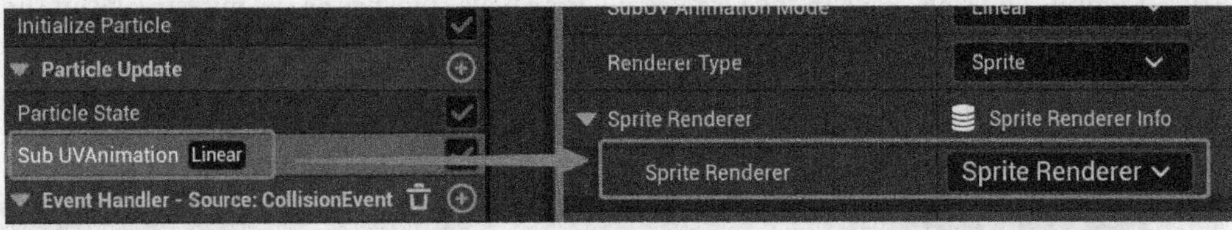

Figure 4.16 - Setting the Sub UVAnimation module

Figure 4.17 shows the completed **Rain_Streaks** and **Splashes** emitters side by side:

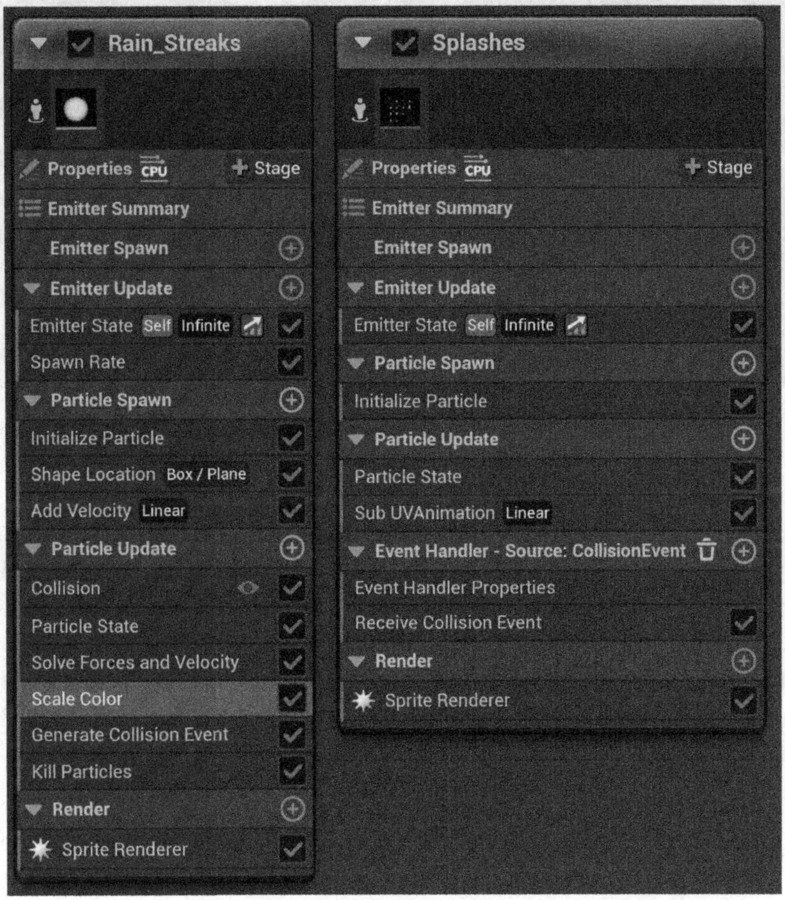

Figure 4.17 - Completed Rain_Streaks and Splashes emitters

10. Compile and save. Back in the Level, you'll now have splashes as the rain streaks hit the ground, as shown in *Figure 4.18*:
11. To change the size of the splashes, increase the **Uniform Size** in the **Splashes** emitter **Initialize Particle** module.

Figure 4.18 - The final rain with splashes

How it works...

In this recipe, you added a second emitter to the same Niagara System, so the rain streaks can create splashes when they hit the ground. The **Rain_Streaks** emitter is responsible for the falling rain, while the **Splashes** emitter reacts when those rain particles collide with the surface. This is why the **Generate Collision Event** module is added to the rain emitter, and the **Event Handler** is added to the splash emitter. The rain particles detect the hit, then send that collision information to the **Splashes** emitter. The **Receive Collision Event** module reads that information, such as where the collision happened, and uses it to spawn a short-lived splash particle at the contact point.

The **Requires Persistent IDs** setting is important because Niagara needs a reliable way to identify particles when passing event data from one emitter to another. Without it, the collision event may not be tracked properly, and the splash emitter may not receive the information it needs. You also switched the rain emitter back to CPU Sim because event-based collision workflows can require CPU simulation, depending on the modules being used. GPU simulation is useful for large numbers of particles, but not every feature works the same way on the GPU. In this case, CPU Sim gives Niagara the information needed to generate and pass collision events more reliably.

The cinematic reason for adding splashes is simple: rain feels disconnected if nothing happens when it touches the ground. Even small splashes help the audience believe the surface is being hit by water. The splash lifetime is kept very short because real rain impacts happen quickly, and the sprite size is kept small, so the effect supports the shot without looking like sparks or debris.

The **Sub UV** splash material gives the splash a quick animated shape, which is more convincing than using a default texture. The main thing to watch is balance: if the splashes are too large or too frequent, they will steal attention from the rain; if they are too subtle, the ground will still feel inactive. The best result is usually a soft, constant layer of tiny impacts that makes the surface feel wet and alive.

There's more...

Once the rain splashes are working, you can change the effect using **User Parameters** by adjusting the splash size, lifetime, and **Spawn Rate** based on the type of rain you want. Light rain should have smaller, softer splashes with fewer particles, while heavy rain can use a higher spawn rate and slightly larger splash particles (as shown in *Figure 4.19*). Be careful not to make the splashes too big, because they can quickly look like sparks, dust, or small explosions instead of water hitting the ground.

Figure 4.19 - Light versus Heavy Rain

See also

To understand **Events** and **Event Handlers** better, check out the Epic Games documentation for additional information: `https://dev.epicgames.com/documentation/unreal-engine/events-and-event-handlers-in-niagara-effects-for-unreal-engine`.

Creating a rain ripple effect

In the previous recipes, you created falling rain streaks and added splashes to show that the rain is hitting the surface. In this recipe, we will add **rain ripples** to complete the surface reaction. Ripples are important cinematically because they make the ground feel wet and alive, especially in close-up or low-angle shots where the surface is visible.

A rain scene can look incomplete if the rain falls and splashes, but the surface stays still. By adding subtle circular ripples, you create another layer of movement that helps sell realism, reflection, and mood. The goal is to keep the effect simple and controlled, so it supports the shot without becoming too busy.

Getting ready

As we will be expanding upon the *Creating a rain splash effect* recipe, please have `NS_Rain` open and ready to go.

How to do it...

Like before, we will build on the existing **Splashes** emitter setup and modify it to create ripple effects.

1. With `NS_Rain` opened in the Niagara Editor, select and duplicate the **Splashes** emitter and rename it to `Ripples`. We will basically use most of the modules in this emitter, but make some slight changes and additions.
2. In the **Ripples** emitter, select the **Initialize Particle** module and change **Lifetime** to `0.5`. We want the ripples to linger for a slightly longer time compared to the splashes.
3. Select **Sprite Renderer** and change the **Material** to `M_Ripples`; this is the round-shaped texture that ripples make after a splash. If you are interested in knowing how this material was created, refer to the *There's more...* section, where I explain how I made it.
4. Change **Sub Image Size** to **X** = 1, **Y** = 1.
5. To align the sprites (round ripple texture) flat onto the ground, add a **Sprite Facing and Alignment** module to the **Particle Spawn** section. Change the **Z** value to `1.0`.

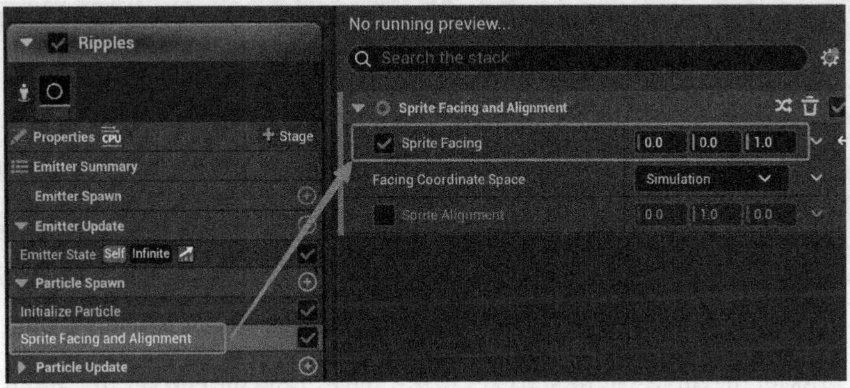

Figure 4.20 - Adding Sprite Facing and Alignment module

6. Next, the ripples need to expand and disappear; to achieve that, we will use the **Scale Sprite Size** and **Scale Color** modules. Add the **Scale Sprite Size** module to the **Particle Update** section.
7. Choose the **Linear Curve** from the **Templates** section. For the first **Key**, set **time** to `0.0` and **value** to `1.0`. For the second **Key**, set **time** to `1.0` and **value** to `3.0`, as shown in *Figure 4.21*. The ripple will scale up as it disappears once we have the **Scale Color** module in place.

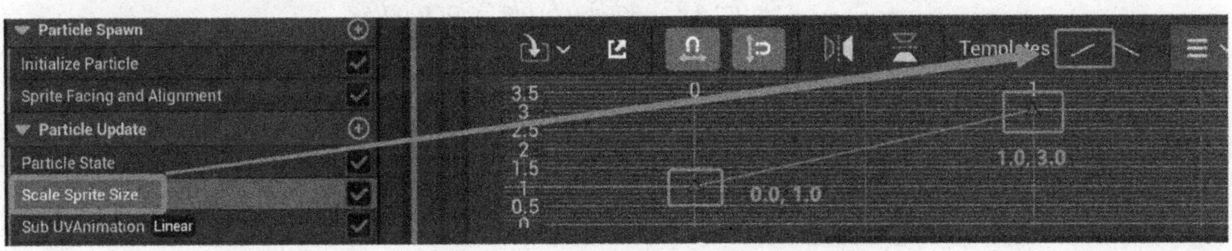

Figure 4.21 - Adding Scale Sprite Size module

8. Now add the **Scale Color** module. Since we need to make the ripple disappear, we only need to adjust the **Alpha** channel. Click the down-pointing arrow for **Scale Alpha** and choose **Float from Curve**.

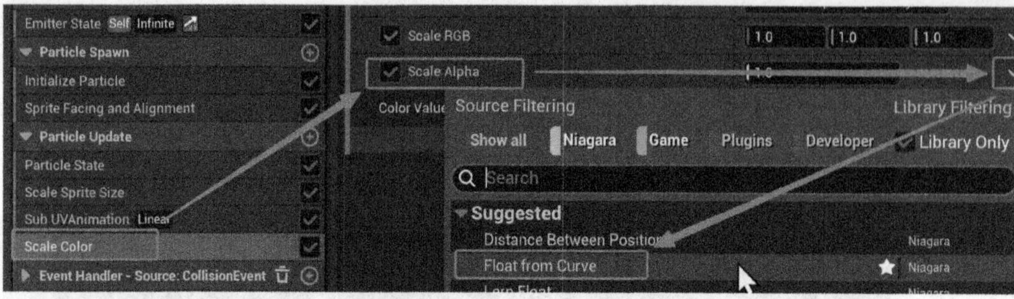

Figure 4.22: Adding Scale Color module

9. As for the curve, set the **start** key to `0.0` and `0.6` and the **end** key to `1.0` and `0.0`, as shown in *Figure 4.23*. This setting will fade off the ripple as it enlarges. Compile and save.

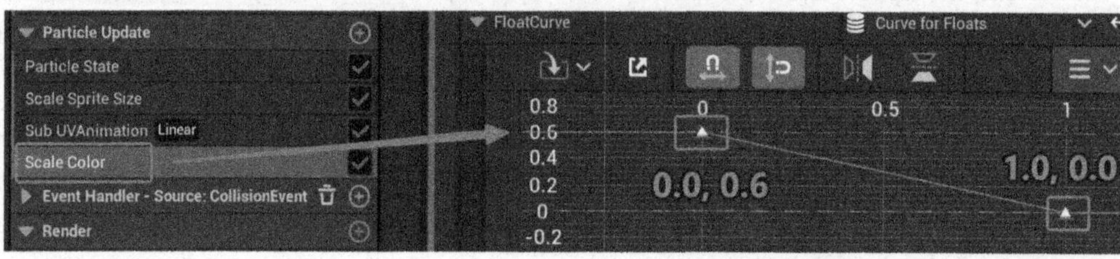

Figure 4.23 - Adding Scale Color module

> **Note**
>
> These numbers are just a guide; you can experiment with your own settings to achieve the look you are going for.

Figure 4.24 shows the final look of the rain streaks, splashes, and ripple effects:

Figure 4.24 - The final rain splashes with ripples

How it works...

In this recipe, you reused the splash setup and adapted it into a ripple emitter. This is a smart workflow because ripples and splashes are both surface reactions caused by rain impact, so they can share the same event-driven timing. By duplicating the **Splashes** emitter, you keep the collision-event structure already in place, then change the look and behavior of the particles. The ripple particles use a circular texture instead of a splash texture, and the **Sprite Facing and Alignment** module turns the sprite so it lies flat on the ground. This is important because a ripple should read like a ring spreading across a wet surface, not like a particle floating upright in the air.

Curves in Niagara matter because they let an effect change smoothly over a particle's lifetime instead of staying constant. For example, a splash can start small, grow quickly, and fade out naturally, while a smoke puff can expand slowly and lose opacity over time. Without curves, effects can feel sudden, flat, or mechanical. Curves give you timing control, helping particles appear, move, scale, and disappear in a way that feels more natural and cinematic.

The **Scale Sprite Size** module makes the ripple expand over its lifetime, while the **Scale Color** module fades it out. These two changes are what sell the idea of water reacting after impact: the ring starts small, spreads outward, and slowly disappears. The ripple lifetime is slightly *longer* than the splash lifetime because ripples need time to be seen, especially in close-up or low-angle shots. Cinematically, ripples add a quieter layer of realism. The rain streaks show falling water, the splashes show impact, and the ripples show the surface responding after the impact.

The key is to keep the ripples subtle. If they are too bright or too dense, the ground becomes visually noisy. They should support the wet look, not turn into the main effect.

There's more...

In *step 3* of the *How to do it* section, I mentioned the `M_Ripples` material and how it was made. It was made in image-editing software with a transparent background, with a resolution of 1024 x 1024, and saved as a PNG file format.

Figure 4.25 - The ring texture for the ripple effect

Let me take you through the process of making the ripple material:

1. In the `Materials` folder, right-click and select **Material**, and rename it to `M_Ripple2` (because `M_Ripples` already exists).
2. Double-click to open the Material Editor. With the main material node still selected, in its **Details** panel, change **Blend Mode** to **Translucent**. This will enable the **Opacity** control option, which is required since our Texture has an alpha channel (transparency).

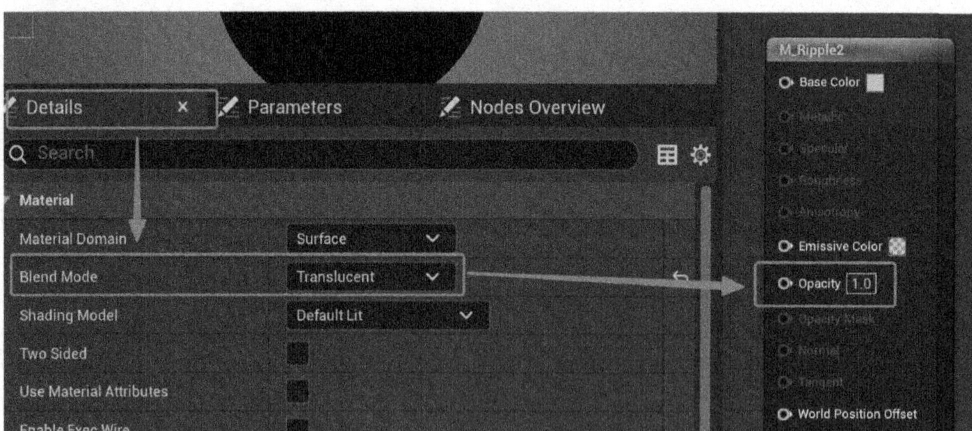

Figure 4.26 - Enabling the Translucent Blend Mode

3. Press *Ctrl* + *Space* to access the **Content Browser**, then from the **Textures** | **Chapter 4** folder, drag and drop the `RainRipple_C` texture into the Material Editor.

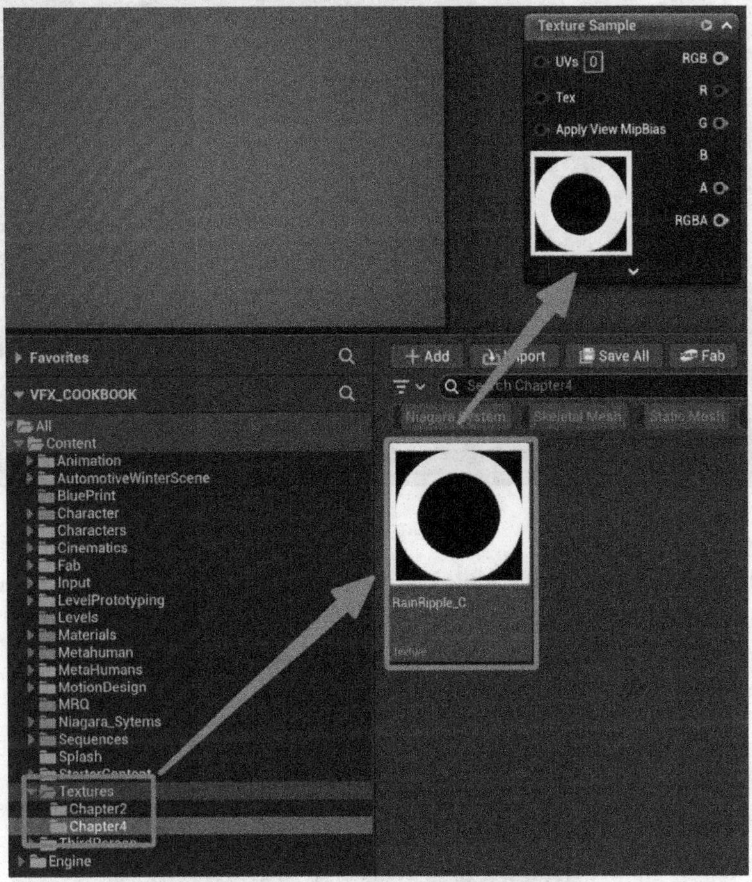

Figure 4.27 - Adding the RainRipple_C texture into the Material Editor

4. Right-click anywhere in the material graph area and search for and add a **Particle Color** node, then add two **Multiply** nodes and attach the nodes as shown in *Figure 4. 28*:

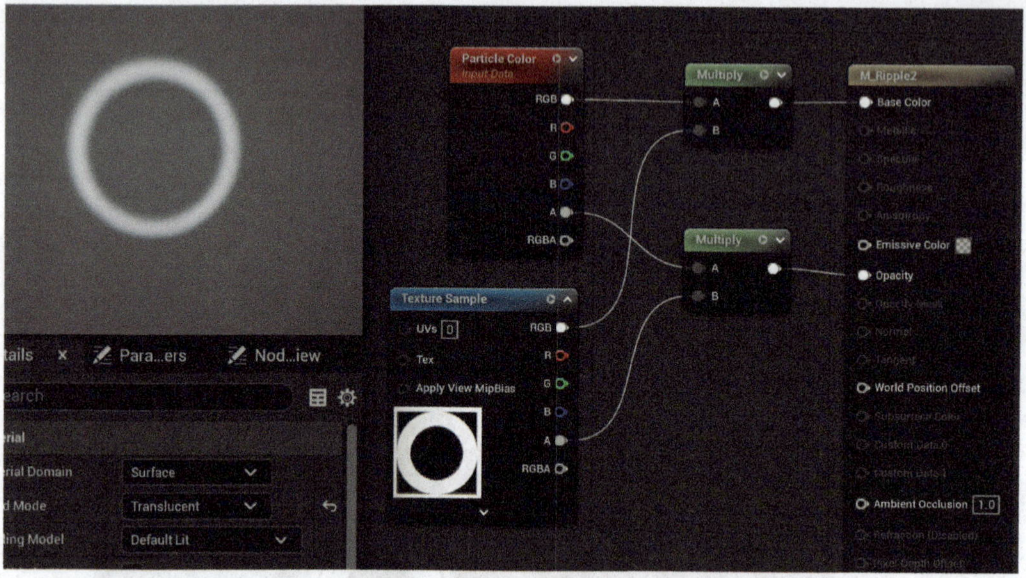

Figure 4.28 - Connecting the nodes

5. Optionally, to make the ripple texture appear more opaque, in the **Translucency** section, change the **Lighting Mode** to **Volumetric Directional.**

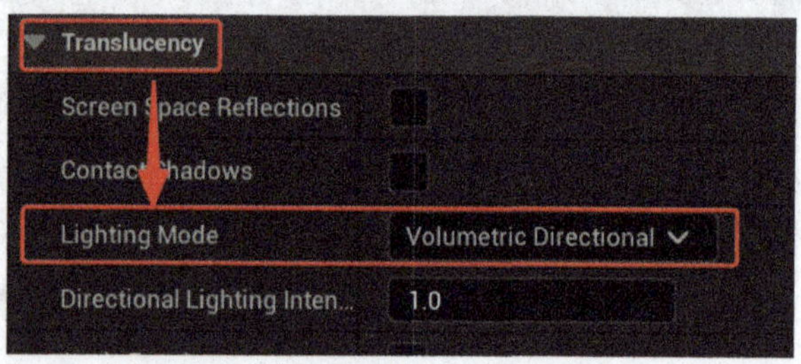

Figure 4.29 - Changing the Lighting Mode

6. Click **Apply** and save, and you're done!

See also

If you would like to have a deeper understanding of Unreal Engine **Material nodes and expressions**, here's a highly recommended reference: `https://dev.epicgames.com/documentation/unreal-engine/unreal-engine-material-expressions-reference`.

Creating a cinematic rain puddle effect

In the previous recipes in this chapter, you created the main rain streaks, added splashes, and built ripples to show how rain reacts when it hits the ground. In this recipe, we will complete the rain setup by creating **rain puddles**. Puddles are important cinematically because they add reflections, shine, and contrast to the ground, making the whole scene feel wetter and more atmospheric.

For this recipe, we will not use Niagara. Instead, we will create the puddle effect using materials only. This keeps the setup simple and allows us to focus on surface appearance, such as roughness, reflection, opacity, and shape. By the end of the recipe, you will have a simple puddle material that can be placed into any scene to support the rain, splashes, and ripples created earlier.

Getting ready

In order to achieve the best aesthetics of the complete rain, splashes, ripples, and puddles effect, there is a level just for that. In the **Content Browser | Levels**, open the `LV_VFX_Puddles` level. I've added a wet surface and texture made from Quixel Megascans available from **Fab** (`https://www.fab.com/`).

How to do it...

In this section, we will create the puddle effect using a material instead of Niagara. Since puddles are mainly about how the ground looks and reflects light, a material-based approach is more suitable than a particle system. We will build a simple **decal material** that can be placed on the floor, adjusted through a Material Instance, and used to support the rain streaks, splashes, and ripples created earlier.

1. To get a good angle of the puddle's effect once it's ready to view, I've set a bookmark. Either press the *1* key on your keyboard or select **Camera Options | Bookmarks | Bookmark 1**.

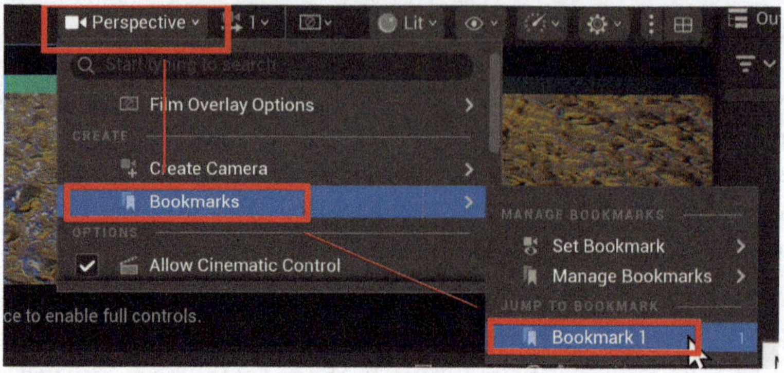

Figure 4.30 - Selecting Bookmark 1

2. In the `Materials` folder, right-click and make a new Material and rename it to `M_Puddles` and open it in the Material Editor.
3. Select the **Output** node and in its **Details** panel, change **Material Domain** from **Surface** to **Deferred Decal** and **Blend Mode** from **Opaque** to **Translucent**. We will be using the **Decal** method to create the puddle effect, as it can be used on any surface – how useful!

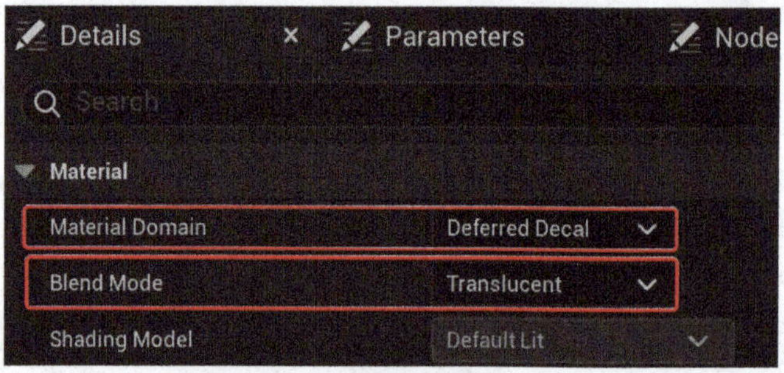

Figure 4.31 - Setting Material Domain and Blend Mode

4. For the **Base Color**, add a **Constant 3 Vector** node and a **Scalar Parameter** node and connect them as shown in *Figure 4.32*. Rename the **Constant 3 Vector** to `Water color` and the **Scalar Parameter** to `Color`.

> **Note**
>
> If you are new to the Material Editor, you can add nodes either by right-clicking in the graph or by pressing the *Tab* key, then searching for the appropriate nodes.

5. Set the **Water color** to `0.5,0.5,0.5,1.0`, and set the **Color** parameter's **Default Value** to `0.1`.

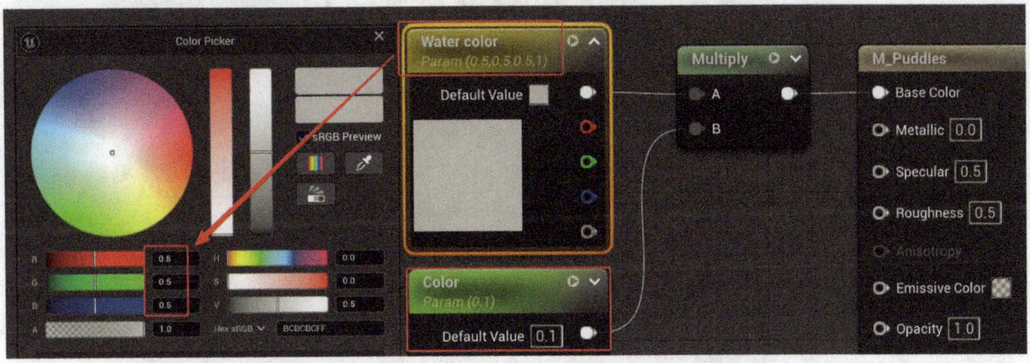

Figure 4.32 - Base Color output nodes

6. Next, we will work on the **Roughness** and **Opacity** output. Add the following nodes and connect them as shown in *Figure 4.33*:
   - 1 **World Position** (Absolute World Position)
   - 1 **Scalar** parameter, renamed to `Scale` with a value of `1.0`
   - 1 **Constant**, with a value of `100`
   - 1 **Multiply** node
   - 1 **Divide** node

   Connect the **Scale** output pin to the **A** input and the **Constant** output to the **B** input of the **Divide** node. Connect the **Absolute World Position XYZ** pin to the **A** input of the **Multiply** node, as follows:

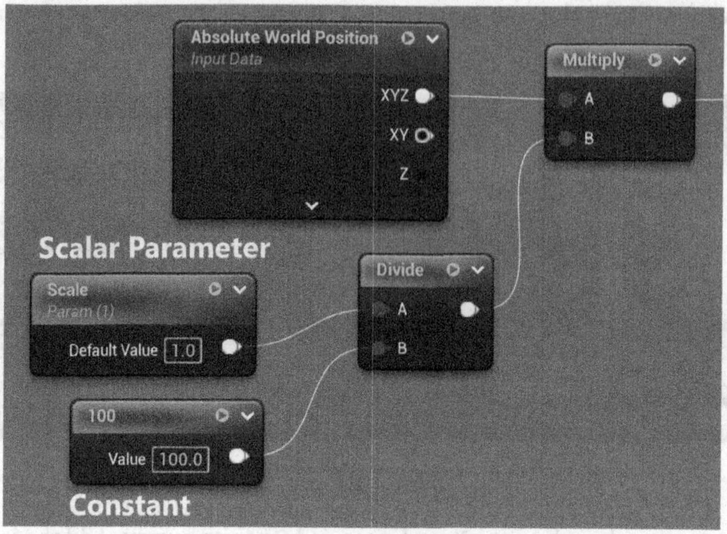

Figure 4.33 - Creating Roughness and Opacity nodes

7. Next, add the following nodes and connect them as shown in *Figure 4.34*:
   - 1 **Noise**
   - 1 **One-minus** (1-x)
   - 2 **Multiply**
   - 2 **Scalar Parameters**, renamed to `Roughness` with a value of `0` and **Opacity** with a value of `1.0`

   Connect the **Multiply** output pin from *Figure 4.33* to the **World Position** of the **Noise** node. Output of the **Noise** node goes into **One-Minus** and **Multiply (1) A** input pins. **Opacity** node connects to **Multiply (2) B** pin. **Roughness** output connects to the **Multiply (1) B** pin, and the **One-minus** output pin connects to the **Multiply (1) A** pin:

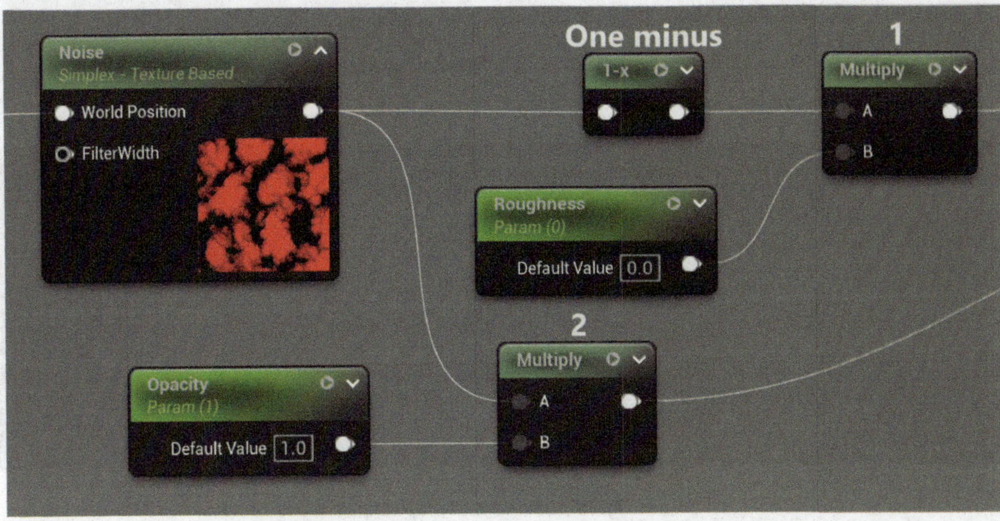

Figure 4.34: Creating Roughness and Opacity nodes (continued)

8. To complete the connection, connect the **Multiply** output pin (see *Figure 4.33*) to the **World Position** pin of the **Noise** node. Connect the **Multiply (1)** output pin (see *Figure 4.34*) to the **Roughness** pin of the main node and the **Multiply (2)** output pin to the **Opacity** of the main node, as shown in *Figure 4.35*:

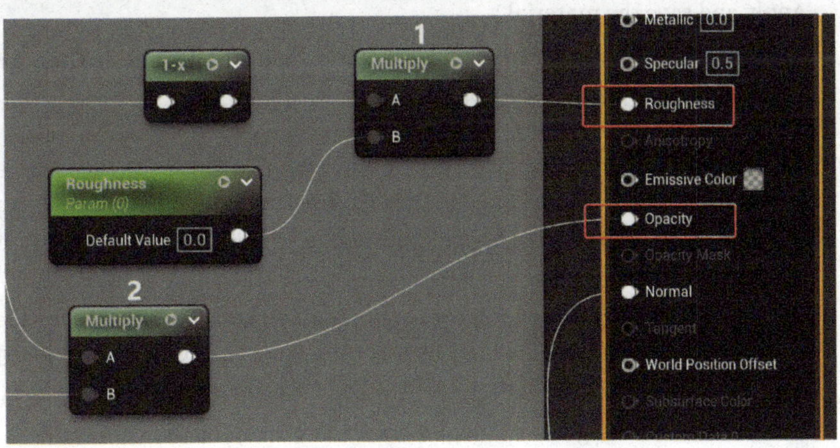

Figure 4.35 - Creating Roughness and Opacity nodes (continued)

9. Lastly, we will add the **Normal** output nodes. Add the following nodes and attach them as shown in *Figure 4.36*:
   - 1 **Flatten Normal** node
   - 1 **One-minus** node

- 1 **Scalar** Parameter (renamed to `Normal Amt`)
- 1 **Texture** sample (using the **T_Ground_Grass_N** texture from the `Starter Content` folder)

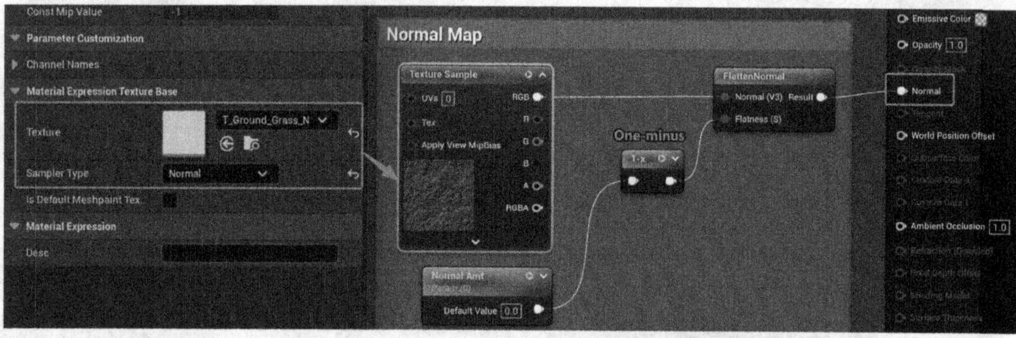

Figure 4.36 - Normal map output nodes

> **Note**
>
> The **Normal Map** will give bumpy effects on the puddle water if you tweak the **Normal Amt** parameter.

10. Apply and save the material.
11. Back in the `Materials` folder, right-click on `M_Puddles` and choose **Create Material Instance** and rename it to `MI_Puddles`.

> **Note**
>
> Material Instances and Niagara **User Parameters** are similar because both give you a cleaner way to control an effect without rebuilding it from scratch. A **Material Instance** lets you adjust exposed material values such as color, roughness, opacity, or normal strength, while Niagara **User Parameters** let you adjust exposed particle values such as spawn rate, size, speed, color, or wind. In a production workflow, both act like artist-friendly controls: instead of opening the full material graph or Niagara stack every time, you tweak only the important settings needed for the shot.

12. Double-click on `MI_Puddles` to open the Material Instance. In the **Details** panel, you'll have access to all the parameters you just created in the `Puddles` master material.

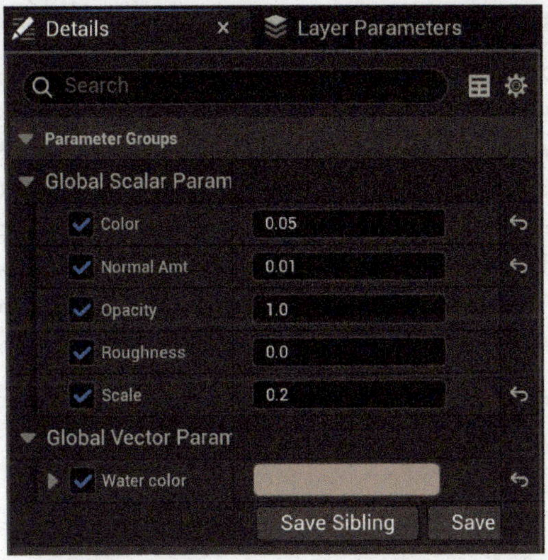

Figure 4.37 - Editing the MI_Puddles Material Instance

13. Drag `MI_Puddles` into the level, rotate it to `-90` on the **Y** axis, and set **Scale** to `2.0` on the **Y** and **Z** axes.
14. You can now tweak the settings and make them look the way you want them to look.

Figure 4.38 - The final rain effect with a puddle

How it works...

In this recipe, you completed the rain setup by adding puddles using a material instead of Niagara. This is the right choice because puddles are mainly a surface look, not a particle effect. By setting the **Material Domain** to **Deferred Decal** and the **Blend Mode** to **Translucent**, the puddle can be projected onto the ground and blended with the existing surface. This makes it flexible, because the same puddle material can be placed on different areas without replacing the floor material. The **Base Color** controls the water tint, while **Opacity** controls how strong the puddle appears. **Roughness** is especially important because it controls how shiny or mirror-like the wet area feels.

The Material Instance makes the setup practical for production because you can adjust the puddle without rebuilding the master material. You exposed useful controls such as **Color**, **Opacity, Roughness**, **Scale**, and **Normal Strength,** which give you quick control over the final look. The normal map adds a small surface disturbance, so the puddle does not look like a flat painted patch.

In the *There's more...* section, adding a slow **Panner** to the normal map gives the water a very subtle movement, which helps the puddle feel alive without using Niagara. Cinematically, puddles help tie the whole rain scene together. They catch highlights, create reflections, and make the ground feel wet enough to support the rain streaks, splashes, and ripples you built earlier.

There's more...

To take the Puddle effect one step further, let's add a subtle movement of the puddle's water surface. This can be achieved very easily by adding *two extra nodes* to the **Normal** output. Follow these steps:

1. In the `M_Puddles` Material Editor, add a **Panner** node and a **Scalar Parameter** node. Rename the **Scalar Parameter** to `Speed` and set its default value to `0.01`. Connect the **Panner** so it gently moves the **Normal** texture over time. This creates a very subtle movement on the puddle surface, helping the water feel alive without looking like it is flowing too strongly. Attach as shown in *Figure 4.39*:

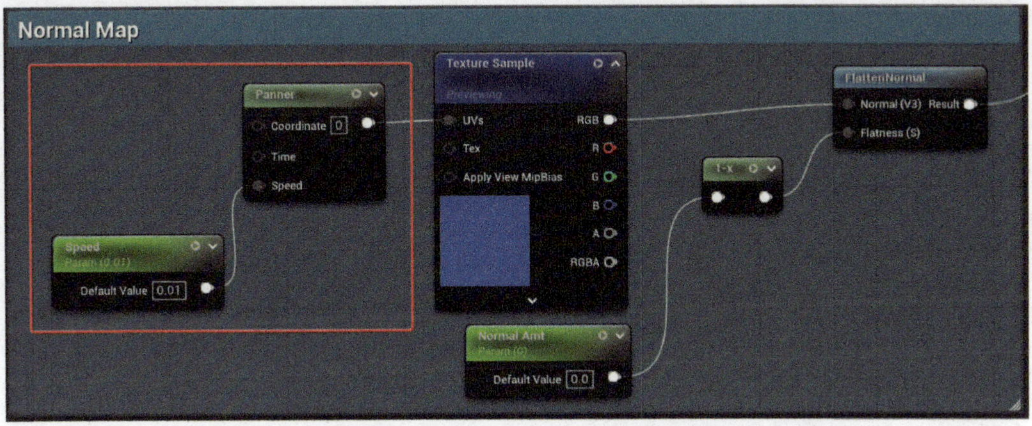

Figure 4.39 - Adding Panner and Scalar Parameter nodes

2. You can now tweak the movement using the `MI_Puddles` parameters. Be sure to set the **Normal Amt** to at least `0.05` to see the slow-moving ripples.

Figure 4.40 - Final look of slow movement to puddle water surface

See also

Conveniently, Material Instances let you reuse the same puddle material while adjusting values such as roughness, normal strength, opacity, and panning speed without rebuilding the material from scratch. To understand this better, here's an in-depth resource about **Material Instances**: `https://dev.epicgames.com/documentation/unreal-engine/instanced-materials-in-unreal-engine`.

5

Niagara Snow for Cinematics

Snow has a powerful cinematic effect because it can completely change the mood of a scene. A light snowfall can make a shot feel quiet, emotional, or peaceful, while heavy snow or a blizzard can create tension, danger, and scale. Snow also helps show depth in a frame because flakes move between the camera, subject, and background, giving the shot a stronger sense of atmosphere.

In this chapter, we will create several snow effects using Niagara, starting with a simple light snowfall and then building toward heavier and more dramatic variations. You will learn how to control snowflake size, speed, density, direction, and movement, so the effect remains readable through the camera without becoming too noisy. We will then create a blizzard pass, a localized snow swirl around objects, and a ground kick-up effect for impacts or movement. Each recipe is designed to stay practical, reusable, and suitable for cinematic shot work.

Throughout this chapter, the focus will be on building systems that can be easily art-directed, adjusted for different shot requirements, and rendered reliably as part of a cinematic production workflow.

Therefore, in this chapter, we'll cover the following recipes:

- Creating light snowfall (soft drift)
- Creating a blizzard pass (foreground/mid/background layers)
- Creating a localized snow swirl around objects
- Creating a snow kick-up burst (ground interaction)

Technical requirements

Before starting this recipe, ensure the following are set up:

- Make sure that **Unreal Engine 5.6** is installed (see *Chapter 1* for details).

- A project with **Niagara** and **Niagara Sim Caching** plugin enabled.
- A test environment or sandbox level where the effect can be previewed—you may use the sandbox environment we created in the *Setting up a reusable VFX "Sandbox" level for cinematic lookdev* recipe in *Chapter 1*.
- Maintain the folder structure to keep the assets organized, as shown below:
    - `Content`
        - `Niagara_Systems`
        - `Sequences`
        - `Textures`
        - `Materials`
        - `MRQ`

You can download the example project for this book by following the instructions in the *Download the example code/resource files* section in the *Preface* of this book.

The complete example project is included in the downloadable code/resource bundle.

Creating a light snowfall (soft drift)

In this recipe, you will create a simple light snowfall effect using Niagara. This will be the foundation for the snow effects in this chapter, so we will keep it clean and easy to control. Unlike rain, which usually falls quickly in straight streaks, snow moves more slowly and softly. Snowflakes drift, float, and change direction more easily, so the effect needs to feel lighter and less aggressive than the rain effects from *Chapter 4*.

You will control the snowflake size, fall speed, density, and subtle side movement, so the snowfall feels natural through the camera. This effect works well for quiet cinematic scenes, emotional moments, or establishing shots where you want to add atmosphere and depth without overwhelming the subject.

Getting ready

Before starting, set up your test environment by opening the `LV_VFX_Sandbox` level.

How to do it...

In this recipe, we will create a simple Niagara snowfall effect using soft sprite particles. We'll keep the setup light and focus on slow movement, gentle drift, and camera readability. Follow these steps:

1. In the **Content Browser**, go to your `Niagara_Systems` folder, right-click, and create a new Niagara System.
2. In the **Niagara System** creation window, select **Minimal** Niagara emitter. When prompted, rename the system to `NS_Snow`**.** A **Minimal** emitter is a basic emitter with essential modules already enabled.
3. Double-click `NS_Snow` to open it in the Niagara Editor.
4. Select the **Properties** module. Enable **Determinism,** change **Sim Target** to **GPUCompute Sim**, and set **Calculate Bounds Mode** to **Fixed**. The snow effect needs many particles, so using the GPU helps keep the effect efficient.
5. In the **Emitter State** module, change **Life Cycle Mode** to **Self**, then ensure the **Loop Behavior** is set to **Infinite**. This allows the snow to keep falling continuously while you preview and adjust the effect.

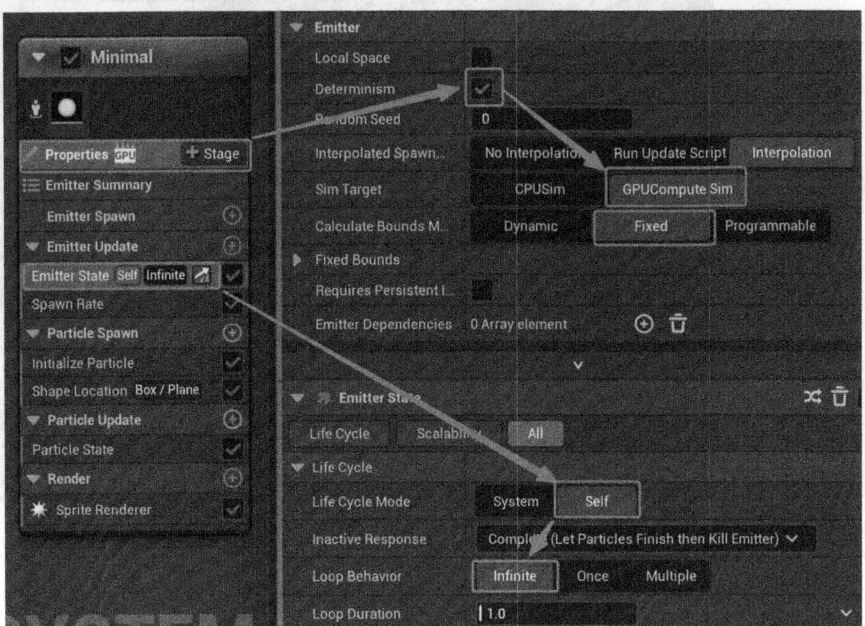

Figure 5.1 - Properties and Emitter State modules settings

6. In the **Emitter Update** section, add a **Spawn Rate** module if it is not already there. Start with a value of around `1500` to `3000`**.** You can increase or decrease this later, depending on how heavy you want the snow to look.
7. In the **Particle Spawn** section, select **Initialize Particle.** Set the **Lifetime Mode** to **Random** and use a longer lifetime, such as `1.0` to `10` seconds. Snow particles move slowly, so they do need to stay alive for a little longer.
8. Change **Color Mode** to **Direct Set** and set to the default white. Set the **Alpha** to `0.4`. This is because snow is not 100 percent opaque.
9. Still in the **Initialize Particle**, change the **Sprite Size Mode** to **Random Uniform,** with **Uniform Sprite Size Min** to `0.5` and **Max** to `3.0`**.** This will set the snowflakes to vary in size.

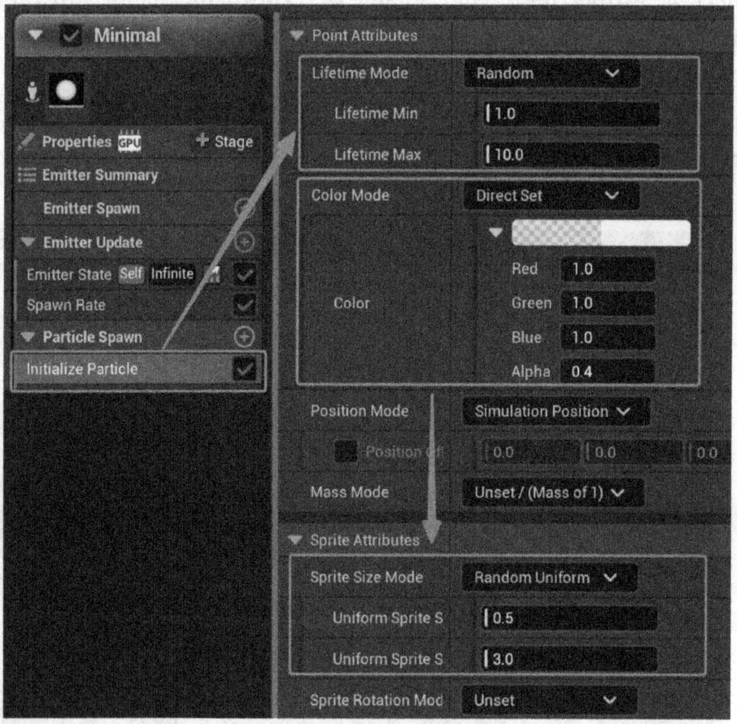

Figure 5.2 - Initialize Particle module settings

10. In the **Particle Spawn** section, add a **Shape Location** module. Change the **Shape Primitive** (in **Shape Location**) to **Box.** Use this box as the snow spawn area above the scene. For larger areas, use larger numbers. A good starting value is **X** = `2000`, **Y** = `2000`, **Z** = `20`.

11. Then, add an **Add Velocity** module. When prompted, click the first **Fix issue** button. This will automatically add the required **Solve Forces and Velocity** module.

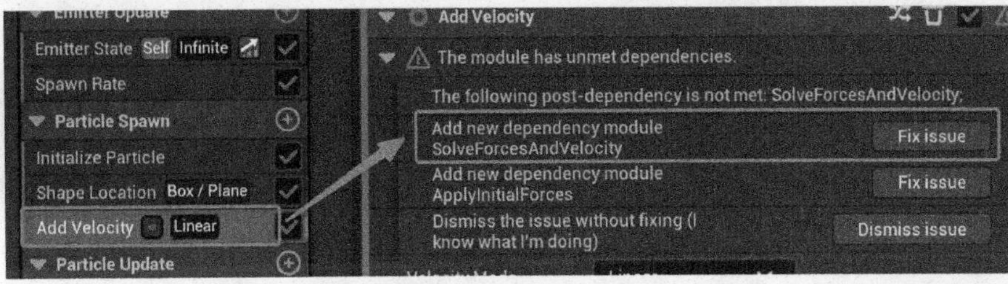

Figure 5.3 - Fixing the Add Velocity module

12. Using the down-pointing arrow on the **Velocity** property, choose **Random Range Vector**. Set **Minimum** to **X** = `0.0`, **Y** = `0.0`, **Z** = `-10` and **Maximum** to **X** = `0.0`, **Y** = `0.0`, **Z** = `-100`. This will add some variable downward movement to the snowflakes.

13. To have the snowflakes collide with the floor, in the **Particle Update** section, add a **Collision** module and change **Restitution** to `0.0`. This will stop the snowflakes from bouncing off the floor.

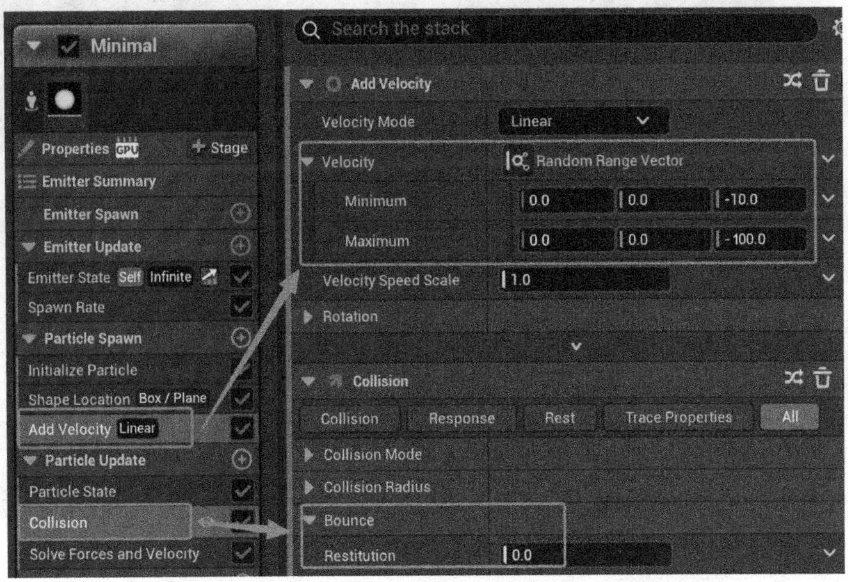

Figure 5.4 - Add Velocity and Collision module settings

14. To mimic real life, let's add some swirly movement to the falling snow. In the **Particle Spawn** section, add a **Curl Noise Force**. If you're prompted to **Fix issue**, please do so.

Set **Noise Strength** to 200 and **Noise Frequency to 210**. You can experiment with these numbers to go for the effects you're looking for.

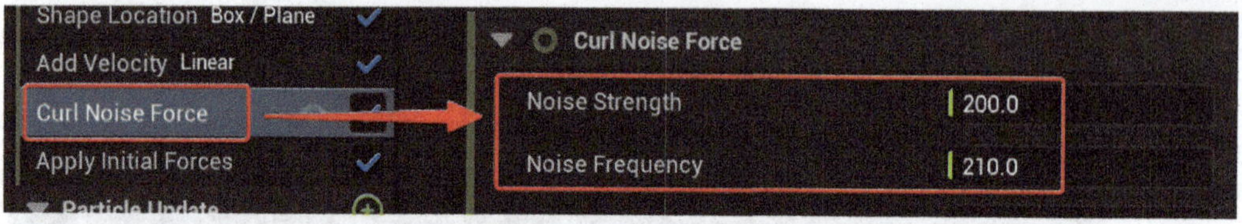

Figure 5.5 - Curl Noise Force module settings

You're done! The final look for light snowfall, as shown in *Figure 5.6*:

Figure 5.6 - The final look for light snowfall

I've gone ahead and added **User Parameters** to the necessary settings, as shown in *Figure 5.7*:

> **Note**
>
> If you have jumped straight into this chapter and are unsure how to set up **User Parameters**, see the more direct and faster workflow covered in the *There's more...* section of the *Creating a post-impact debris dust layer for aftershock effects* recipe in *Chapter 3*.

These parameters can now be adjusted directly from the level or keyframed in **Sequencer**, making it easier to control the snow density, size, speed, and direction over time. This will also be useful when preparing the effect for **Movie Render Queue** (**MRQ**), as you can fine-tune the snowfall for the final camera view before rendering.

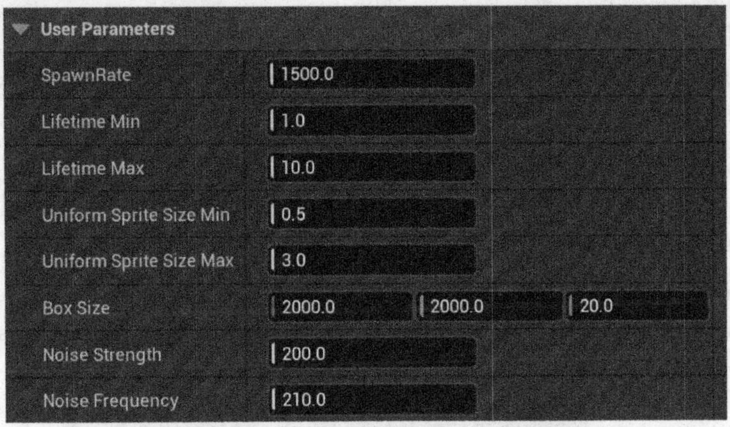

Figure 5.7 - Suggested User Parameters for the Snow effect

How it works...

In this recipe, you created a light snowfall effect using simple sprite particles. The system starts with a **Minimal** Niagara emitter, so the setup stays clean and easy to understand. **GPUCompute Sim** is used because snowfall can require many particles on screen at the same time, and using the GPU helps keep the effect more efficient.

The emitter is set to loop infinitely because snow is a continuous weather effect, not a one-time burst. The longer random lifetime allows each snowflake to stay visible long enough to drift slowly through the frame, which is different from rain, where particles usually move quickly and disappear much faster.

The small random sprite size gives the snow natural variation, so every flake does not look the same. *Larger flakes* work well for close-up or medium shots because they read better in camera and add depth near the subject. *Smaller flakes* are better for wide shots because they help fill the environment without becoming too distracting. The **Shape Location** box controls where the snow is spawned, while the **Add Velocity** module gives the flakes slow downward movement.

Collision is added so the particles stop when they reach the floor instead of bouncing, which helps the snow feel more grounded. The **Curl Noise Force** adds gentle, uneven motion, giving the flakes a soft, drifting behavior instead of falling in a straight line.

By exposing the key values as **User Parameters**, you can adjust the snow density, size, speed, and drift from the level or keyframe in **Sequencer**. This makes the system easier to tune for different camera angles and final **Movie Render Queue (MRQ)** renders.

There's more...

If you move too far away in the level Viewport, you may notice that the snow effect disappears. This usually happens because the emitter's **Bounds** setting is too small, causing Unreal Engine to stop drawing the particles once they fall outside that area. Let's fix this:

1. In the level, select `NS_Snow` from the **Outliner.** In the **Details** panel, search for `Bounds`, then increase the **Bounds Scale** value to `100`.
2. Now move and rotate around the Viewport again. You should find that the snow effect remains visible from a much wider viewing area and no longer disappears unexpectedly.

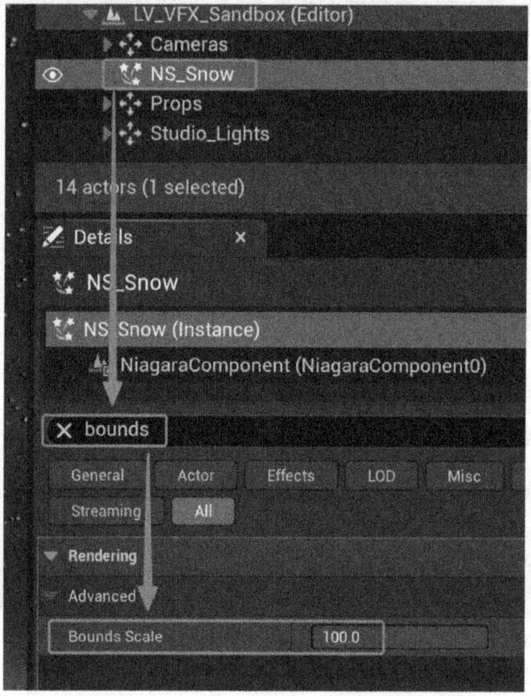

Figure 5.8 - NS_Snow Bounds Scale settings

See also

If you're looking for a real snowfall reference, **Pexels** (`https://www.pexels.com/search/videos/snowfall`) has a useful collection of free snowfall videos that can help you study how snow moves in camera. Look at the flake size, fall speed, drift direction, density, and how snow becomes more visible against darker backgrounds or strong lights before finalizing your Niagara settings.

Creating a blizzard pass (foreground/mid/background layers)

In the previous recipe, you created a light snowfall effect designed for calm, atmospheric shots. That setup works well when you want snow to gently add mood and depth without distracting from the subject. In this recipe, we will push the same idea further by creating a blizzard pass, where the snow becomes heavier, faster, and more aggressive.

A **blizzard** effect is useful when the weather needs to become part of the storytelling, not just background detail. Unlike light snowfall, which adds a quiet atmosphere, a blizzard can reduce visibility, hide parts of the environment, create tension, and make the scene feel colder and more dangerous. For cinematic shots, this also gives the camera more depth because the snow moves at different distances from the viewer.

To achieve this, we will layer the snow in the foreground, midground, and background. *Foreground snow* can move faster and appear larger, creating energy close to the camera. *Midground snow* helps connect the subject to the environment, while *background snow* fills the distance and adds scale. This layered approach gives more control and a more natural result than using one heavy emitter, which can easily make the shot look flat, noisy, or too dense.

Getting ready

I've prepared an environment especially for this recipe (see *Figure 5.9*), as it needs a snowy environment to go with it. This environment was created using free Fab assets (`https://www.fab.com/?lang=en`). I used Quixel's `Fresh Windswept Snow` for the ground surface. The trees and mountains are from the `Automotive Winter` scene, and the cabin from the `Winter Wood House` pack. Links to these assets are provided in the *See also* section.

Figure 5.9 - The LV_VFX_Snowscape level

How to do it...

To achieve the blizzard-pass look, we will use *two* Niagara Systems:

- The first is a tweaked version of the snow effect you created in the *Creating a light snowfall (soft drift)* recipe, which will provide the falling snow layer.
- The second is a blowing mist effect, built using workflows you have already learned in previous chapters.

These Niagara Systems will be placed in strategic locations within the environment so we can control where the snow and mist appear in camera, helping us shape the final cinematic look instead of covering the whole scene unnecessarily. Let's begin.

Creating the directional snow layer

Let's start by creating the falling snow layer:

1. Before starting, in the Levels folder, open the `LV_VFX_Snowscape` level.
2. To see the view as shown in *Figure 5.9*, press the *2* key on your keyboard (not Numpad) to set the view from **Bookmark2**.
3. In the `Niagara_Systems` folder, select `NS_Snow` and press *Ctrl* + *D* to duplicate it, rename as `NS_SnowBlizzard`. Double-click on `NS_SnowBlizzard` to open it in the Niagara Editor.

4. In the **Particle Update** section, add a **Wind Force** node. Click the top **Fix issue** button to automatically add a **Drag** module. You can use the settings in the **Drag** module to slow down the snowflakes, but not for now.

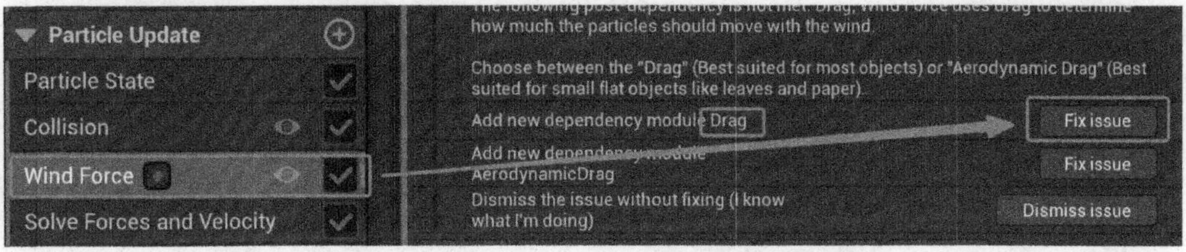

Figure 5.10 - Fixing Wind Force error

5. The parameters we will require to make the snow move fast in any direction will be tweaking the **Wind Speed** to **X** = `0.0`, **Y** = `1000`, **Z** = `0.0`. You'll be able to change this once you've set up the **User Parameters**.
6. Let's also randomize the wind speed. Click the down-pointing arrow for **Wind Speed Scale** and select **Random Range Float**. Set **Minimum** to `1` and **Maximum** to `10`.
7. Lastly, set **Turbulence Mode** to **Curl Noise**. This will make the snow particles swirl as they move. I'd suggest converting all these parameters to **User Parameters**, as you'll need to tweak the direction and speed of the wind once placed in the environment.

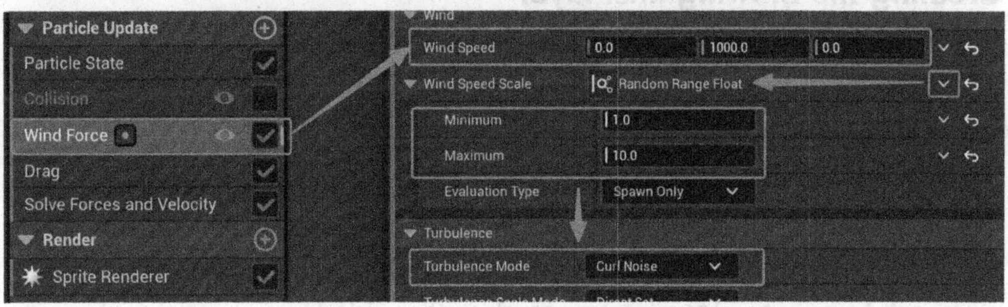

Figure 5.11 - Setting Wind Force parameters

8. Compile and save, then drag the `NS_SnowBlizzard` into the level. Place it toward the upper left to have the snow move from screen left to screen right in the environment, as shown in *Figure 5.12*:

Figure 5.12 - Adding NS_SnowBlizzard to the environment

Creating the blowing mist layer

Now we'll work on the blowing mist that persists in a blizzard:

1. Right-click in the `Niagara_Systems` folder and add a Niagara System, select the **Minimal** emitter, and rename `NS_BlowingMist`.
2. In the **Properties** module, enable **Local Space** and **Determinism.**
3. In the **Emitter Update** section, add a **Spawn Rate** module, set the **SpawnRate** to `50`.
4. In the **Initialize Particle** section, change **Lifetime** to **Random Range Float** and set **Minimum** to `5` and **Maximum** to `15`. This will vary the blowing mist size.
5. Set **Color Mode** to **Direct Set** and leave color as pure white.
6. Set **Sprite Size Mode** to **Random Uniform**. Set **Uniform Sprite Size Min** to `900` and **Uniform Sprite Size Max** to `1200`.

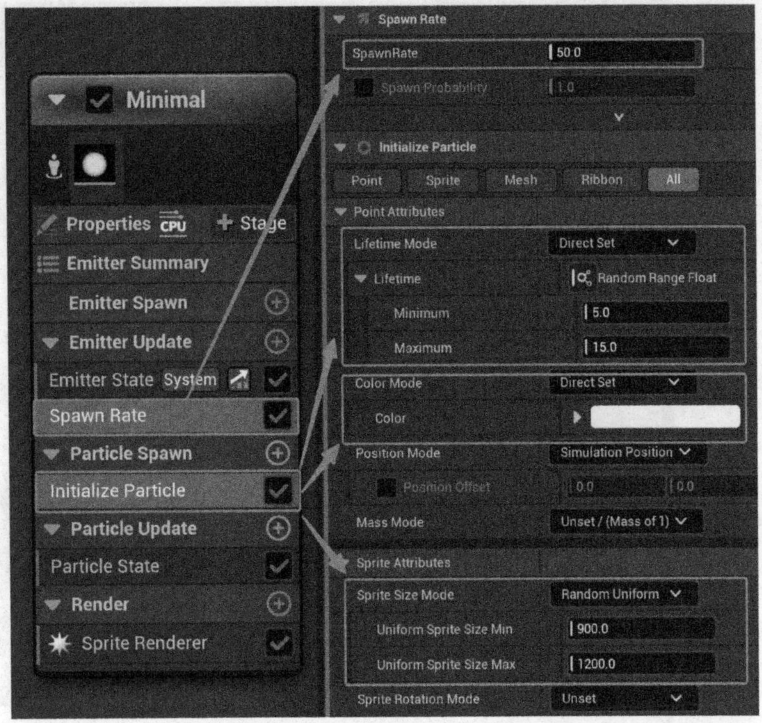

Figure 5.13 - Adding Spawn Rate and Initialize Particle parameters

7. In the **Particle Spawn** section, add a **Shape Location** module, change **Shape** Primitive to **Box / Plane**, and set **Box** Size to **X** = `50`, **Y** = `1000`, **Z** = `50`.
8. Select the **Sprite Renderer** module and change the **Material** to `MI_Smoke_Puff_A`. Change **Sub Image Size** to **X** = 8, **Y** = 8, and enable **Sub UV Blending Enabled** and **Use Material Cutout Texture** checkboxes.

Figure 5.14 - Sprite Renderer settings

9. In the **Particle Update** section, add the **Sub UV Animation** module. Set **Sprite Renderer** to **Sprite Renderer**.
10. Now, to force the particles to move fast, in the **Particle Update** section, add the **Wind Force** module. This will also require clicking on both **Fix issue** buttons to automatically add **Drag** and **Solve Forces and Velocity** modules.
11. Set **Wind Speed** to **X** = `150`, **Y** = `0`, **Z** = `0`. Change **Wind Speed Scale** to **Random Range Float** and set **Minimum** to `1` and **Maximum** to `5`. Set **Turbulence Mode** to **None.** Turbulence is not needed here as we are using UV textures instead of default sprites.

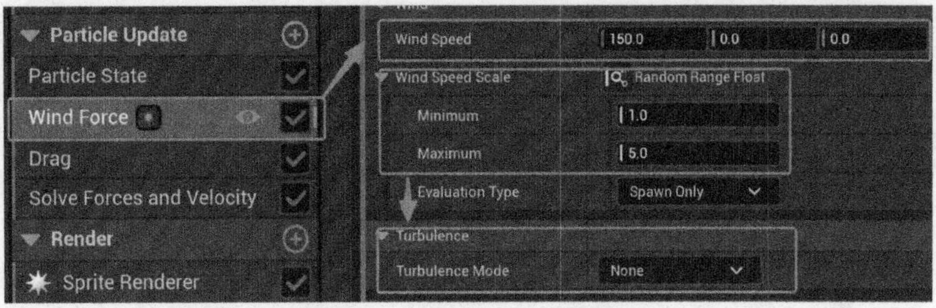

Figure 5.15 - Wind Force settings

12. To vary the size of the blowing mist, in the **Particle Update** section, add a **Scale Sprite Size** module and set the curve as shown in *Figure 5.16*:

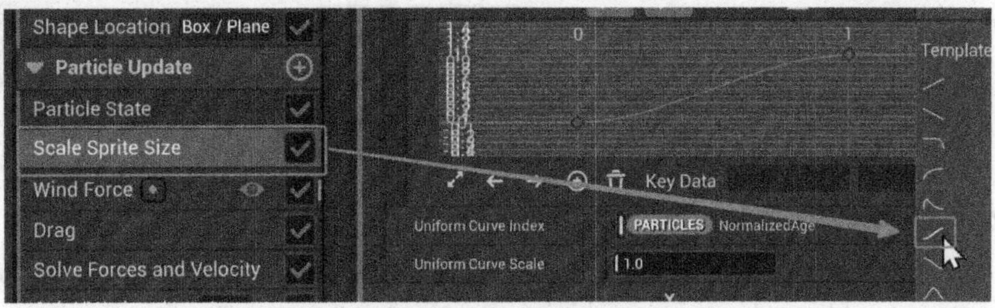

Figure 5.16 - Scale Sprite Size settings

13. To fade the smoke as it moves, add the **Scale Color** module. For **Scale Alpha**, click the down-pointing arrow and select **Float From Curve** as shown in *Figure 5.17*. The chosen curve will rapidly enlarge the blowing mist texture and gradually fade away, as any real-life mist/smoke.

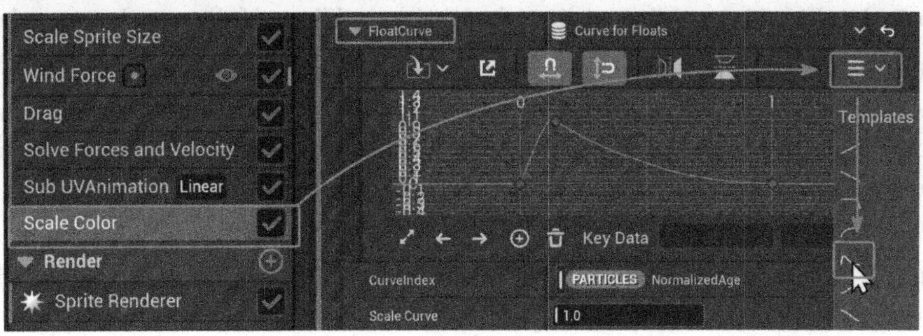

Figure 5.17 - Scale Color settings

14. Compile and save. Add the `NS_BlowingMist` into the environment. I've placed a few in the foreground, mid, and background environments as shown in *Figure 5.18*:

Figure 5.18 - The final blizzard pass

How it works...

In this recipe, you turned the calm snowfall from the *Creating a light snowfall (soft drift)* recipe into a stronger blizzard pass by combining two Niagara Systems. The first system, `NS_SnowBlizzard`, is a modified version of the original snow effect. Instead of only falling gently, it now uses **Wind Force** to push the particles across the scene. This is what makes the snow feel more aggressive and directional.

The **Wind Speed** controls the main movement direction, while the random **Wind Speed Scale** adds variation, so the flakes do not all move at the same speed. Setting the **Turbulence Mode** to **Curl Noise** adds a swirling quality, which helps the blizzard feel more chaotic and natural.

The second system, `NS_BlowingMist`, adds the soft white haze that usually comes with heavy snow and strong wind. Large **SubUV** smoke-style sprites are used because blowing mist is less about individual flakes and more about creating moving layers of atmosphere. The mist has a longer lifetime, large sprite size, wind movement, scale changes, and alpha fade, so it grows and disappears softly as it moves through the shot.

Placing mist in the foreground, midground, and background helps create depth, which makes the blizzard feel more cinematic. The foreground adds movement near the camera, the midground connects the weather to the subject, and the background adds distance and scale. This layered approach also gives you more control than using one heavy emitter, keeping the shot dramatic but still readable.

There's more...

Jumping back to the `MI_Smoke_Puff_A` material used in the **Sprite Renderer** module, it is a Material Instance, which has two parameters that can be adjusted: the **Value** and **Color**. Let's have a closer look:

1. In the `Materials` folder, double-click to open `MI_Smoke_Puff_A`. As you can see, the **Value** has been set to `2.0`, and the **Color** is a hint of blue (**RGBA** `0.7`, `0.8`, `1.0`, `1.0`) to mimic the cold winter look.
2. Now let's look at the main material to study how this material was constructed by double-clicking on the parent material thumbnail:

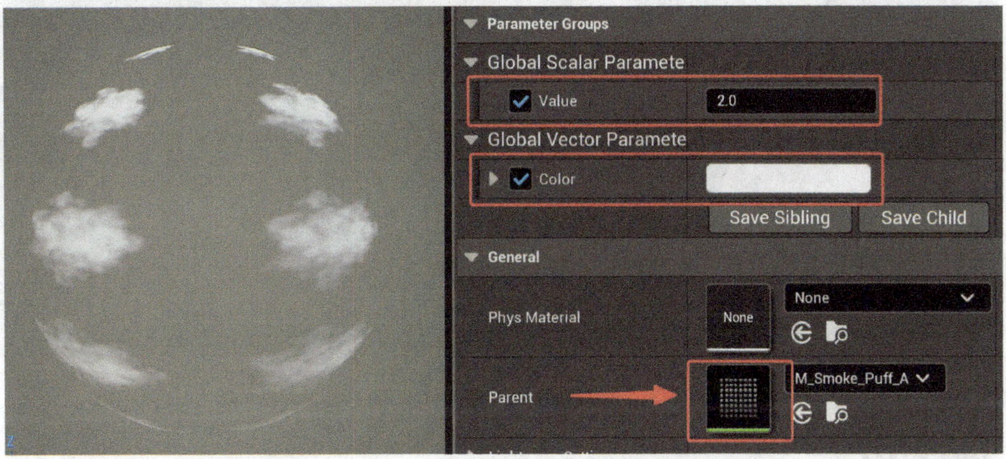

Figure 5.19 - The MI_Smoke_Puff_A Material Instance

3. As you can see, it's a simple material setup, a workflow that was already covered in previous chapters, specifically the *There's more...* section of the *Creating a rain ripple effect* recipe in *Chapter 4*. You can also clearly see where the **Color** and **Value** parameters originate:

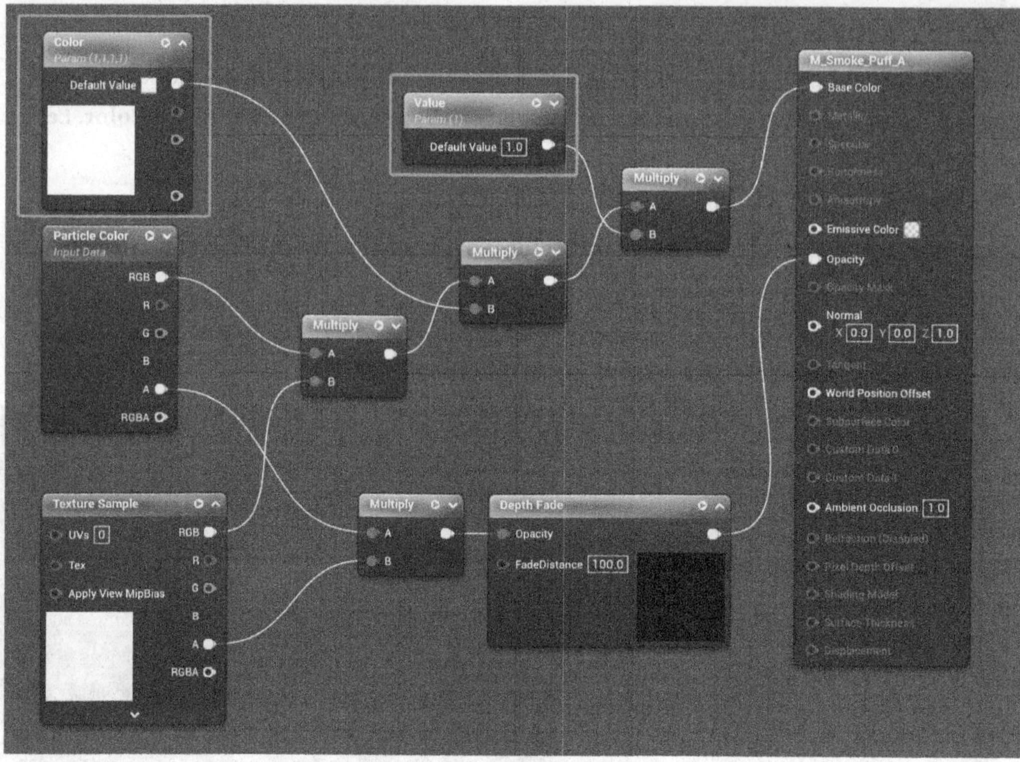

Figure 5.20 - The MI_Smoke_Puff_main material

See also

- For additional visual reference, you may refer to real blizzard or snowstorm footage on **Pexels** (`https://www.pexels.com/search/videos/snow%20storm/`) to see how heavy snow behaves on camera. This is useful when comparing the look of your Niagara snow layers against real-world movement, density, and visibility before finalizing the shot.
- Here are the links to the assets used in the Snowscape level:
  - `Automotive Winter Scene`: `https://fab.com/s/98b1a621ecd3`
  - `Winter House`: `https://fab.com/s/6957ab7bec2c`
  - `Fresh Windswept Snow`: `https://fab.com/s/2087ebcc78ae`

Creating a localized snow swirl around objects

In the previous recipes, we used Niagara to create a light snowfall and a heavier blizzard pass. In this recipe, we will switch gears and use one of my favorite Unreal Engine features: *Motion*

Design. Unreal Engine **Motion Design** is a real-time toolset for creating animated graphics and procedural motion directly inside Unreal Engine. It includes tools such as Cloners, Effectors, splines, shapes, and modifiers, making it useful for motion graphics and art-directed cinematic effects without relying heavily on Blueprints.

So instead of building the swirl with Blueprints or adding more Niagara complexity, we will keep things simple by using **Motion Design** tools and splines to create an art-directed snow swirl.

This approach is useful for cinematic work because it gives you direct control over the shape, direction, and placement of the swirl. Rather than relying on random particle movement, you can design the motion around a subject, object, or camera angle. By using splines, we can guide the particles into a more intentional path, making the effect easier to control, easier to revise, and more suitable for shot-based work.

More importantly, this workflow is not limited to snow. You can use the same **Motion Design** and spline-based approach for other projects, such as dust trails, magical particles, energy streaks, or any effect where you need controlled motion without setting up Blueprints.

Figure 5.21 - The final Localized Snow Swirl effect

Getting ready

In this section, we will build the effect in *two parts*:

- First, we will create particles using **Motion Design** tools.
- Then, we will apply those particles to a spline so we can control the swirl shape more deliberately using **Sequencer**.

As you work through the **Motion Design** properties, you will notice some familiar Niagara-style terms, as **Motion Design** also uses particle-related settings such as spawn, lifetime, size, velocity, and color.

For this recipe, you'll need to open the `LV_VFX_Sandbox` level, which was created in the *Setting up a reusable VFX "Sandbox" level for cinematic lookdev* recipe in *Chapter 1*, and install the **Motion Design** plugin. If not already installed, let's install the plugin first:

1. From the **Edit | Plugins** menu, search for **Motion Design** and enable the **Motion Design** plugin. You may need to restart the editor if prompted.

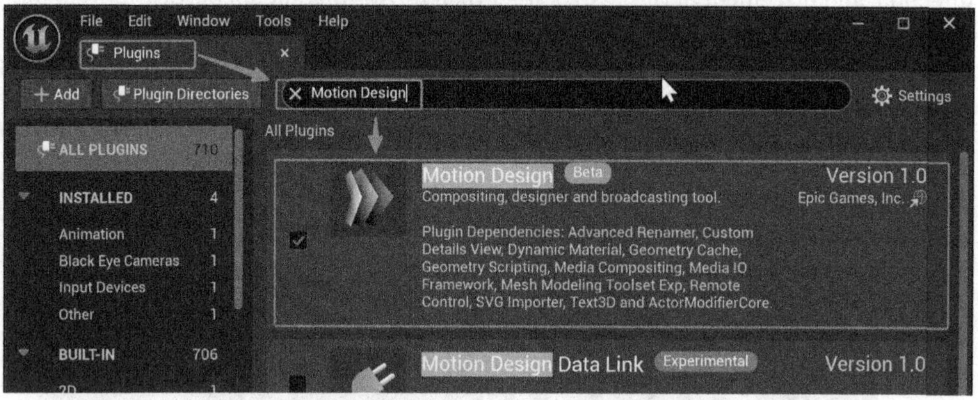

Figure 5.22 - Enabling Motion Design plugin

2. If the installation was successful, you will be able to access the **Motion Design** mode from the mode selection drop-down or by pressing *Shift + 9*.

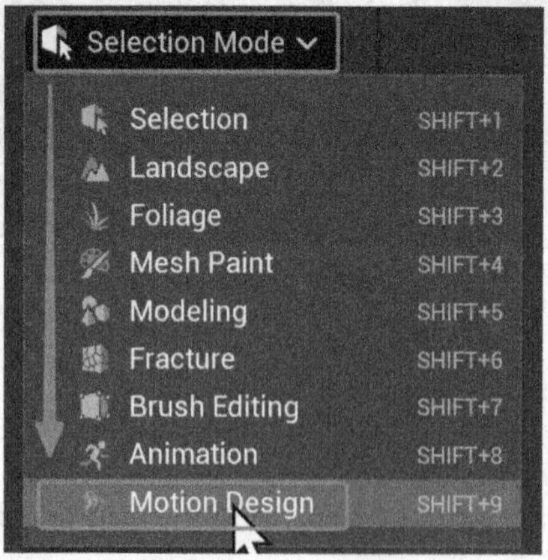

Figure 5.23 - Selecting the Motion Design mode

How to do it...

Let's start by creating the particles that will form snow swirls. At this stage, we are not shaping the motion yet; we are simply building the small visual elements that will later travel along the spline. Using **Motion Design**'s **Cloner** tools, we can quickly generate many small particles, adjust their size, lifetime, and emission rate, and prepare them for the swirl movement in the next part of the recipe.

Creating the particle system

Let's start by creating the particles that will form the snow swirl:

1. Once you've activated the **Motion Design** mode, you'll be presented with a panel on the left of the editor UI that consists of all the Motion Design tools. Select the **Cloners** section and click **once** on **SphereRandom**, then click **once** in the Viewport.

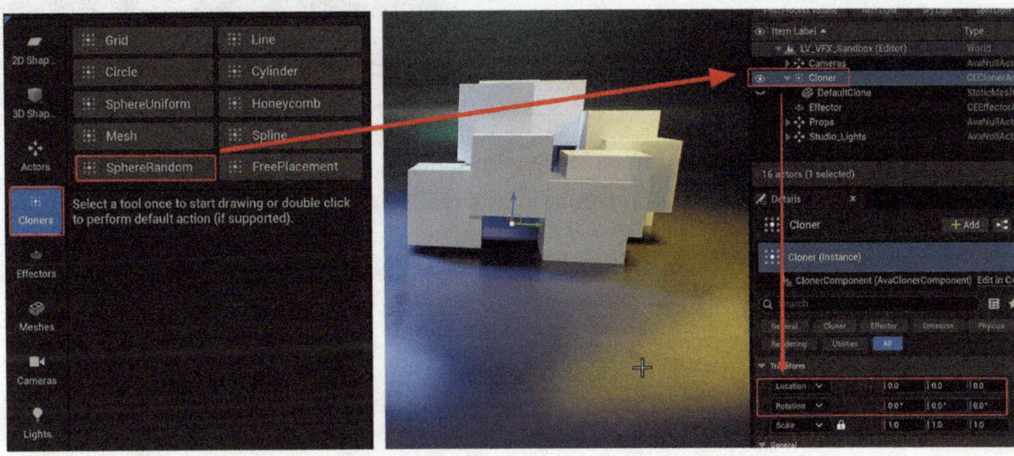

Figure 5.24 - Adding SphereRandom cloner

2. In the **Outliner**, select **Cloner** and reset **Location** and **Rotation** to `0,0,0`. In the Viewport, you will have some random cubes, but we'll need to change them to tiny spheres that will become particles.
3. Back to the **Motion Design** panel, select the **3D Shape** section and double-click on **Sphere**. Then, drag the **Sphere** in the **Outliner** onto the **Cloner**, then delete the **DefaultClone** mesh. Dragging the **Sphere** onto the **Cloner** will make the **Sphere** a child of the **Cloner**. So if we change any properties in the **Cloner**, it will automatically affect the spheres.

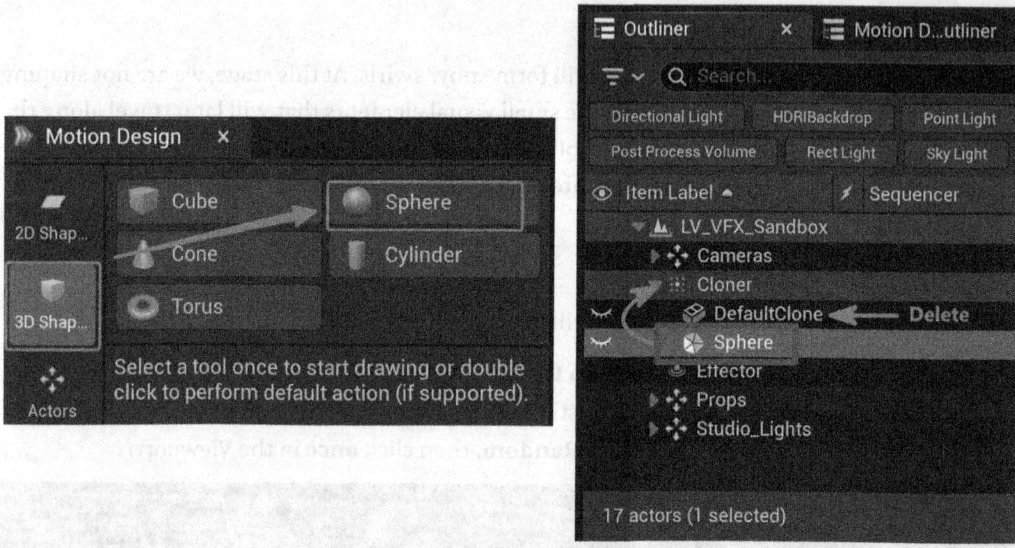

Figure 5.25 - Adding sphere object

4. The random cubes have been replaced with spheres, but they are too large. With the **Sphere** still selected in the **Outliner**, in its **Details** panel, in the **Shape** category, change **Mesh Size** to `1.0` on **X**, **Y**, **Z**.

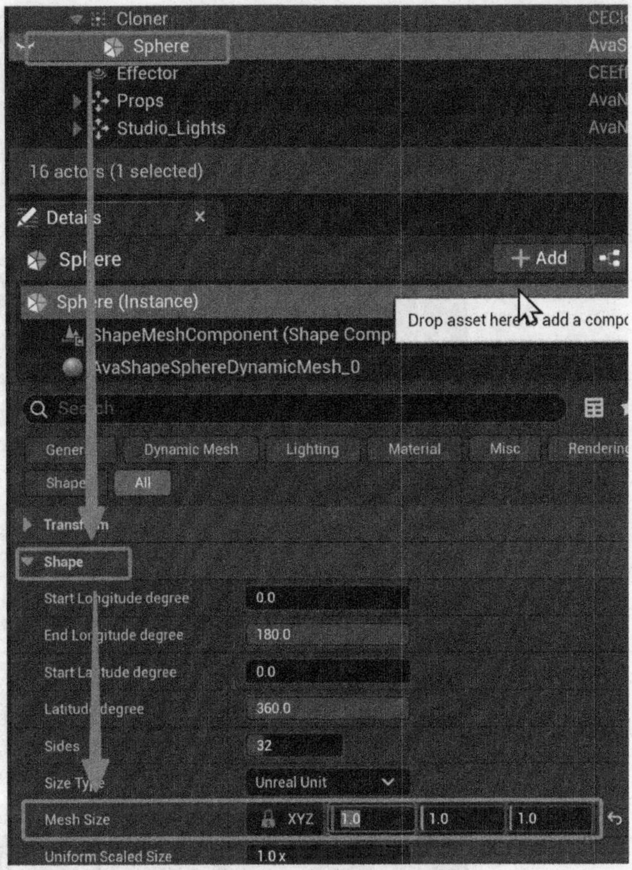

Figure 5.26 - Changing Sphere size

5. You'll now have tiny particles (Spheres). Next is to replicate them and make them come alive. With the **Cloner** still selected, in the **Spawn** section, change **Emission Mode** to **Infinite** (sounds familiar?), **Emission Style** to **Rate**, and **Emission Rate** to `200`**.** You'll now see some sparkly particles in the Viewport. **Emission Rate** here relates to the **Spawn Rate** in Niagara.
6. Disable **Use Local Space** and enable **Lifetime**, set **Min** to `1.0` and **Max** to `1.5`**.** With **Use Local Space** disabled, the particles will leave a trail as they move, and their lifetime will be determined by the **Min** and **Max** settings. The larger the **Max** number, the longer they are going to stick around.

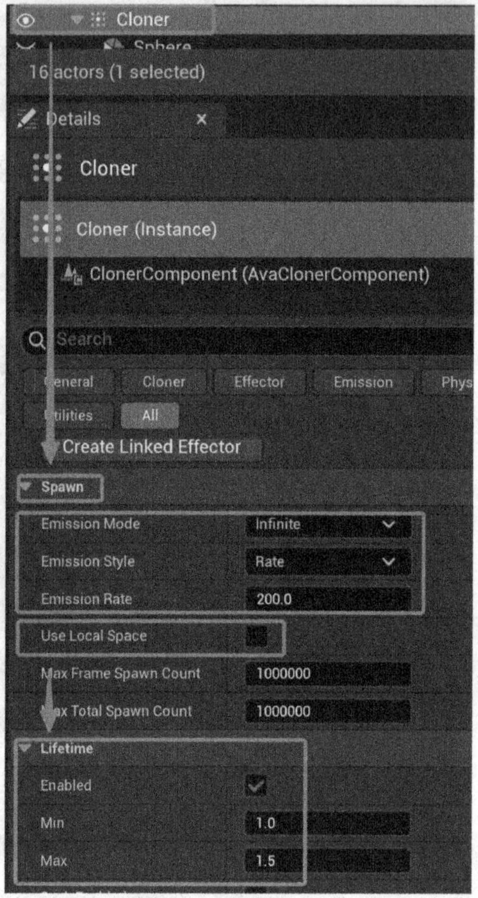

Figure 5.27 - Cloner Spawn and Lifetime settings

7. Scroll up to the **Layout** section, ensure **Layout** is set to **SphereRandom,** and set Radius to `10`**.** This setting will determine how close or far apart the particles are from each other.

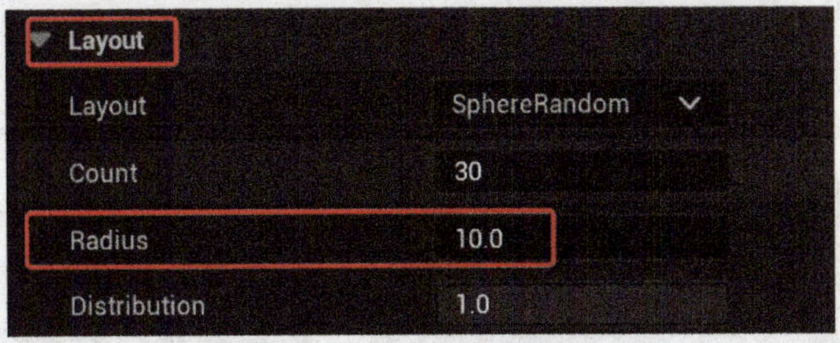

Figure 5.28 - Cloner Radius setting

8. Now grab and move one of the **Cloner**'s *X*, *Y*, or *Z* gizmo tools in the Viewport, and you'll see that the particles are leaving a trail. This is exactly what we need.

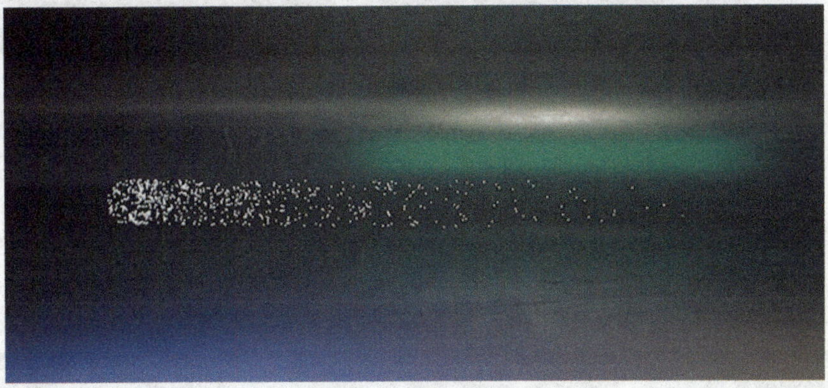

Figure 5.29 - Testing the particles

Creating and animating the spline path

Now that the particles are ready, the next step is to control how they move through the scene. Rather than animating the particles by hand, we will use the **Spline Actor** available in **Motion Design**. This allows us to define a clear path for the particles to follow, making the snow swirl easier to art-direct and adjust for the shot.

> **Note**
>
> In Unreal Engine **Motion Design**, a **spline** is a curved path that you can draw and edit in the Viewport. Think of it as a guideline for motion or placement. Instead of moving particles or objects manually, you shape a spline, then use **Motion Design** tools to place or guide elements along that path.

Let's get started:

1. From the **Motion Design** panel, click the **Actors** category, and double-click **Spline Actor**. In the **Outliner**, you have an **AvaSplineActor**; let's rename it to `Spline1`.

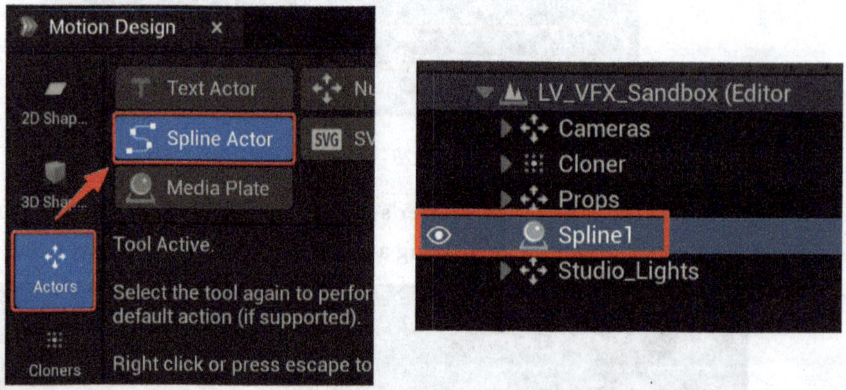

Figure 5.30 - Adding a Spline Actor

2. In the Viewport, you now have a spline with little squares at both ends (endpoints). You can start editing the spline by selecting and dragging the endpoints using the *X*, *Y*, *Z* **gizmo** tool, but this will only make the spline move in straight, diagonal, or up/down directions.

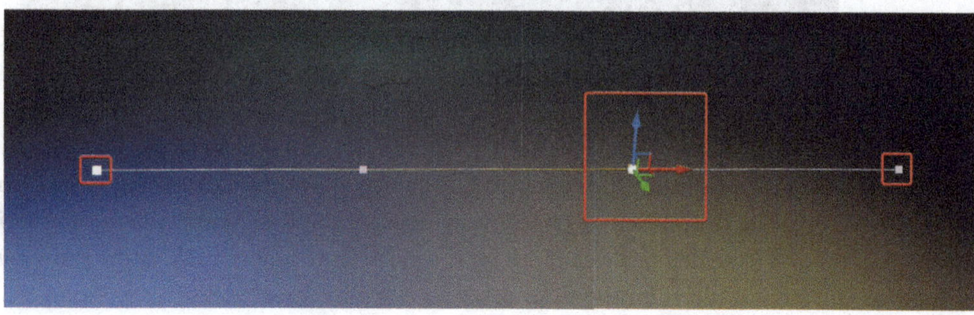

Figure 5.31 - Manipulating the spline actor endpoints

3. Notice that once you have selected the end point, the **Bézier curve** (the *purple-ish* one) lines appear on both sides. If you move these endpoints, you'll now be able to bend the spline.

> **Note**
>
> A **Bézier curve** is a smooth curve controlled by points and handles. The spline point sets where the curve passes through, while the Bézier handles control the direction and strength of the curve as it enters or leaves that point. By moving the handles, you can make the spline bend smoothly, curve more sharply, or flow in a specific direction. This makes it easier to shape the snow swirl path in a more controlled and art-directed way.

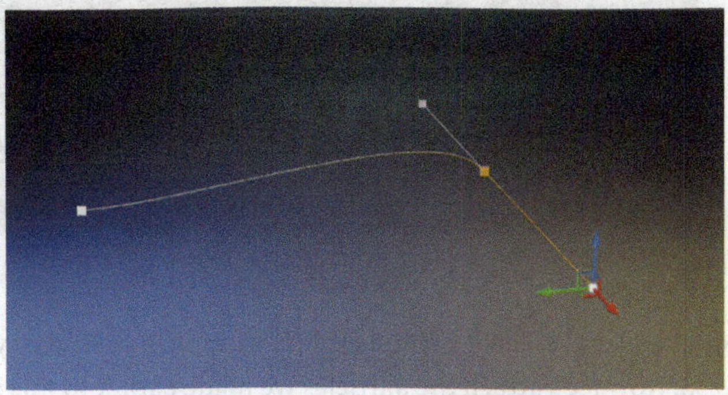

Figure 5.32 - Manipulating the Bézier Curves

4. To add more points, hold down the *Alt* key while dragging any of the endpoints.

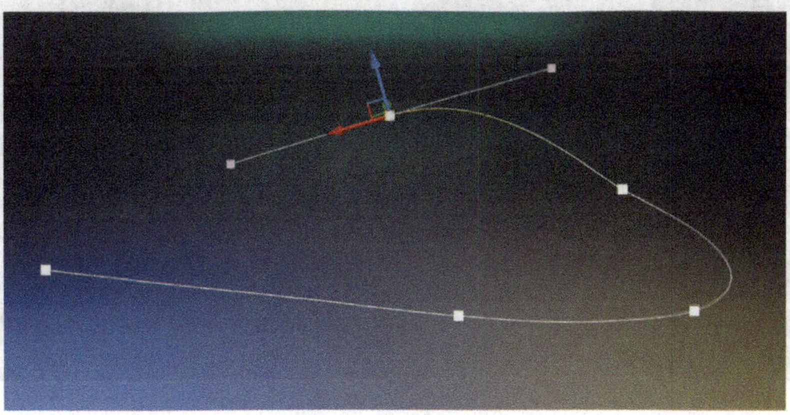

Figure 5.33 - Adding more points

5. Create a spline shape that suits your shot. Once the spline is in place, we will connect the particles to it and then animate the result in **Sequencer**. This workflow may take a little practice at first, especially when shaping the spline and adjusting the particle

placement, but it gives you a much more art-directable way to control the swirl. You can also manipulate the spline using its properties in the **Details** panel, as shown in *Figure 5.34*:

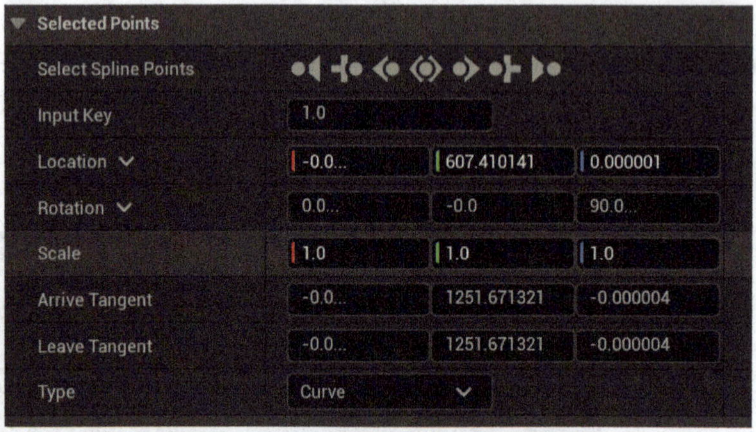

Figure 5.34 - Spline properties

6. I've gone ahead and created a simple spline wrapping around a cylinder as shown in *Figure 5.35*. Now let's attach the particles we made earlier to this spline.

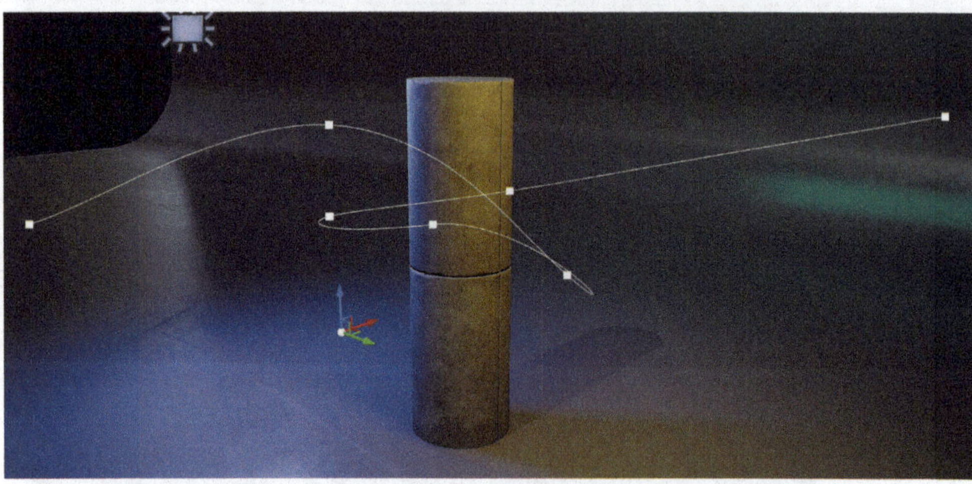

Figure 5.35 - Simple spline around a cylinder

7. With **Cloner** selected, reset its **Location** to `0,0,0`, then from the top left of the UI, open the **Operator Stack** panel.

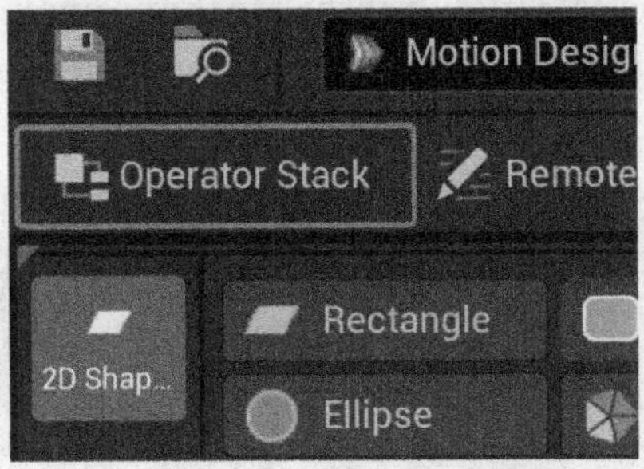

Figure 5.36 - Accessing the Operator Stack panel

8. Click **Add Modifiers** and choose **Spline Path**. Change **Spline Actor Weak** to **Spline1** and change **Sample Mode** to **Time**. Since we will be keyframing this in **Sequencer**, **Time** is a better option.

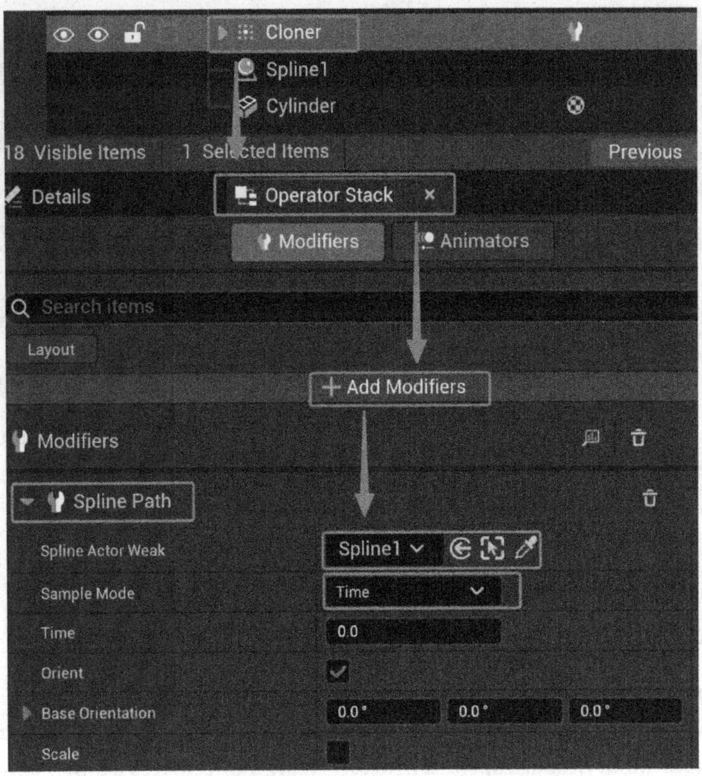

Figure 5.37 - Adding Spline Modifier to the Cloner

9. The **Cloner** (particles) is now attached to the beginning of **Spline1**. To add a keyframe, simply click the **diamond**-shaped icon in the **Time** property. This will add a keyframe to the beginning of the timeline.

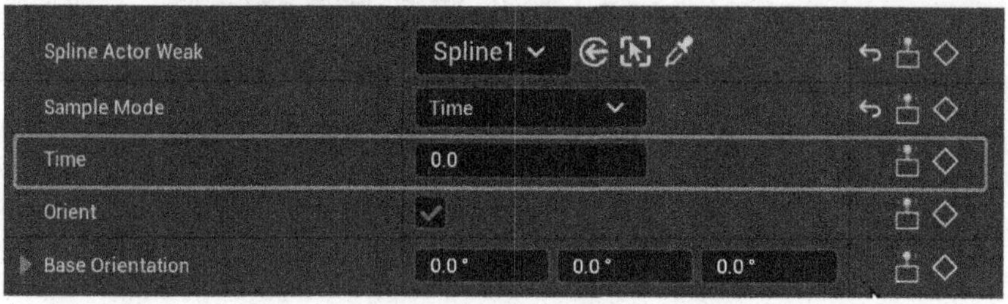

Figure 5.38 - Creating the first keyframe for the Time property

10. Now drag the Playhead to the *end* of the timeline, change **Time** to `1.0`, and add another keyframe.

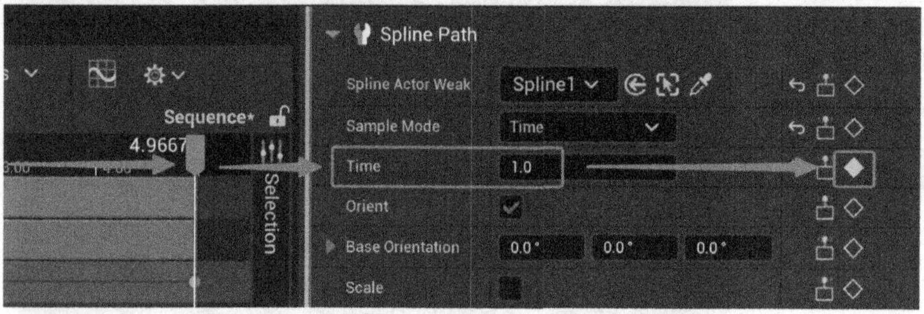

Figure 5.39 - Creating the last keyframe for the Time property

11. Scrub the timeline, and you'll have the particles moving along the spline in the duration of time set in the **Sequencer**. Bring the keyframes close to each other in the timeline if you need fast-moving particles or vice versa.
12. The hard part is done! You can now tweak the particles' size, **Spawn Rate**, radius, color, and, of course, the spline shape.

How it works...

In this recipe, you switched from Niagara to **Motion Design** to create a more art-directed snow swirl. The first part of the setup creates small sphere particles using a **Cloner**. Instead of rendering traditional Niagara sprites, **Motion Design** duplicates a small sphere many times and controls the way those clones (particles in our case) behave. The emission settings create a continuous stream of particles, while the lifetime settings control how long they remain visible.

Disabling **Use Local Space** is important because it allows the particles to leave a trail as the cloner moves, instead of staying locked to the cloner's position. This is what gives the effect its flowing, particle-like behavior.

The second part of the recipe uses a **Spline Actor** to control the motion path. The spline acts like a guide that defines where the particles should travel. By adding the **Spline Path** modifier to the **Cloner** and setting the **Sample Mode** to **Time**, you can animate the particles along the spline in **Sequencer** using simple keyframes. This makes the swirl easy to time, reshape, and direct around an object.

The main advantage of this workflow is control: instead of relying on random particle movement or Blueprint logic, you can design the swirl shape directly for the camera and adjust it like a shot element.

There's more...

The **Motion Design** feature includes many properties, and it can feel a little overwhelming at first. However, you do not need to adjust everything to get a good result. For this section, we will focus only on a few useful settings that help improve the look and movement of the particles. These small adjustments will make the swirl feel more polished and cinematic without making the setup too complicated. Let's continue:

1. In the **Outliner**, select the **Cloner**. Then, in the **Lifetime** section, enable **ScaleEnabled.** Just like in Niagara, a curve will be activated, and you can change the shape of the curve if you wish. This shape will determine how the particles fade away.

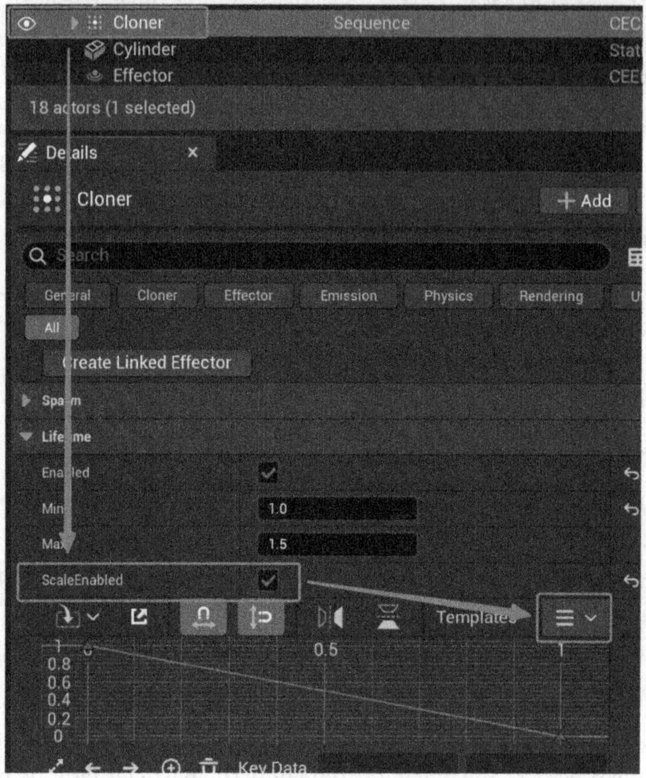

Figure 5.40 - Enabling ScaleEnabled

2. Then, under **Effector,** click the **Create Linked Effector** button. This will create an **Effector** assigned to the **Cloner**.

> **Note**
>
> In Motion Design, an **Effector** is a control object that changes how cloned particles or objects behave. It can affect their position, rotation, scale, color, or randomness. For this recipe, the **Effector** helps us shape the snow movement without manually animating each particle or creating a Blueprint setup.

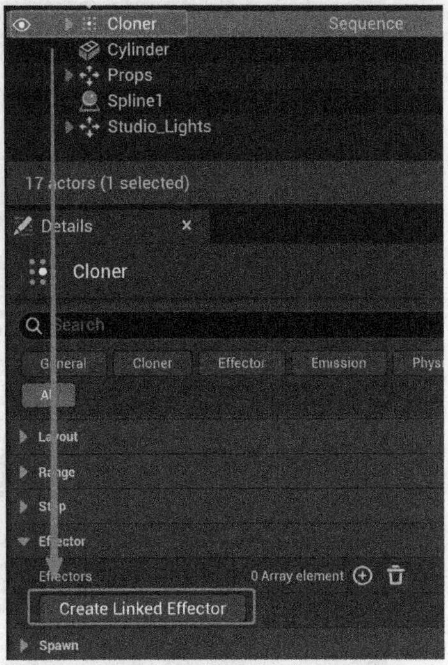

Figure 5.41 - Creating an Effector

3. Select the **Effector** in the **Outliner**. Under the **Shape** section, change **Shape** to **Unbound**. Then, in the **Forces** section, click the **Enabled** button and the **Curl Noise Force Enabled** checkmark. This will make the particles swirl more aggressively then fade away. Try setting a higher or lower number to see the difference.

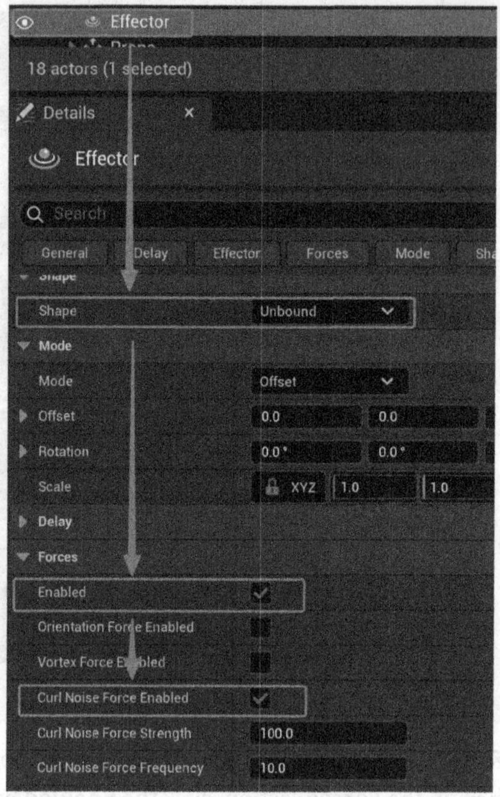

Figure 5.42 - Changing Effector Shape and Forces

4. Notice that after adding the **Effector**, the particle color changed to *red*. The reason is that in the **Color** section of the **Effector**, the color is set to red by default. Yes, you can change the color here, but I have a better suggestion.

Figure 5.43 - Particle turns red

5. Let's change the particle color and add some glow. Select the **Sphere** (parented to the **Cloner**), in its **Material** section, change **Material** type to **Material Designer**.
6. From the **Material Designer** panel, select **Emissive** and press **Continue**.

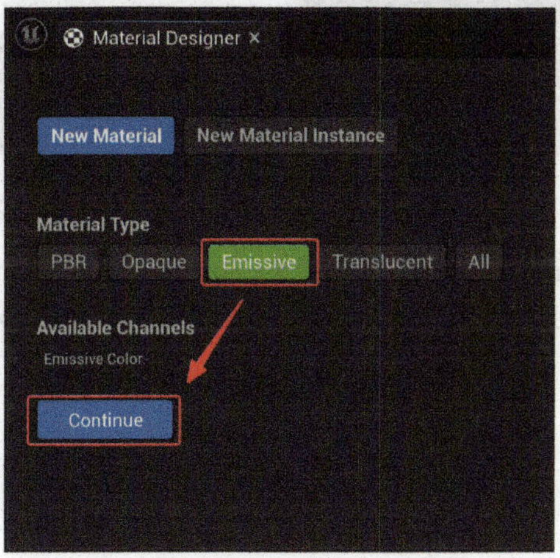

Figure 5.44 - Choosing Emissive in the Material Designer

7. In the next panel, select **Emissive Color** and then click the **checkered** icon (Texture) and choose **Solid Color**.

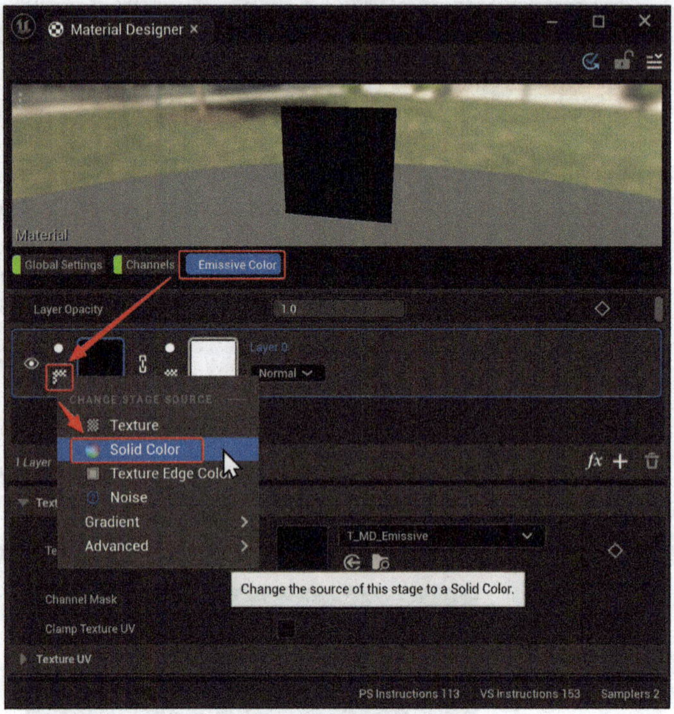

Figure 5.45 - Changing from Texture to Solid Color

8. Click the **Color Picker** box, choose a color, and to make it glow, change the **Value** to `30~50`. The higher this number, the brighter the glow. Close the **Material Designer** panel.

Figure 5.46 - Choosing color and glow value

9. You now have a glowing particle with a color of your choice, as shown in *Figure 5.47*:

Figure 5.47 - Final particle color with glow

See also

This reference is useful if you want to understand how **Cloners** and **Effectors** work together in Motion Design. In this recipe, we used them to build an art-directed snow swirl without using

Blueprints. Epic's documentation explains how these tools can control movement, rotation, scale, randomness, and color, making them helpful for many other cinematic effects too: `https://dev.epicgames.com/documentation/unreal-engine/motion-design-cloners-and-effectors-in-unreal-engine`.

Creating a snow kick-up burst (ground interaction)

In the previous recipes, you created falling snow, a heavier blizzard pass, and an art-directed snow swirl. In this recipe, we will add **ground interaction** by creating a **snow kick-up burst** that appears when a character's foot touches the ground. This effect is useful in cinematics because it helps connect the character to the environment. Without it, a character can look like they are sliding over the snow instead of stepping into it.

We will use a simple Niagara burst effect triggered by the character's movement, so the snow reacts at the right moment. The goal is not to create a complex snow simulation, but to add a believable powdery burst that sells weight, contact, and motion. Although we are using snow in this recipe, the same workflow can be used with many other effects, such as dust, sand, water splashes, sparks, or debris. Once you understand how to trigger an effect from movement or contact, you can reuse the method in many cinematic situations.

The main objective of this recipe is to learn how to trigger Niagara effects from character contact events. The MetaHuman, running animation, and snow environment are supporting elements, but the core workflow is timing the Niagara burst so it appears exactly when the character's foot hits the ground.

Getting ready

For this recipe, we will start with the standard `LV_VFX_Sandbox` created in *Chapter 1*. This keeps the setup simple while we build and test the snow kick-up burst without distractions from a full environment.

To demonstrate the effect clearly, we will use a running animation that comes with Unreal Engine, so we have clear foot-contact moments to trigger the snow burst.

Once the effect is working correctly, we will move it into the snow level used earlier in this chapter, place it with a pre-made MetaHuman character, and time the action in **Sequencer** to create a more cinematic ground interaction shot.

How to do it...

In the following steps, we will create a simple Niagara burst effect for the snow kick-up, then use a pre-made running animation available in Unreal Engine to test the timing. This gives us a clear foot-contact moment, so we can trigger the snow burst exactly when the character's foot hits the ground.

Creating the Niagara burst

Let's begin by creating the snow kick-up effect itself:

1. From the **Content Browser**, open the `LV_VFX_Sandbox` level and press the *1* key to jump to **Bookmark1**. This is the same level we've been using throughout this book.
2. In the `Niagara_Systems` folder, right-click, select **Niagara System**, and in the pop-up panel, choose the **Directional Burst** template. Click **Create**. Rename as `NS_Snow_Kickup`.

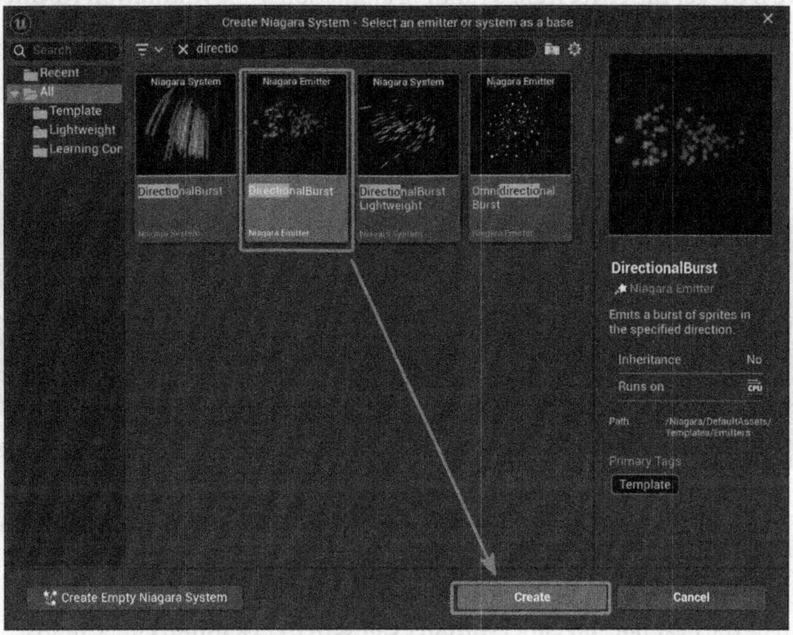

Figure 5.48 - Creating a Directional Burst emitter

3. Double-click to open it in the Niagara Editor. From the Preview panel, you'll notice a sideways burst of particles every few seconds. The only setting we need to change for now is the direction of the burst.
4. Select the **Add Velocity** module, change **Cone Axis** to **X** = `0.0`, **Y** = `0.0`, **Z** = `1.0`. This will make the particle burst upwards. We will leave all other settings as they are right now. Click **Save**.

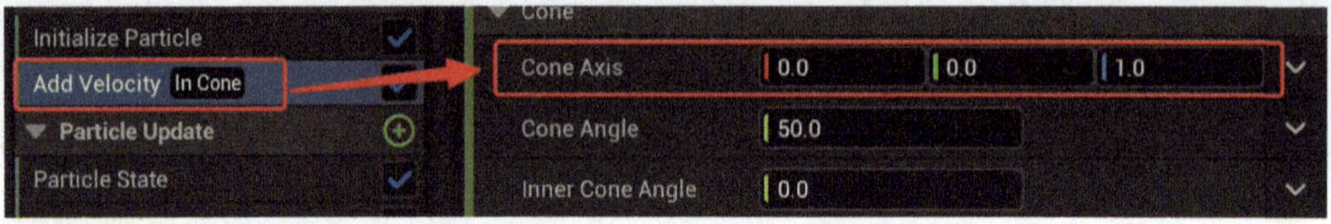

Figure 5.49 - Adding the Velocity module

Setting up Animation Notifies

Next, we'll trigger the effect from a running animation using **Animation Notifies**:

1. Back in the **Content Browser**, click the **+Add** icon, and select **Add Feature or Content Pack**. From the pop-up panel, choose **Third Person** and click **Add to Project**. On the bottom right notification, click **Import.**

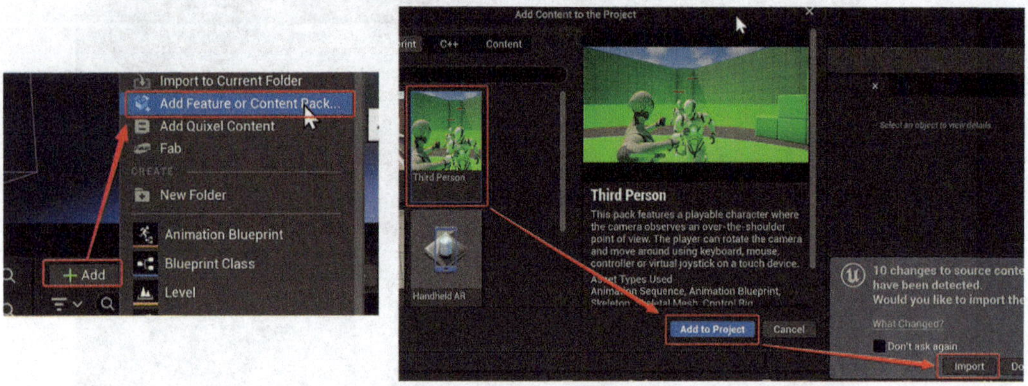

Figure 5.50 - Adding ThirdPerson Content

2. For the next pop-up panel (**Import Content**), click **Import** once more.

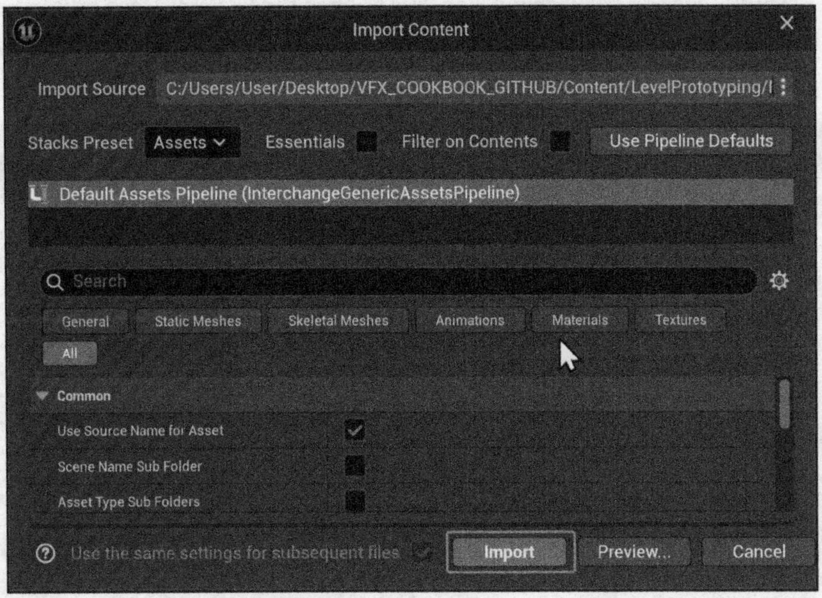

Figure 5.51 - Importing the ThirdPerson content

3. You'll now have a new `Characters` folder, which comes with an assorted range of animations. The one we are interested in is `MF_Unarmed_Jog_Fwd`.

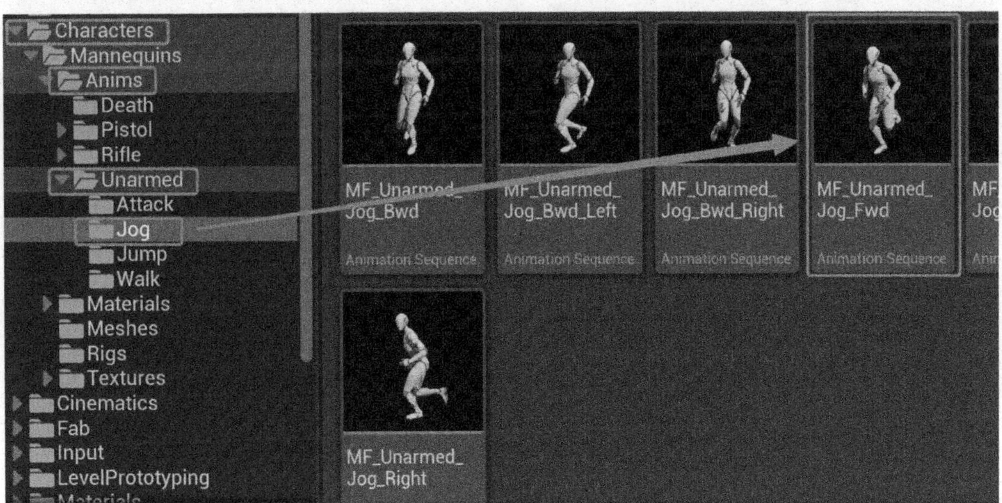

Figure 5.52 - Accessing the Jog Animation

4. Double-click on `MF_Unarmed_Jog_Fwd` to open the Skeletal Mesh Editor. Select the **Animation** icon and in the **Asset Browser**, ensure the `MF_Unarmed_Jog_Fwd` is selected. Adjust the Viewport so that you can view the run animation as shown in *Figure 5.53*:

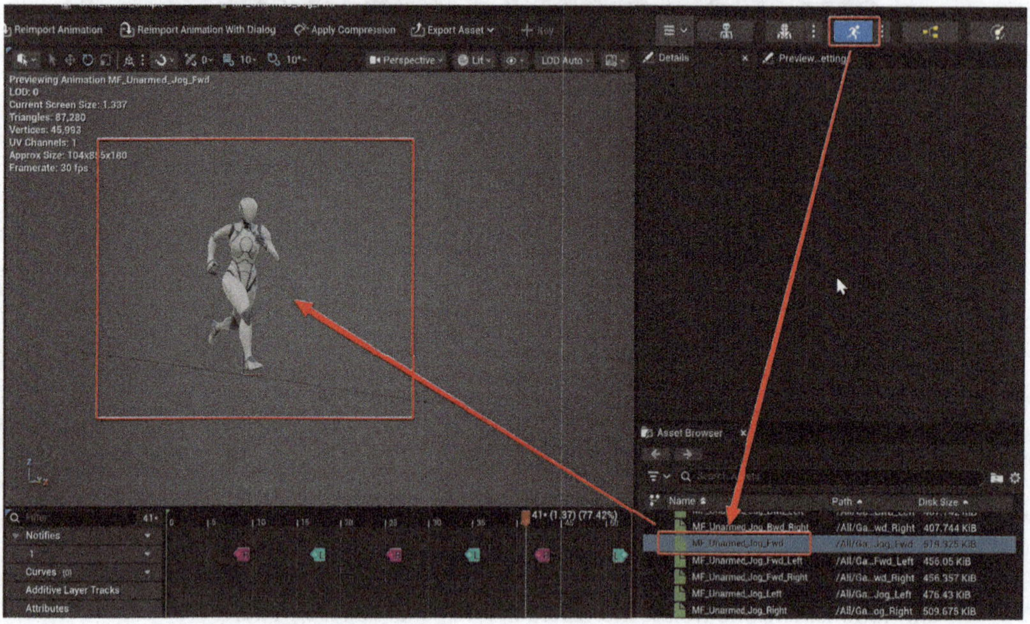

Figure 5.53 - Opening the Skeletal Mesh Editor

5. In the **Timeline** panel, stop the playback. You'll notice that every time the character's feet touch the ground, there is an **R** and an **L** marker. This will be our cue to activate the `NS_Snow_Kickup` effect.

6. Click the track drop-down and choose **Add Notify Track**. Rename it to `Footsteps`. Drag the play head to the first keyframe (**R**), right-click in the **Footsteps** track and select **Add Notify**, then choose **Play Niagara Particle Effect**.

> **Note**
>
> An **Animation Notify** is a marker placed on an animation timeline. It is used to trigger something at a specific frame during the animation, such as playing a sound, spawning a particle effect, or calling gameplay logic. In this recipe, we use a **Notify** to trigger the Niagara snow kick-up exactly when the character's foot touches the ground, so the effect matches the contact moment.

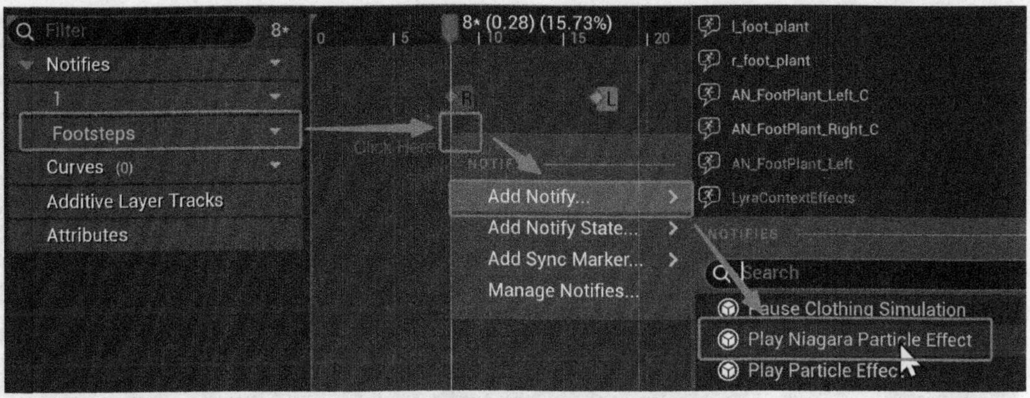

Figure 5.54 - Adding Notify keyframes

7. Click once on the keyframe you just made, in the **Details** panel, in the **Niagara System** drop-down menu, choose the Niagara System you made earlier (`NS_Snow_Kickup`), and in the **Socket Name**, type `Root`. This will attach the effect to the character's root bone (near its feet). Repeat this process for all the keyframes. If the keyframe falls into another track, simply redo or drag the keyframe into the **Footsteps** track. It might take a few tries.

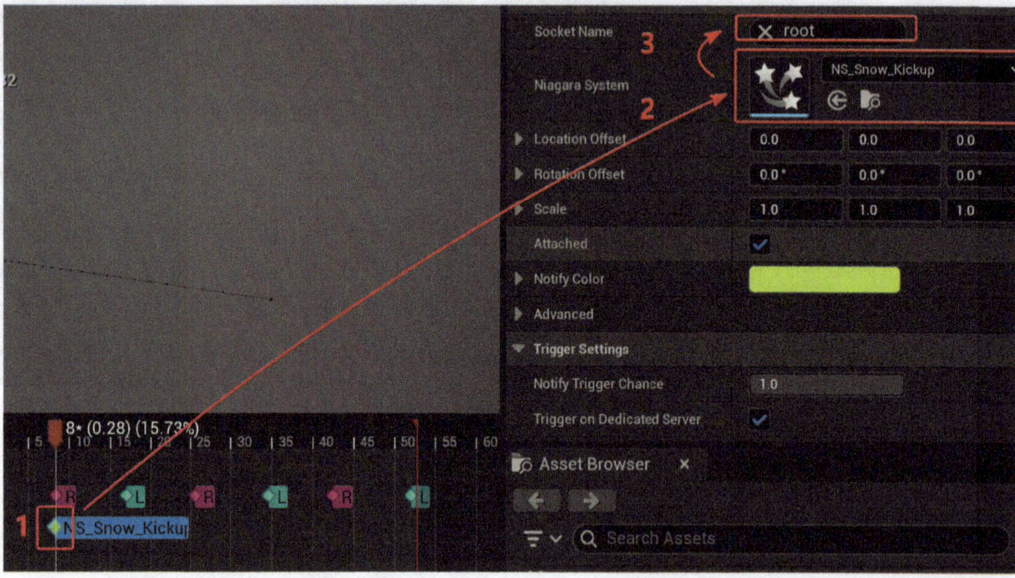

Figure 5.55 - Setting the Niagara System and Socket Name

8. Once completed, scrub the timeline to ensure you have the right timing every time his feet touch the ground. Click **Save**. The hard part is done!

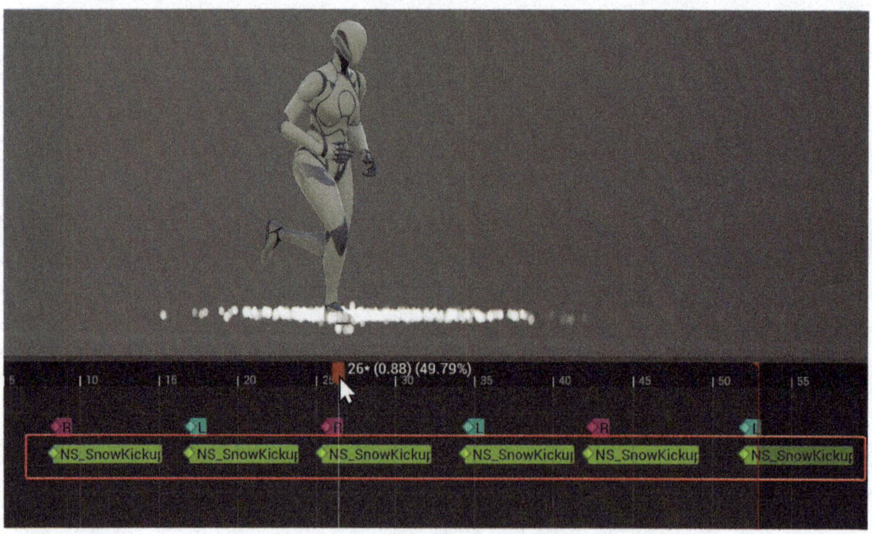

Figure 5.56 - The completed Notify keyframes

Testing in Sequencer

Now let's test the effect in **Sequencer** and check the timing:

1. For testing purposes, let's use a default character from the `Characters` folder. In the **Characters** | **Mannequins** | **Meshes** folder, drag `SKM_Manny_Simple` into the Level. Reset its **Location** to `0,0,0`.

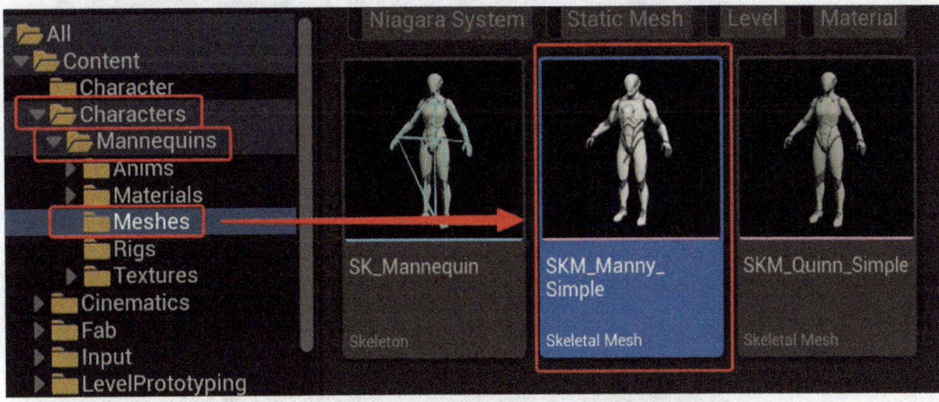

Figure 5.57 - Accessing the Manny Skeleton Mesh

2. From the top menu, click the **clapperboard** icon and choose **Add Level Sequence**. Rename it to `LS_SnowKickup` and save it in the `Sequences` folder.

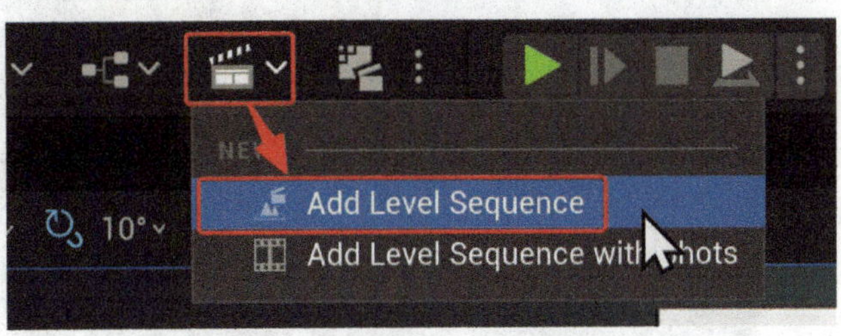

Figure 5.58 - Creating a Level Sequence

3. Once the **Sequencer** is created, drag `SKM_Manny_Simple` into the timeline. Delete the `CR_Mannequin_Body` track – we won't be using the Control Rig.

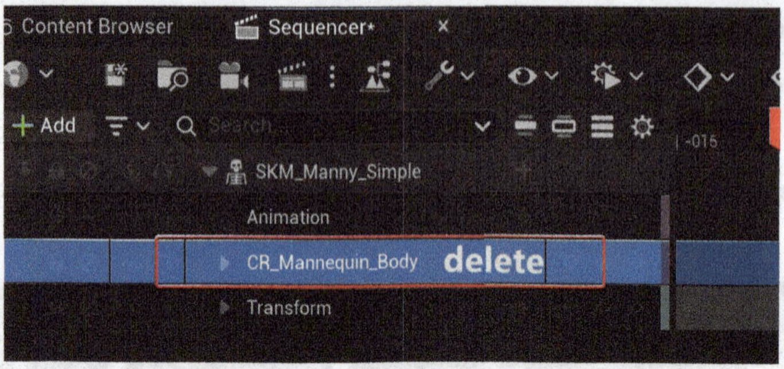

Figure 5.59 - Deleting the Control Rig

4. In the **Animation** track, click the **+** sign and search for and click on `MF_Unarmed_Jog_Fwd`. This is the animation we added to the Burst Niagara effect earlier. Press *spacebar* (or click the **Play** button). If you have done everything correctly, you will now see Niagara particles emitting from the character's feet as he runs.

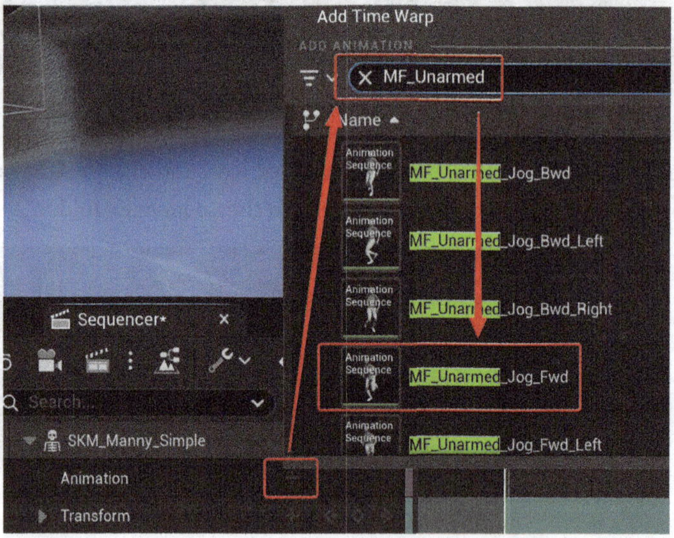

Figure 5.60 - Adding the animation track

> **Note**
>
> You will not see the effect if you simply scrub the Playhead.

5. We have two issues now:
    - The character is running in place.
    - The particles are way too explosive.

   Let's handle the first problem. Stop playback, right-click on the animation track (the *purple* track) and choose **Properties**, then in the **Start Location Offset**, change the **X** value to `1.0`.

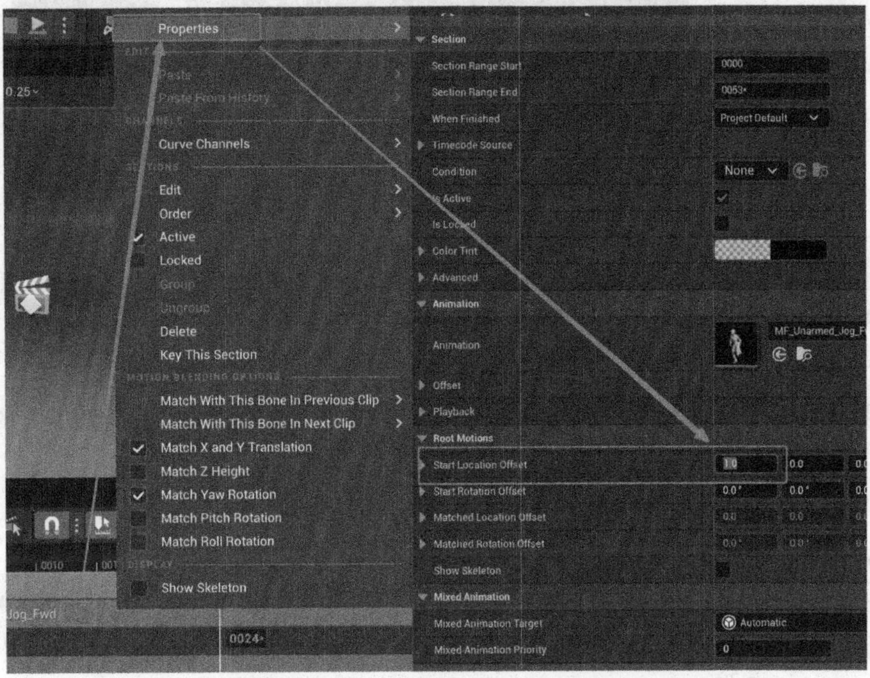

Figure 5.61 - Setting the Start Location Offset

6. Start playback; the character is now running with particles emitting as he runs. It looks cool, but snow does not kick up in such a manner. Let's fix this next.

Figure 5.62 - Testing the snow kick-up animation

Refining the snow kick-up effect

The timing is working, so let's refine the burst to better match loose snow:

1. In the `Niagara_Systems` folder, double-click to open `NS_Snow_Kickup`. Let's change some settings:
   - In the **Properties** module, enable **Determinism**.
   - In the **Burst Instantaneous** module, set **Spawn Count** to `1000`.
   - In the **Initialize Particle** module, set **Lifetime Min** to `0.5` and **Lifetime Max** to `2.0`. Change **Sprite Size Mode** to **Non-Uniform** and set **Sprite Size** to **X** = `5.0`, **Y** = `20`.
   - In **Add Velocity**, set **Velocity Speed Minimum** to `100` and **Maximum** to `350`, and Set **Cone Angle** to `150`.
   - In **Particle Update**, add a **Collision** module. Set **Restitution** to `0.0`.

> **Note**
>
> These settings are meant to be adjusted based on the look you want to achieve. Use the techniques you have learned throughout this book to experiment with particle size, speed, lifetime, color, and fade until the snow kick-up feels right for your shot.

2. Finally, let's swap the character with a pre-made MetaHuman. From the **MetaHuman | MH_Character** folder, drag `BP_MH_Character` into the level, place it beside the Manny character, then drag the MetaHuman character from the **Outliner** into the **Sequencer**.
3. Delete the **MetaHuman_ControlRig** and **Face** tracks. Click the + sign on the **Body** track, select **Animation**, then `MH_Unarmed_Jog_Fwd`. Right-click on the animation track (the *purple* track) and choose **Properties**, then in the **Start Location Offset**, change the **X** value to `1.0`.

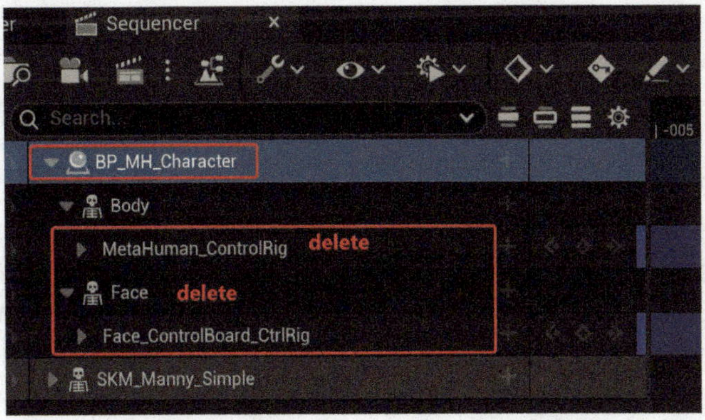

Figure 5.63 - Deleting the Control Rig and Face tracks

4. Start playback, and now you'll have both the Manny and MetaHuman characters running with snow kick-up.

Figure 5.64 - Testing the snow kick-up animation with MetaHuman

> **Note**
>
> Creating a MetaHuman from scratch is a separate process and can take some time, so we will not cover it in this recipe. To keep the focus on the snow kick-up effect, I have provided a pre-made MetaHuman character with clothing assets sourced from Fab (`https://www.fab.com/`). You can use this character to follow along immediately and concentrate on timing the Niagara burst to the running animation. If you would like to create or customize your own MetaHuman later, I have included useful documentation links in the *See also* section.

How it works...

In this recipe, you created a simple snow kick-up effect that reacts to the character's foot contact. The **Directional Burst** template is a good starting point because a footstep kick-up is a short, sudden effect, not a continuous particle system. By changing the **Add Velocity** direction so the burst moves upward, the particles behave more like powder being pushed out of the snow when the foot hits the ground. This gives the movement a clear visual reaction and helps the character feel connected to the surface instead of simply running over it.

The important part of this workflow is *timing*. The snow burst must happen on the frame where the foot touches the ground, because even a small timing mistake can make the effect feel disconnected from the animation. Using the running animation gives you clear foot-contact moments to work with, and triggering the Niagara burst from those moments makes the effect feel more believable. The snow should appear quickly, lift slightly, and then fade away, just like loose powder being disturbed by movement.

Testing the effect first in the sandbox level keeps the setup simple because you can focus only on the burst direction, size, timing, and readability. Once the effect works, moving it into the Snowscape level with the MetaHuman turns it into a proper cinematic shot. The same idea can also be reused for other character-driven effects.

By changing the material, color, velocity, and lifetime, this snow kick-up setup can become dust, sand, water splashes, sparks, or debris. The key production habit is always the same: find the contact moment first, then make the effect support the character's weight and movement.

There's more...

Once the snow kick-up effect is working in the sandbox level, try placing the MetaHuman character into the Snowscape level used earlier in this chapter. This will let you test the effect in a more cinematic environment, with falling snow, blowing mist, lighting, and snow-covered ground already in place. The snow kick-up can also be layered with the earlier snowfall, blizzard, or snow swirl systems to create a more complete snow scene. The falling snow adds atmosphere, the blizzard or swirl adds environmental movement, and the kick-up provides the close contact detail when the character's foot hits the ground.

Add the character to the level and use **Sequencer** to create a camera shot, as shown in *Figure 5.65*. This is a good way to check whether the burst feels believable in a real shot, rather than only in a clean test scene.

Figure 5.65 - The final snow kick-up effect

See also

If you would like to create or customize your own MetaHuman character, refer to Epic Games' *Getting Started with MetaHuman Creator* documentation (`https://dev.epicgames.com/documentation/metahuman/getting-started-with-metahuman-creator`). It explains how to set up **MetaHuman Creator** inside Unreal Engine and begin creating characters for your project.

6

Niagara Lightning and Electrical Effects for Cinematics

Lightning and **electrical effects** are powerful cinematic tools because they can add instant energy, danger, tension, and visual impact to a shot. In film, animation, and VFX, these effects are rarely just decorative. A lightning bolt can reveal a character for a split second, an electrical arc can show power moving between objects, and character-based crackle or sparks can make an animated performance feel charged, unstable, or dangerous.

In this chapter, we will build a set of practical Niagara lightning and electrical effects designed for cinematic shot work. We will start with a **Sequencer**-cued lightning bolt that can be timed to exact frames with a controllable flicker. We will then create an electrical arc between two points using user-controlled endpoints, followed by a character-based crackle and spark effect that attaches electricity to an animated Skeletal Mesh.

Each recipe focuses on timing, control, readability, and reusability, so the effects can be adjusted for different cinematic situations.

In this chapter, we'll be covering the following recipes:

- Creating a cinematic lightning bolt (Sequencer-cued)
- Connecting an electrical arc between two points
- Applying surface crackle/character sparks

Technical requirements

Before starting this recipe, ensure the following is set up:

- Make sure **Unreal Engine 5.6** is installed (see *Chapter 1* for details).
- A project with **Niagara** and **Niagara Sim Caching** plugin enabled.

- You may use the sandbox environment we created in the *Setting up a reusable VFX "Sandbox" level for cinematic lookdev* recipe in *Chapter 1*.
- Maintain the folder structure to keep the assets organized, as shown below:
    - `Content`
        - `Niagara_Systems`
        - `Sequences`
        - `Textures`
        - `Materials`
        - `MRQ`

You can download the example project for this book by following the instructions in the *Download the example code/resource files* section in the *Preface* of this book.

The complete example project is included in the downloadable code/resource bundle.

Creating a cinematic lightning bolt (Sequencer-cued)

In this recipe, you will create a basic cinematic lightning bolt effect that can be timed precisely in **Sequencer**. Unlike continuous effects such as rain or snow, lightning is usually a fast, high-impact moment that appears for only a few frames. Because of that, *timing* is just as important as the look of the effect.

We will build a **controllable lightning bolt** using Niagara and set it up so it can be triggered at a specific point in the shot. The goal is to create a bolt that feels sharp, bright, and energetic, with enough flicker and variation to avoid looking static. This type of effect is useful for storm scenes, magical attacks, Sci-Fi power surges, dramatic reveals, or any cinematic moment that needs a sudden burst of visual energy.

Getting ready

For this recipe, we will use the **Basic Level Template** that comes with Unreal Engine 5. This keeps the scene simple so we can focus on building, timing, and previewing the lightning bolt without extra distractions. Once the effect is working, you can place it into any cinematic scene and trigger it from the **Sequencer** at the exact frame needed.

How to do it...

In this recipe, we will create a simple Niagara lightning bolt using the **Ribbon Renderer**. We will keep the setup focused and practical, with emphasis on creating a jagged bolt shape, adding brightness and flicker, and timing the effect clearly in **Sequencer**. Follow these steps in the subsequent sections.

> **Note**
>
> A **Ribbon Renderer** connects particles together to create a continuous strip or trail. It is useful for effects such as lightning, energy arcs, beams, and motion streaks.

Building the base lightning bolt

In this section, you'll create the core lightning effect by setting up a Niagara beam, shaping its appearance, and adding the jitter and width variations that give it an energetic look:

1. Go to **File | New Level**, from the pop-up panel, choose **Basic**, and click **Create**. Since we'll be creating a lightning effect, this is an appropriate level to be in. Go back to **File | Save Current Level As...** and set the name as `LV_LightningBolt`, then click **Save**.

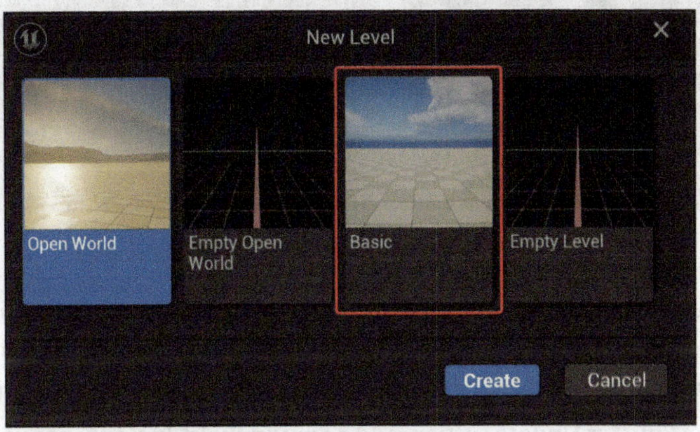

Figure 6.1 - Creating the Basic level

2. Press the *1* key on your keyboard to set **Bookmark 1**, then press the *G* key to hide the overlay icons and select the **Directional Light** to change its **Intensity** to `0.5` lux. This will create a dark environment for our lightning bolts.
3. To achieve a glow effect later in the scene, add the **Post Process Volume** and set the **Bloom** Method to **Standard** and **Intensity** to `2.0`.

Figure 6.2 - Creating the Basic level

4. In the `Niagara_Systems` folder, right-click and select **Niagara System**. From the pop-up window, choose the **Minimal** emitter. Rename it to `NS_LightningBolt` and double-click to open the Niagara Editor.

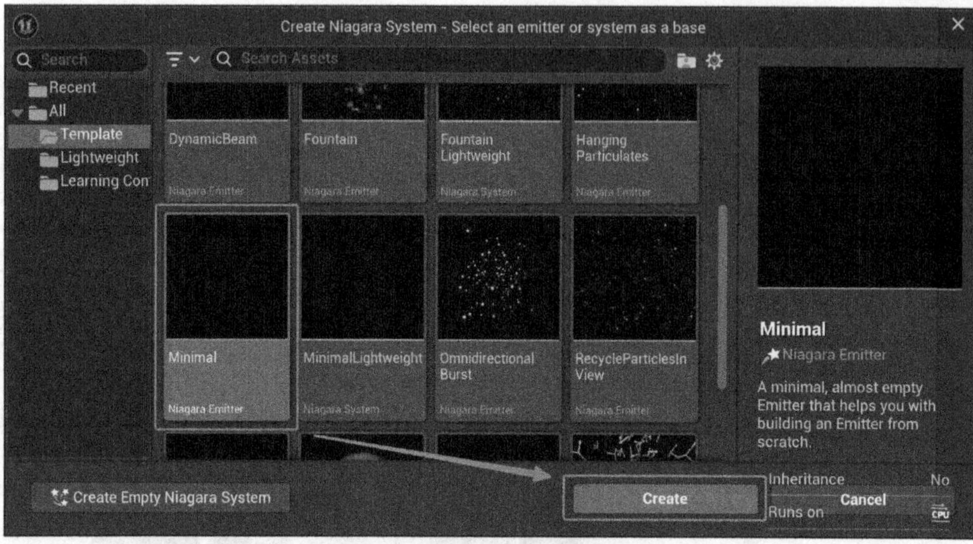

Figure 6.3 - Creating the Minimal emitter

5. Select the **Properties** module and enable **Local Space** and **Determinism**. **Local Space** will allow you to place the Niagara effect anywhere in the level, and **Determinism** will return the same results for the same configuration in the **Sequencer** timeline.
6. In the **Emitter Update** section, add a **Spawn Burst Instantaneous** module. Change **Spawn Count** to `45`. Lightning strikes within a split-second; thus, using **Spawn Burst Instantaneous** is the best choice here.
7. In the **Render** section, add the **Ribbon Renderer** module and disable the **Sprite Renderer** module.
8. In the **Particle Spawn** section, add a **Spawn Beam** module and click **Fix issue**. You'll now see a beam in the Preview pane. This is the start of our lightning bolt.

Figure 6.4 - Adding modules to the emitter

9. Back to the **Beam Emitter Setup** module, change the **Beam End Z** value to `500` – this sets the height of the lightning bolt. I suggest using a high value if you are placing the lightning far in the background.
10. Enable **Use Beam Tangents** to expose the **Beam Start Tangent and Beam End Tangent**.
11. For **Beam Start Tangent** using the down-pointing arrow, choose **Random Range Vector.** Leave **Minimum** and **Maximum X, Y, Z** values as they are, set **Beam End Tangent** to **X** = `0`, **Y** = `0`, **Z** = `0`.

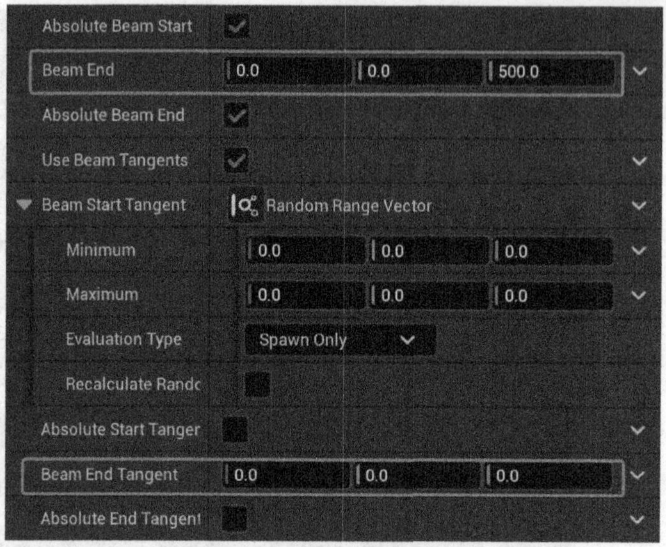

Figure 6.5 - Setting the Beam emitter Setup

12. Select **Initialize Particle**, change **Lifetime** to `1`. The lightning will only appear for 1 second. Change **Color Mode** to **Direct Set** and choose a color for your lightning. I suggest setting **R** = `0`, **G** = `12`, **B** = `50`, as shown in *Figure 6.6*. Take note of the **Value** setting of `50`; this will add glow to the lightning bolt.

Figure 6.6 - Lightning color setup

13. In the **Particle Spawn** section, add a **Beam Width** module. Using the down-pointing arrow for **Beam Width**, select **Float from Curve**.

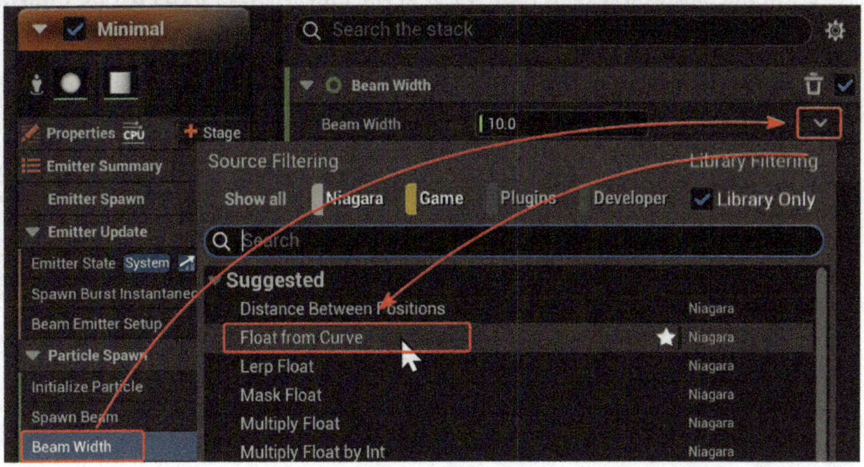

Figure 6.7 - Adding Float from Curve for Beam Width

14. Select the **Linear Ramp Down Curve** and set **Scale Curve** to `10`. This will give the lightning bolt a sharp edge at the end. The **Scale Curve** applies thickness to the lightning bolt.

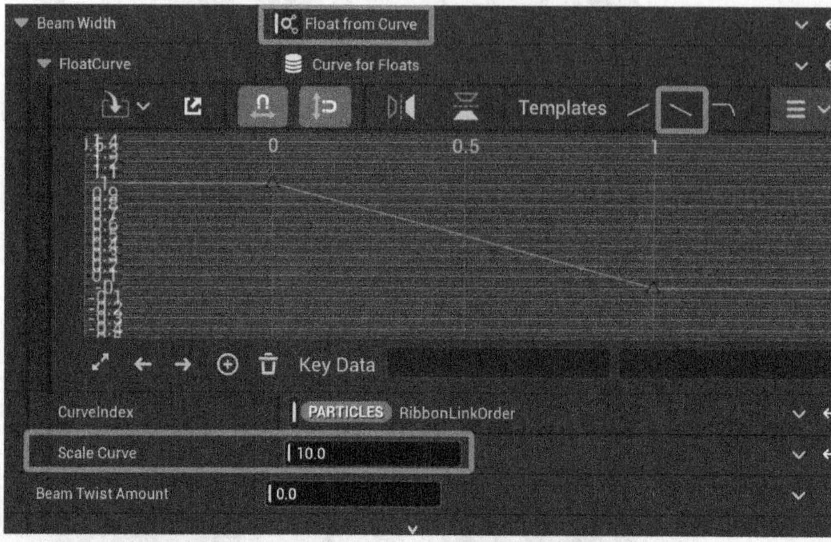

Figure 6.8 - Using Linear Ramp and setting the Scale Curve amount

15. In the **Particle Update** section, add a **Jitter Position** module, change **Jitter Amount** to `20`, and **Jitter Delay** to `0.1`. You'll now see some random jitteriness in the Preview window.

16. From the **Parameters tab** (lower left of the Editor), drag **PARTICLES Lifetime** between the **Particle State** and **Jitter Position**.

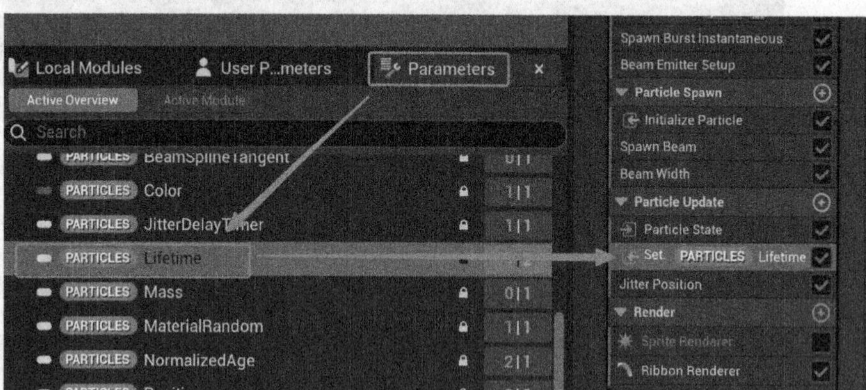

Figure 6.9 - Adding Particles Lifetime

17. In the **PARTICLES Lifetime** details panel, click the down-pointing arrow and choose **Random Range Float**, and set the **Minimum** to `0.1` and **Maximum** to `0.2`. The lightning bolt will now appear for a brief second and disappear.

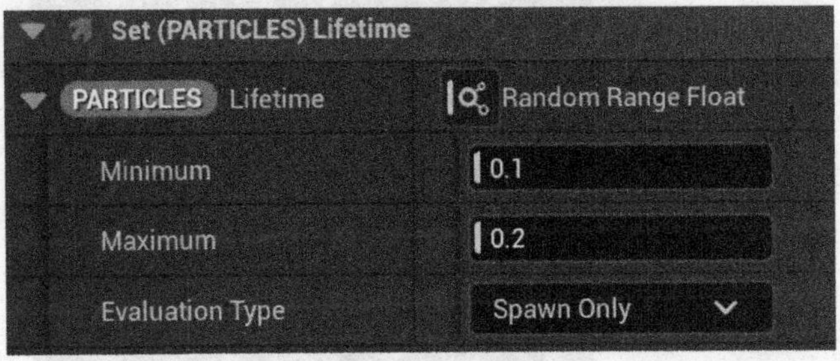

Figure 6.10 - Setting Random Range Float values

18. For preview purposes, in the `NS_LightningBolt` system module, change **Loop Duration** to `1.0`. Compile and save.

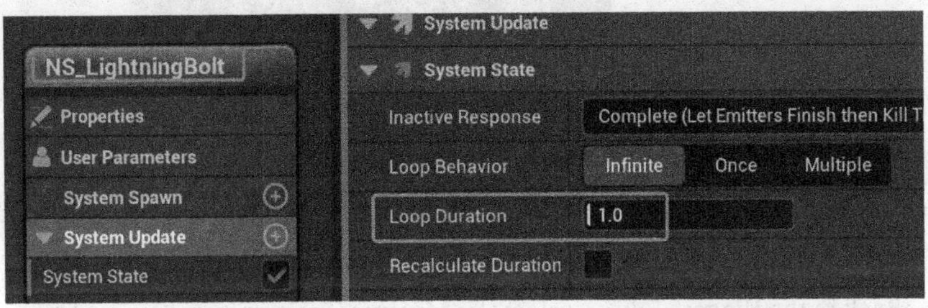

Figure 6.11 - System module Loop Duration setting

19. In the Main Level, drag `NS_LightningBolt` into the scene. You'll now have a basic-looking lightning bolt, but we're not done yet. Lightning has branches spreading out. Let's work on that next.

Figure 6.12 - The beginning of the lightning bolt

Creating the branching lightning effect

In this section, to create multiple branches of the lightning, you'll need to duplicate and modify the emitter, which will give the bolt a more natural, irregular silhouette.

1. Back in the Niagara Editor, select the **Minimal** emitter, press *F2*, and rename it to `Bolt1`. For `Bolt1`, change the following:
   - **Beam Emitter Setup**: Change **Beam End** to `-1000`
   - **Beam Start Tangent**: Set **Maximum** value to **X** = `0`, **Y** = `0`, **Z** = `0`
   - **Beam End Tangent**: Set **X** = `0`, **Y** = **0.3**, **Z** = `0`
2. Select `Bolt1`, press *Ctrl* + *D* to duplicate the emitter. Rename it to `Bolt2` and change the following:
   - **Beam Emitter Setup**: Change **Beam End** to `500`
   - **Beam Start Tangent:** Set **Minimum** and **Maximum** value to **X** = `0`, **Y** = `0`, **Z** = `0`
   - **Beam End Tangent**: Set **X** = `0`, **Y** = `0`, **Z** = `0`
3. Select `Bolt2`, press *Ctrl* + *D* to duplicate the emitter. Rename it to `Bolt3` and change the following:
   - **Beam Emitter Setup**: Change **Beam End** to `800`

- **Beam Start Tangent**: Set the **maximum** value to **X** = `0`, **Y** = `0`, **Z**=`0`
- **Beam End Tangent**: Set **X** = `0`, **Y** = `0`, **Z** = `0`

4. Select `Bolt3`, press *Ctrl* + *D* to duplicate the emitter. Rename it to `Bolt4` and change the following:
    - **Beam Emitter Setup**: Change **Beam End** to `-900`
    - **Beam Start Tangent**: Set the **Maximum** value to **X** = `0`, **Y** = `0`, **Z** = `0`
    - **Beam End Tangent**: Set **X** = `0`, **Y** =`-0.4`, **Z** = `0`
5. Select `Bolt4`, press *Ctrl* + *D* to duplicate the emitter. Rename it to `Bolt5` and change the following:
    - **Beam Emitter Setup**: Change **Beam End** to `-600`
    - **Beam Start Tangent**: Set the **Maximum** value to **X** = `0`, **Y** = `0`, **Z** = `0`
    - **Beam End Tangent**: Set **X** = `0`, **Y** = `-0.2`, **Z** = `0`

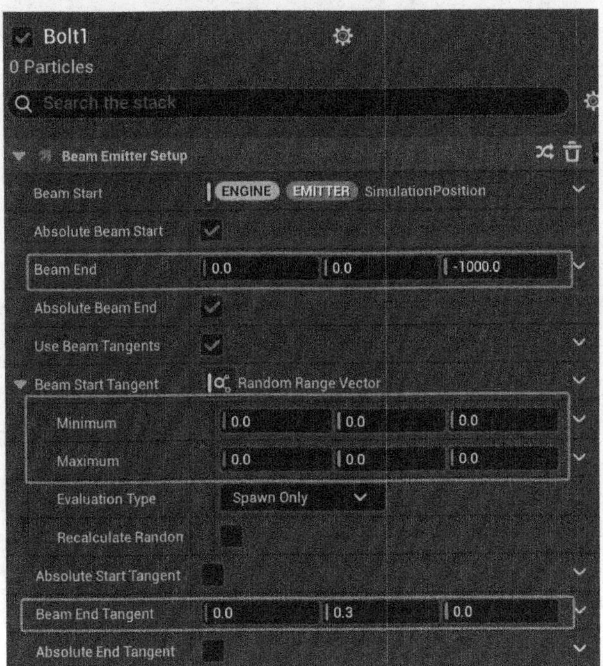

Figure 6.13 - Beam Emitter Setup for Bolt1

6. Compile and save. You now have a lightning bolt with 5 random branches. The more emitters you duplicate, the more branches you will have.

Note

In this recipe, we are using the **Ribbon Renderer** to create lightning bolts. The **Beam End** value controls where the ribbon ends. If the value is *negative*, the beam points downward; if the value is *positive*, it points upward. **Beam Start Tangent** controls the direction from where the beam begins, while **Beam End Tangent** controls the direction where the beam finishes.

Some of the bolt emitters use positive values, and others use negative values, so a few branches point upward while others point downward. This helps break up the lightning shape and makes it look less uniform.

I have also used different **Beam End Tangent** values to create the branching effect near the bottom of the lightning. You can adjust these values to spread the branches farther apart or bring them closer together, depending on the look you want.

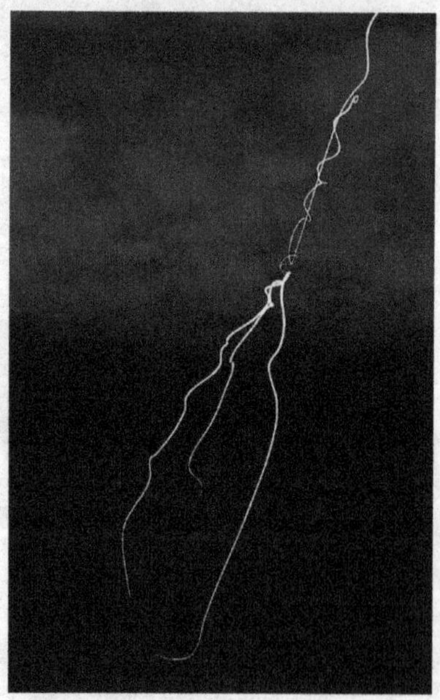

Figure 6.14 - The finished lightning bolt

There is one last thing we need to add. When there is lightning, there usually is a bright flash of light. Let's add that to our effect.

7. Back in the Niagara Editor. In the **Bolt 1 Render** section, add a **Light Renderer** module and change the following:
   - **Source Mode**: Change to **Emitter**
   - Disable **Use Inverse Squared Falloff**
   - **Radius Scale**: Set to `500` – radius of the light
   - **Diffuse Scale**: Set to `2.0` – the brightness of the light
   - **Color Add**: Change **X** = `0`, **Y** = `0`, **Z** = `2.0` – the color of the light

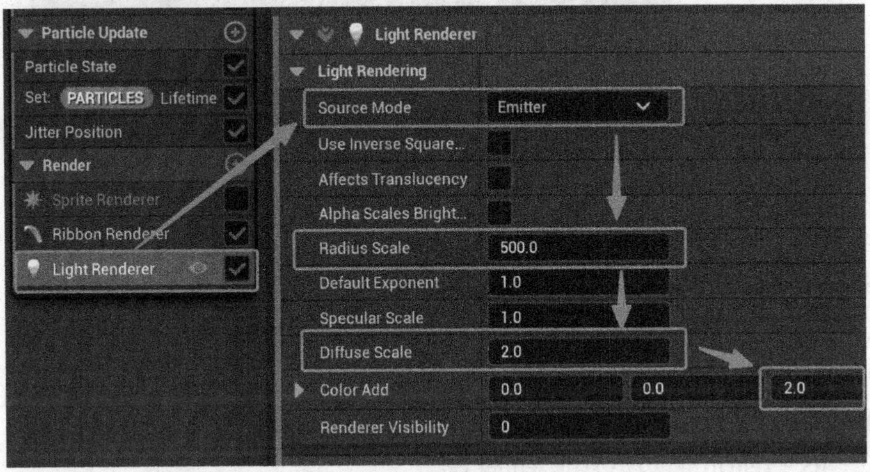

Figure 6.15 - Light Renderer setup

The bright flash of light will now be part of the lightning bolt, as shown in *Figure 6.16*:

Figure 6.16 - The finished lightning bolt

Timing the effect in Sequencer

Finally, we are ready to add the lightning bolt to the **Sequencer** and trigger it at a specific point in a shot. Follow these steps:

1. Add a Level Sequence and rename it as `LS_Lightning_Bolt`. Add the `NS_LightningBolt` to the sequence.
2. On the `NS_LightningBolt` track click the **+** sign and add a **NiagaraComponent0**.

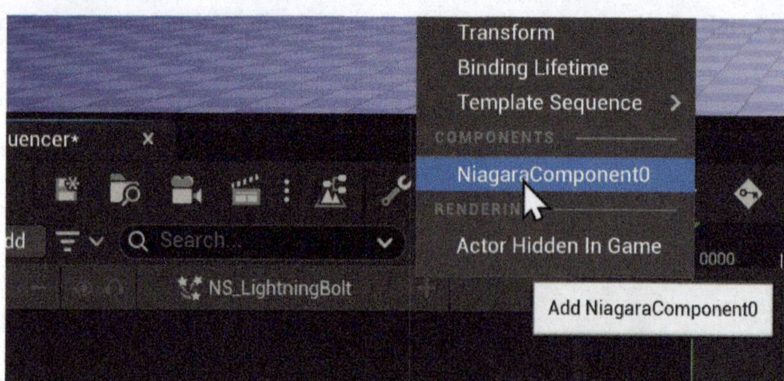

Figure 6.17 - Adding the Niagara Component

3. Click the + sign on the **NiagaraComponent0** and choose **Niagara System Life Track Cycle**. In the **System Life Cycle** track, change **Tick Delta Time** to **Desired Age**.

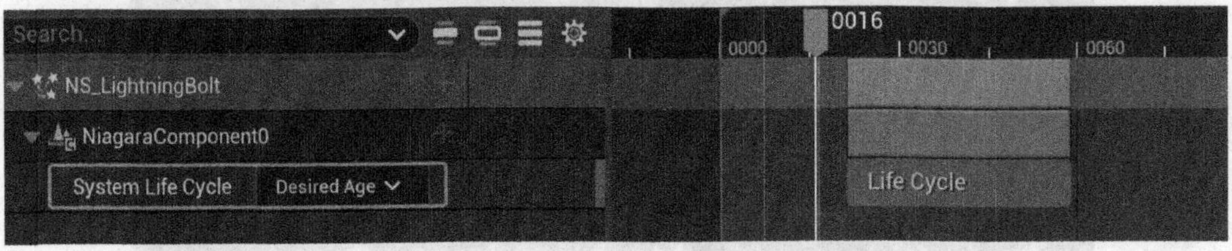

Figure 6.18 - Adding the System Life Cycle track

> **Note**
>
> This workflow and the reason behind it were covered in detail in the *Making Niagara effects stable for scrubbing and repeatable playback (repeatable takes)* recipe in *Chapter 1*.

4. Press play to test the effect. Trim the track so the effect only plays once. Incidentally, the bright flash of light will remain for the duration of the track, so timing it by trimming the track is crucial.
5. Duplicate the effect in the **Outliner** and add it to the **Sequencer**. You can move, scale, and rotate the effect in the scene. Add as many as required for your shot.

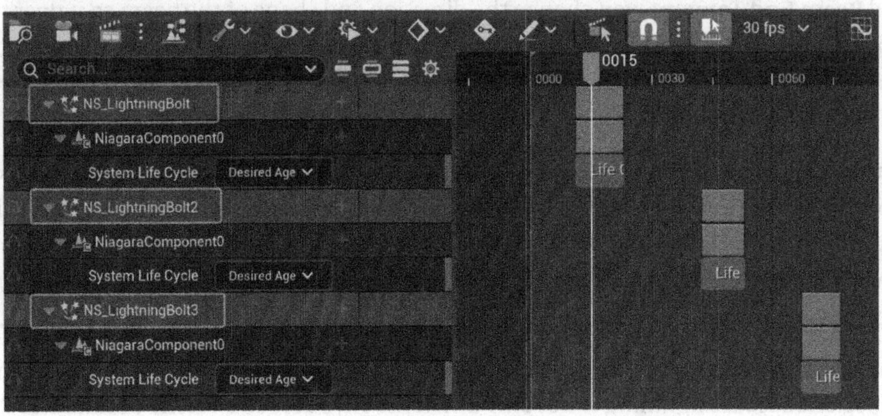

Figure 6.19 - Adding multiple lightning effects

Your customizable lightning bolt effect is now ready for use in any cinematic scene. Well done!

Figure 6.20 - The final lighting effects timed in the Sequencer

How it works...

In this recipe, you created a cinematic lightning bolt using Niagara's **Ribbon Renderer**. Instead of using sprite particles, the **Ribbon Renderer** connects particles together to form a continuous streak. This makes it suitable for lightning because the effect needs to look like a sharp, connected electrical path rather than separate particles floating in space.

The **Spawn Beam** module gives the lightning its basic start and end points, while the **Beam End** value controls the direction and height of the bolt. By adjusting the **Beam Start Tangent** and **Beam End Tangent**, you change the direction and shape of the beam so it does not look perfectly straight. This is important because natural lightning usually has an uneven, jagged shape. The **Jitter Position** module adds extra movement and randomness, helping the bolt feel unstable and energetic.

Duplicating the original emitter into several bolt emitters creates the branching structure. Each duplicated emitter has slightly different **Beam End** and **Beam End Tangent** values, so the branches spread in different directions. This gives the lightning a more natural and cinematic look without needing to build a very complex system. The **Beam Width** curve also helps shape the bolt by making it thicker in some areas and sharper toward the ends.

The **Light Renderer** adds the flash that usually happens during a lightning strike. This is important because lightning is not only a visible bolt, but it also briefly illuminates the scene around it. By adding light directly inside the Niagara System, the effect feels more connected to the environment and less like a flat graphic placed in front of the camera.

Finally, the **System Life Cycle** track in **Sequencer** allows the lightning to be timed to an exact frame. This is what makes the effect useful for cinematic work. You can place the strike on a cut, a reveal, a character reaction, or a music beat. Trimming the **System Life Cycle** section is also important because the light flash remains active for the duration of the track, so the timing needs to be controlled carefully.

There's more...

So far in this recipe, we have created a lightning bolt using Niagara by cloning emitters and adding a flashing light. However, one important element is still missing: *storm clouds*.

In many cinematic storm scenes, lightning is not always seen directly. Instead, it often flashes from behind or inside the clouds, briefly illuminating their shape and creating a dramatic bloom effect. We'll now add this extra layer to our setup and expand the effect further. Let's begin:

1. In the **Outliner**, select the **VolumetricCloud** asset. In its **Details** panel, scroll down to the **Material** section and click on the **Browse to** icon.

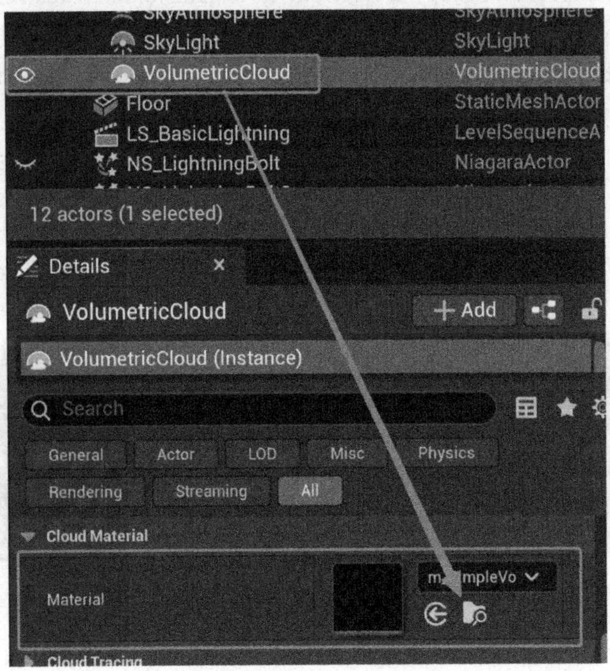

Figure 6.21 - Accessing the VolumetricCloud material

2. By pressing the **Browse To** icon, you'll be led to the **Engine Sky | VolumetricClouds** folder, which contains the `m_SimpleVolumetricCloud_Inst` material. Select the material and drag it into the `Materials` folder. When prompted, select **Copy**.

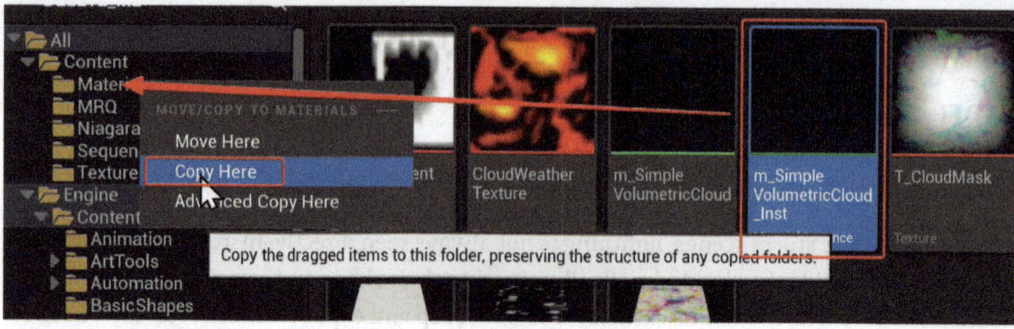

Figure 6.22 - Copying the VolumetricCloud material

> **Note**
>
> It is important to copy assets from the `Engine` folder instead of editing or moving the original files. Unreal Engine uses these assets for its default project setup, so changing them directly may affect other projects or cause unexpected issues later.

3. Once copied into the `Materials` folder, rename the material to `MI_StormClouds`.
4. While it is still selected, click the **Use Asset Selected From The Content Browser** icon. This will assign the assets we just copied to **VolumetricCloud**.

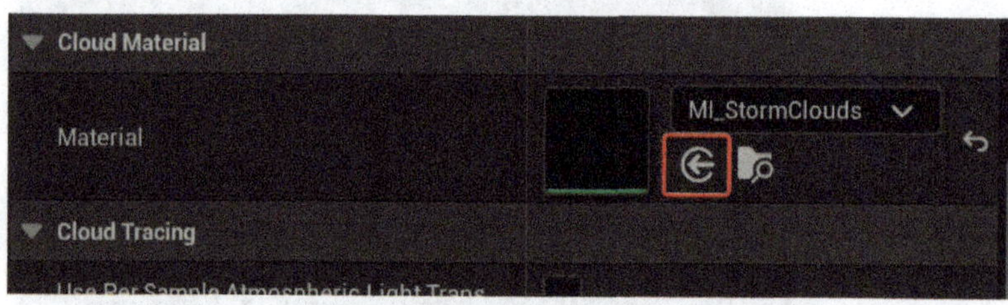

Figure 6.23 - Assigning the new material

5. To see this effect better, I suggest taking the **Direction Light**'s **Intensity** down to `0.5` lux (darker scene).
6. Now select the **VolumetricCloud** and double click the **Materials** icon or double click the `MI_StormClouds` material in the **Content Browser**. Arrange the panel so it looks like *Figure 6.24*:

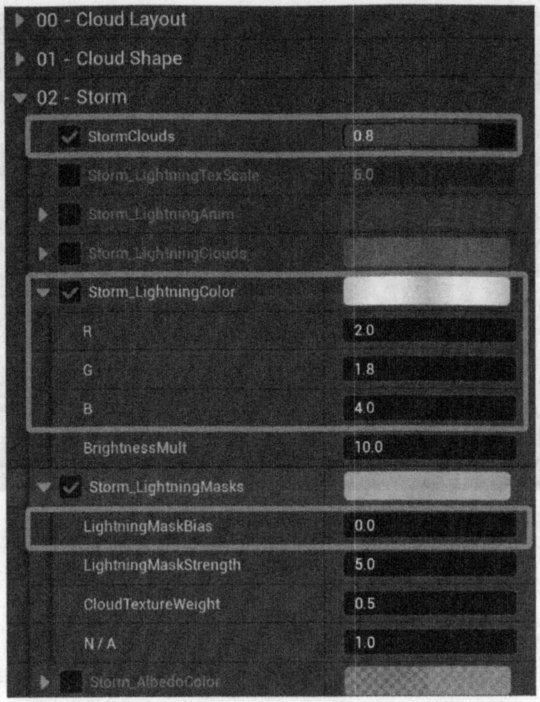

Figure 6.24 - Changing the material parameters

7. Activate and change the parameters as follows:
   - **StormClouds:** `0.4~0.8`
   - **Storm_LightningColor: R** = `2.0`, **G** = `1.8`, **B** = `4.0`
   - **LightningMaskBias:** `0.0`
8. Instant animated storm clouds! You may tweak the other parameters for the look you are going for.

Figure 6.25 - The stormy cloud final look

See also

For more control over the final lightning look, refer to Unreal Engine's **Post Process Effects** documentation: `https://dev.epicgames.com/documentation/unreal-engine/post-process-effects-in-unreal-engine?application_version=5.6`. This is useful when adjusting bloom, exposure, tone mapping, and overall scene brightness for lightning flashes and cloud illumination.

Connecting an electrical arc between two points

In this recipe, you will create an electrical arc that connects two points in the scene. Unlike the lightning bolt from the previous recipe, which was designed as a quick cinematic strike, this effect is more controlled and directional. It can be used to show electricity between two objects, energy transferring from one device to another, or a Sci-Fi power connection building tension in a shot.

We will build the arc using Niagara and set it up with user-controlled endpoints, so the start and end positions can be adjusted more easily. This makes the effect useful for cinematic work because the arc can be placed exactly where the shot needs it, whether it is between two props, a character and an object, or part of a larger electrical sequence. The focus of this recipe is control, timing, and readability, so the arc feels like it belongs in the scene rather than appearing as a random bolt.

Figure 6.26 shows the electrical arc effect as follows:

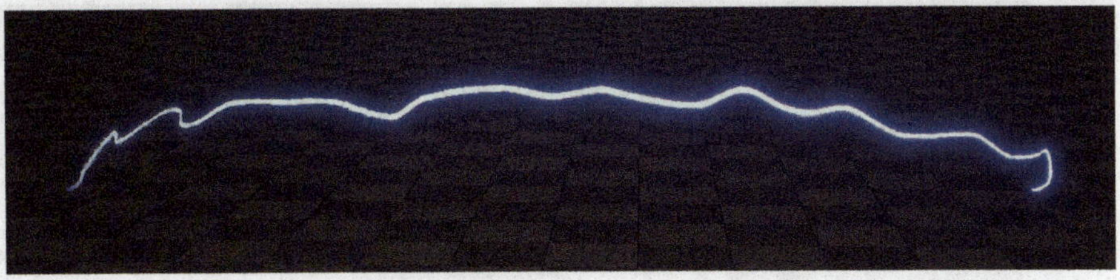

Figure 6.26 - The Electrical Arc effect

Getting ready

Before starting, you'll need to set up your test environment. Locate the `LV_VFX_Sandbox` from the **Content Browser**. This is the level that we've been using throughout this book.

How to do it...

With the `LV_VFX_Sandbox` level open, follow along:

1. In the `Niagara_Systems` folder, right-click and create a Niagara System. Then, choose the **StaticBeam** emitter, and rename it as `NS_ElectricalArc`.
2. Drag `NS_ElectricalArc` into the level and double-click to open it in the Editor. It is always good to drag your Niagara System into the level. It will give you a chance to see every change and edit you make in real time.
3. In the **Render** section, select the **Ribbon Renderer** module, scroll down to the **Ribbon Tessellation** section, and set the **Curve Tension** to `0.5`. This will affect how spiky the effect is. The higher the value, the sharper the curves.

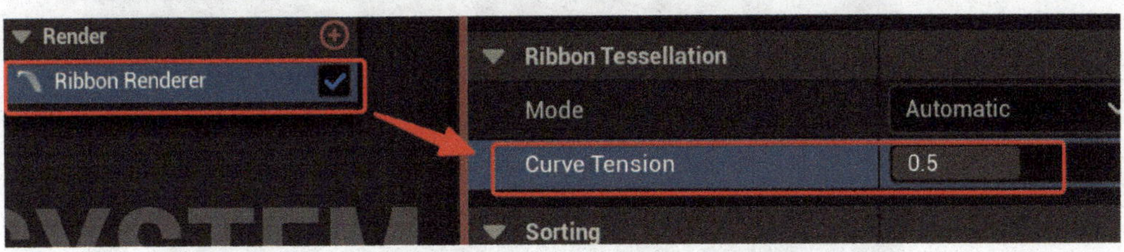

Figure 6.27 - Setting the Curve Tension

4. Select the **Emitter State** module. For **Loop Duration**, use the dropdown arrow, and choose the **Random Range Float**. This adds the **Minimum** and **Maximum** fields.

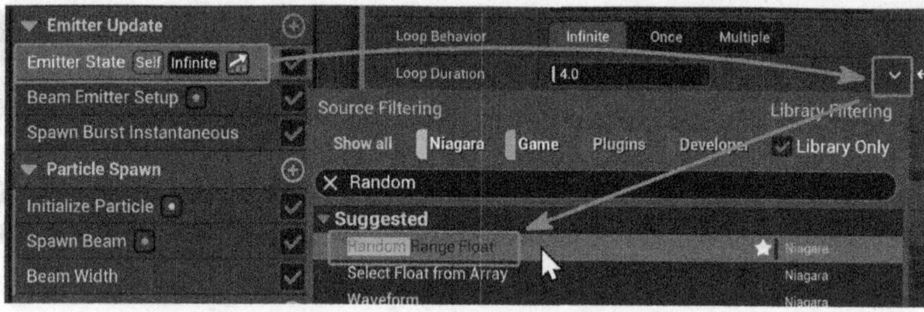

Figure 6.28 - Adding Random Range Float

5. Set **Loop Duration Minimum** to `0.1` and **Maximum** to `0.2`. This will add some randomness to the **Loop Duration**.

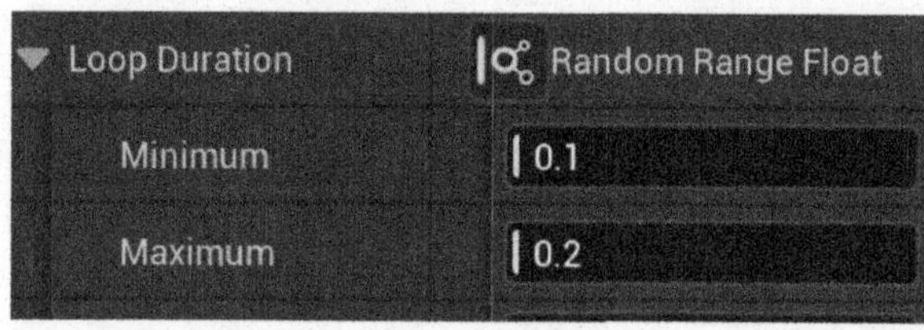

Figure 6.29 - Loop Duration values

6. Next, select the **Beam Emitter Setup** module. You'll need to click on **Fix issue** and **Dismiss**, then enable **Absolute Beam End** and **Use Beam Tangents**.

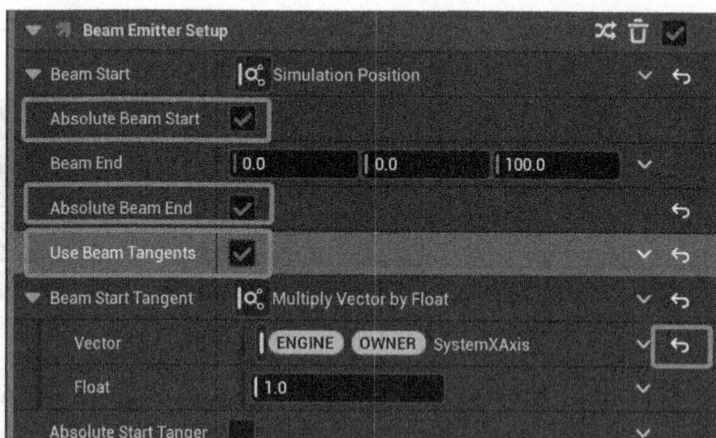

Figure 6.30 - Enabling Beam Start and Beam End

7. For **Beam Start Tangent**, click the reset to the default icon as shown in *Figure 6.31*. Then, use the dropdown arrow to choose **Multiply Vector by Float**. Set the **Beam**

Start Tangent Vector to **X** = 0, **Y** = 0, **Z** = 1.0, and **Float** to 0.5. Set the **Beam End Tangent** Vector to **X** = 0, **Y** = 0, **Z** = 1, and **Float** to 1.0.

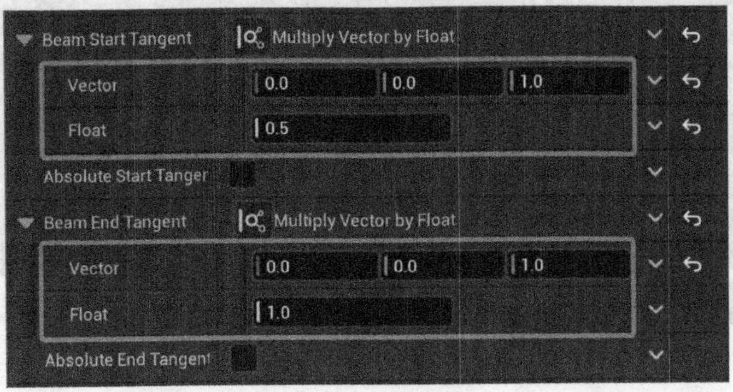

Figure 6.31 - Enabling Beam Start and End Tangents

8. Select the **Burst Instantaneous** module and set **Spawn Count** to 35. Then select the **Initialize Particle** module and click the top (first) **Fix issue** button. It seems the current **Initialize Particle** module has been deprecated, but by clicking **Fix issue**, a new **Initialize Particle 001** was created. Click on it and set **Lifetime** to 0.2.

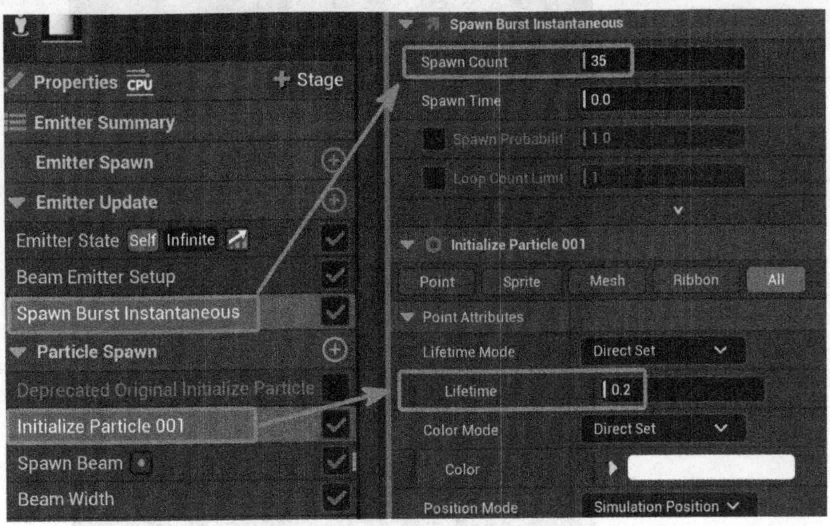

Figure 6.32 - Spawn Burst and Initialize Particle 001 settings

9. Now, select the **Spawn Beam** module and click on **Fix issue** and **Dismiss**. Then select the **Beam Width** module. This module sets the width of the beam. For now, using the dropdown icon, select the **Ramp Up Down** curve. This will make the beam thick in the middle and sharp on the edges. Set **Scale Curve** to 5.

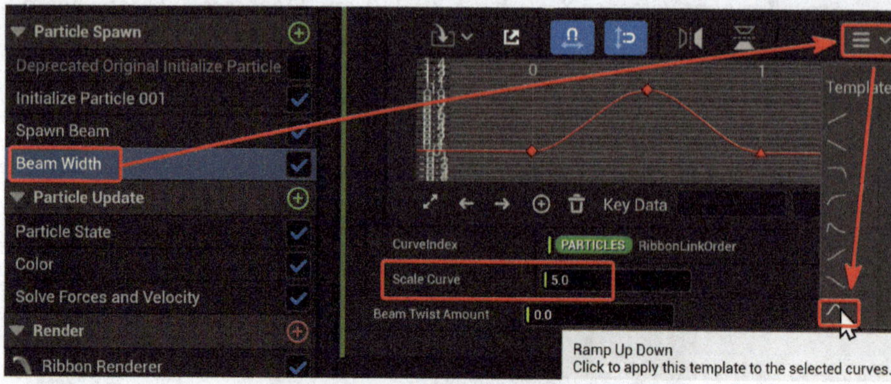

Figure 6.33 - Beam Width settings

10. Next, let's set the color. In the **Particle Update** section, select the **Color** module. Click on the color picker and use the following settings: **R** = `0.6`, **G** = `0.3`, **B** = `30`. This will give the beam a glowing *purple-blue* color. Click **OK**.

Figure 6.34 - Setting Beam color

11. Let's make the beam jitter like an electrical beam. In the **Particle Update** section, add the **Update Beam** and **Jitter Position** modules. Leave the **Jitter Amount** and **Jitter Delay** at default. We will revisit these settings if needed.

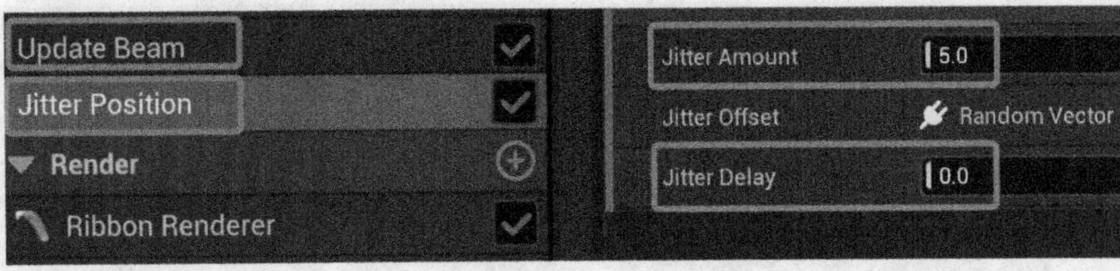

Figure 6.35 - Adding Update Beam and Beam Jitter modules

Now, let's work on getting the beam ends attached to an actor (any object) in the level. We will be jumping into the Blueprint world—don't worry, we'll only use a few nodes, and I promise it'll be a simple setup! No prior Blueprint knowledge required. Let's get started:

1. Select the **Beam Emitter Setup** module. Click the dropdown arrow next to the **Beam End,** then search for `Scratch` and select **New Scratch Dynamic Input**. This will open a scratch pad with a basic setup.

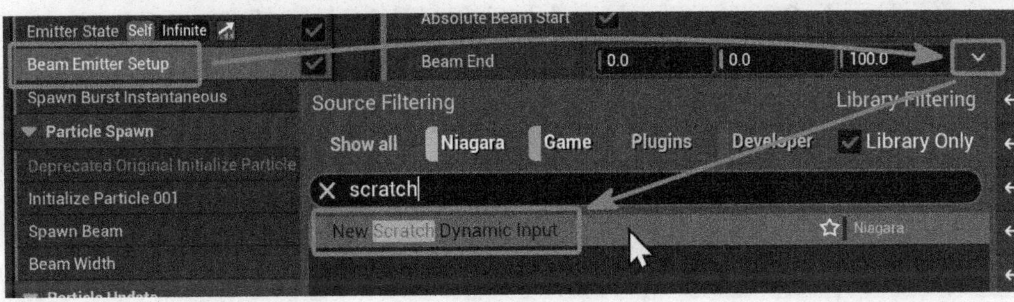

Figure 6.36 - Adding Scratch Pad module

2. In the Scratch pad interface, you'll have three nodes: **Input Map**, **Map Get**, and **Output Dynamic Input.** Right-click on the **INPUT Default** pin and select **Remove Pin**. It is not needed.

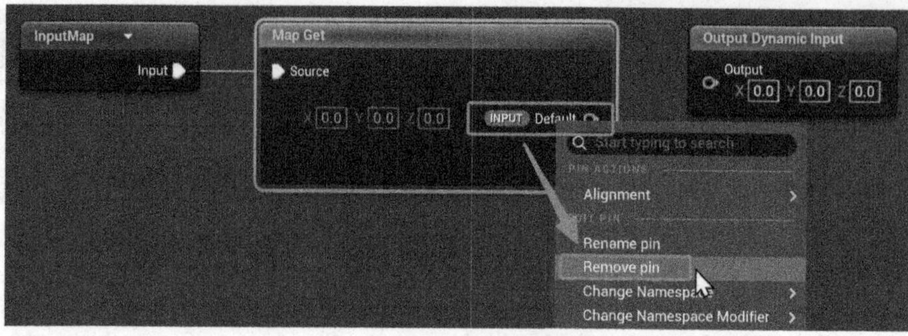

Figure 6.37 - Removing the INPUT Default pin

3. On the **Map Get** node, click the + sign and search for `Actor Component Interface` node. On the **Actor Component Interface** pin (blue), click and drag and search for `Get Transform` node (type `transform`). In the **Get Transform** node, attach the **Position** pin (pink) to the **Output** pin (pink), and that is it! Click **Apply** and **Save**.

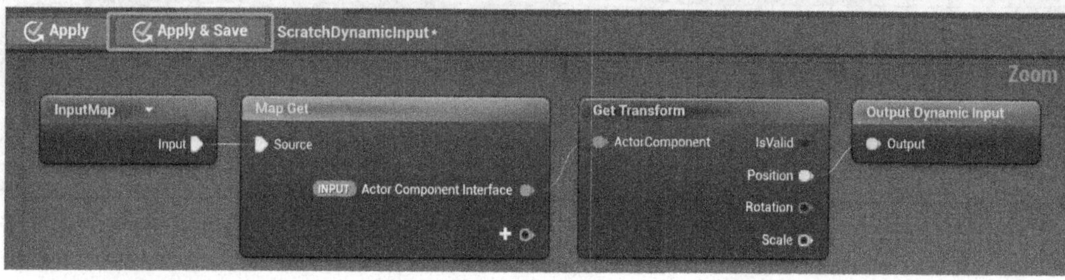

Figure 6.38 - The completed Blueprint

Click on the **System Overview** tab to get back to the Niagara Editor. In the **Beam Emitter Setup** module, in the **Beam End** properties, you now have an **Actor Component Interface**, which allows the selection of an Actor outside of the Niagara System. Let's first make this into a User Parameter so we can make the selection from the main level.

1. Click the dropdown arrow for the **Beam End** and search for and add **Read from new User parameter**.

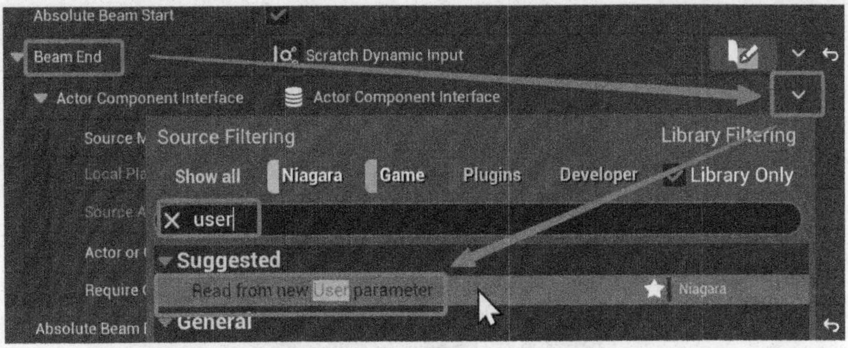

Figure 6.39 - Creating User Parameter for Beam End

2. In the **User Parameters** tab (lower left of the interface), you now have an **Actor Component Interface_Beam End User Parameter**. Disable **Use Beam Tangent** as it is not needed for this effect.

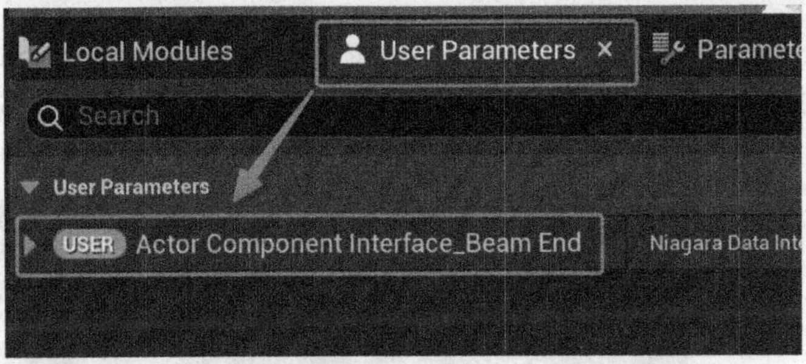

Figure 6.40 - Locating the new User Parameter

3. Let's test our Niagara effect. Back in the main level, add a Sphere and rename it to `Sphere_BeamEnd`. Place it anywhere *but* the center of the level. Change its scale to `0.5`.

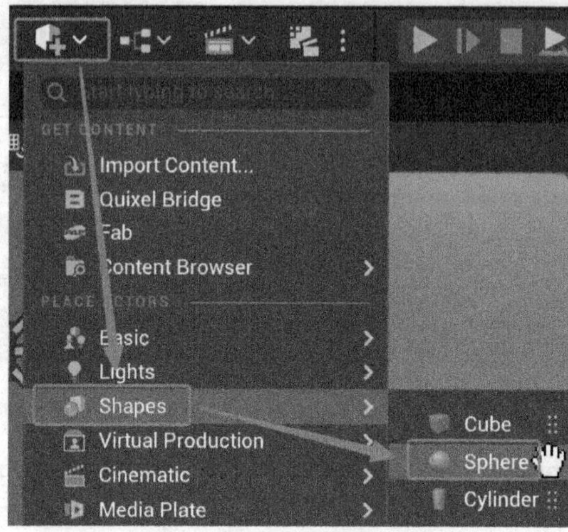

Figure 6.41 - Creating a basic Sphere

4. In the **Outliner**, select `NS_ElectricalArc`, raise it in the *Z* position. Then, in its **Details** panel, scroll down to the **User Parameters** section, in **Source Actor** select `Sphere_BeamEnd`**.** You'll see the electrical beam attached to the Sphere.

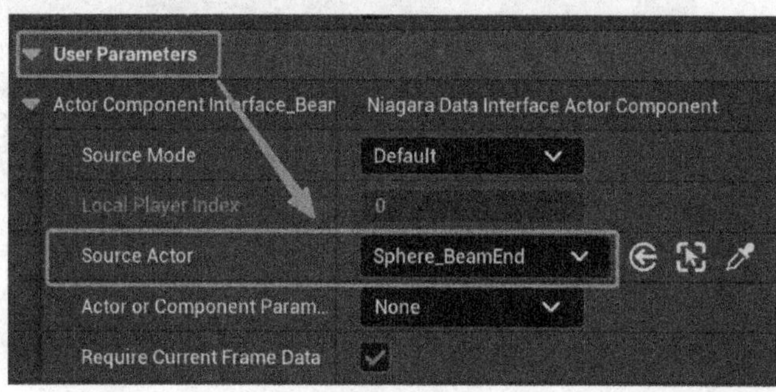

Figure 6.42 - Selecting the Sphere_BeamEnd

5. Move the sphere around, and the beam will follow along. Decrease the **Directional Light** to have a better view of the effect, as shown in *Figure 6.43*:

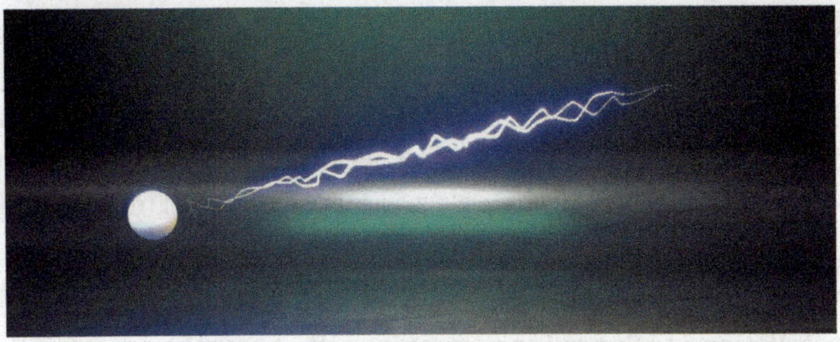

Figure 6.43 - Beam_End attached to a Sphere

6. Let's do the same for the **Beam Start.** Back in the Niagara Editor, select the **Beam Emitter Setup** module, right-click on the **Beam_End Scratch Dynamic Input**, copy, and paste onto **Beam_Start (Simulation Position)**. We are just copying/pasting the same Blueprint.
7. Again, using the drop-down arrow, convert it to a User Parameter. Just like in *step 3*, add another sphere and assign it to **Actor Component Interface_Beam Start.**

Once both ends are attached to separate Actors, the electrical arc will connect the two points, as shown in *Figure 6.44*:

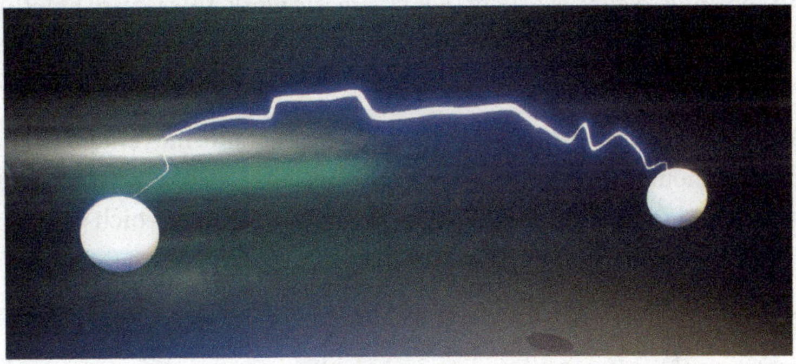

Figure 6.44 - Both ends are connected to a Sphere (Actor)

> Tip
>
> **Things to try**
>
> You can now tweak settings such as **Spawn Count, Beam Width, Jitter Position**, and **Color**. To have a curved beam, in the **Beam Emitter Setup**, enable **Beam Tangents.** Also, try disabling the **Update Beam** module to get a different look.

How it works...

In this recipe, you created a controlled electrical arc between two points using a Niagara beam setup. Unlike the lightning bolt from the previous recipe, this effect is designed to stay connected between two objects. This makes it useful for energy transfer, Sci-Fi machinery, magical power links, or any shot where electricity needs to travel from one point to another.

The **StaticBeam** emitter gives you a good starting point because it already behaves like a beam-style effect. The **Ribbon Renderer** draws the arc as a connected streak, while the **Ribbon Tessellation** and **Curve Tension** settings affect how sharp or smooth the beam appears. A *higher* curve tension can make the arc feel more jagged and electrical, while a *lower* value can make it feel softer and more controlled.

The **Beam Emitter Setup** controls the main start and end positions of the arc. By enabling **Absolute Beam End** and using **Beam Tangents**, you gave the beam a clearer direction and shape. The **Beam Width** curve gives the arc thickness in the middle and sharper edges at the ends, which helps the effect feel more like electrical energy rather than a simple line.

The scratch dynamic input and Blueprint setup are what make the arc more useful in a shot. Instead of manually typing a fixed **Beam End** value, the arc can read the position of another object in the level. This means the start and end points can be moved, adjusted, or animated, and the arc will continue to connect them. For cinematic work, this is very helpful because the effect can follow props, characters, or moving objects without having to rebuild the Niagara System each time.

The **Update Beam** and **Jitter Position** modules add the unstable movement that makes the arc feel alive. Electricity should not feel perfectly still, especially in close-up or dramatic shots. The short loop duration and random timing help the arc flicker quickly, which gives it a more energetic feel.

There's more...

So far in this recipe, we have created an electrical arc that connects two points using Niagara. The arc gives us the main energy connection, but it can still feel a little too clean on its own. To make the effect feel more active and believable, we will complement the arc with small spark particles along the beam.

Although optional, these sparks help sell the idea that the electricity is reacting with the objects in the scene, adding extra detail, movement, and cinematic energy to the shot. Let's begin:

1. In the Niagara Editor, for `NS_ElectricalArc`, right-click to add a **Minimal** emitter and rename it to `Sparks`. In the **Emitter State** module, change **Life Cycle Mode** to **Self** and set **Loop Duration** to `0.1`.

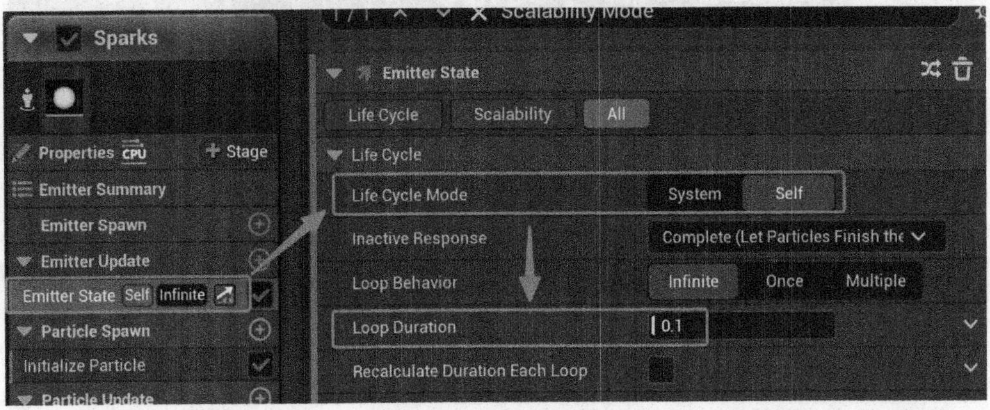

Figure 6.45 - Emitter State settings

2. In the **Initialize Particle** module, change **Lifetime Mode** to **Random**, set **Lifetime Min** to `0.1`, and **Lifetime Max** to `0.3`.
3. Set **Color Mode** to **Direct Set** and set **Color** to be the same as the beam, and for the **Sprite Size Mode**, change it to **Uniform** and set **Uniform Sprite Size** to `0.2`. This will create short-lived tiny particles.

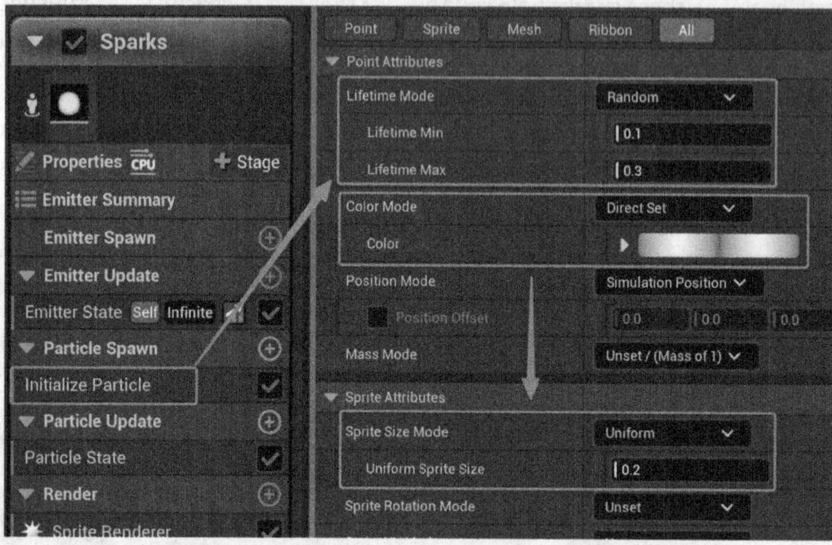

Figure 6.46 - Initialize Particle settings

4. Since we need to add these sparks along the electrical beam, we will need to make a reference to it in the **Sparks** emitter. In the **Emitter Update** section, add the **Spawn Particles from Other Emitter** module. Click **Fix issue**. This will also add a **Sample Particles from Other Emitter** module in the **Particle Spawn** section.

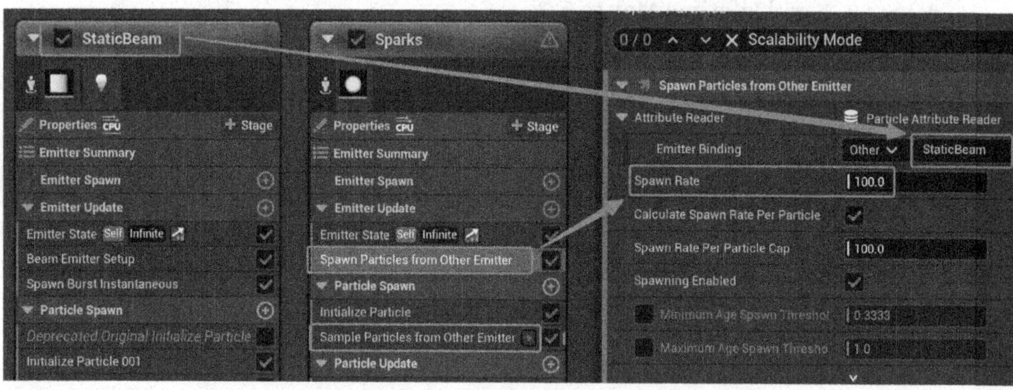

Figure 6.47 - Adding Spawn Particles from the Other Emitter module

5. For the **Spawn Particles from Other Emitter** module, in its **Emitter Binding**, type the name of the Beam Emitter: `StaticBeam` in this case. Then change the **Spawn Rate** to `100`, as shown in *Figure 6.47*.

6. For the **Sample Particles from Other Emitter** module, click **Fix issue**.

7. In the **Particle Spawn** section, add an **Add Velocity** module, change **Velocity Mode** to **From Point**, and change **Velocity Speed** to `100`.
8. To make the particles fall, in the **Particle Update** section, add a **Gravity Force** module. Then, add a **Scale Color** module and, for **Scale Alpha**, choose **Float from Curve** to make the particles fade away.

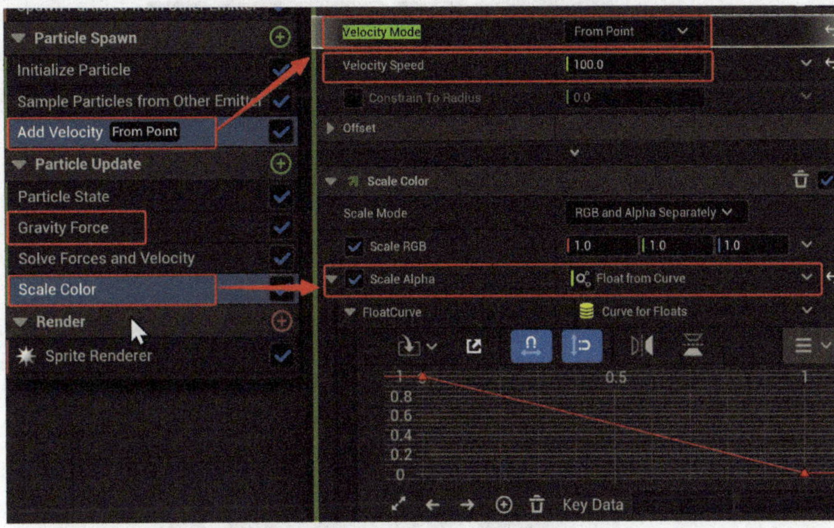

Figure 6.48 - Adding Add Velocity, Gravity Force, and Scale Color modules

9. You're done! As mentioned previously, you may tweak various properties for the look you're going for.

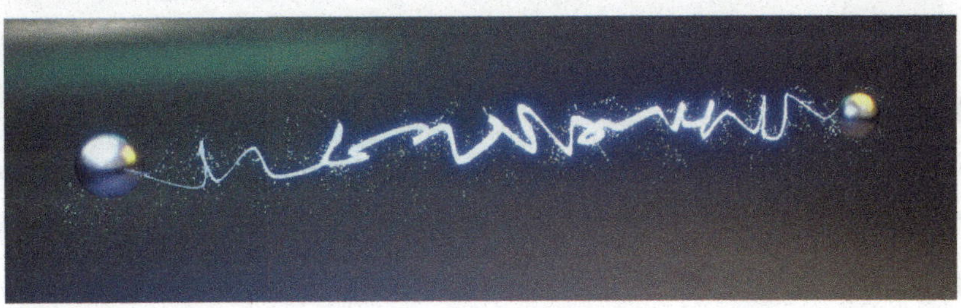

Figure 6.49 - The final look

Applying surface crackle/character sparks

In this recipe, you will create a lightning crackle effect where lightning and sparks appear around an animated Skeletal Mesh character. Instead of placing the crackle on a static surface, we will use the moving character as the surface for the electrical effect. This allows the lightning to feel connected to the body and follow the performance during the shot.

This type of effect is useful for magical attacks, Sci-Fi shock effects, power overloads, energy surges, or any cinematic moment where a character is being charged or hit by electricity. The goal is to create a controlled electrical layer that adds danger and energy without hiding the animation underneath.

Figure 6.50 shows a representation of the effect as follows:

Figure 6.50 - The outcome of this section

Getting ready

Before starting, you'll need to set up your test environment. Locate the `LV_VFX_Sandbox` from the **Content Browser**. This is the same level that we've been using throughout this book.

How to do it...

With the `LV_VFX_Sandbox` level open, implement these steps in the subsequent sections.

Building the electrical effect

In this section, we'll create the core Niagara System by sampling a Skeletal Mesh and generating electrical beams that travel across the character's surface:

1. In the `Niagara_Systems` folder, right-click and create a Niagara System. Choose the **Minimal** emitter when prompted to do so and save it as `NS_Electrocute`. Drag `NS_Electrocute` into the level.
2. Double-click to open the Niagara Editor. Rename the emitter as `Lightning 1`.

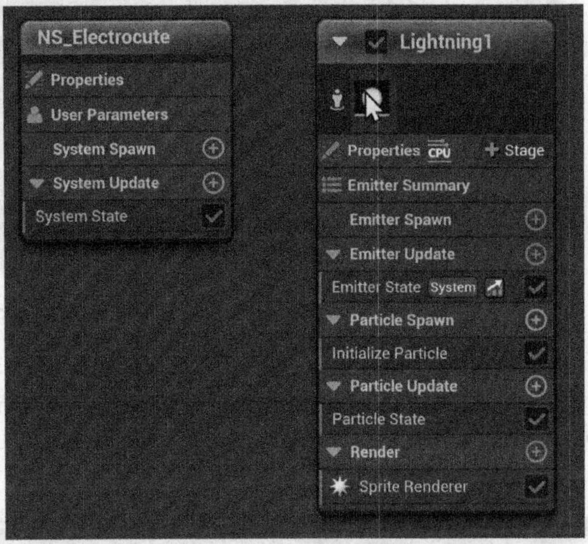

Figure 6.51 - Creating a Minimal emitter

3. In the **Emitter Properties** module, enable **Local Space** and **Determinism**. This will allow the emitter to move with the character without leaving particle traces behind.
4. In the **Emitter State** module, change **Life Cycle Mode** to **Self** and change **Loop Duration** to `0.1`.

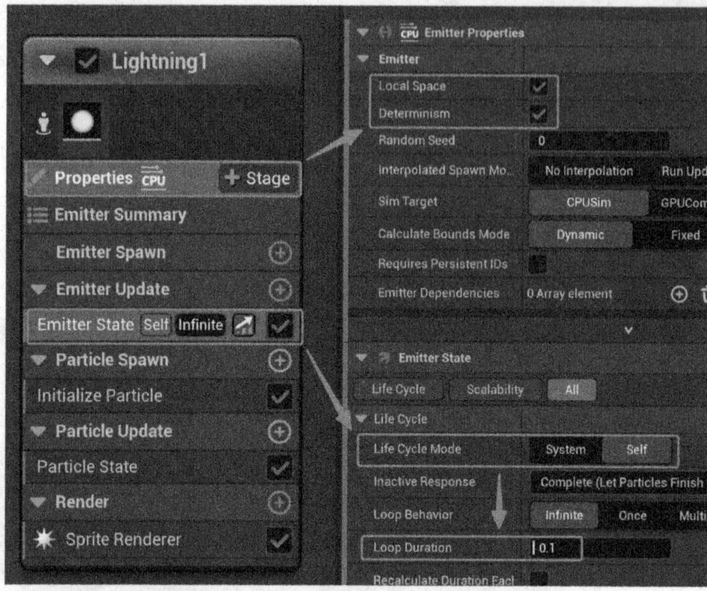

Figure 6.52 - Properties and Emitter State settings

5. Since we are creating a lightning crackle type effect on an animated character, in **Emitter Update**, add the **Sample Skeletal Mesh** module. Change **Source Mode** to **Attach Parent**. In **Preview Mesh**, select `SKM_Quinn_Simple` for both **Preview Mesh** and **Default Mesh**.

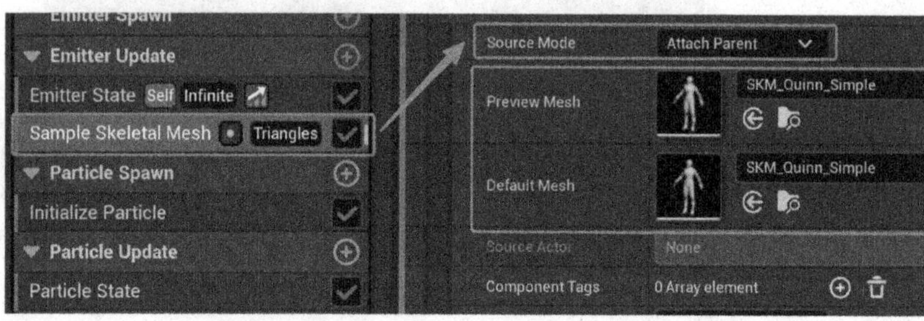

Figure 6.53 - Adding Sample Skeletal Mesh module

> **Note**
>
> If `SKM_Quinn_Simple` does not appear in the dropdown, you'll have to use the **Add Feature** or **Content Pack** from the **Content Browser**. This topic was covered in the *Creating a snow kick-up burst (ground interaction)* recipe in *Chapter 5*.

6. Still in the same module, scroll down to the **Sampling** section, change **Mesh Sampling Type** to **Surface (Triangles)**; **Triangle Sampling Mode** to **Random (All Triangles)**; and **Random Evaluation** to **Every Frame**. This is the best choice for making maximum lightning beams.

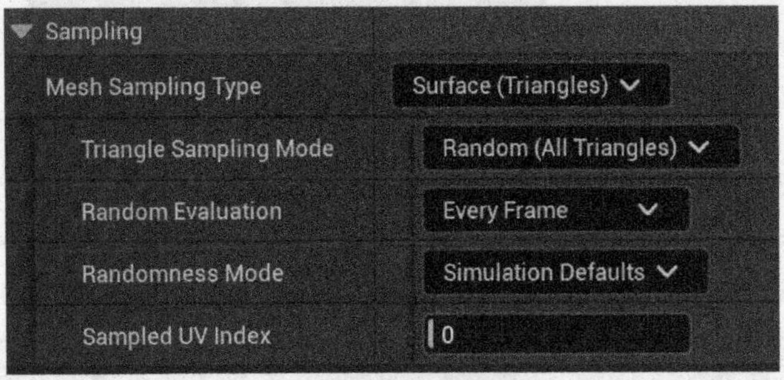

Figure 6.54 - Sampling settings

7. For us to be able to select any Skeletal Mesh at the main level, let's convert the Skeletal Mesh selection into a User Parameter. In the same module, click the dropdown for the **Skeletal Mesh** section and select **Read from new User parameter**. The User Parameter will now appear in the **User Parameters** tab in the lower left of the editor.

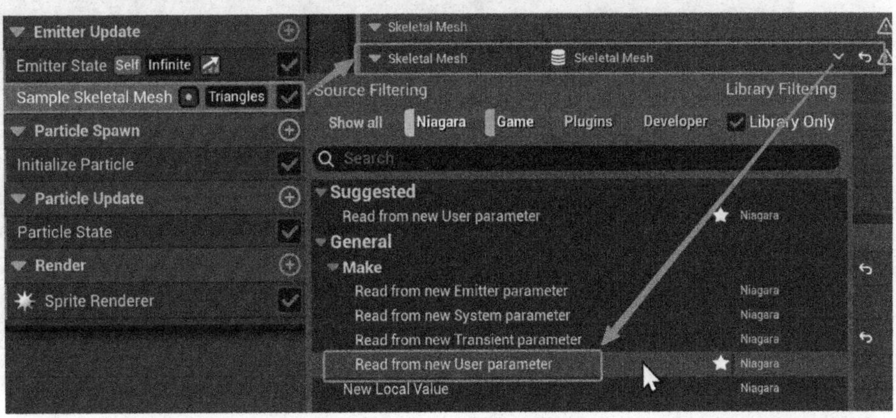

Figure 6.55 - Converting to User Parameter

8. Our effect requires the lightning to exit from one part of the character's body and enter another part of the body; as such, we will have to duplicate the **Sample Skeletal Mesh** by selecting the module and copying with *Ctrl* + *C* and pasting with *Ctrl* + *V*. You should now have **Sample Skeletal Mesh 001** in the emitter.

9. In the **Render** section, add a **Ribbon Renderer** module. In the **Emitter Updat**e section, add a **Beam Emitter Setup** module.

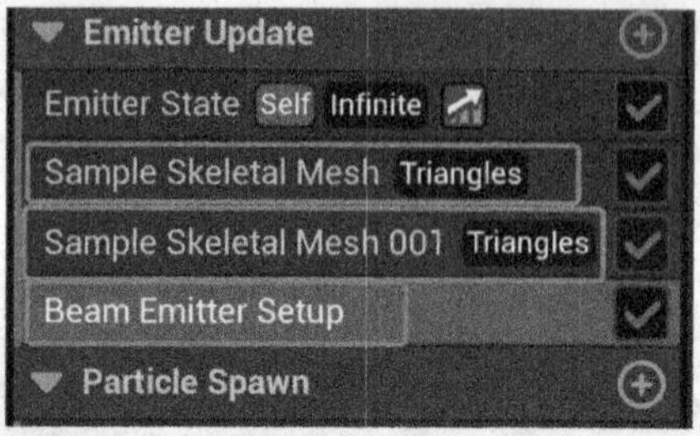

Figure 6.56 - Duplicating the Sample Skeletal Mesh module

10. In the **Emitter Setup** module, for **Beam Start**, click the dropdown arrow and select **Link Inputs | Emitter | SAMPLE SKELETAL MESH SampledPosition**.

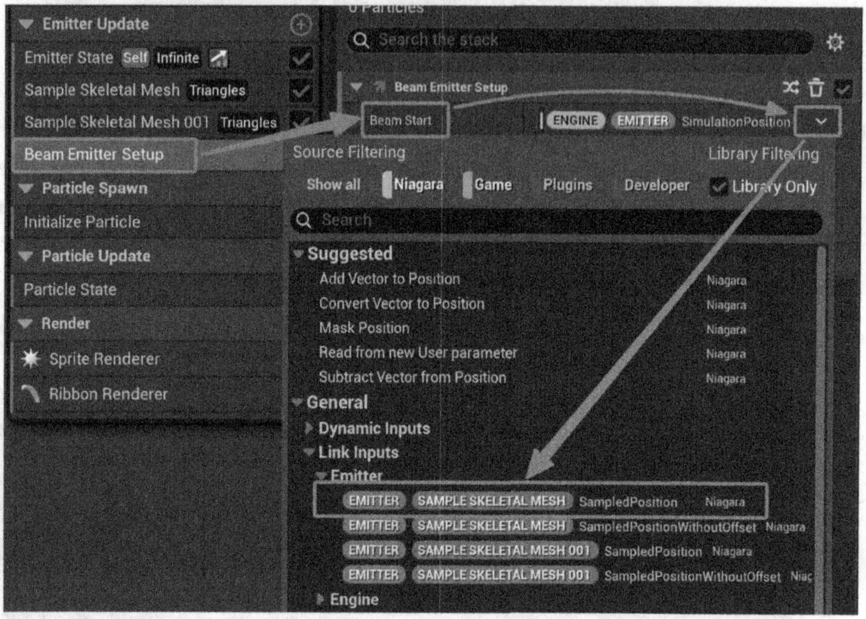

Figure 6.57 - Linking the Beam Start to the Skeletal Mesh

11. Now let's repeat the same process with **Beam End**. Click the dropdown arrow for **Beam End**, select **Link Inputs | Emitter | Sample Skeletal Mesh 001** Sample Position. Then enable **Absolute Beam End**.

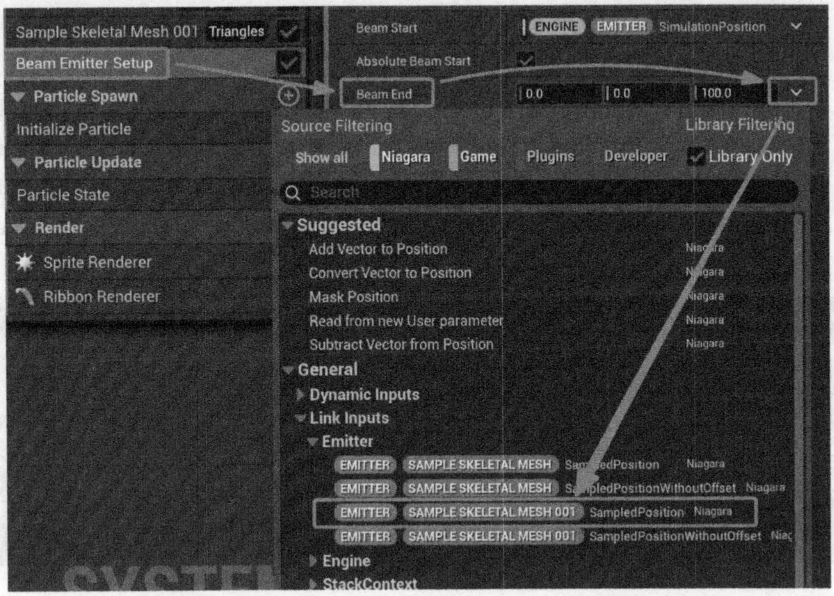

Figure 6.58 - Linking the Beam End to the Skeletal Mesh

12. Again, in the **Emitter Update**, add a **Spawn Burst Instantaneous** module. Using the dropdown arrow for **Spawn Count**, select **Random Range Int** and change **Minimum** to 5 and **Maximum** to 15. Drag it underneath the **Beam Emitter Setup** module.

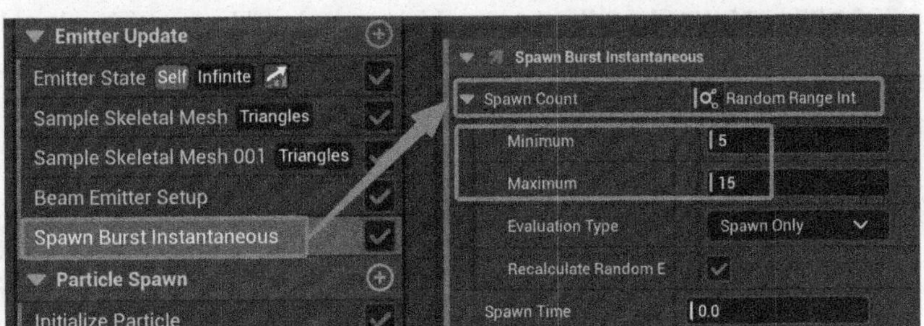

Figure 6.59 - Spawn Burst Instantaneous settings

13. In the **Particle Spawn** module, select **Initialize Particle** module, set the following:
    - **Lifetime** to `0.25`
    - **Color Mode** to **Direct Set**
    - **Set color** to **R** = `0`, **G** = `100`, **B**=`80`

   - **Sprite Size Mode** to **Uniform**
   - **Uniform Sprite Size** to `2.0`

14. In the **Particle Spawn** section, add **Spawn Beam** and **Beam Width** modules. For **Beam Width**, using the dropdown arrow, select **Float from Curve** and select the **Ramp Up Down** curve. Increase the **Value** properties for each end to `0.3`. This will give a beam-shaped thickness in the middle. You may experiment with the other curves, too.

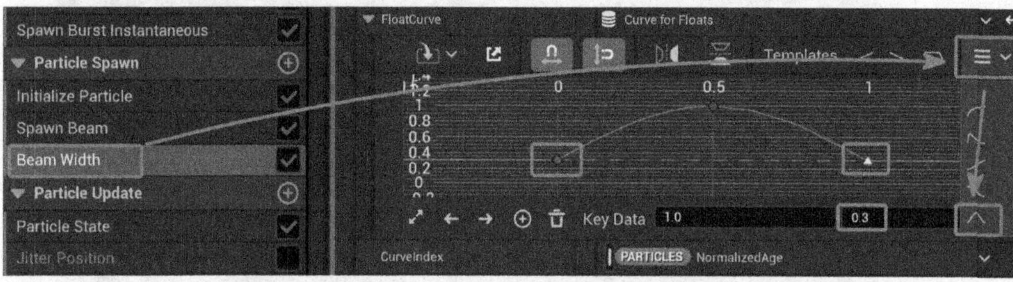

Figure 6.60 - Setting Beam Width thickness

15. For the **CurveIndex**, click the dropdown arrow and search for `RibbonLinkOrder`. Change **Scale Curve** to `2.0` for a thicker beam effect. Uncheck **Sprite Renderer**.

> **Note**
>
> **RibbonLinkOrder** tells Niagara which order the ribbon particles should be connected in. In a **Ribbon Renderer**, particles with the same **RibbonID** are joined together to form one continuous ribbon.

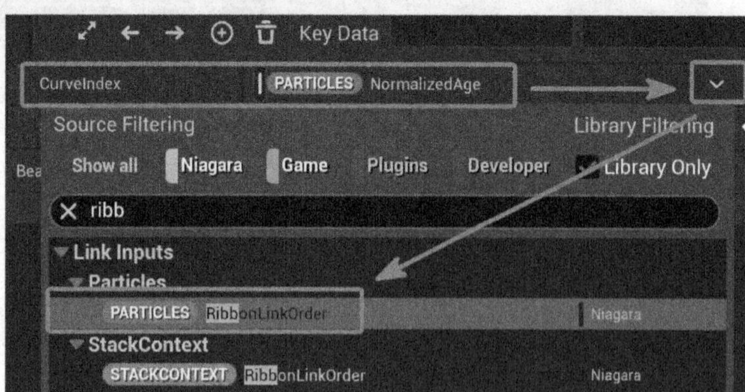

Figure 6.61 - Adding RibbonLinkOrder

16. In the **Particle Update** section, add a **Jitter Position** module. You'll now have some squiggly dancing lines in the Preview window that do not look like lightning. Let's change that. Click the dropdown arrow for **Jitter Amount** and select **Float from Curve**, choose the **Ramp Up Down** curve, then shape the curve as you did in *step 14*.

17. Let's test the effect we have created so far. In the main level, from the **Characters | Mannequin | Meshes** folder, drag `SK_Mannequin` into the level and reset its **Location** to `0,0,0`.

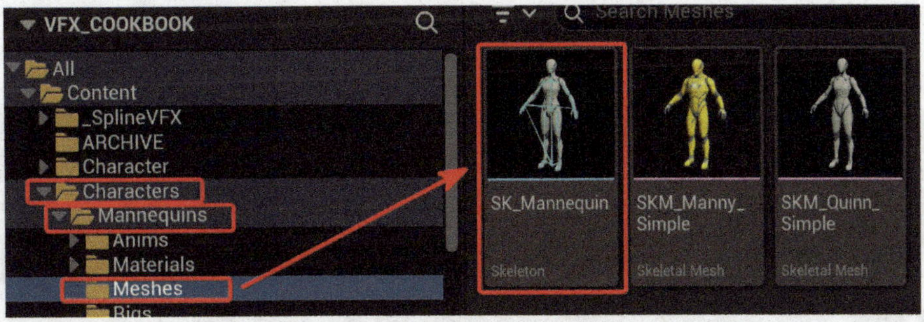

Figure 6.62 - Accessing the SK_Mannequin character

18. Drag `NS_Electrocute` into the level and reset its location to `0,0,0`. You'll now have a sneak peek at how this effect will present itself. We're not done just yet; there is more to learn. Let's continue.

Figure 6.63 - Testing the effect on a character

If you move the character away from its location, you'll realize they are not connected. We will solve that in the next steps by using an animated character that was sourced from **Mixamo** (`https://www.mixamo.com/`). The cool thing about this effect is that it will work with any character that has a skeleton and a root bone. An explanation of what a root bone is can be found in the *See also* section.

Attaching the effect to an animated character

Now you'll attach the Niagara effect to an animated character using an **Animation Notify** so it plays at the correct moment during the performance. Let's continue:

1. Remove `SKM_Quinn_Simple` and `NS_Electrocute` from the **Outliner**. In the **Character** | **Exo_Gray** folder, double-click on the `Standing_Taunt_Battlecry_Exo_Gray_Anim` Animation Sequence.

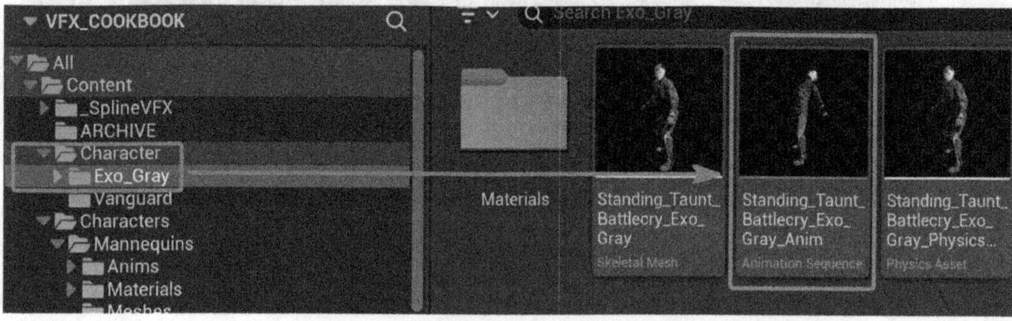

Figure 6.64 - Accessing the Exo Gray character folder

2. In this Skeletal Mesh Animation Editor, you now have an animated character: Exo Gray doing a battle cry. We will need to assign the Niagara System we made to this character. In fact, its workflow was already covered in the *Creating a snow kick-up burst (ground interaction)* recipe in *Chapter 5*.

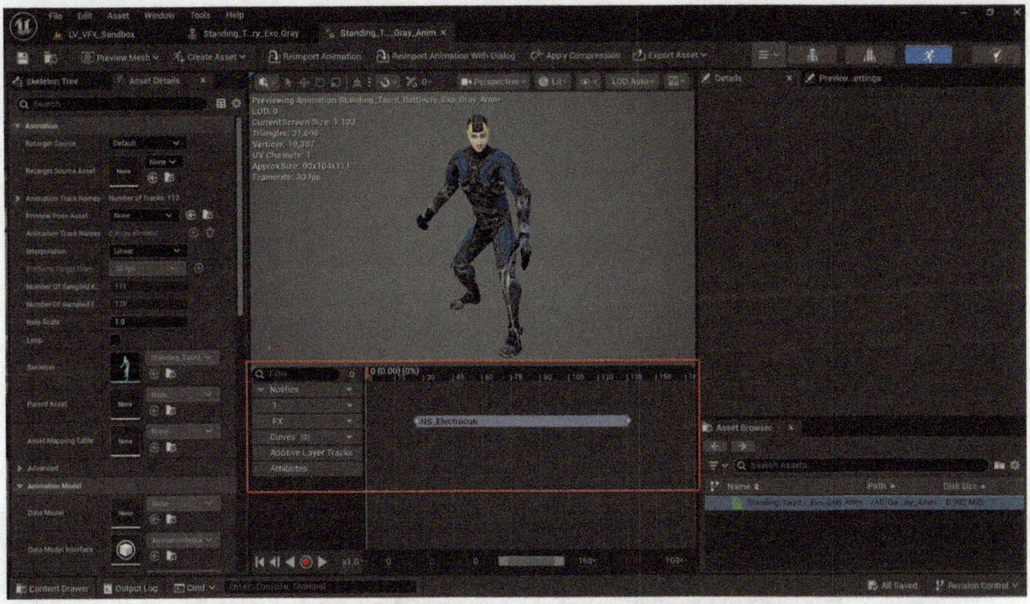

Figure 6.65 - The Skeletal Mesh Animation Editor interface

3. In the timeline panel, click the dropdown arrow for the **Notifies Track** and choose **Add Notify Track**. Rename the track as FX.

Figure 6.66 - Adding the Notify Track

4. On the **FX** track, right-click on the timeline, choose **Add Notify State | Timed Niagara Effect**.

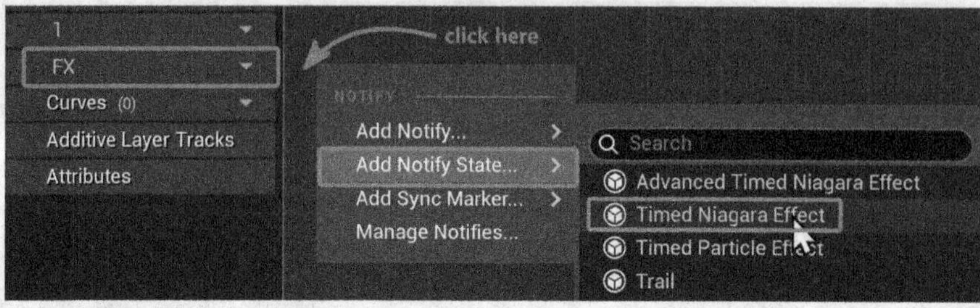

Figure 6.67 - Adding the Timed Niagara Effect

5. You'll now notice two keyframes. Drag the start keyframe to approximately Frame **26** and the end keyframe to Frame **111**. This placement will depend on the animation you are working with. The beginning keyframe is where Exo starts to open his arms to release energy/lightning, and the effect we make will fade toward the end.

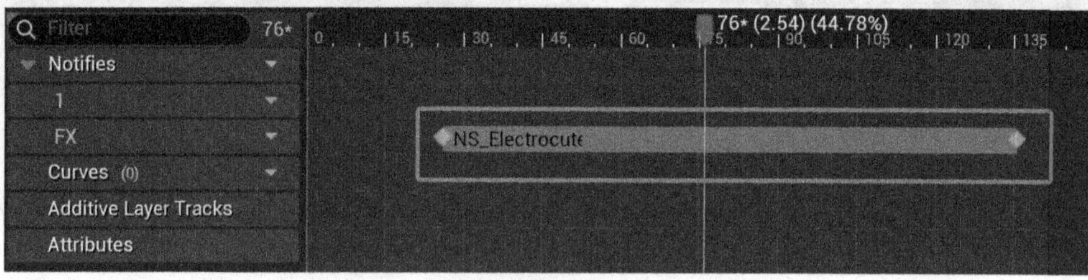

Figure 6.68 - Setting the first and last keyframe

6. Now let's add the effect. Select the *blue* **FX** track, in the **Details** panel | **Niagara System**, and choose `NS_Electrocute`.

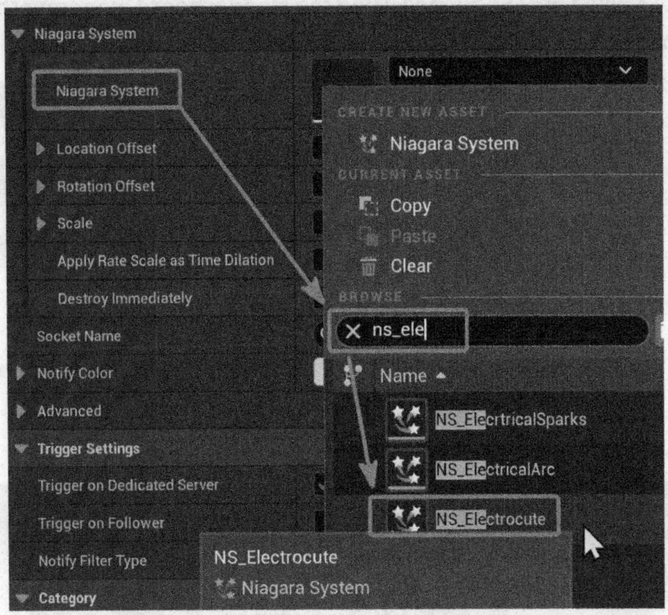

Figure 6.69 - Choosing the NS_Electrocute effect

7. In the **Socket Name**, type `Root`. This will attach the Niagara effect to the character's root bone, so if the character moves, the effect will follow. Click on **Save**.

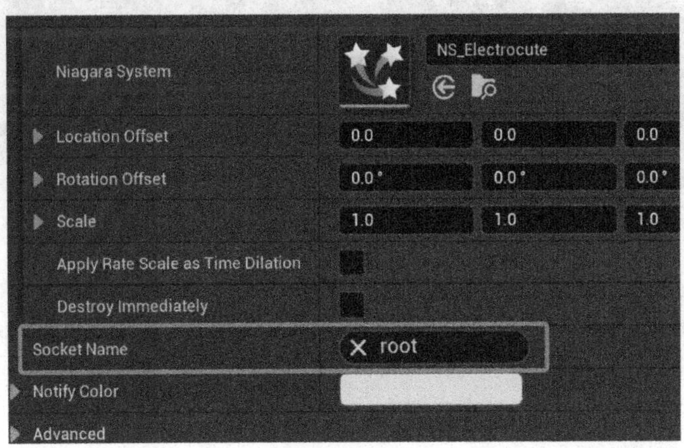

Figure 6.70 - Adding root to the socket name

8. Back in the main level, from the `Character` folder, add `Exo_Gray` to the level, rotate him to face forward (90 degrees on the *Z*).

9. Create a new **Level Sequence** using the **clapperboard** icon from the top menu bar, rename it as `LS_Electrocute`, and save it in the `Sequences` folder.

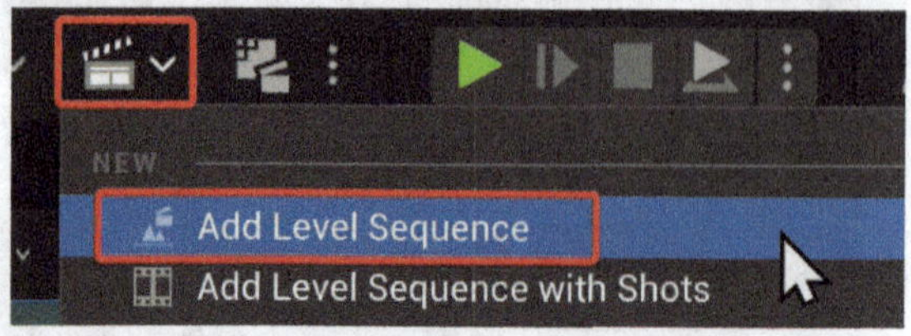

Figure 6.71 - Creating a Level Sequence

10. Drag Exo Gray into the Sequence. Click the + sign on the **Animation** track and choose `Standing_Taunt_Battlecry_Exo_Gray_Anim`. Drag the end of the timeline *red* bar to the end of the animation.

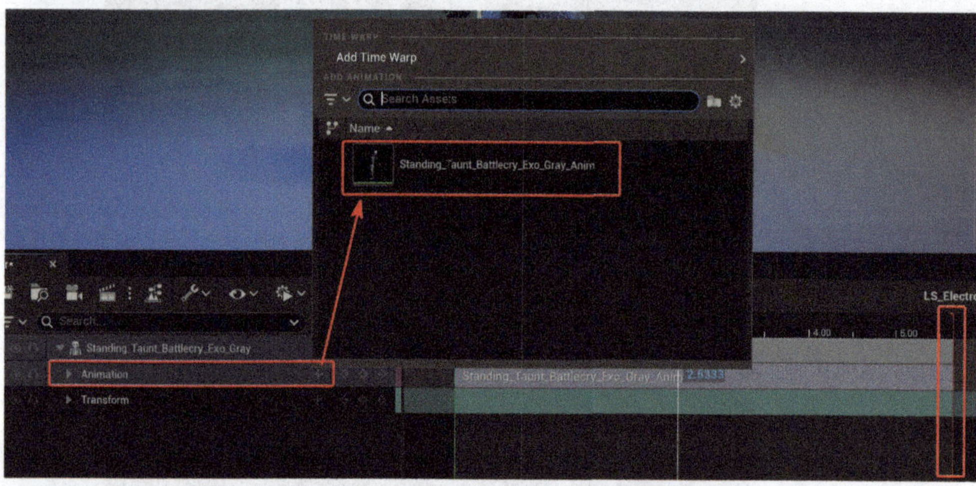

Figure 6.72 - Adding the Character Animation

11. Tap the *spacebar* or click the **play** button, and you'll now have Exo Gray with a lightning bolt coming out of him, but we're not done yet. We can make this ten times better.

Figure 6.73 - The preliminary effect

To avoid uniformity, let's add a secondary lightning with different attributes.

Enhancing the final effect

Let's make the effect look more dynamic and believable. Follow these steps:

1. Back in the Niagara Editor, duplicate **Lightning 1** and rename it to `Lightning 2`, and change the following:
    - **Spawn Burst Instantaneous Minimum =25**, **Maximum =40** – this will give the beams a higher resolution, thus more curves.
    - In **Beam Width**, reduce **Scale Curve** to `1.0` to have slightly thinner beams.
2. As a finisher, let's add some sparks. In the Niagara Editor, right-click and add a **Minimal** emitter and rename it to `Sparks`.
3. In **Properties**, enable **Local Space** and **Determinism.**
4. Select **Emitter State**, change **Life Cycle Mode** to **Self,** and set **Loop Duration** to `0.1`.
5. In the **Emitter Update**, add **Spawn Particles from Other Emitter** module (this is the same workflow we learned in the earlier section in this chapter). Click **Fix issue**, and in the **Emitter Binding**, type `Lightning1`.

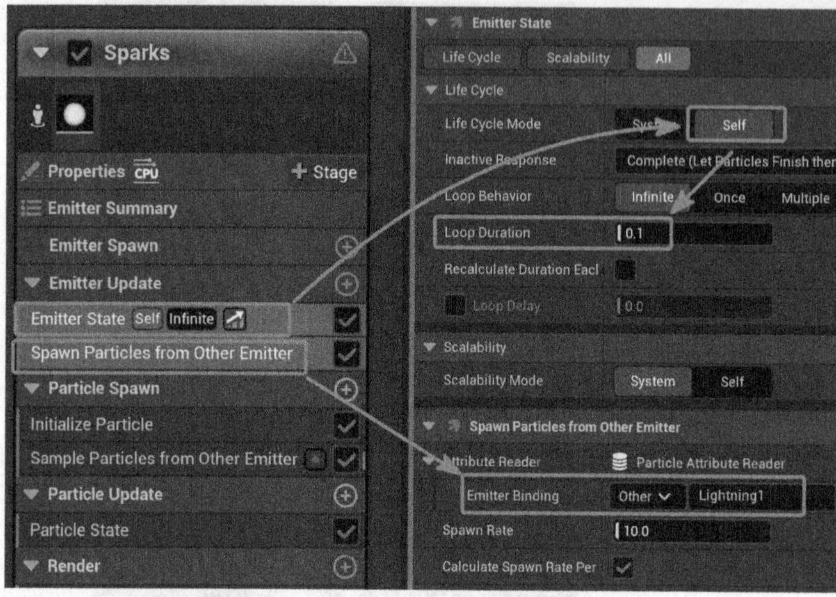

Figure 6.74 - Emitter State and Spawn Particles from Other Emitter settings

6. Select **Initialize Particle** and set the following:
   - **Lifetime Mode** to **Random**, **Lifetime Min** to `0.8`, and **Lifetime Max** to `1.5`
   - **Color Mode** to **Direct Set** and use the same color as the beams
   - **Sprite Size Mode** to **Random Uniform**, **Uniform Sprite Size Min** to `0.2`, and **Uniform Sprite Size Max** to `0.5`
7. In the **Particle Spawn** section, add the **Add Velocity** module. Click **Fix issue,** change **Velocity Mode** to **From Point.** Set **Velocity Speed** to `200`**.** For **Origin Offset**, change the **Z** value to `100`. This will place the particle at the center of the Character's body.

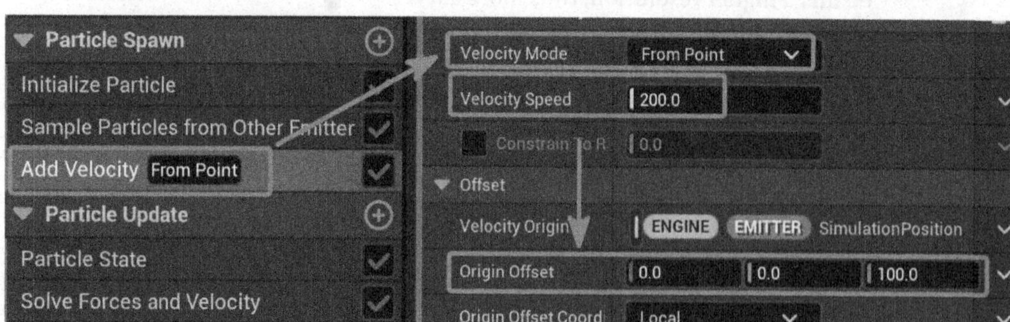

Figure 6.75 - Add Velocity settings

8. To make the particle fall to the floor, in the **Particle Update** section, add a **Gravity Force** module. Now let's add collision.
9. In the same section, add the **Collision** module and change **Restitution** to `0.2`. The final effect should resemble *Figure 6.76*:

Figure 6.76 - The completed effect

How it works...

In this recipe, you created a lightning crackle effect that follows an animated Skeletal Mesh character. Instead of placing electricity on a static surface, the character becomes the moving surface for the effect. This makes the lightning feel connected to the body and allows it to support the performance rather than sitting separately in the scene.

The Niagara System uses multiple emitters to create the final look. The lightning emitters provide short electrical arcs around the character, while the spark emitter adds small bursts of energy. Together, these layers make the effect feel more active and dangerous. The lightning gives the main electrical shape, while the sparks add finer detail and flickering motion.

Local Space is important in this setup because the effect needs to move with the character. If the particles were left behind in **World Space**, the electricity could separate from the body as the animation plays. By keeping the effect attached to the animated character, the electricity appears to belong to the performance.

The **Sample Skeletal Mesh** module is the key part of the setup because it allows Niagara to use the Skeletal Mesh as a source for the effect. Instead of spawning particles from a simple point or box shape, the particles can appear around the character's body. This helps the electrocution effect feel more natural because the energy is distributed across the animated mesh.

The **Timed Niagara Effect** notify is used to control when the electrocution begins and ends during the animation. This is more precise than simply placing the effect in the level and hoping the timing lines up. By adding the Niagara effect directly to the animation **Notify** track, you can trigger it at the moment the character starts releasing or receiving energy, then fade or stop it when the performance ends.

Using the **Root** socket attaches the Niagara System to the character's root bone. This gives the effect a stable reference point, so it follows the character as the animation moves. The root bone acts as the main foundation of the Skeletal Mesh, which makes it useful when attaching effects that need to stay with the whole character instead of a specific hand, foot, or weapon.

There's more...

So far in this recipe, we have created a lightning crackle effect that follows an animated Skeletal Mesh character, using lightning arcs and spark accents to make the electricity feel attached to the body.

To finish the effect and give it a more cinematic impact, we will now add a **Light Renderer**. This will allow the electrical particles to cast small flashes of light, helping the effect illuminate the character and feel more integrated into the shot. Follow along these steps:

1. Open the Niagara Editor for `NS_Electrocute`.
2. In the **Render** section for **Lightning1**, add a **Light Renderer** module.
3. Do the same for **Lightning2** and the **Sparks** emitters.
4. Compile and save, and you're done!

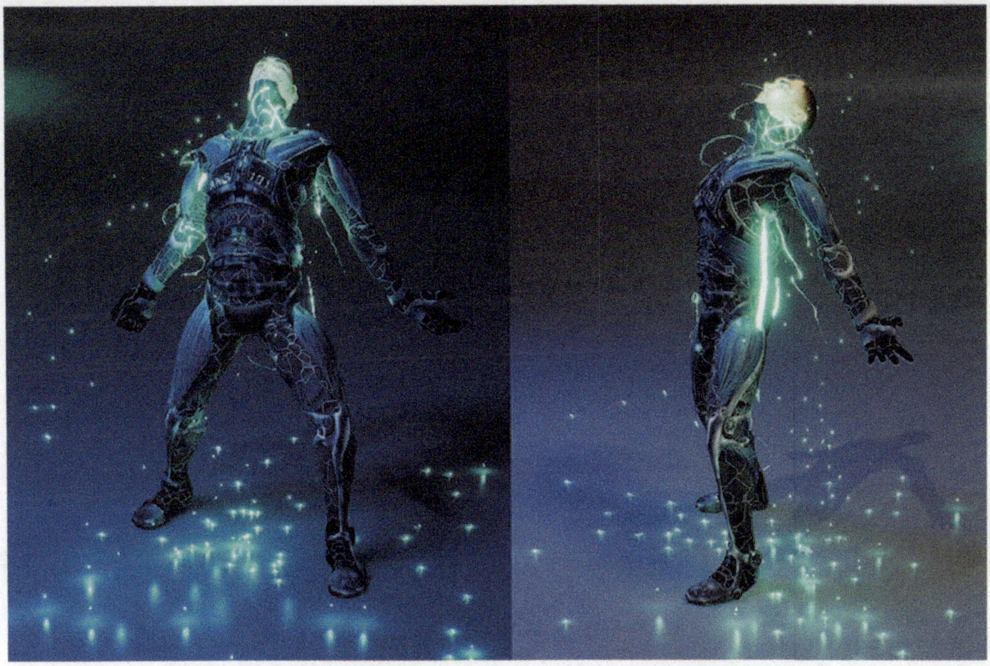

Figure 6.77 - The completed effect with the Light Renderer module

See also

For more information about the **root bone** and how it relates to character movement, refer to Unreal Engine's **Root Motion** documentation: `https://dev.epicgames.com/documentation/unreal-engine/root-motion-in-unreal-engine`. This is useful for understanding how the root bone acts as the main reference point for a Skeletal Mesh and why it matters when attaching or timing effects to an animated character.

7

Niagara Fluids for Cinematic Volume Effects

In this chapter, we will move from sprite-based Niagara effects into **Niagara Fluids**, which allows us to create volume-based effects such as fog, smoke, fire, gas, and explosions. Unlike flat sprites or texture cards, Niagara Fluids simulates density, heat, velocity, and motion in 3D space, giving the effect greater depth and presence in the scene.

We will primarily use the **Grid3D_Gas_Master_Emitter**, which serves as a 3D simulation container. A simple Niagara emitter can feed particles into this container, and the **Grid3D_Gas_Master_Emitter** turns that source data into volumetric fog, smoke, fire, or explosive motion.

In this chapter, you will create low-lying volumetric fog, a cinematic explosion, a high-rising storm cloud, and fire on Static Meshes. These recipes will give you practical volume-based workflows that can be reused in cinematic VFX shots and will also prepare you for the destruction effects in the next chapter.

Therefore, we'll cover the following recipes in this chapter:

- Creating low-lying volumetric fog with object collision
- Building a cinematic explosion using Niagara Fluids
- Creating a high-rising volumetric storm cloud using Niagara Fluids
- Applying fire to Static Meshes using Niagara Fluids

Technical requirements

Before starting this recipe, ensure the following are set up:

1. Make sure **Unreal Engine 5.6** is installed. Refer to *Chapter 1* for setup details. If you are using a different version of Unreal Engine, some settings, interface options, or results may vary.
2. A project with **Niagara**, **Niagara Sim Caching**, and **Niagara Fluids** plugins enabled.
3. Maintain the folder structure to keep the assets organized, as shown below:
    - `Content`
        - `Niagara_Systems`
        - `Sequences`
        - `Textures`
        - `Materials`
        - `MRQ`

You can download the example project for this book by following the instructions in the *Download the example code/resource files* section in the *Preface* of this book.

The complete example project is included in the downloadable code/resource bundle.

> **Note**
>
> Niagara Fluids can be more demanding than regular sprite-based Niagara effects because the simulation is processed on the GPU. For best results, use a higher-end PC with a capable graphics card, especially when working with 3D gas, smoke, fire, or liquid simulations. If performance becomes slow, reduce the simulation size, lower the resolution, or work with shorter preview ranges while building the effect.

Creating low-lying volumetric fog with object collisions

This recipe is designed as a simple introduction to Niagara Fluids. You will create a simple, low-lying fog effect using Niagara Fluids. In earlier chapters, we created atmospheric effects using sprites, cards, UV textures, and transparent materials. Those methods are useful, fast, and easy to art-direct, but they are still mostly flat visual layers. They can suggest fog very effectively, but they do not behave like a real volume inside the scene.

Niagara Fluids gives us a different approach. Instead of using flat sprite particles, we can create volume-based fog that has depth, thickness, and movement within 3D space. This allows the fog to interact naturally with the environment, especially when it moves around objects, reacts to collisions, and catches light in a more dimensional way. It can be more expensive to simulate and render, but it gives a richer cinematic result when used carefully.

Niagara Fluids is the better choice when the effect needs real volume, depth, lighting interaction, collision, or movement through 3D space, such as close-up fog, rolling smoke, fire, explosions, or hero atmospheric shots. For simpler background haze or distant smoke, sprite-based Niagara effects may be faster and easier to control, but Niagara Fluids gives a more dimensional result when the shot needs it.

We will keep the setup focused on a low ground fog effect so you can understand the basic idea without getting lost in a complex simulation. This recipe introduces Niagara Fluids **3D Gas** basics, density, dissipation, fog movement, collision with simple 3D objects, lighting through volume, and the difference between sprite-based fog and true volumetric fog.

Figure 7.1 - The outcome of this section

Getting ready

For this recipe, we will use the **Basic Level Template** that comes with Unreal Engine 5. This keeps the scene simple so we can focus on building, timing, and previewing the effect without extra distractions. Once the effect is working, you can place it into any cinematic scene and trigger it from **Sequencer** at the exact frame needed.

How to do it...

Let's start by creating a new basic level:

1. Go to **File** | **New Level**. From the pop-up panel, choose the **Basic** template, and click **Create**. Save the level as `LV_GroundFog`.

2. Press the *G* key to hide all the overlay icons. In the `Niagara_Systems` folder, right-click and choose **Niagara System**. From the pop-up panel, search for `Minimal` emitter, and click **Create**. Rename it to `NF_GroundFog` (NF = Niagara Fluids).

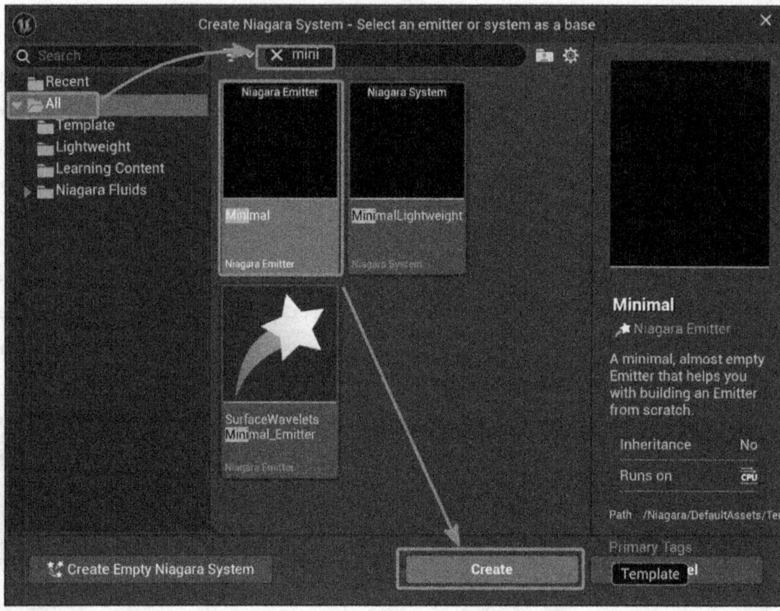

Figure 7.2 - Creating the Minimal emitter

3. Drag `NF_GroundFog` into the level and double-click to open the Niagara Editor. This is the same editor we've been using throughout this book.
4. In the next few steps, we'll configure the **Minimal** emitter. In the **Properties** module, enable **Local Space** and **Determinism**. Set **Sim Target** to **GPUCompute Sim**. Set **Calculate Bounds Mode** to **Fixed**. We will be utilizing the GPU processing power to create this effect.
5. In **Emitter Update**, add the **Spawn Rate** module and set the **Spawn Rate** to `500`.
6. Select the **Initialize Particle** module, set **Lifetime** to `1.0`, and **Sprite Size Mode** to **Uniform**, as well as **Uniform Sprite Size** to `2.0`.
7. In the **Particle Spawn** section, add a **Shape Location** module. Change **Shape Primitive** to **Box/Plane**. Adjust **Box Size** to **X** = `20`, **Y** = `500`, **Z** = `100`.
8. In the same section, add the **Add Velocity** module, and click **Fix issue**. Set **Velocity** to **X** = `50`, **Y** = `0`, **Z** = `0`. In the Preview panel, you now have particles moving in the X (*red arrow*) direction, as shown in *Figure 7.3*:

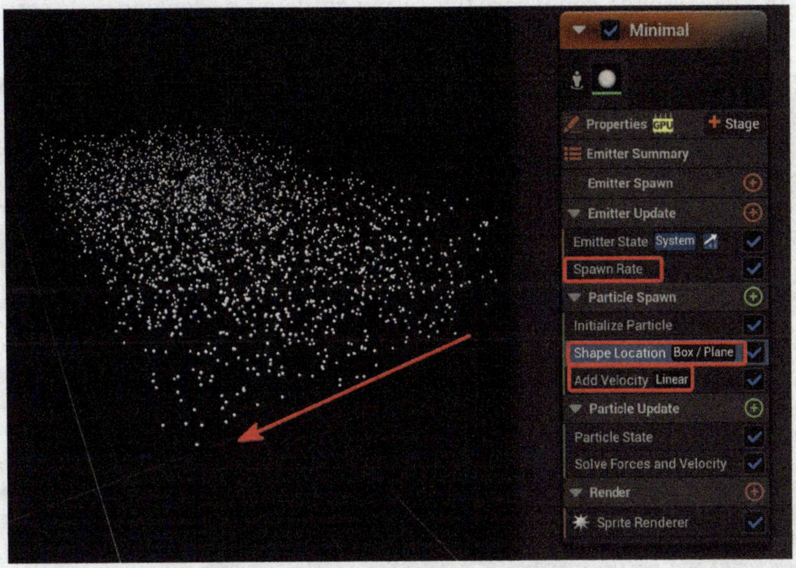

Figure 7.3 - Setting up the Minimal emitter

We are using the sprite emitter as a source to drive the fluid simulation. The particles from this emitter act as small moving emitters that feed density and motion into the Niagara Fluids gas emitter, helping the fog spread and move through the scene instead of remaining static. Let's continue:

1. In the **Particle Update** section, add **Set Fluid Source Attributes**. This will set the default attributes used within the fluid/gas simulation sourcing modules. Leave its properties at default for now.
2. Extend the timeline to **20** seconds to have a longer preview of the effect.

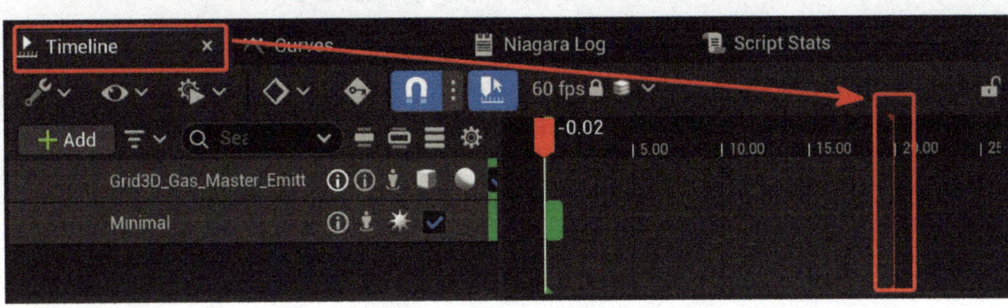

Figure 7.4 - Extending the timeline

3. Right-click anywhere in the node panel, select **Add Emitter**, and search for `Master`. Select the **Grid3D_Gas_Master_Emitter**. Click **Add**.

In a few seconds, you'll have this seemingly daunting-looking node appear in the editor. The preview pane will show dense smoke belching out of a sphere.

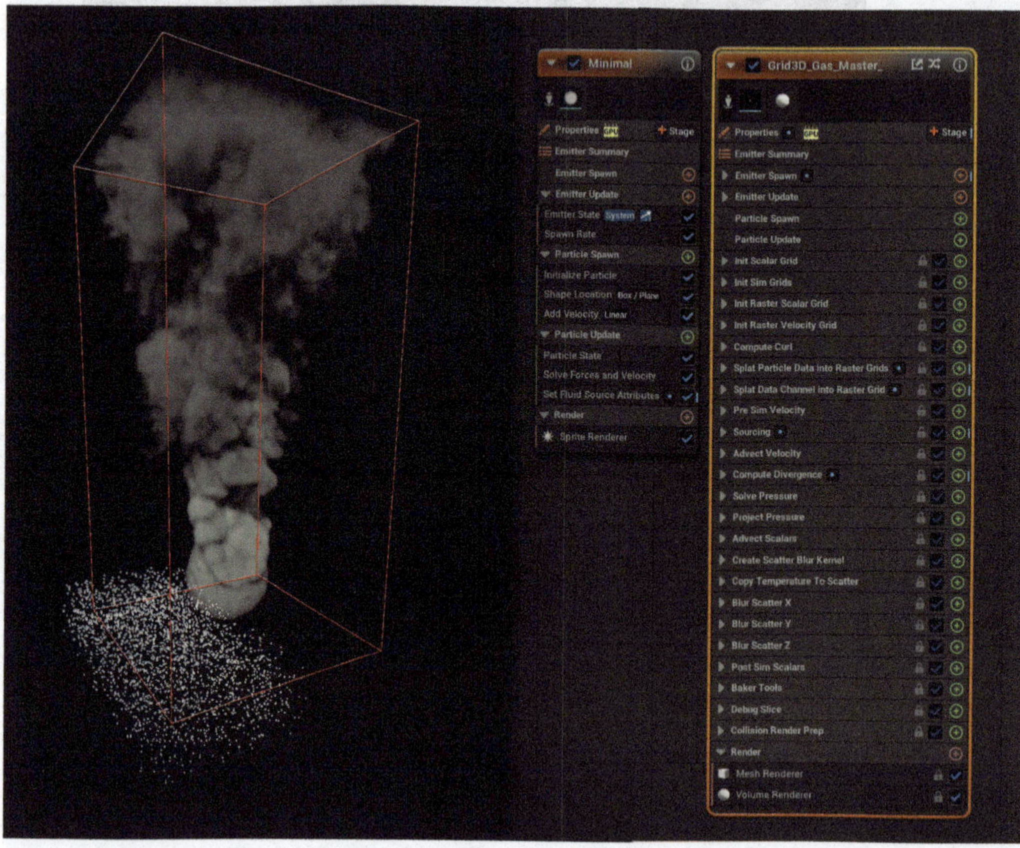

Figure 7.4 - The Grid3D_Gas_Master_Emitter

4. Don't be intimidated by the complexity of the node; we will only need *one module* to create the ground fog effect. In the **Grid3D_Gas_Master_Emitter** node, select the **Emitter Summary** module. You'll notice the following tabs: **Simulation**, **Source**, **Forces**, **Collisions**, and **Render**. These are the only attributes we are interested in.

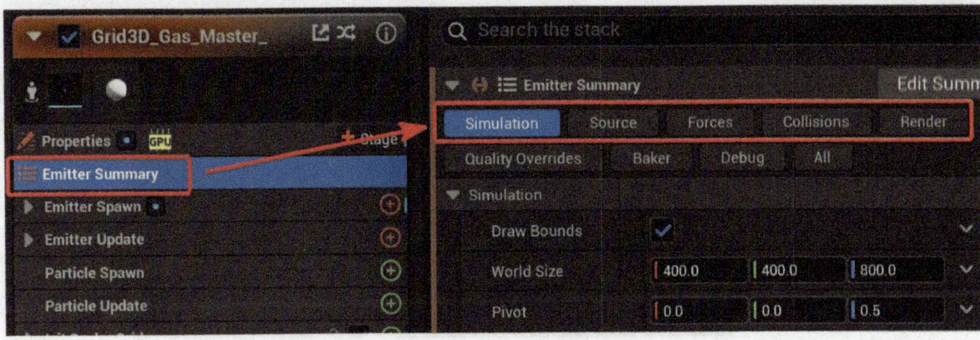

Figure 7.5 - Accessing the Emitter Summary tabs

5. First, let's reshape the **Draw Bounds** box (*red* box) to have a wider flat box. In the **Emitter Summary** module, select the **Simulation** tab. For **World Size**, set **X** = `1500`, **Y** = `500`, **Z** = `500`. Keep an eye on the Preview panel as we make changes.

6. The Sphere and Sprites are right in the middle of the box. Let's push them to the far side of the box. For **Pivot** set, **X** = `0.5`, **Y** = `0`, **Z** = `0.5`. The Sphere and Sprites are now pushed to the other end of the box.

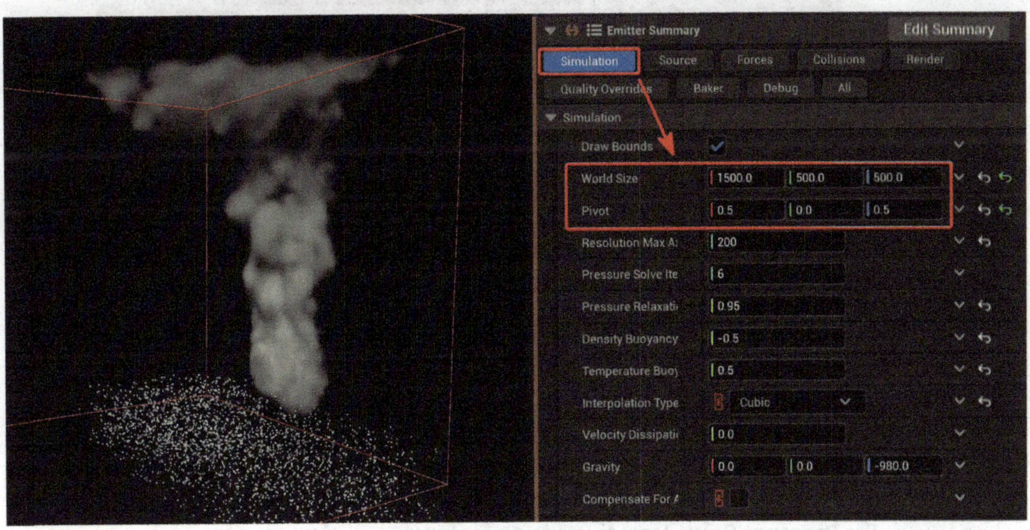

Figure 7.6 - Setting the Simulation tab

7. Now let's assign the **Minimal** emitter as the source of smoke/gas. In the **Source** tab, open the **Sphere Source** section and uncheck **Enable**. The Sphere will now disappear. Under the **Particle Source** section, for **Particle Source Type**, change to **Emitter**.

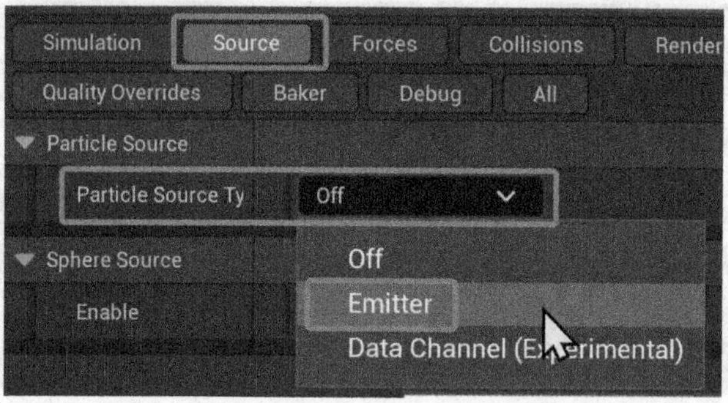

Figure 7.7 - Setting the Source tab

8. More properties will be revealed. In the **Particle Reader** section for **Emitter Binding**, delete the **Grid3D_Gas_Master_Emitter** and replace it with **Minimal**. This is the name of the sprite emitter we created earlier.

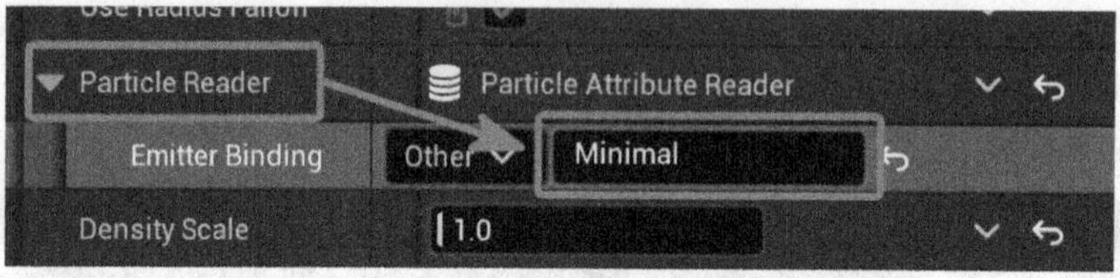

Figure 7.8 - Changing the Emitter Binding

You'll now have smoke in the shape of the **Shape Location** box we created in the **Minimal** emitter earlier, but the smoke is rising upwards. We need it to flow on the ground. Let's fix that.

1. Disable the **Sprite Renderer** module in the **Minimal** emitter; we won't be needing it anymore. Back in the **Grid3D_Gas_Master_Emitter** node's **Emitter Summary**, select the **Simulation** tab and change the following:
   - Setting **Resolution Max Axis** to `350` will increase the detail of the smoke, but it is GPU-intensive. Stick to `200` if you have a low-powered PC or if the simulation starts to lag.
   - Set **Pressure Solve Iterations** to 12 for better collision accuracy.
   - Set **Density Buoyancy** to `0.1`– using a positive value will make the smoke/gas flow downwards.
   - Change **Gravity** values to **X** = `0`, **Y** = `0`, **Z** = `20`.
   - Uncheck **Draw Bounds**.

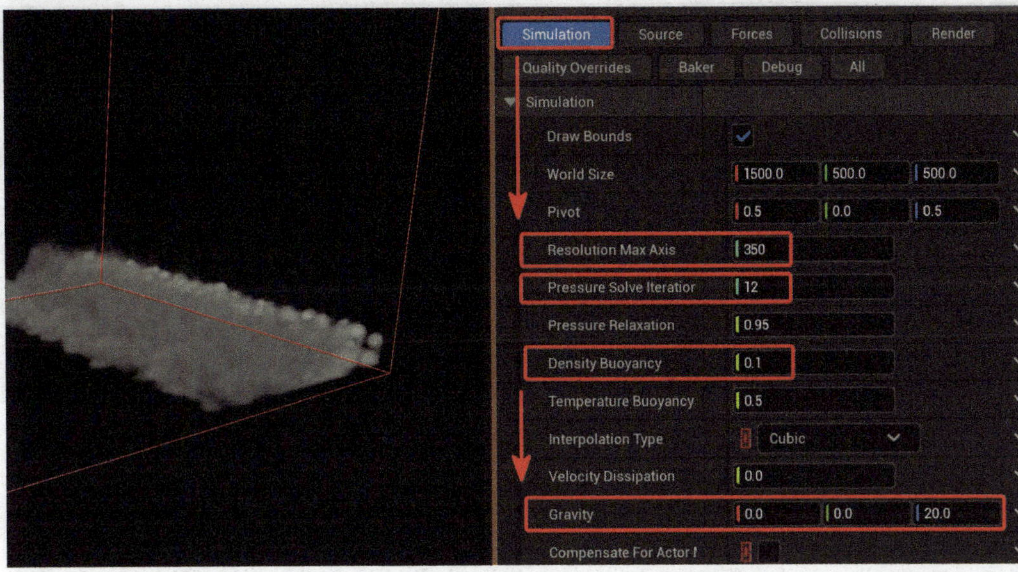

Figure 7.9 - Completing the Simulation settings

2. The smoke seems stuck on the far side. Let's make it travel further. In the **Collisions** tab, scroll down to the **Boundary** section and uncheck the **Open Boundary –Z.** The smoke will now collide with the floor. Now we need the smoke to travel all the way to the other side of the box.
3. In the **Forces** tab, under the **Wind** section, enable **Calculate Wind**. Set **Wind Magnitude** to `10`. Much better. Let's increase the smoke.

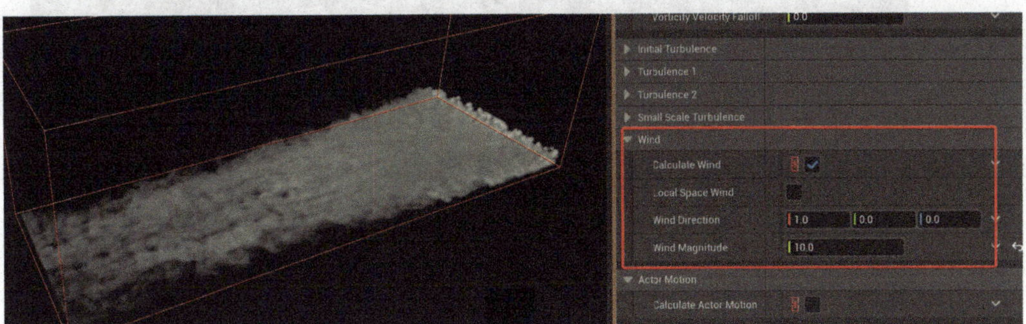

Figure 7.10 - Adding Wind

4. In the **Minimal** emitter node, for the **Set Fluid Source Attributes** module, increase **Radius** to `20`. You can also experiment with the **Density** properties to have less or denser smoke. Now we have much denser smoke travelling on the ground.

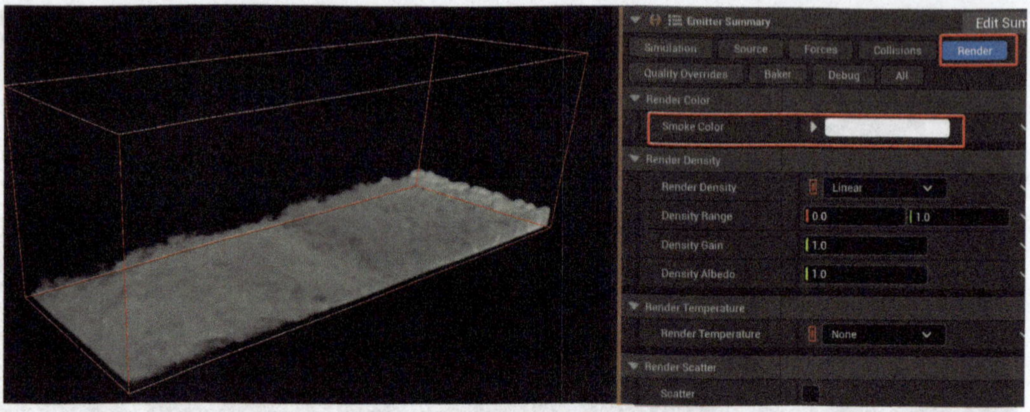

Figure 7.11 - Changing smoke color from the Render tab

5. You can change the color of the smoke using the **Smoke Color** properties in the **Render** tab.
6. To finally test the effect, back in the main level, disable the **Directional Light**, and add two **Rect Lights** to give a moody look. Place the **Rect Lights** above the Ground Fog and add a basic cylinder to collide with the fog as shown in *Figure 7.12*:

Figure 7.12 - Disabled Directional light with two Rect lights

7. One final but important step is to select **RectLight**, then go to the **Details** panel and search for `Cast`. Enable **Cast Volumetric Shadow**. Repeat this for the other lights in

your scene if you want them to affect the fog in the same way. This allows the volumetric fog to receive shadow detail from the lights, making the scene feel deeper and more cinematic. However, this setting can be GPU-intensive, so use it carefully and disable it on lights that do not need to contribute to the fog.

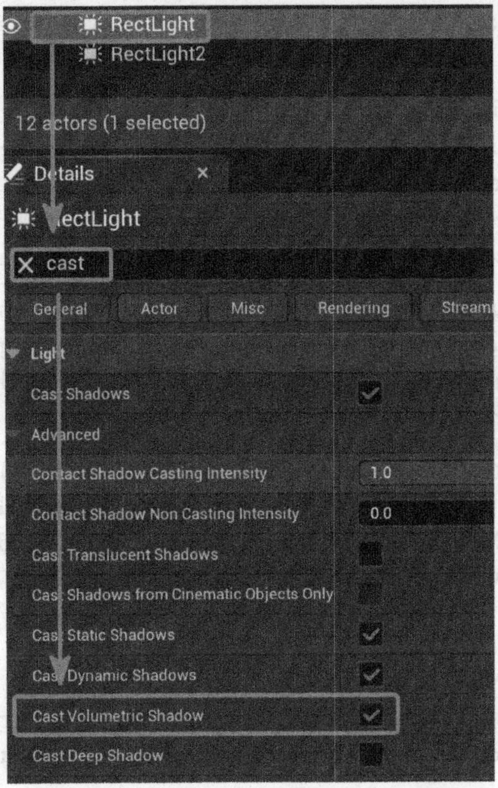

Figure 7.13 - Enabling Cast Volumetric Shadow

At this stage, the low-lying volumetric fog setup is working and interacting with the object in the scene. You can now begin adjusting the settings to match the look you want. Try changing the fog density, color, dissipation, movement speed, and lighting to create different moods, such as soft ground mist, thick cinematic haze, or heavier fantasy-style fog. Once you are happy with the result, this setup can be reused in any scene where low-lying fog is needed. Small changes can make a big difference, so always judge the final result through the camera.

How it works...

In this recipe, you used a simple sprite emitter as the source for the Niagara Fluids simulation. The sprite particles are not the final visible fog. Instead, they act as moving source points that feed density (smoke), velocity, and other fluid attributes into the

Grid3D_Gas_Master_Emitter. This is why the **Sprite Renderer** can be disabled after the fog is working, because the visible result is now coming from the volumetric gas simulation.

The **Grid3D_Gas_Master_Emitter** is responsible for turning that source data into a volume. By changing the **World Size**, you reshaped the simulation container into a wide, low area suitable for ground fog. The **Pivot** setting was used to move the source position within the container, so the fog begins from one side and has room to travel across the scene.

The **Simulation** settings control how the fog behaves once it enters the volume. Increasing the **Resolution Max Axis** gives the fog more detail, but also makes the effect more demanding on the GPU. **Pressure Solve Iterations** help improve how the gas reacts inside the simulation, especially when collision is involved. **Density Buoyancy** and **Gravity** are used here to keep the fog low, so it spreads across the floor instead of rising upward like smoke.

The **Collision** settings allow the fog to interact with the floor and simple objects in the scene. By changing the boundary behavior, the fog is prevented from simply escaping through the bottom of the simulation box. The **Wind** setting then helps push the fog across the ground, giving it slow movement and making the effect feel less static.

The lighting step is important because volumetric fog becomes much more cinematic when light passes through it. Using **Rect Lights** with **Cast Volumetric Shadow** enabled allows the fog to receive more shadow detail, which helps reveal its depth and thickness. This is one of the main differences between sprite-based fog and Niagara Fluids fog: *the volume can catch light and feel like it exists inside the 3D space.*

There's more...

If you are going to use the effect in broad daylight, whereby your scene is lit using the **Directional Light**, you'll find the fog color looks more like a sandstorm instead of fog, as shown in *Figure 7.14*:

Figure 7.14 - Sandstorm-looking fog

Here's a quick remedy: Select the **Directional Light**, then in its **Details** panel, scroll down to **Volumetric Scattering Intensity** and raise the value until you get the color you desire. This result will look something like *Figure 7.15*:

Figure 7.15 - Color-corrected fog using Volumetric Scattering Intensity

See also

For more information about Niagara Fluids, refer to Unreal Engine's **Niagara Fluids documentation** (`https://dev.epicgames.com/documentation/unreal-engine/niagara-fluids-in-unreal-engine`). This is useful for understanding how Unreal Engine handles fluid-style effects such as smoke, fire, gas, and liquid simulations.

Building a cinematic explosion using Niagara Fluids

No cinematic VFX book would feel complete without an explosion! **Explosions** are one of the most recognizable effects in film, animation, games, and visual effects because it combines fire, smoke, light, force, and timing into one dramatic moment. Even a small explosion can add danger, scale, and impact to a shot when it is timed and framed properly.

Since you now have the basics of Niagara Fluids, in this recipe, we will create a cinematic explosion using Niagara Fluids. We will keep the setup simple and focused, so the goal is not to build a huge destruction sequence yet. Instead, we will create a compact fire-and-smoke burst that is easy to understand, easy to adjust, and impressive enough to use as a starting point for cinematic work. This recipe also prepares us for *Chapter 8*, where explosion effects can be combined with destruction, debris, impacts, and larger action scenes.

Getting ready

For this recipe, we will use the **Basic Level Template** that comes with Unreal Engine 5. This keeps the scene simple so we can focus on building, timing, and previewing the effect without extra distractions. Once the effect is working, you can place it into any cinematic scene and trigger it from **Sequencer** at the exact frame needed.

How to do it...

Let's start by creating a new basic level:

1. Go to **File** | **New Level** and choose the **Basic** template, then click **Create**. Save the level as `LV_Explosion`.
2. Press the *G* key to hide all the overlay icons. In the `Niagara_Systems` folder, right-click and choose **Niagara System**. From the pop-up panel, search for `Minimal` emitter, and click **Create**. Rename as `NF_Explosion` (NF = Niagara Fluids).

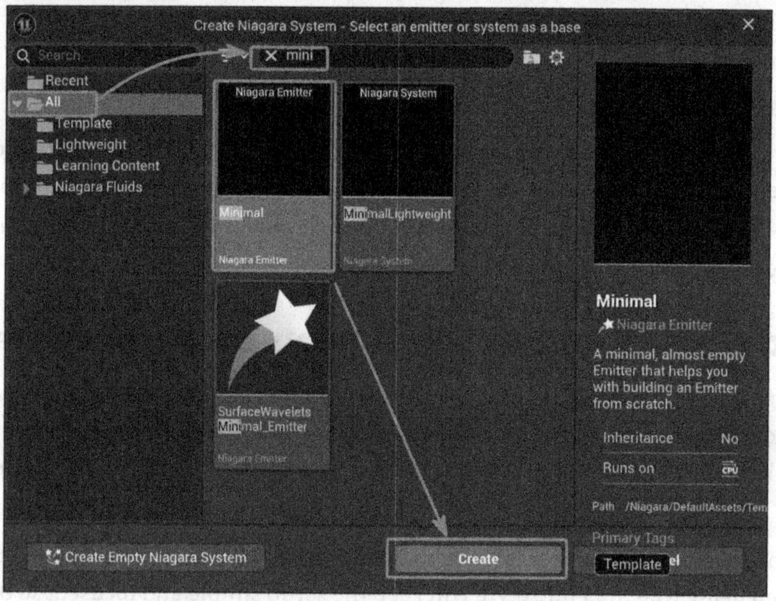

Figure 7.16 - Adding the Minimal emitter

3. Drag `NF_Explosion` into the level and double-click to open the Niagara Editor. This is the same editor we've been using throughout this book.
4. Just like in the previous recipe, we will use a sprite emitter as a source to drive the fluid simulation. In the next few steps, we'll configure the **Minimal** emitter.

5. In the **Properties** module, enable **Local Space** and **Determinism**, then set **Sim Target** to **GPUCompute Sim** and **Calculate Bounds Mode** to **Fixed**. We will be utilizing the GPU processing power to create this effect.
6. Since it's an explosion, we will use the **Spawn Burst Instantaneous** module. In the **Emitter Update** section, add **Spawn Burst Instantaneous** and set **Spawn Count** to `15`.
7. For the **Initialize Particle** module, set **Lifetime** to **Random Range Float** and set **Minimum** to `0.3` and **Maximum** to `0.7`. Set **Sprite Size** to **Uniform** and **Uniform Sprite Size** to `2.0`.

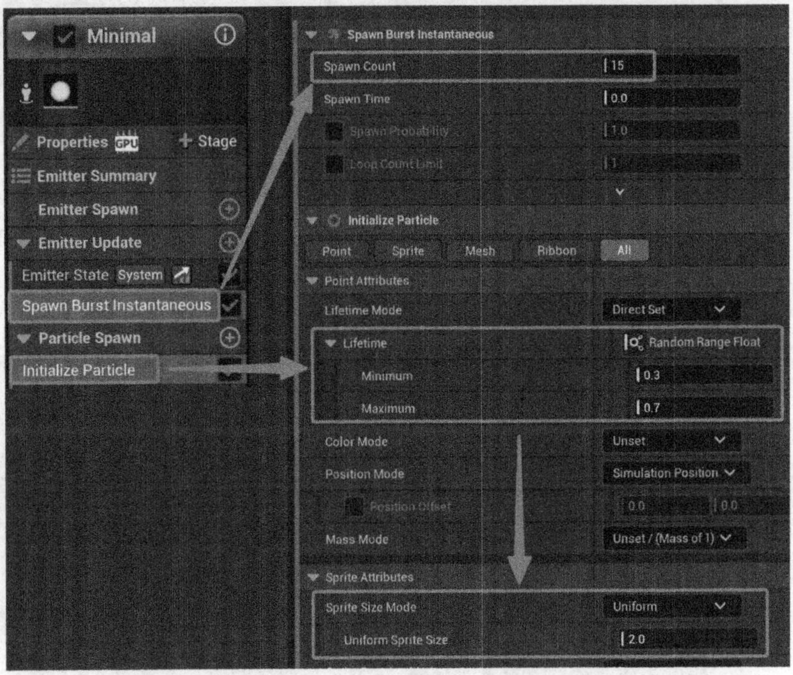

Figure 7.17 - Setting the Emitter Update and Initialize Particle modules

8. Since an explosion is basically a ball of fire, in the **Particle Spawn** section, add a **Shape Location** module. Set **Sphere Radius** to `50` and **Sphere Surface Distribution** to `1.0`. This will make the particles emit from the surface of the sphere.
9. In the same section, add the **Add Velocity** module. Click the top **Fix issue** button. Change **Velocity** to **X** = `0`, **Y** = `0`, **Z** = `100`. This will move the particles upwards.

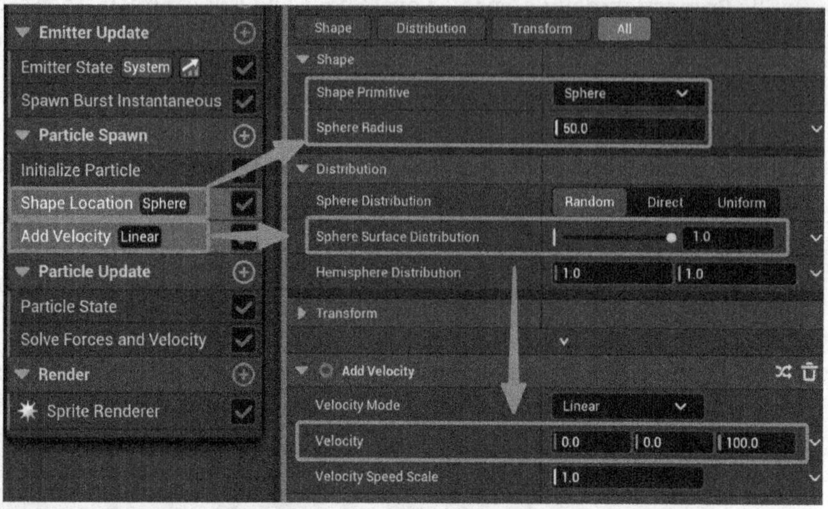

Figure 7.18 - Adding Shape Location and Add Velocity modules

10. In the **Particle Update** section, add **Curl Noise Force**. Set **Noise Strength** to `100` and **Noise Frequency** to `40`. Add another **Curl Force Noise** module and set its **Noise Strength** to `300` and **Noise Frequency** to `40`.

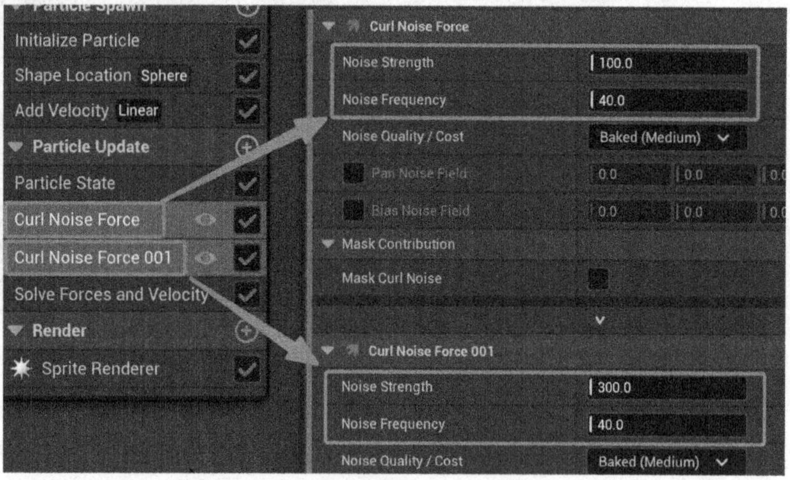

Figure 7.19 - Adding Curl Noise Force modules

11. Since we will be using the **Grid3D_Gas_Master_Emitter**, add the **Set Fluid Source Attributes** module and set the following:

    - Set **Density** to **Random Range Float** as well as **Minimum** to `0.8` and **Maximum** to `1.2`
    - Set **Temperature** to **Random Range Float** as well as **Minimum** to `0.08` and **Maximum** to `0.12`
    - Set **Velocity Scale** to **Random Range Float** as well as **Minimum** to `1.2` and **Maximum** to `1.6`
    - Set **Divergence** to **Random Range Float** as well as **Minimum** to `11.0` and **Maximum** to `16.0`
    - Set **Radius** to **Random Range Float** as well as **Minimum** to `8.0` and **Maximum** to `12.0`

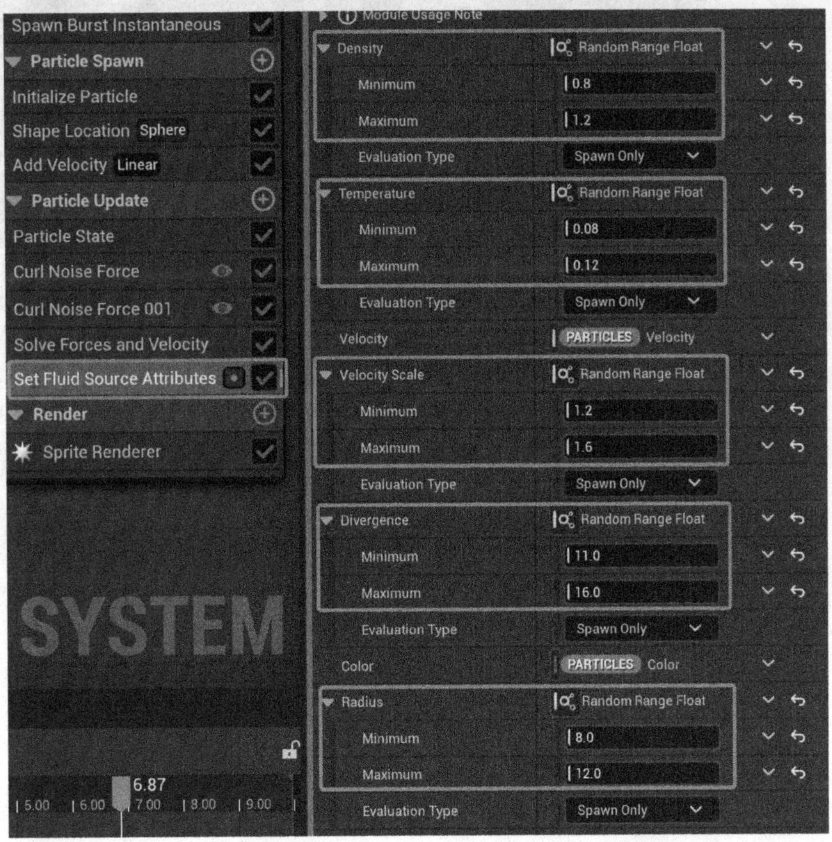

Figure 7.20 - Configuring the Set Fluid Source Attributes module

12. Now add the **Grid3D_Gas_Master_Emitter**. Right-click anywhere in the node panel, select **Add Emitter**, and search for `Master`. Select the **Grid3D_Gas_Master_Emitter**. Click **Add**.

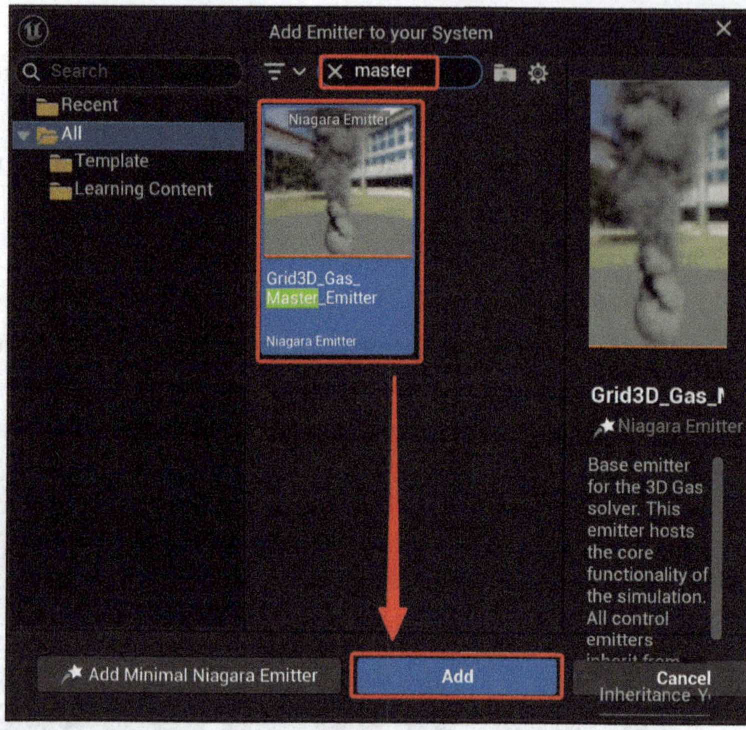

Figure 7.21 - Adding the Grid3D_Gas_Master_Emitter emitter

13. Like the previous section, we will only work with the **Emitter Summary** module. Collapse the node using the *top triangle* (as annotated) so we don't get distracted.

Figure 7.22 - Collapsing the 3D Grid Gas Master Emitter

14. In the **Emitter Summary** of the **Grid3D_Gas_Master_Emitter**, click the **Simulation** tab. Change the **World Size** to **X** = `900`, **Y** = `900`, **Z** = `1000`. This will make a tall, box-shaped bound.
15. Change **Pivot X** = `0`, **Y** = `0`, **Z** = `0.4`, and **Resolution Max Axis** to `300` (do not exceed `500`!). Leave it as `200` if your computer is starting to lag. This is a very GPU-intensive setting.
16. For **Temperature Buoyancy**, use the dropdown arrow to select **Random Range Float** and set **Minimum** to `0.25` and **Maximum** to `0.4`.
17. Set **Velocity Dissipation** to `0.2`. This setting will determine how quickly the velocity will dissipate to 0.

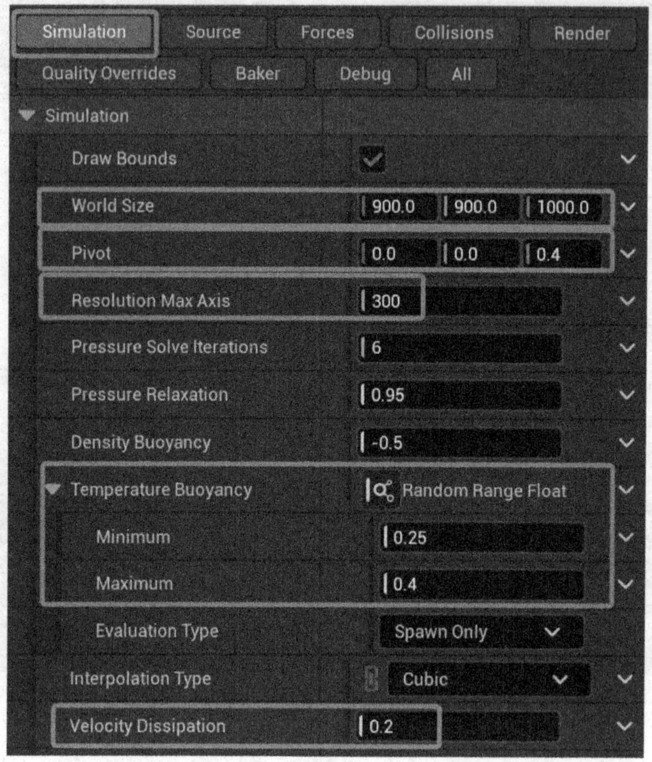

Figure 7.23 - Setting the Simulation properties

> **Note**
>
> The settings used in this recipe are based on my workstation, which has a fairly powerful GPU. Niagara Fluids can be demanding, so your results and performance may vary depending on your PC specifications. If the simulation feels slow or heavy, reduce the grid resolution, lower the emitter size, or work with shorter preview ranges while building the effect. Stopping the playback in the editor timeline also helps, but you need to view the updates from the main level.

18. Now let's assign the **Minimal** emitter as the source of smoke/gas. In the **Source** tab, open the **Sphere Source** section and uncheck **Enable**. The Sphere will now disappear. Under the **Particle Source** section, for **Particle Source Type**, change to **Emitter**.

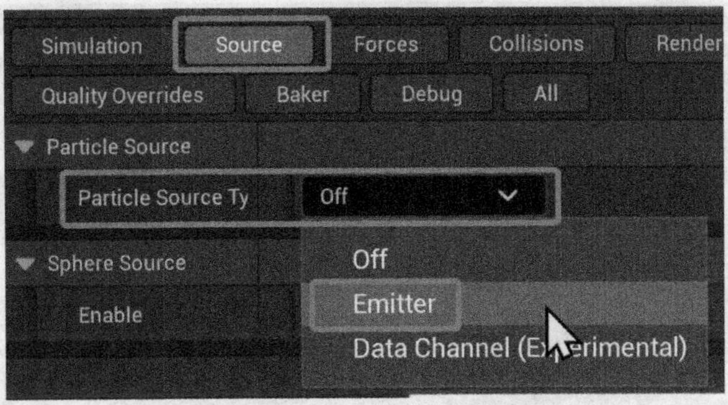

Figure 7.24 - Accessing the Source module

19. More properties will be revealed. In the **Particle Reader** section for **Emitter Binding**, delete the **Grid3D_Gas_Master_Emitter** and replace it with **Minimal**. This is the name of the sprite emitter we created earlier.

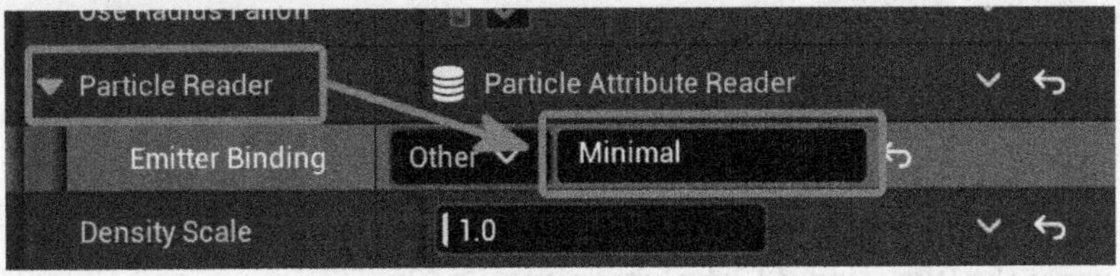

Figure 7.25 - Setting up the Minimal emitter

20. Still in the **Source** tab, enable **Read Divergence** and set **Divergence Scale** to 15. This setting will give the pushing effect of explosions. Conversely, a negative value will cause an implosion.
21. Now, let's jump into the **Forces** tab and change the following:
    - For **Initial Turbulence**, enable **Calculate Turbulence**, set **Turbulence Frequency** to `0.15`, and **Turbulence Gain** to `100`
    - For **Turbulence1**, enable **Calculate Turbulence**, set **Turbulence Frequency** to `0.2`, and **Turbulence Gain** to 25
    - For **Small Scale Turbulence**, just enable **Calculate Turbulence**

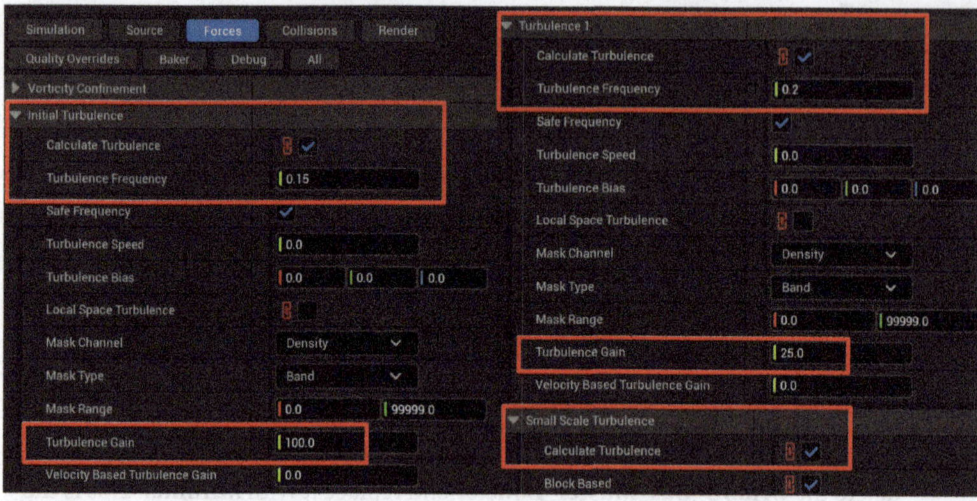

Figure 7.26 - Configuring the Forces properties

22. In the **Render** tab, change the **Render Temperature** to **Black Body**.
23. In the **Simulation** tab, disable **Draw Bounds** to hide the *red* bounding box, then click **Save**.
24. Back in the main level, you can now admire your explosion! If the scene is too bright, lower the **Directional Light Intensity** to `2.0` lux.

Figure 7.27 - The final explosion

25. In the **Render** tab, you can change the **Smoke Color** and **Fire Color**. Experiment with different colors to find the best outcome for your shot. Warmer colors can make the explosion feel more intense and fiery, while cooler or darker smoke tones can make the effect feel heavier, more dramatic, or more stylized. Since we have **Local Space** enabled in the **Minimal** emitter, you can position this effect anywhere in the scene.

How it works...

In this recipe, the **Minimal** emitter is used as the source of the explosion. We added a Burst Instantaneous module. The burst of particles creates the initial shape and motion, while the **Grid3D_Gas_Master_Emitter** turns that particle data into a fire and smoke volume. This is a useful way to think about Niagara Fluids: *one emitter provides the source of information, and the gas emitter simulates the visible volumetric result.*

The **Shape Location** module creates a spherical source, which gives the explosion its starting form. The **Add Velocity** module pushes the particles upward, while the **Curl Noise Force** modules add uneven motion, so the burst does not look too clean or mechanical. These source particles are short-lived, but they provide the information needed to start the fire and smoke reaction.

The **Set Fluid Source Attributes** module controls what the source particles contribute to the gas simulation. **Density** adds smoke; **Temperature** adds heat and fire behavior; **Velocity Scale** strengthens the movement; **Divergence** creates the outward pushing force of the blast; and **Radius** controls how much area each source particle affects. Together, these settings define the character of the explosion before the gas simulation takes over.

Inside the **Grid3D_Gas_Master_Emitter**, the **Simulation** settings control the size, detail, and behavior of the explosion volume. The **World Size** creates enough space for the explosion to expand upward, while **Resolution Max Axis** controls how detailed the volume appears. **Temperature Buoyancy** helps the heated fire and smoke rise, and **Velocity Dissipation** controls how quickly the movement loses energy after the initial burst.

The **Source** settings connect the **Minimal** emitter to the **Grid3D Gas** simulation. By setting **Particle Source Type** to **Emitter** and binding it to the **Minimal** emitter, the gas system reads the particles as the source for the explosion. Enabling **Read Divergence** allows the simulation to use the divergence values from **Set Fluid Source Attributes**, creating the outward blast effect. This is what gives the explosion its push instead of making it behave like a normal smoke plume.

The turbulence settings in the **Forces** tab add breakup and motion inside the volume. **Initial Turbulence**, **Turbulence1**, and **Small Scale Turbulence** work together to disturb the fire and smoke at different levels. This helps the explosion feel more natural and chaotic, while the

Render settings let you control the final **Fire Color** and **Smoke Color** for different cinematic looks. Don't forget to set **Render Temperature** to **Black Body**.

The **Data Channel** workflow in the *There's more...* section shows another useful way to drive the same gas simulation. Instead of keeping the source emitter inside the same Niagara System, a separate emitter writes source data to a **Data Channel**, while the **Grid3D Gas** system reads that data to generate the explosion. This gives you more flexibility, because you can modify or swap the source emitter to create different explosion shapes without rebuilding the main fluid simulation.

There's more...

Since we're all about explosions, here's another neat workflow that uses the **3D Grid Master** emitter that will work with any of the existing template emitters. Follow along these steps:

1. Remove `NF_Explosion` from the **Outliner**, so we have a scene without any explosions going on. In the `Niagara_Systems` folder, duplicate `NF_Explosion` and rename it to `NF_ExplosionData`.
2. Right-click in the same folder and create another Niagara System. Use the **Omnidirectional Burst** template and rename it as `NS_EmitterData`. I'm giving both a name that has the word "Data" for ease of identification. Double-click to open `NS_EmitterData`.
3. As the name suggests, you'll see an omnidirectional burst of particles in the preview window. In the **Particle Update** section, add a **Set Fluid Source Attributes** module, then enable **Write to Data Channel**.

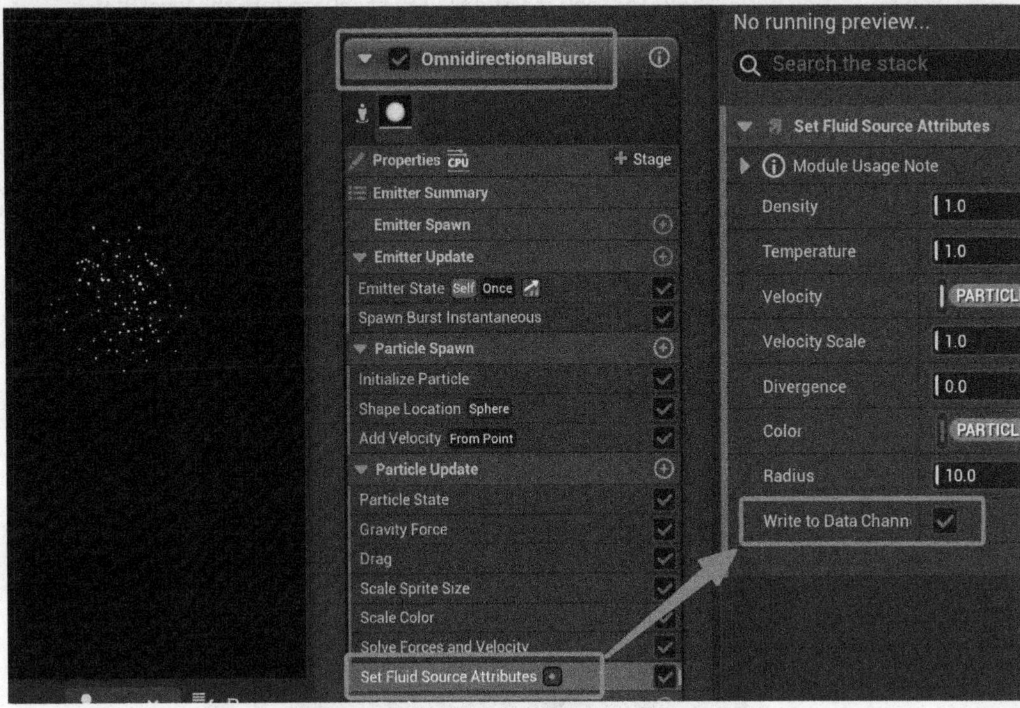

Figure 7.28 - Enabling Write Data Channel

4. Now double-click to open `NF_ExplosionData`, select the **Grid3D_Gas_Master_Emitter**, then select the **Source** tab and change **Particle Source Type** to **Data Channel (Experimental)**.

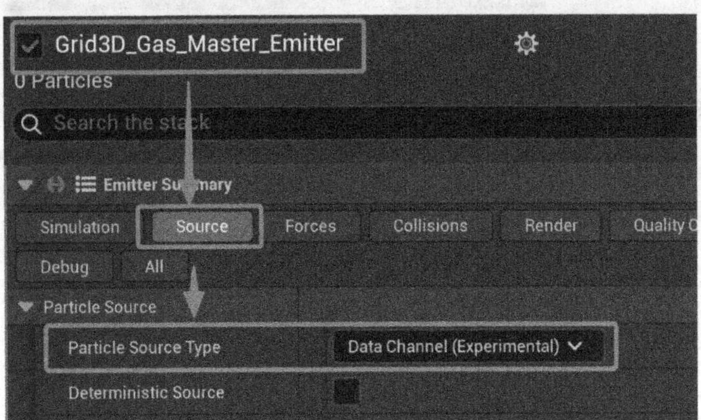

Figure 7.29 - Setting the Particle Source Type

5. You must drag both `NF_ExplosionData` and `NS_EmitterData` into the level. Raise `NS_EmitterData` up to about `500` units in **Z**. Use the **Auto Activate** checkbox to toggle the explosion.

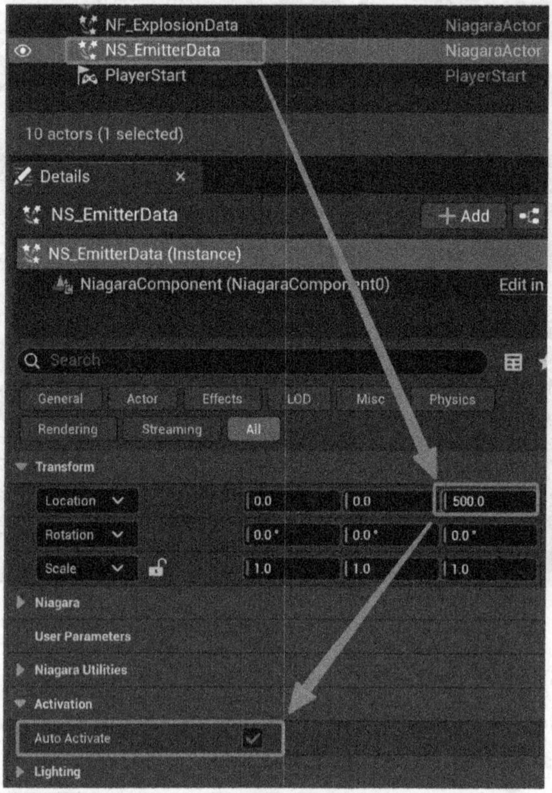

Figure 7.30 - Auto-Activating the NS_EmitterData

6. The Fire seems too bright, let's fix that. Back in `NF_ExplosionData`, access the **Grid3D_Gas_Master_Emitter**'s **Source** tab and lower the **Temperature Scale** to 2.

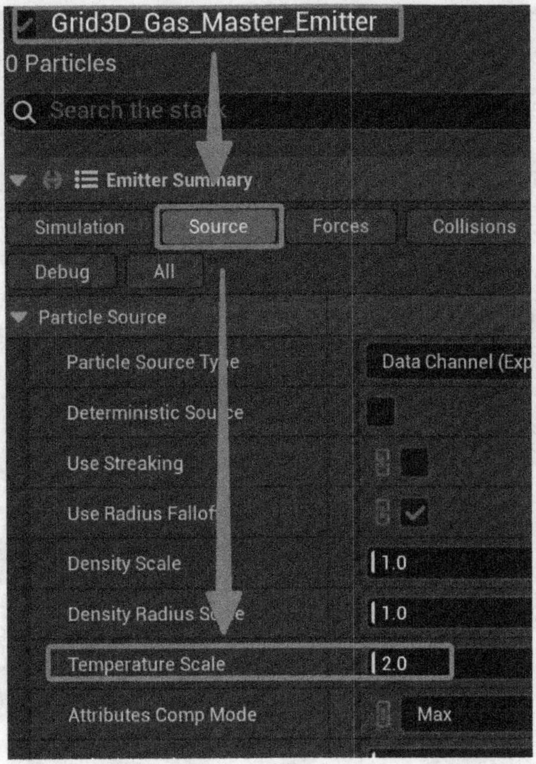

Figure 7.31 - Adjusting the Fire temperature

What is happening here is that although the emitters are separate assets, the **Grid3D_Gas_Master_Emitter** (`NF_ExplosionData`) is using the source emitter (`NS_EmitterData`) to generate the explosion. The source emitter feeds data into the gas simulation, which then creates the fire and smoke volume. Now you can simply add or modify emitters inside `NS_EmitterData` to create different explosion looks, such as a wider burst, stronger upward plume, or more directional blast.

Figure 7.32 - Explosion using the Spawn Burst Instantaneous emitter

See also

You can refer to the **Niagara Fluids Quick Start Guide** and **Niagara Fluids Reference** for more details on the **Grid3D Gas** templates, including how explosion-style systems are created and adjusted: `https://dev.epicgames.com/documentation/unreal-engine/niagara-fluids-quick-start-guide-for-unreal-engine`.

Creating a high-rising volumetric storm cloud using Niagara Fluids

In this recipe, you will create a **high-rising volumetric storm** cloud using Niagara Fluids. This effect is inspired by the large atmospheric volume seen in the background on the *book cover*, where smoke, cloud, and energy appear to rise through the scene.

We will keep the setup simple by starting with a rising gas volume, then shaping it into a taller and more dramatic storm-like column. The goal is not to create a physically perfect tornado, but to build a cinematic volume effect with height, movement, density, and atmosphere. This builds on the earlier fog and explosion recipes, while showing how Niagara Fluids can be used for larger background effects that add scale and mood to a shot.

Figure 7.33 - The outcome of this section

Getting ready

For this recipe, we will use the **Basic Level Template** that comes with Unreal Engine 5. This keeps the scene simple so we can focus on building, timing, and previewing the effect without extra distractions. Once the effect is working, you can place it into any cinematic scene and trigger it from **Sequencer** at the exact frame needed.

How to do it...

Let's start by creating a new basic level:

1. Go to **File** | **New Level** and choose the **Basic** template, then click **Create**.

2. Press the *G* key to hide all the overlay icons. In the `Niagara_Systems` folder, right-click and choose **Niagara System**. From the pop-up panel, search for `Minimal` emitter, and click **Create**. Rename as `NF_Tornado` (NF = Niagara Fluids).

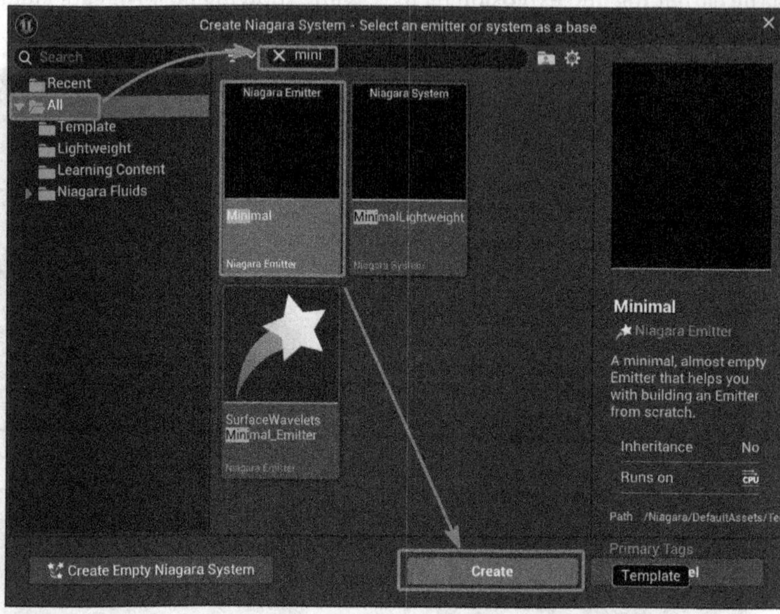

Figure 7.34 - Adding the Minimal emitter

3. Drag `NF_Tornado` into the level and double-click to open the Niagara Editor. This is the same editor we've been using throughout this book.
4. Just like in the previous recipe, we will use a sprite emitter as a source to drive the fluid simulation. For the **Minimal** emitter set the following:
    - In the **Properties** module, enable **Local Space** and **Determinism,** then set **Sim Target** to **GPUCompute Sim** and **Calculate Bounds Mode** to **Fixed.** We will be utilizing the GPU processing power to create this effect.
    - In the **Emitter Update** section, add the **Spawn Rate** module and set **Spawn Rate** to `2000`.
    - For the **Initialize Particle** module, set the **Lifetime** to **Random Range Float** and set **Minimum** to `2.0` and **Maximum** to `3.0`. Set **Sprite Size** to **Uniform** and change **Uniform Sprite Size** to **Random Range Float.** Set **Minimum** to `1.0` and **Maximum** to `3.0`.

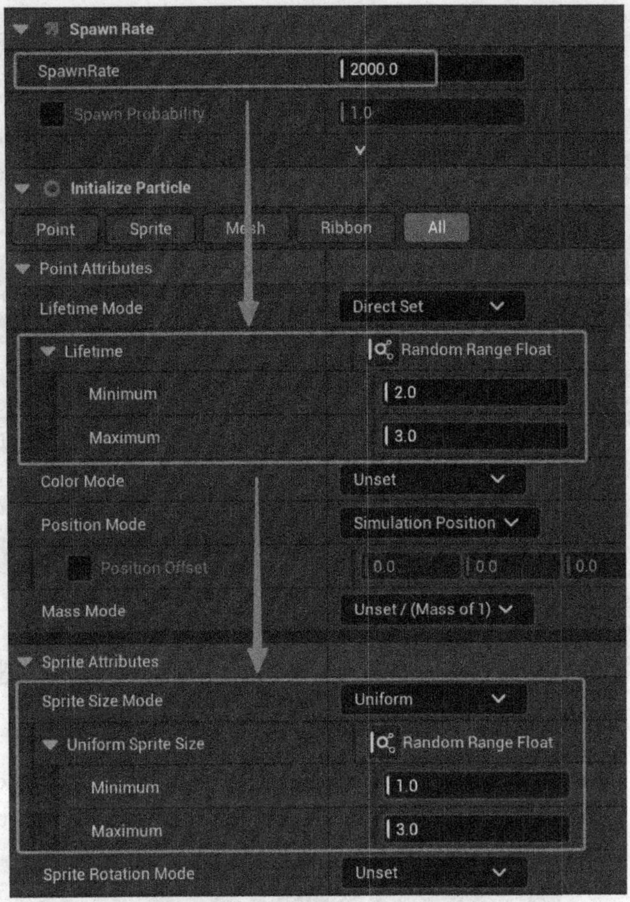

Figure 7.35 - Spawn Rate and Initialize Particle settings

- Since the effect is in a cylindrical shape, add a **Shape Location** module, and change **Shape Primitive** to **Cylinder**. Set **Cylinder Height** to `1000`, **Radius** to `20`, and **Cylinder Height Midpoint** to `0.0`.
- In the **Particle Update** section, add the **Vortex Force Amount** module, click **Fix issue**, and set **Vortex Force Amount** to `200`.
- Add another **Vortex Force**, set **Vortex Force Amount** to `200`, but this time enable **Vortex Origin Offset** and set the **Z** value to `1000` (same as the height of the Cylinder).

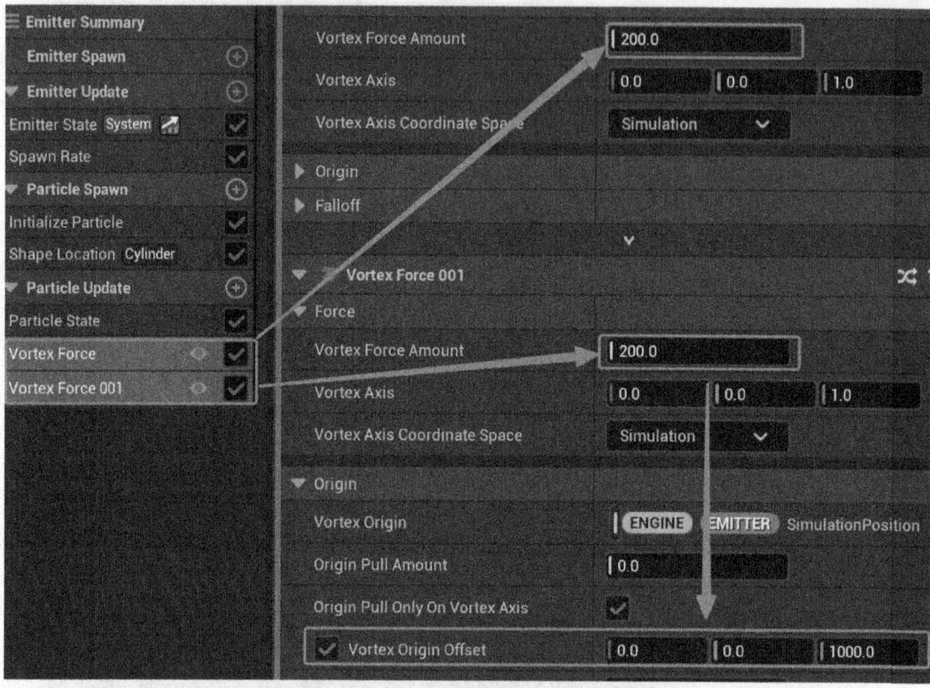

Figure 7.36 - Adding Vortex modules

- Finally, in the **Particle Update** section, add the **Set Fluid Source Attributes** module. Set **Density** to `1.5`. Leave the rest of the properties as default.

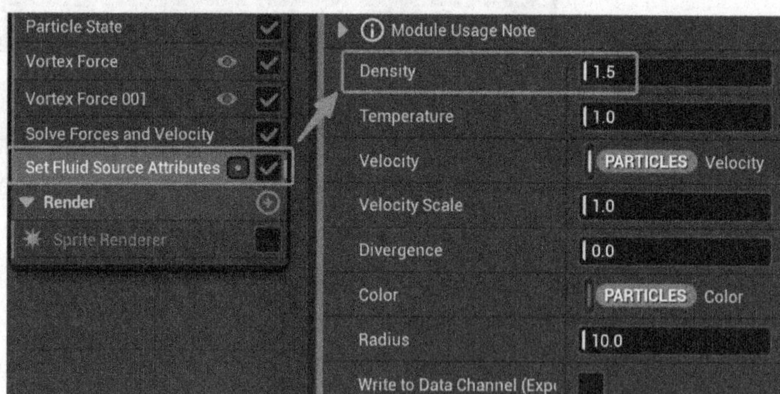

Figure 7.37 - Set Fluid Source Attributes settings

5. Now add the **Grid3D_Gas_Master_Emitter**. Right-click anywhere in the node panel, select **Add Emitter**, and search for `Master`. Select the **Grid3D_Gas_Master_Emitter**. Click **Add**.

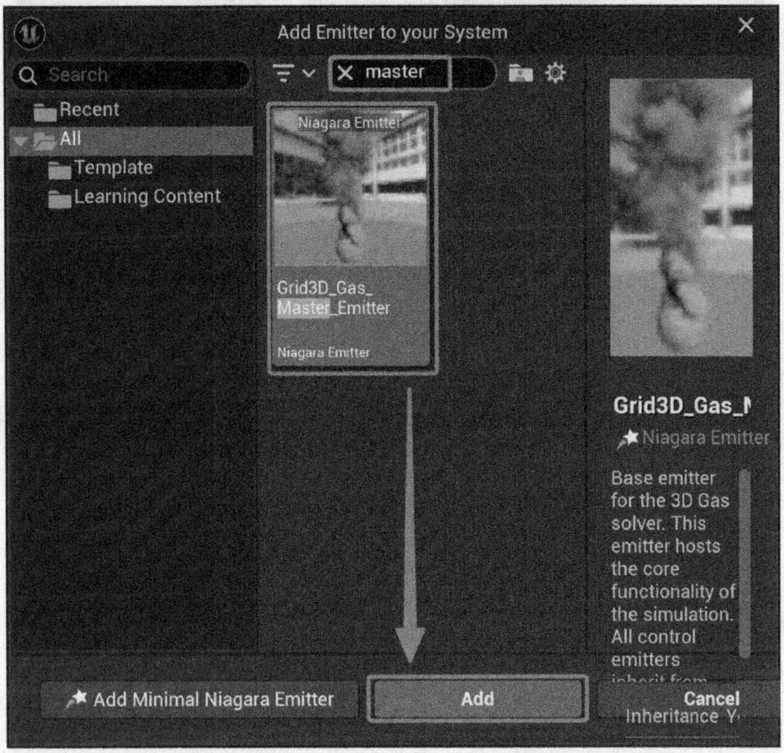

Figure 7.38 - Adding the Grid3D_Gas_Master_Emitter

6. Like the previous section, we will only work with the **Emitter Summary** module. Collapse the node using the top triangle (as annotated) so we don't get distracted.

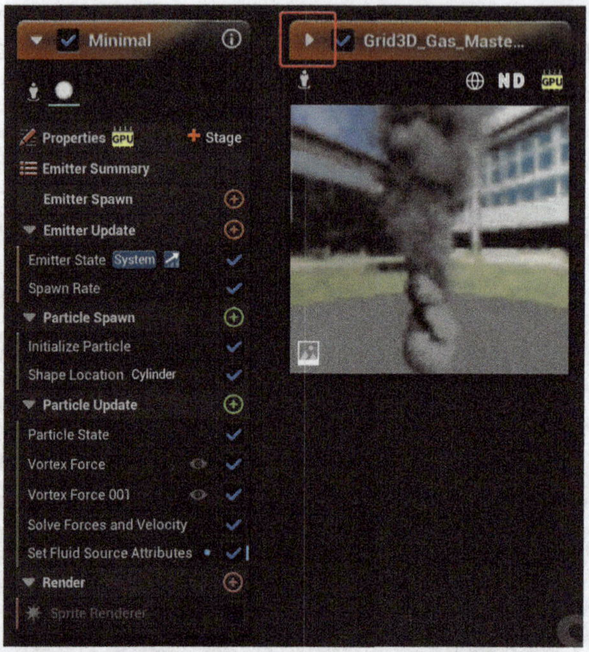

Figure 7.39 - Collapsing the Grid3D_Gas_Master_Emitter

> **Tip**
>
> **Pro-Tip**: If your system starts to lag while making changes to the **Grid3D_Gas_Master_Emitter**, I suggest stopping the playback in the editor timeline and starting to view the updates from the main level.

7. Select the **Grid3D_Gas_Master_Emitter** and, in the **Simulation** tab, change the following:
   - Disable **Draw Bounds**.
   - **World Size**: **X** = `1000`, **Y** = `1000`, **Z** = `1000`.
   - **Resolution**: `300`.
   - **Pressure Solver Iterations**: `12`.
   - **Density (Smoke) Buoyancy**: `0.0`.
   - **Temperature (Fire) Buoyancy**: `0.0`.
   - In the **Attributes** section, change **Dissipation Rate Density** to `1.0`. This will gradually fade the smoke (**Density**).

8. Now, let's assign the **Minimal** emitter as the source of smoke/gas. In the **Source** tab, open the **Sphere Source** section and uncheck **Enable**. The Sphere will now disappear. Under the **Particle Source** section, for **Particle Source Type**, change to **Emitter**.

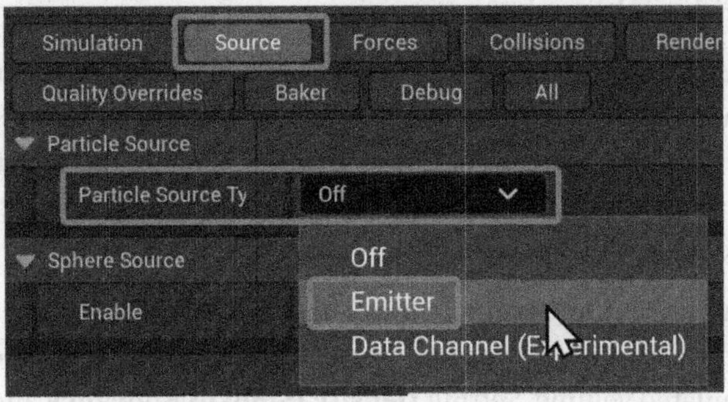

Figure 7.40 - Accessing the Source module

9. More properties will be revealed. In the **Particle Reader** section for **Emitter Binding**, delete the **Grid3D_Gas_Master_Emitter** and replace it with **Minimal.** This is the name of the sprite emitter we created earlier.

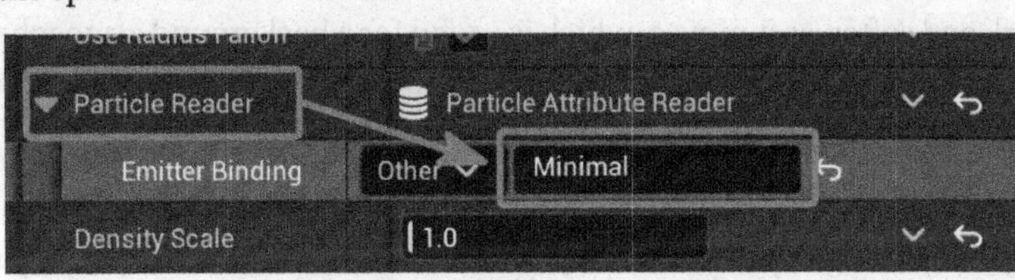

Figure 7.41 - Setting up the Minimal emitter

10. You can now disable the **Sprite Renderer** in the **Minimal** emitter to hide the source particles. You may also tweak settings such as **Spawn Rate**, **Sprite Size**, and **Vortex Force Amount** to control the shape, density, and swirling motion of the rising cloud.

This effect is intended to work as a background atmospheric element, so it does not need to show too much fine detail up close. Higher values can create a stronger and more dramatic column, while lower values will give you a softer and more subtle background effect.

How it works...

In this recipe, you created a high-rising storm cloud by using particles as a source for a **Grid3D Gas** simulation. The **Minimal** emitter provides the moving source particles, while the **Grid3D_Gas_Master_Emitter** converts those particles into a larger volumetric cloud. This follows the same basic idea as the earlier fog and explosion recipes, but the source shape and forces are designed to create a taller background effect.

The **Cylinder Shape Location** is important because it defines the vertical source area for the cloud. Instead of emitting from a flat plane or a small sphere, the particles are distributed inside a tall cylinder. This gives the gas simulation a clear vertical structure from the start and helps form the rising column shape.

The **Vortex Force** modules create the swirling motion. One vortex affects the lower part of the source, while the second vortex uses an offset so the twisting motion also affects the upper part of the column. This gives the volume a more tornado-like movement without needing a complex physical tornado setup. The goal is not accuracy, but a strong cinematic shape that reads well in the background of a shot.

The **Grid3D Gas Simulation** settings control how the cloud fills the volume. A larger **World Size** gives the storm cloud enough space to rise and spread, while the **Resolution** controls the detail of the simulated volume. Setting **Density (Smoke) Buoyancy** and **Temperature (Fire) Buoyancy** to `0` helps keep the shape more art-directed, so the vortex and source motion define the look rather than having the cloud rise too quickly on its own.

The **Dissipation Rate Density** setting helps the cloud fade over time. Without dissipation, the volume can become too dense and lose its shape. With controlled dissipation, the cloud can build, swirl, and soften as it moves, which is useful for a background atmospheric effect. Since this effect is not intended for close-up detail, the focus is on silhouette, movement, and mood.

The flickering light added in the *There's more...* section gives the cloud more cinematic energy. The `BP_LightFlicker` Blueprint uses a **Point Light** with changing intensity values to create the feeling of lightning or power building inside the volume. This is especially useful for a storm cloud effect because the light does not need to show a visible bolt. It only needs to briefly illuminate the volume from within.

Adding the effect to **Sequencer** and using a **Niagara Life Cycle Track** makes the storm cloud easier to control in a cinematic shot. Caching the Niagara simulation allows the effect to play back more smoothly, especially because Niagara Fluids can be expensive to simulate in real time. Once cached, you can scrub the timeline more reliably and review the cloud timing, lighting, and final camera framing with less delay.

There's more...

In this section, we will enhance the scene by adding a flickering light inside the volumetric storm cloud. This will help create the impression of energy building within the cloud and add more cinematic drama to the shot. We will then add the effect to **Sequencer**, control its timing using a **Niagara Life Cycle Track**, and use **Niagara Cache** for smoother and more stable playback.

The **Niagara Life Cycle Track** and **Niagara Cache** workflows were covered in detail in the *Making Niagara effects stable for scrubbing and repeatable playback (repeatable takes)* recipe in *Chapter 1.*

Let's continue where we left off:

1. With the scene still open, in the **Content Browser | Blueprint** folder, drag `BP_LightFlicker` into the level. Reset its **Location** to `0,0,0`, and set its **Z** location to `1000` (the height of the Tornado).

> **Note**
>
> `BP_LightFlicker` is made of a Point Light in a simple Blueprint script to randomly change the intensity of the light with a delay. The Blueprint also allows you to set the color of the light from the **Details** panel. We will not cover how the Blueprint is made, but you may inspect the script by double-clicking it.

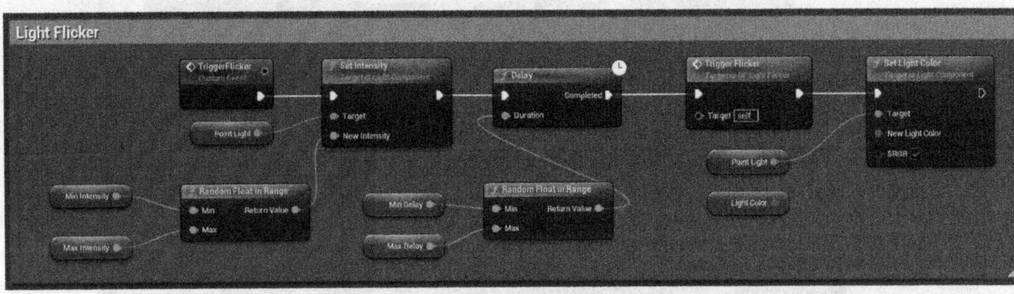

Figure 7.42 - An overview of the Light Flicker Blueprint

2. You may control the Light's **Min Intensity** and **Max Intensity,** as well as **Min Delay** and **Max Delay** and **Light Color** from the **Details** panel.

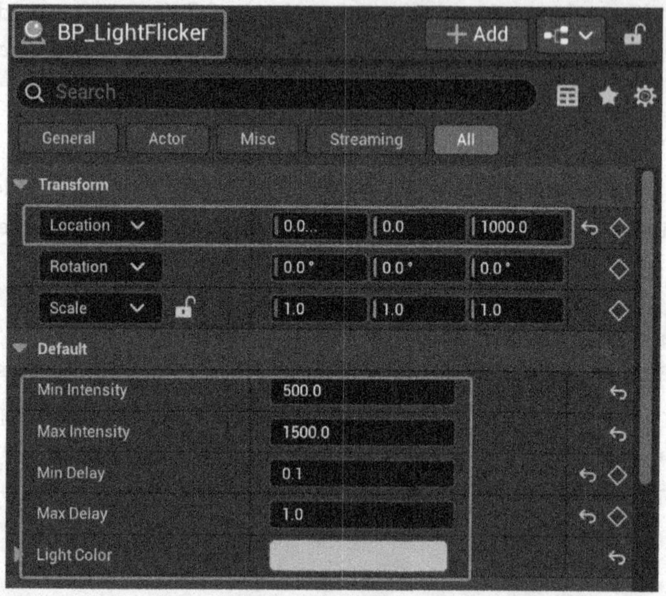

Figure 7.43 - The LightFlicker Blueprint settings

3. Now let's add the effect to the **Sequencer** to set up a smoother playback using the **Niagara LifeCycle Track** and **Niagara Cache**. From the top menu, click the **clapperboard** icon and choose **Add Level Sequence**. Save it in the `Sequences` folder as `LS_Tornado`. Click **Save**.

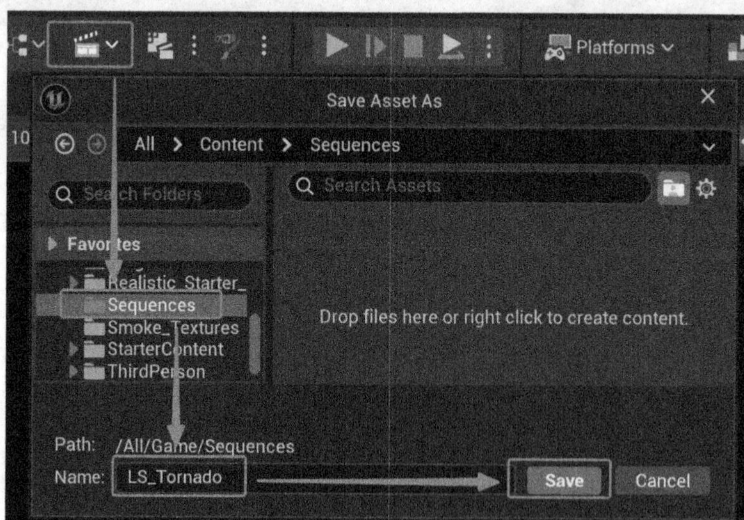

Figure 7.44 - Creating a new Level Sequence

4. Drag `NF_Tornado` from the **Outliner** into the **Sequencer**. Click the + sign on the `NF_Tornado` track and choose **NiagaraComponent0**. Click the + sign on **NiagaraComponent0** and choose **Niagara System Life Cycle Track**. Change **System Life Cycle** to **Desired Age**.

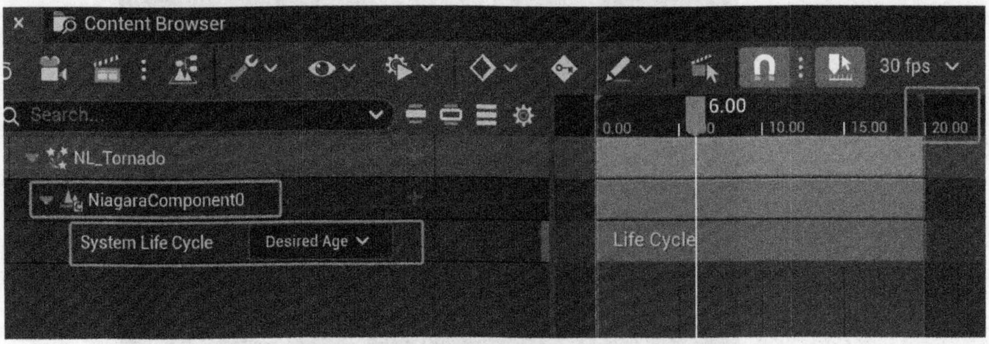

Figure 7.45 - Adding Niagara Life Cycle Track

5. Set the timeline to be around **20** seconds. The Tornado will fully form around the **6** seconds, so trim the start marker (the *green* vertical line) to **6** seconds on the timeline. Click the **NiagaraComponent0**'s + sign one more time and choose **Niagara Cache**. Now click the **red** button to start caching the effect. It might take a few minutes, so please be patient. Once completed, you can now scrub the timeline without any lag or delay.

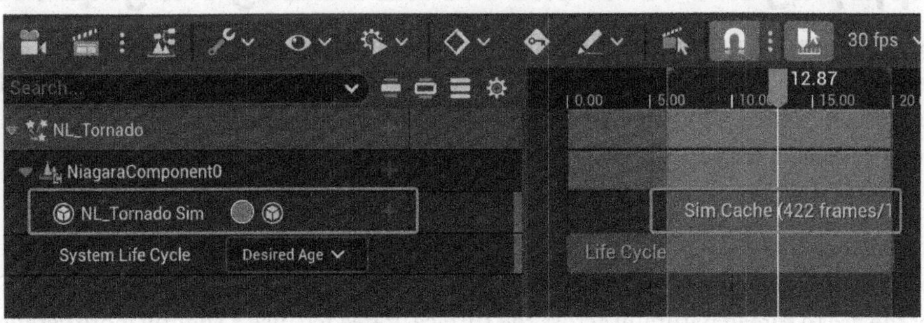

Figure 7.46 - Adding Niagara Cache

6. Save your project and admire your amazing volumetric storm cloud effect with flickering light!

Figure 7.47 - The completed Volumetric Storm Cloud Niagara effect

Applying fire to Static Meshes using Niagara Fluids

In this recipe, you will create a fire effect that appears to burn from the surface of a Static Mesh using Niagara Fluids. Instead of placing a fire effect in only one position, we will use the mesh itself as the source, allowing the flames and smoke to feel connected to the object. This makes the effect useful for burning props, vehicles, buildings, wreckage, or even text meshes in a cinematic shot.

For this workflow to look convincing, the mesh should have enough surface detail or triangles for Niagara to sample from. A very simple low-poly mesh may not give enough useful points for the fire to spread naturally across the surface. If needed, use a slightly more detailed mesh or subdivide the object so the effect has more areas to emit from.

We will keep the setup simple and focused, using Niagara Fluids to create fire and smoke that can be adjusted for different cinematic situations. By the end of the recipe, you will have a reusable workflow for adding volume-based fire to static objects, which can also be combined with destruction, debris, sparks, and smoke in later shots.

Getting ready

For this recipe, we will use the **Basic Level Template** that comes with Unreal Engine 5 and a free Fab asset, which can be downloaded here: `https://fab.com/s/1f80a0bb3c3c`.

Figure 7.48 - Asset downloadable from Fab

Once the effect is working, you can place it into any cinematic scene and trigger it from **Sequencer** at the exact frame needed.

How to do it...

Let's start by setting up a new level:

1. Go to **File** | **New Level** and choose the **Basic** template, then click **Create**.
2. Press the *G* key to hide all the overlay icons. In the `Niagara_Systems` folder, right-click and choose **Niagara System**. From the pop-up panel, search for `Minimal` emitter, and click **Create**. Rename it as `NF_MeshFire` (NF = Niagara Fluids).

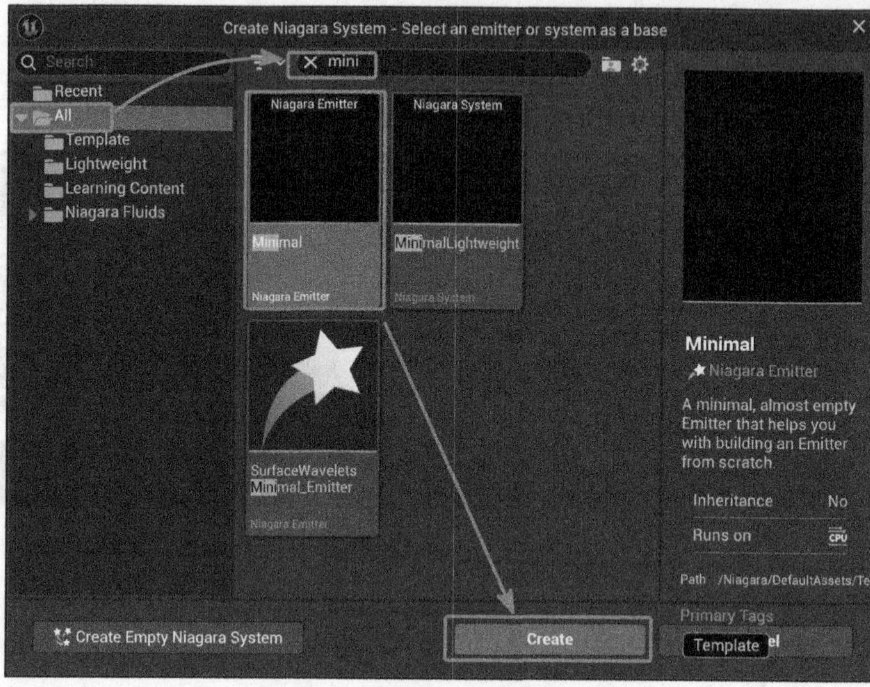

Figure 7.49 - Adding the Minimal emitter

3. Drag `NF_MeshFire` into the level and double-click to open the Niagara Editor. This is the same editor we've been using throughout this book.
4. Just like in the previous recipe, we will use a sprite emitter as a source to drive the fluid simulation. For the **Minimal** emitter set the following:
   - In the **Properties** module, enable **Local Space** and **Determinism,** then set **Sim Target** to **GPUCompute Sim** and **Calculate Bounds Mode** to **Fixed**. We will be utilizing the GPU processing power to create this effect.
   - In the **Emitter Update** section, add the **Spawn Rate** module and set the **Spawn Rate** to `400`.
   - For the **Initialize Particle** module, set the **Lifetime** to **Random Range Float** and set **Minimum** to `2.5` and **Maximum** to `6.0`. Set **Sprite Size** to **Random Uniform** and change **Uniform Sprite Size** to **Random Range Float.** Set **Minimum** to `50` and **Maximum** to `100`.

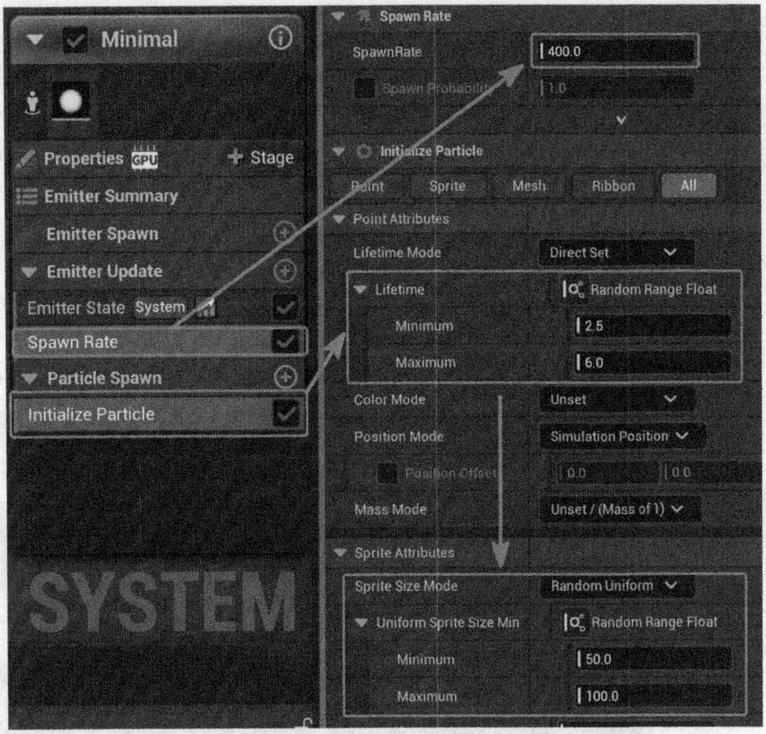

Figure 7.50 - Spawn Rate and Initialize Particle properties

- In the **Particle Spawn** section, add a **Static Mesh Location** module. Change **Source Mode** to **Attach Parent**. In **Preview Mesh**, search for `Wooden House` and select the `wooden_house_house_in_the_woods_project` asset (you downloaded from Fab).

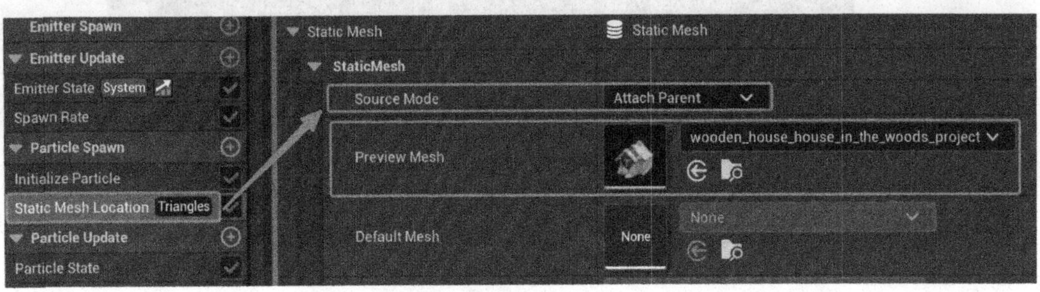

Figure 7.51 - Static Mesh Location settings

> **Note**
>
> The **Static Mesh Location** module allows Niagara to use a Static Mesh as a particle source. In this recipe, it helps the fire emit from the surface of the mesh, so the flames and smoke feel connected to the object instead of coming from a single point.

5. To be able to swap to any mesh from the **Details** panel, in the **Minimal** emitter, select the **Static Mesh Location** module. Click on the dropdown arrow for **Static Mesh**, then under **General | Make**, choose the **Read from new user parameter** option.

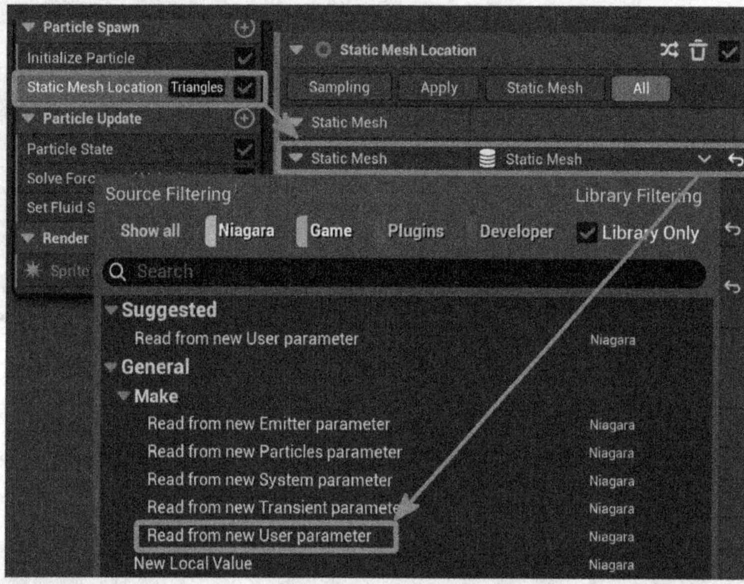

Figure 7.52 - Static Mesh Location settings

6. In the **Particle Update** section, add the **Set Fluid Source Attributes** module and leave all its properties as default.
7. Now add the **Grid3D_Gas_Master_Emitter**. Right-click anywhere in the node panel, select **Add Emitter**, and search for `Master`. Select the **Grid3D_Gas_Master_Emitter**. Click **Add**.

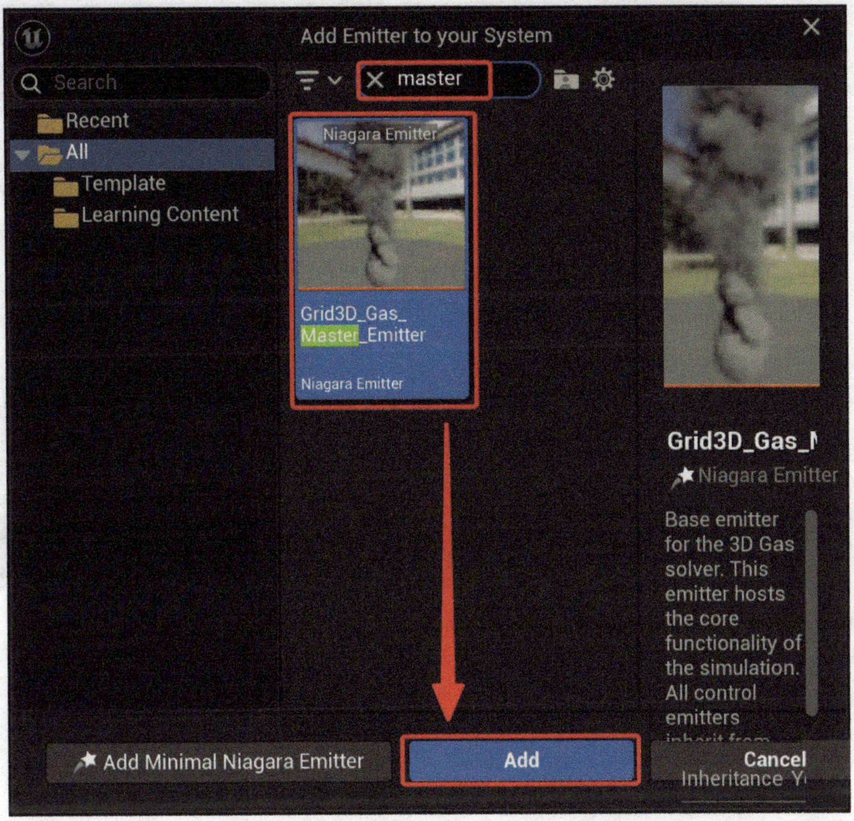

Figure 7.53 - Adding the 3D Grid Gas Master emitter

8. Like in the previous recipe, we will only work with the **Emitter Summary** module. Collapse the node using the top triangle (as annotated) so we don't get distracted.

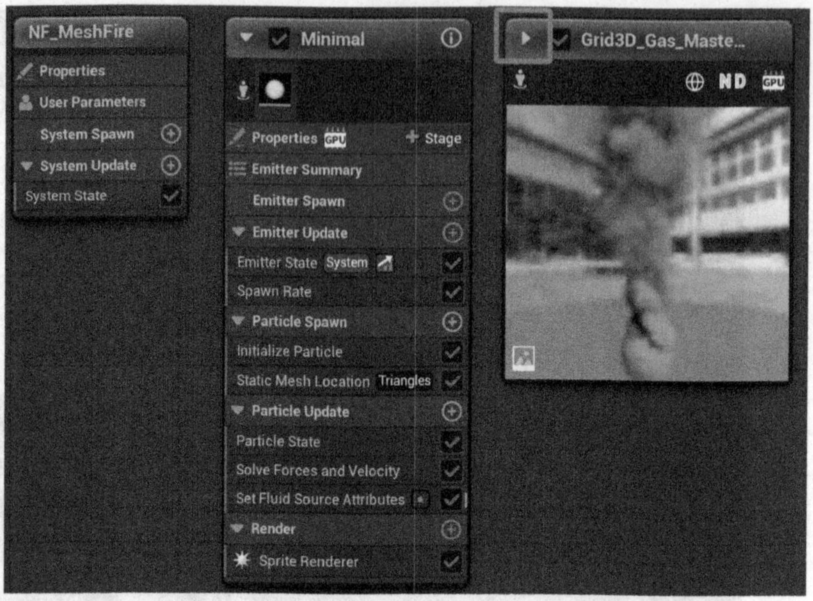

Figure 7.54 - Collapsing the Grid3D_Gas_Master_Emitter

Tip

Pro-Tip: If your system starts to lag while making changes to the **Grid3D_Gas_Master_Emitter**, I suggest stopping the playback in the editor timeline and starting to view the updates from the main level.

9. Select the **Grid3D_Gas_Master_Emitter** and in the **Simulation** tab, change the following:
    - **World Size**: **X** = `1000`, **Y** = `1500`, **Z** = `1800`.
    - **Resolution** = `300`.
    - **Pressure Solver Iterations** = `12`.
    - **Density (Smoke) Buoyancy** = `-0.25`.
    - **Temperature (Fire) Buoyancy** = `0.2`.
    - In the **Attributes** section, change **Dissipation Rate Density** to `0.3`. This will gradually fade the smoke (**Density**).

10. Now, let's assign the **Minimal** emitter as the source of smoke/gas. In the **Source** tab, open the **Sphere Source** section and uncheck **Enable**. The Sphere will now disappear. Under the **Particle Source** section, for **Particle Source Type**, change to **Emitter**.

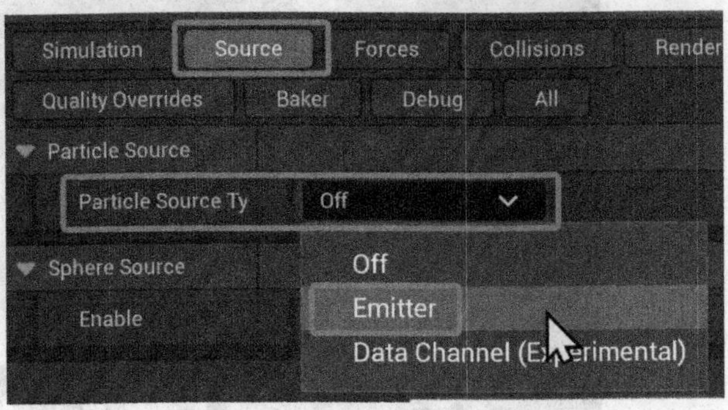

Figure 7.55 - Accessing the Source module

11. More properties will be revealed. In the **Particle Reader** section for **Emitter Binding**, delete the **Grid3D_Gas_Master_Emitter** and replace it with **Minimal.** This is the name of the sprite emitter we created earlier.

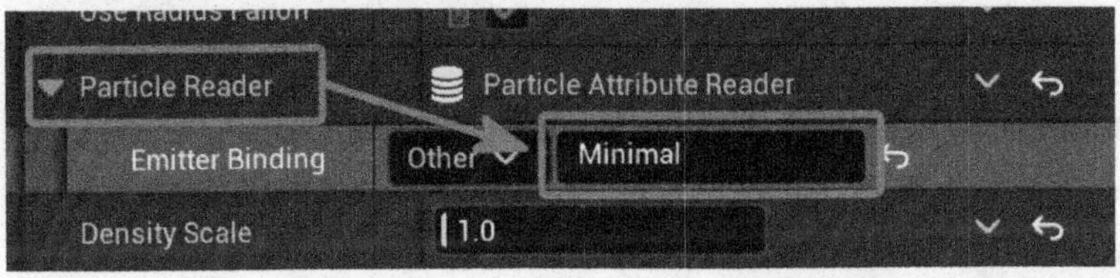

Figure 7.56 - Setting up the Minimal emitter

12. In the **Render** tab, under **Render Temperature**, change **Render Temperature** to **Curve**.
13. If the fire is too bright for your taste, in the **Minimal** emitter | **Set Fluid Sources Attributes** module, change **Temperature** to `0.5`.
14. The Preview panel will now show fire in the form of the house selected in the **Static Mesh Location** module. Disable the **Sprite Renderer** in the **Minimal** emitter. Click **Save**.

Figure 7.57 - Niagara Editor Preview

15. Back in the main level, drag the Wooden House into the level (from the `Fab` folder), reset its **Location** to `0,0,0`. Then, from the `Niagara_Systems` folder, drag `NF_MeshFire` into the level and reset its **Location** to `0,0,0`.
16. Drag `NF_MeshFire` onto the `wooden_house` asset to parent them together. This will allow both assets to be moved as one unit.

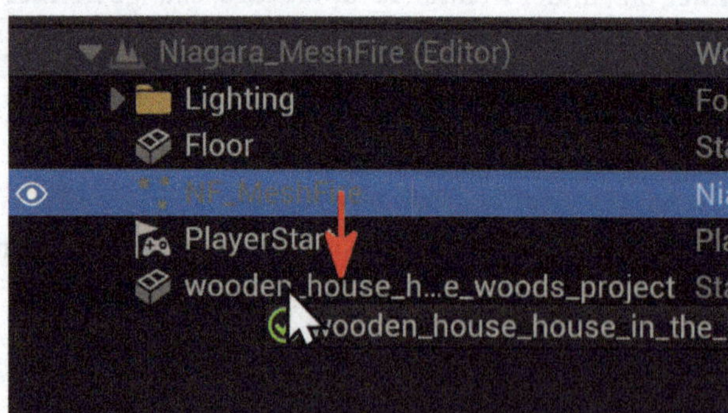

Figure 7.58 - Niagara Editor Preview

17. At this stage, the fire-on-mesh effect is working, but you can continue experimenting with the settings to achieve different results. Try adjusting the **Set Fluid Source**

Attributes values to change how much fire, smoke, and heat are generated from the mesh. You can also add or modify **Forces** such as **Turbulence** and **Wind** to make the flames feel more active, directional, or chaotic. These small changes can help you create different looks, from a gentle surface burn to a more aggressive cinematic fire effect.

Figure 7.59 - The completed Fire on Mesh using Niagara Fluids

How it works...

In this recipe, you created a fire and smoke effect that emits from the surface of a Static Mesh. The key module is **Static Mesh Location**, which allows the **Minimal** emitter to use a mesh as its particle source. Instead of spawning fire from a single point, the particles are distributed across the selected mesh surface, making the flames feel connected to the object.

The mesh needs enough surface detail for this workflow to look convincing. If the mesh has too few triangles, Niagara has fewer surface points to sample from, and the fire may appear patchy or uneven. A mesh with more triangles gives the emitter more areas to sample, which helps the fire and smoke spread more naturally across the object.

Converting the **Static Mesh** selection into a User Parameter makes the system more reusable. This allows you to swap the mesh from the **Details** panel without reopening the Niagara

System. For production work, this is useful because the same fire setup can be tested on different props, vehicles, buildings, wreckage, or text meshes.

The **Set Fluid Source Attributes** module defines how the mesh source contributes to the gas simulation. These values control how much density, heat, velocity, and source radius are sent into the **Grid3D Gas** system. In practical terms, this controls how smoky, fiery, wide, or aggressive the fire feels as it comes from the mesh surface.

The **Grid3D_Gas_Master_Emitter** creates the final volumetric fire and smoke. The **Simulation** settings define the size and detail of the volume, while **Density (Smoke) Buoyancy** and **Temperature (Fire) Buoyancy** affect how the smoke and fire rise. **Dissipation Rate Density** helps the smoke fade over time, preventing the volume from becoming too thick and unreadable.

In the level, parenting the Niagara System to the wooden house keeps the effect aligned with the mesh. This makes the fire appear attached to the object rather than floating separately in the scene. Once the base setup is working, changing **Set Fluid Source Attributes**, **Turbulence**, and **Wind** allows you to create different looks, from a small surface burn to a stronger cinematic fire.

The Skeletal Mesh extension in the *There's more...* section uses the same core idea but replaces **Static Mesh Location** with **Skeletal Mesh Location**. This allows Niagara to sample from an animated mesh instead of a static object. Using the Skeletal Mesh surface as the source, fire and smoke can follow a moving character or creature, which makes the effect useful for burning characters, magical transformations, or animated destruction shots.

There's more...

Now that the fire effect is working on a Static Mesh, we can apply the same idea to a **Skeletal Mesh**. This is useful when you want fire and smoke to appear on animated objects, characters, or creatures instead of only on props or environment pieces. In this example, we will keep the setup simple and focus on using the Skeletal Mesh as the source for the Niagara Fluids effect, so the fire and smoke can follow the animated mesh and feel connected to its movement.

This is a practical extension of the main recipe because the core idea remains the same: the mesh provides surface information, while Niagara Fluids creates the fire and smoke volume. The result can be used for burning characters, damaged creatures, magical transformations, or any cinematic shot where fire needs to stay attached to a moving subject. Follow along:

1. Go to **File** | **New Level** and choose the **Basic** template, then click **Create**. Press the *G* key to hide all the overlay icons. Save the level as `LV_DancingExo`.
2. From the **Character** | **Exo Gray**, drag `Hip_Hop_Dancing` into the Level. Reset its **Location** to `0,0,0` and rotate `90` degrees on **Z**, so he faces forward.

3. Create a new Level Sequence and rename it as `LS_DancingExo`. Add the `Hip_Hop_Dancing` asset into the level sequence.
4. Click the **+** sign on the **Animation** track and select the `Hip_Hop_Dancing` animation, then click **Play**. Exo Gray is dancing his troubles away! Save the project.

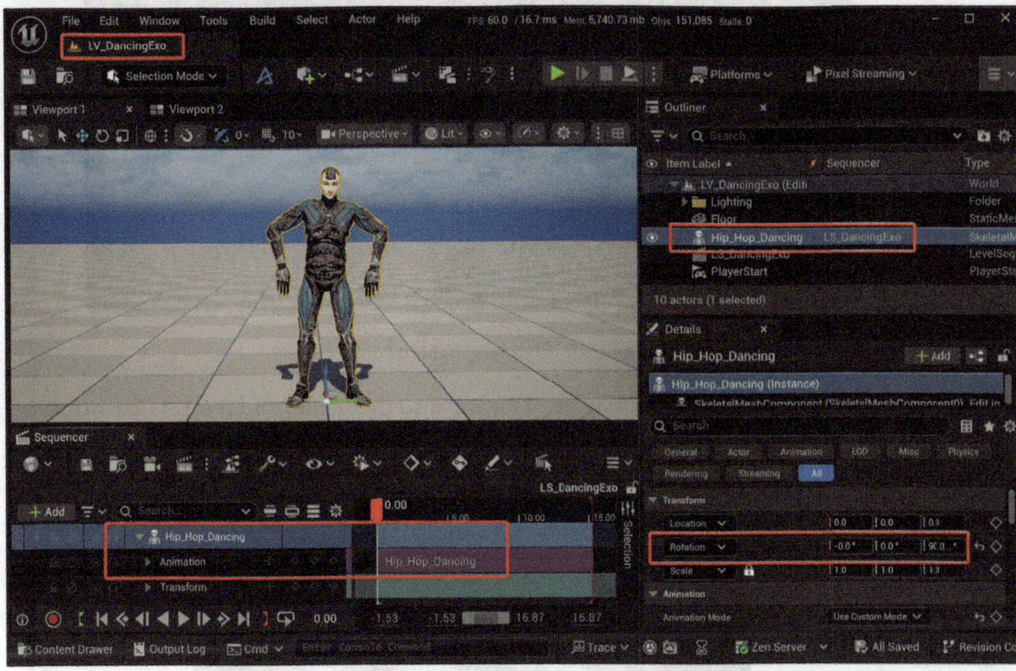

Figure 7.60 - Setting up the Skeletal Mesh

5. In the `Niagara_Systems` folder, duplicate `NF_MeshFire` and rename it as `NF_Dancing`, and double-click to open the Niagara Editor.
6. Since we'll be using a Skeletal Mesh instead of a Static Mesh, in the **Minimal** emitter, delete the **Static Mesh Location** module.
7. In the **Particle Update** section, add a **Skeletal Mesh Location** module. Change **Source Mode** to **Attach Parent** and for the **Preview Mesh**, search for `Exo` and select **Standing Taunt Battlercry Exo Gray**.
8. Under the **Sampling** section, change **Mesh Sampling Type** to **Surface Triangles**. In the preview pane, you should see the shape of the character now.
9. Instead of setting him on fire, let's make cool-looking fluids on him. Select the **Grid3D_Gas_Master_Emitter**, then in the **Render** tab, ensure the **Render**

Temperature is set to **Curve**, then click the **Temperature Color Curve** triangle. Change the color scheme as shown in *Figure 7.61*:

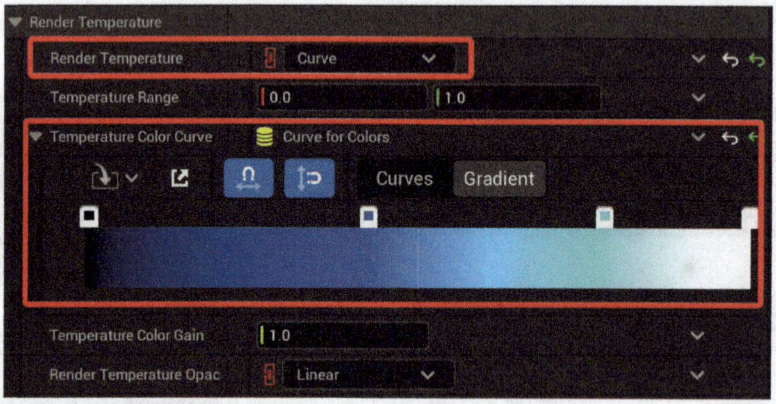

Figure 7.61 - Changing the fire color scheme

10. Jump back to the main level, drag `NF_Dancing` into the scene, and reset its **Location** to `0,0,0`. Just like in the main recipe, parent `NF_Dancing` to `Hip_Hop_Dancing` asset. When prompted to select a bone, choose **None**.
11. Click the **Play** button, and you'll have Exo engulfed in cool-looking fluids.

Figure 7.62 - Skeletal Mesh with cool-looking Niagara Fluids

Use the workflow you've learned throughout this chapter and spend some time tweaking to get the effect you're going for. It's loads of fun!

8

Chaos Destruction and Cloth for Cinematics

In the previous chapter, we used Niagara Fluids to create cinematic volume effects, such as fog, explosions, storm clouds, and fire. These effects are useful on their own, but they become even more powerful when combined with physical destruction and motion in a scene. In this chapter, we will move into **Chaos**, Unreal Engine's physics-based toolset for creating destruction and cloth simulation.

Chaos Destruction is useful in cinematic shots because it adds weight, impact, and scale. A wall breaking apart can instantly make a scene feel more dangerous and believable. However, destruction should not be treated as random pieces flying everywhere. For cinematic work, the timing, fracture shape, debris direction, smoke pass, and camera framing all need to support the story moment.

We will begin by exploding a wall using Chaos Destruction, controlled debris, and a Niagara Fluids smoke pass. This connects directly back to the volumetric smoke workflows covered in *Chapter 7*. We will then look at caching Chaos Destruction so the simulation can be played back, scrubbed, timed, and rendered more reliably in **Sequencer**. Finally, we will create a Chaos Cloth flag or curtain setup for close-up shots, where subtle fabric movement can add realism, atmosphere, and life to the scene.

By the end of this chapter, you will have a practical foundation for combining destruction, debris, smoke, cached simulation playback, and cloth movement in cinematic Unreal Engine shots.

In this chapter, we'll cover the following recipes:

- Exploding a wall with Chaos Destruction and Niagara Fluids smoke

- Caching Chaos Destruction for repeatable cinematic playback
- Creating Chaos Cloth flag/curtain for close shots

Technical requirements

Before starting this recipe, ensure the following are set up:

1. Make sure **Unreal Engine 5.6** is installed. Refer to *Chapter 1* for setup details. If you are using a different version of Unreal Engine, some settings, interface options, or results may vary.
2. A project with **Niagara**, **Niagara Sim Caching, Niagara Fluids**, and **Chaos** plugins enabled.
3. Maintain the folder structure to keep the assets organized, as shown below:
    - `Content`
        - `Niagara_Systems`
        - `Chaos`
        - `Sequences`
        - `Textures`
        - `Materials`
        - `MRQ`

You can download the example project for this book by following the instructions in the *Download the example code/resource files* section in the *Preface* of this book.

The complete example project is included in the downloadable code/resource bundle.

Exploding a wall with Chaos Destruction and Niagara Fluids smoke

In this recipe, you will create a simple example of **Chaos Destruction**. We will use the **Basic Level** template again, so the scene stays clean and easy to follow. The focus here is not to create a complex destruction shot yet, but to understand the basic principles behind **Chaos**, **Geometry Collections**, and **Fracture Mode**.

Before we build a more cinematic wall explosion, it is important to understand the terminology and workflow. You will learn how a Static Mesh is converted into a **Geometry Collection**, how **Fracture Mode** is used to break the wall into pieces, and how those pieces can be controlled so the destruction feels readable on camera.

Once these foundations are clear, we can take the effect further by shaping the debris, controlling the impact moment, and layering it with smoke, dust, or explosion effects in later steps.

> **Note**
>
> Chaos Destruction can be demanding on your computer, especially when working with many fractured pieces. The more fragments you create, the more calculations Unreal Engine needs to process for physics, collision, and movement. For best results, use a high-end PC when working with complex destruction effects. If the scene becomes slow, reduce the number of fracture pieces, fracture only the area that needs to break, or test the simulation in smaller stages before building the final cinematic shot.

Getting ready

For this recipe, we will use the **Basic Level Template** that comes with Unreal Engine 5. This keeps the scene simple so we can focus on building, timing, and previewing the effect without extra distractions. Once the effect is working, you can place it into any cinematic scene and trigger it from **Sequencer** at the exact frame needed.

How to do it...

Let's start by creating a new basic level:

1. Go to **File** | **New Level**, from the pop-up panel, choose the **Basic** template, and click **Create.** Save the Level as `ChaosDestruction`.
2. Press the *G* key to hide all the overlay icons. In the **Content Browser**, create a new folder named `Chaos`. Inside the `Chaos` folder, create another folder named `GeometryCollection`. As you'll see shortly, all fractured collections will be stored in this folder for organization purposes.
3. Press the *1* key on the keyboard to reset the view, and let's break some objects!
4. Just to be sure you have the right plugins enabled, go to **Edit** | **Plugins**. In the **Plugins** panel, search for `chaos` and enable *all* plugins related to Chaos. If you get a warning message about some plugins being experimental versions, just click **Yes**. Restart the editor.

Understanding the Chaos fracture workflow

Let's first understand the basic workflow of how the fracture mode works:

1. Add a Sphere into the scene, reset its location to `0,0,0`, and raise it on the **Z** axis, set to `500` units.

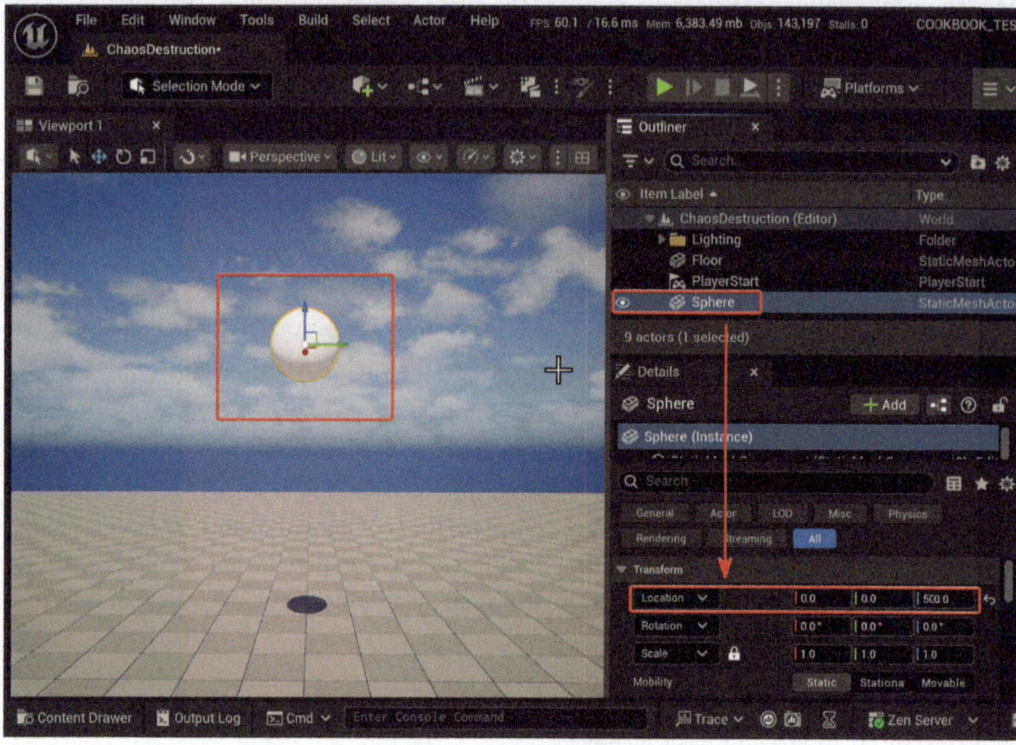

Figure 8.1 - Adding a Sphere to the level

2. From the top left of the editor interface, switch from **Selection Mode** to **Fracture Mode**.

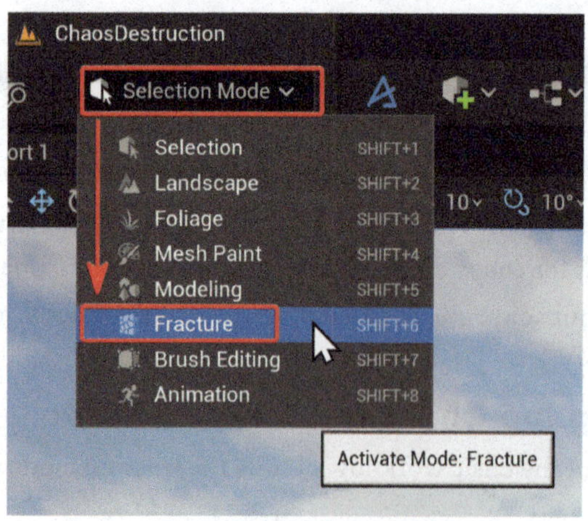

Figure 8.2 - Switching to Fracture mode

Note

If, for some reason, the **Fracture** mode does not appear, please refer to the *Technical Requirements* section.

3. Ensure the user interface is set up as shown in *Figure 8.3*:

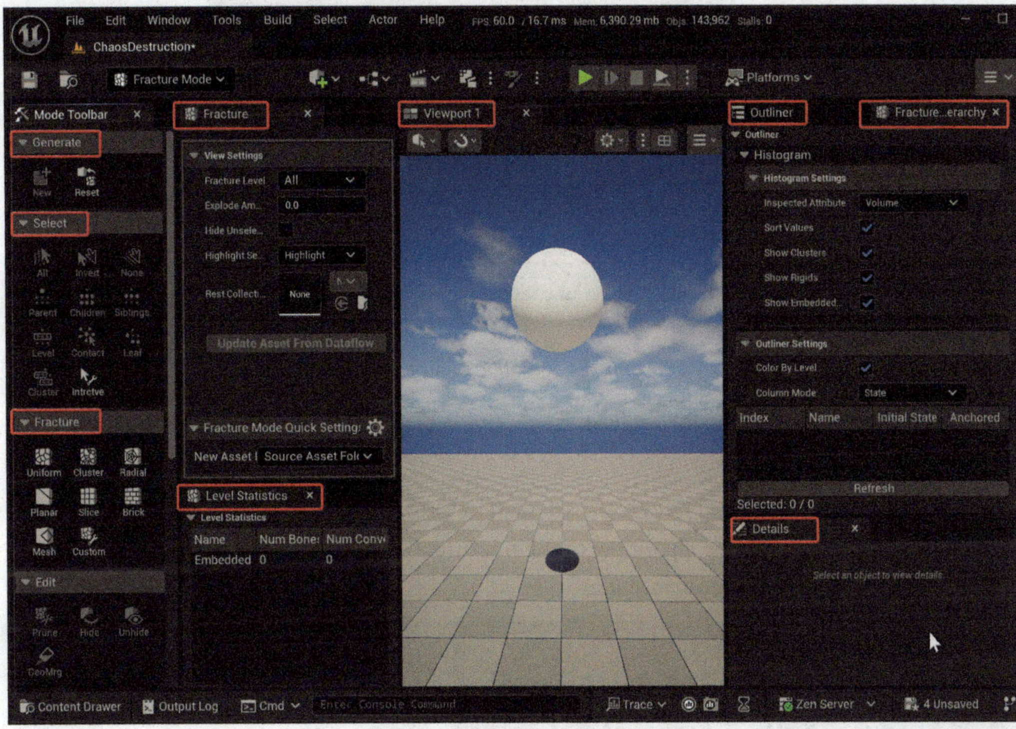

Figure 8.3 - The Fracture Mode interface

There are a lot of panels, but don't worry, we'll go through the workflow step by step. Let's continue.

4. Click on the Sphere in the Viewport. Then, in the **Mode** toolbar, under the **Generate** section, click the **New** button.
5. In the pop-up window, select the `GeometryCollection` folder created earlier. For the **Geometry Collection Name**, type something descriptive; otherwise, the editor will generate one automatically depending on the selected object. Click the **Create Geometry Collection** button.

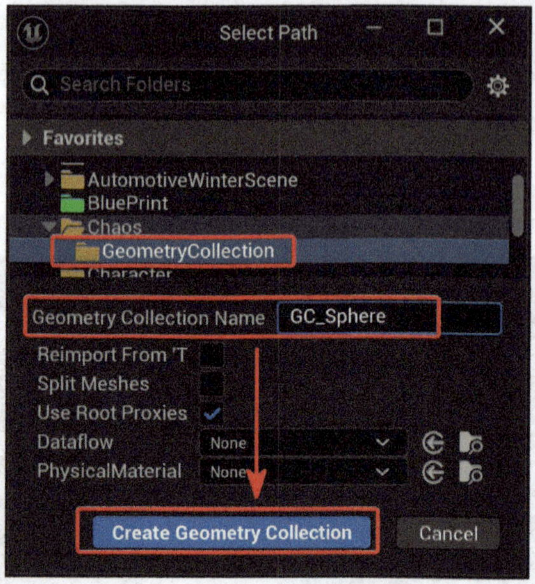

Figure 8.4 - Creating Geometry Collection

6. Look in the **Outliner**, the asset has been converted to a GeometryCollectionActor and is no longer a Static Mesh.
7. With the Sphere (`CG_Sphere`) still selected in the **Fracture** section, click the **Uniform** button once. You'll see a preview of the fracture pattern on the Sphere. Now click the **Fracture** button to confirm the process.

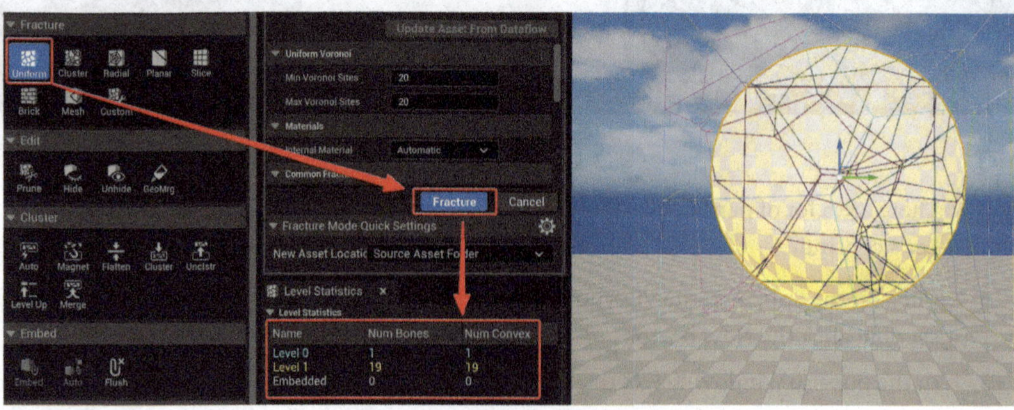

Figure 8.5 - Fracturing the Sphere

8. In the **Level Statistics** panel, you'll notice **Level 0** and **Level 1**. **Level 0** refers to the Sphere, which is *1* object. **Level 2** refers to the number of fractures you just made, which is all *19* of them. In Chaos, fracture fragments are referred to as **Bones**. Go figure!

> **Note**
>
> You can have unlimited levels, but the more levels you make, the slower the process of generating them. As a good rule of thumb, only fracture the section of the object that needs to break. The smaller the selected fracture area, the faster the pieces will be generated and the easier the destruction will be to manage.

9. We will come back to the details later, but for now, we just want the Sphere to break. Zoom out of the Viewport far enough to view the Sphere falling to the floor. Before you click the **Simulate** button, click the **vertical ellipses** (annotated in *Figure 8.6*) and select **Current Camera**, then click the **Simulate** button, and it will run the simulation from the current camera location.

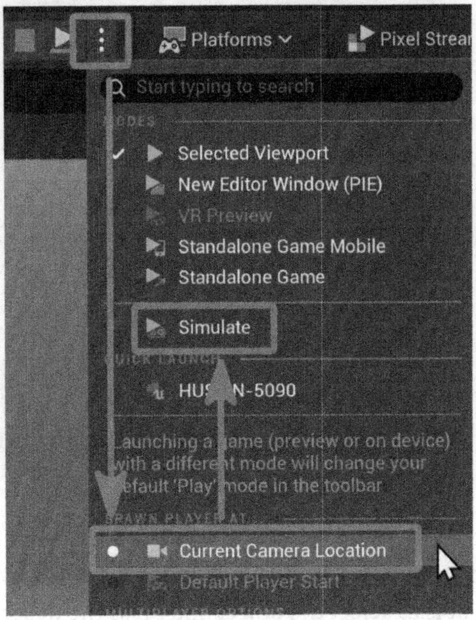

Figure 8.6 - Simulation settings

10. Go ahead and click the **Simulate** button or press *Alt* + *S*. The Sphere will fall and break. Yay! Although a little less dramatic, you managed to make it work. Press *Esc* to end the

simulation mode. Keep simulating to get different results. The Sphere is just a test object to understand the fracture process.

> **Note**
>
> If the Sphere does not break into pieces, position it higher in the *Z* direction (up). Let gravity do its job!

11. Now let's make more fractures (bones). Select the Sphere, click **Uniform**, then **Fracture** once more. Keep an eye on the **Level Statistics** panel. You now have **Level 2** with **106** sub-fractures. Press the **Simulate** button a few times. You'll notice smaller chunks of the Sphere.
12. Select the Sphere and press the *Shift* + *E* keyboard shortcut a few times to see the exploded view. Use *Shift* + *Q* to undo that.

Figure 8.7 - The Exploded view

13. Once objects have been fractured, you will not be able to undo the process. The only way around that is to select the object and press the **Reset** button, next to the **New** button. You can confirm by looking at the **Level Statistics** panel.

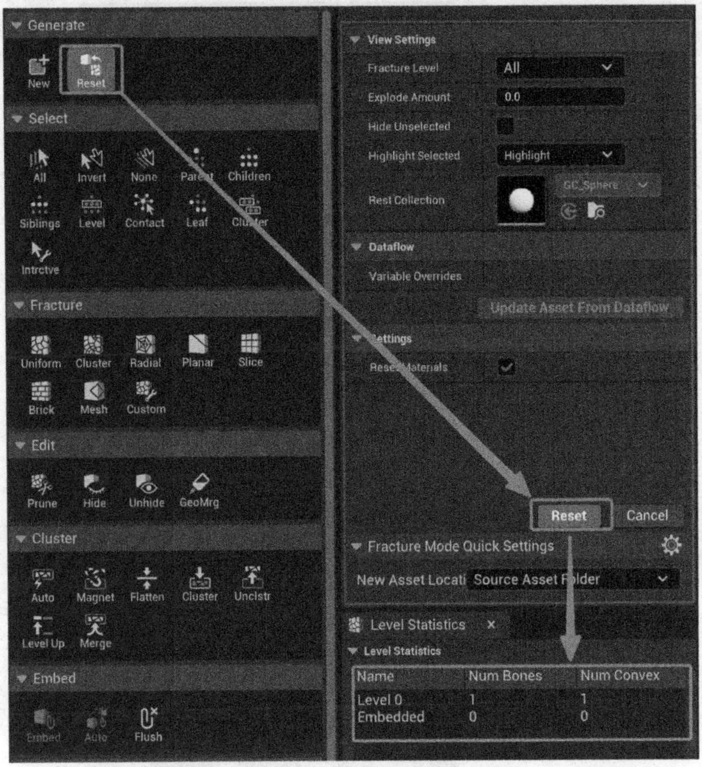

Figure 8.8 - Resetting the fracture operation

14. Until now, the fragments (bones) seem glued together, and we want them to break apart even more. This is achieved by selecting the Sphere (`GC_Sphere`) in the **Outliner** and in its **Detail** panel, searching for `Damage`. In the **Damage Threshold** section, there is **Index [0]**, which refers to **Level 0**; **Index [1]**, which refers to **Level 1**, and **Index [2]**, which in this case refers to **Level 2**—this will depend on how many levels you've created. Change **Index [0]** to `25,000` instead of 500,000. The lower the value, the easier they break apart.

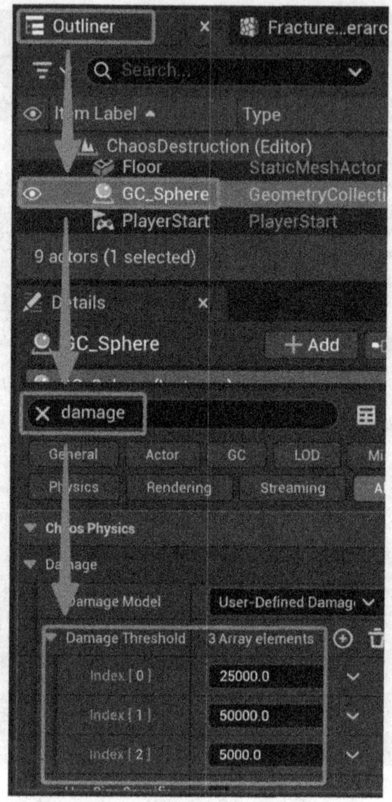

Figure 8.9 - Damage settings

15. Click **Simulate**. Now the **Level 1** fragments are scattered further apart. You can set a lower value to **Index [1]** to have the **Level 2** fragments fall apart too. Try `5000`.
16. Using the method you have learned so far, take a few minutes to reset the Sphere and experiment using the other Fracture types in the **Fracture** category. You can also use any other Static Mesh from the **Content Browser**.

Figure 8.10 - Fracture types

Now that the basic Chaos fracture workflow is clear, we can take the effect further.

Exploding a wall

In this section, we will break a wall and control the exact destruction timing in **Sequencer**. Follow along with these steps:

1. Go to **File | New Level**. From the pop-up panel, choose the **Basic template**, and click **Create**. Save the Level as `WallDestruction`.
2. Press the *G* key to hide all the overlay icons. Press the *1* key on the keyboard to reset the view.
3. Add a Cube into the scene, change its size to **X** = `0.25`, **Y** = 5, **Z** = 5. Set its location to `0,0,250`. From the **Starter Content**, in the `Material` folder, assign the `M_Concrete_Poured`, as shown in *Figure 8.11*:

Figure 8.11 - Assigning wall material

4. I've turned the **Directional Light intensity** to `4.0` Lux so we can see the wall texture better.

Before we start breaking the wall, it is important to understand the shot we are trying to create. The wall should *explode outward* from the middle section, while the outer edges remain mostly intact. This means the center of the wall needs smaller fracture pieces so it can break apart into more detailed fragments, while the surrounding areas stay more stable.

To make the effect feel more cinematic, we will also add a **Niagara Fluids** smoke pass as the wall fragments fall to the ground. This will help sell the impact, add weight to the debris, and connect this recipe back to the volumetric smoke and fire workflows we covered in *Chapter 7*. Let's continue:

1. Select the wall and go into **Fracture Mode**. Under the **Generate** category, click **New**. In the pop-up window, select the **Chaos | GeometryCollection** folder, rename the collection as `GC_Wall`, uncheck **Use Root Proxies**, and press the **Create Geometry Collection** button.

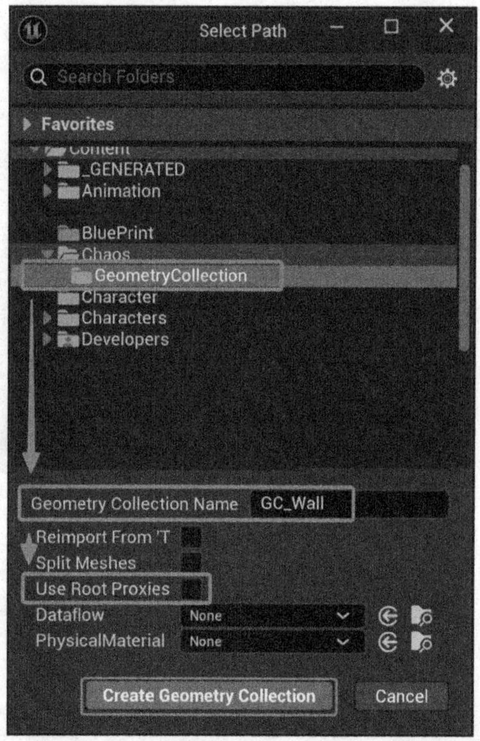

Figure 8.12 - Disabling Use Root Proxies

> **Note**
>
> Make sure **Use Root Proxies** is unchecked before continuing. This step is important because the workflow may not behave correctly if this option remains enabled. In Unreal Engine 5.6, this appears to affect how the fractured wall responds in this setup, although the behavior may differ in later engine versions.

2. In the **Fracture** category, click once on the **Uniform** fracture type. In the next panel, under the **Uniform Voronoi** section, increase **Min Voronoi Sites** and **Max Voronoi Sites** to `100`. This will add more fragments to the wall.
3. Scroll down to the **Noise** section, increase **Amplitude** to 5 and **Frequency** to **1.** Depending on the size of the wall, these settings will add jaggedness to the fragments (bones) so the pieces do not have straight edges.

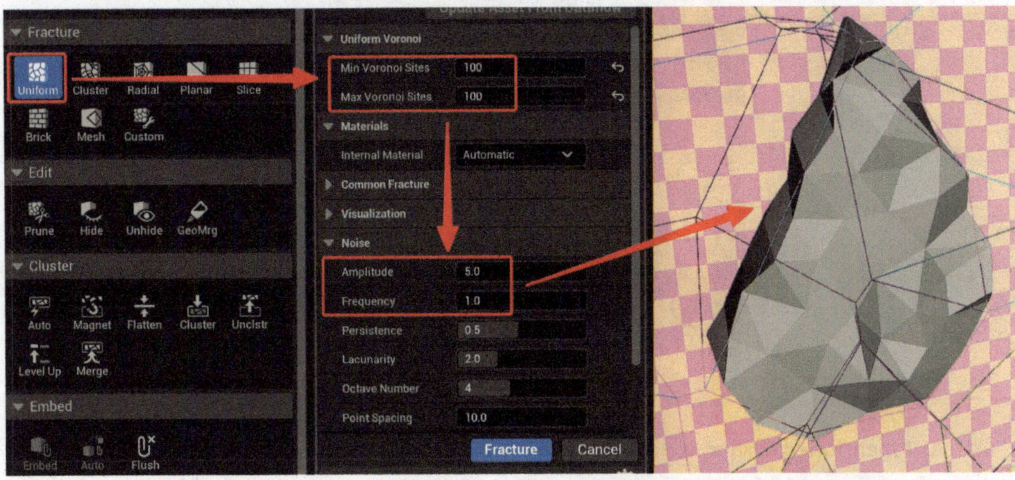

Figure 8.13 - Fracturing the wall

4. Click **Fracture**. You now have colorful pieces of wall fragments. Use the *Shift* + *E* shortcut repeatedly to expand the wall where you can clearly see the uneven fragments. Use *Shift* + *Q* repeatedly to put them back together. Your results may vary.

Figure 8.14 - Exploded view

5. As I mentioned earlier, we need to have smaller fragments in the middle of the wall, where the explosion impact is strongest. In the **Select** category (left side panel), use the **None** button to unselect the wall if it is selected, then select a single middle fragment. In the **Select** category, click the **Contact** button once or twice to *grow* the selection. Use the **None** button again to deselect and reselect if needed.

Figure 8.15 - Selecting the mid-section of the wall

6. With the fragments selected, click **Fracture** again. You'll now have smaller fragments in the mid-section of the wall. Save your project.

> **Note**
>
> As mentioned in the previous section, the higher the number of fragments you create, the longer it will take to create them, especially when using mid-range computers.

7. Switch back to the **Selection** mode. To switch back to the material view, select the wall and in its **Details** panel, under the **General** section, uncheck **Show Bone Colors**.

Although the wall has been fractured, nothing will happen when you click the **Simulate** (*Alt* + *S*) button because no force has been applied to it yet. Earlier, the Sphere broke because gravity caused it to fall and hit the ground. For this wall setup, we need to create a force that pushes the fractured pieces outward. In the next subsection, we will set up the explosion simulation and control how the wall breaks apart.

Controlling wall destruction

In this section, you'll use Chaos Fields to drive the explosion, keep the edges intact, and shape the debris so the destruction reads well on camera:

1. Unreal Engine comes with a few **Chaos-related Blueprints**, but they are well-hidden in the Engine content. To access these Blueprints, ensure you have the **Engine Content** folder visible in the **Content Browser**. If not, click the **gear** icon and enable **Engine Content**, which is accessible from the **Content Browser**.

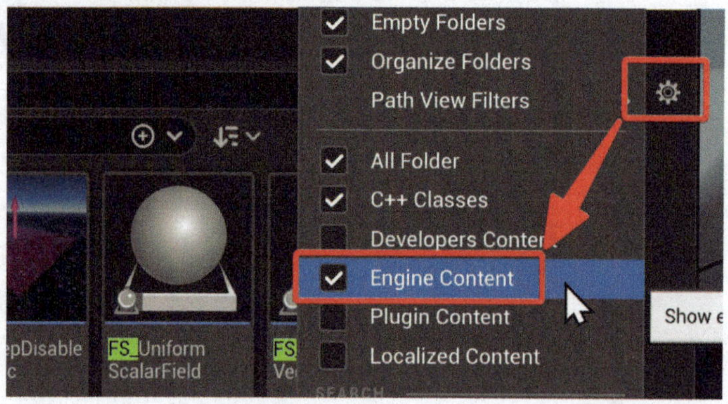

Figure 8.16 - Accessing Engine Content

2. Select the `Engine` folder, in the search bar type `FS_`. Of all these Blueprints, we will use `FS_AnchorField` and `FS_MasterField`. Out of all the available Blueprints, these two are frequently used in this kind of scenario.

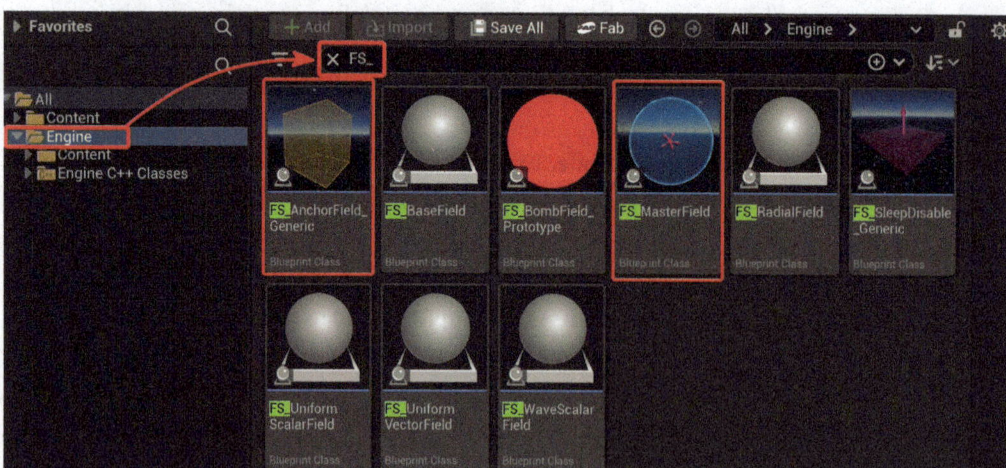

Figure 8.17 - Accessing the Chaos Blueprints

3. Drag `FS_MasterField` into the level and place it in the middle of the wall. If you're unable to view it, press *G*. Stand back and press the **Simulate** button or press *Alt* + *S*. We finally have our exploded wall. The extent of the explosion will depend on the size and placement of the `FS_MasterField` Blueprint. Try placing it in a few different places —forward, back, higher up, or lower down. As long as the Blueprint touches the wall, it will crumble. Press *Esc* to reset and try again.

Figure 8.18 - The exploded wall

4. By adjusting the **Damage** control, we can have the fragments spread further apart. Select the wall, scroll down to the **Damage** section, decrease **Index [0]** to `25,000`, and **Index [1]** to `5000` as we did earlier. Hit the **Simulate** button.

Great! We are making good progress. Let's take it up a notch. Our plan was to have the wall explode outwards from the mid-section, but for the edges to stay intact. This is where the next Blueprint, `FS_AnchorField`, becomes handy. Let's keep going:

1. Drag `FS_MasterField` to the center of the wall, then drag `FS_AnchorField` into the level. Make four copies, position and scale it so it encapsulates only the edges of the wall, as shown in *Figure 8.19*:

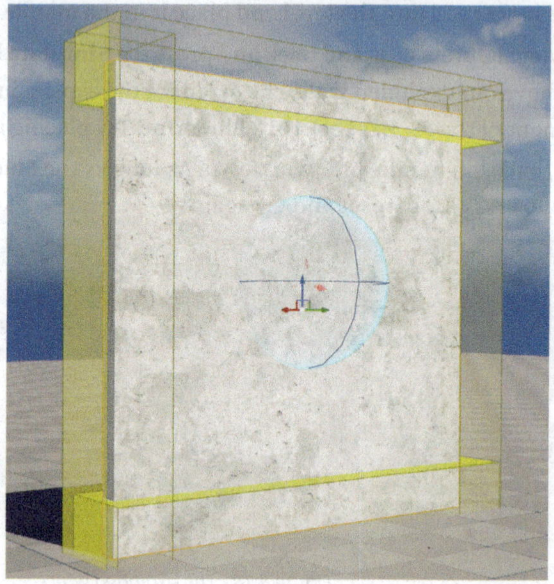

Figure 8.19 - Adding the FS_AnchorField Blueprints

2. Before hitting the **Simulate** keyboard shortcut, there is one more step we need to take. Select `GC_Wall` in the **Outliner**. Then, in its **Details** panel, under the **Initialization** section, click the + sign four times (for four Anchor Fields), then assign **Index [0]** to `FS_AnchorField_Generic` and complete all indexes as shown in *Figure 8.20*.

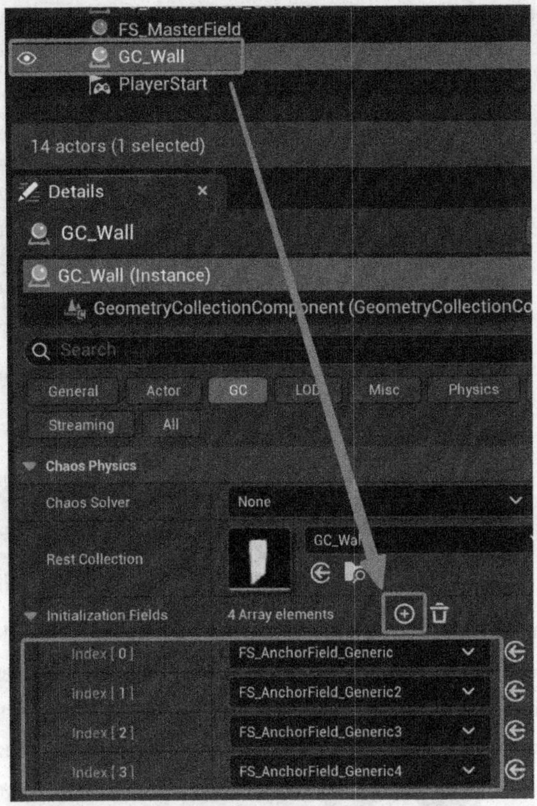

Figure 8.20 - Initializing the Anchor Fields

3. Press *Alt* + *S* to test if the wall breaks from the middle and the edges stay intact. As shown in *Figure 8.21*, reposition the `FS_MasterField` and `FS_AnchorField` if needed.

Figure 8.21 - Exploded wall with intact edges

4. Now let's make the fragments explode outwards. Select `FS_MasterField`, and in its **Details** panel, scroll to the **Apply Linear And Angular Velocities** section and enable **Use Directional Vector**. The Blueprint will now show arrows, which are facing upwards. Rotate the Blueprint so the arrows *face forward*. Press *Alt* + *S* to simulate.

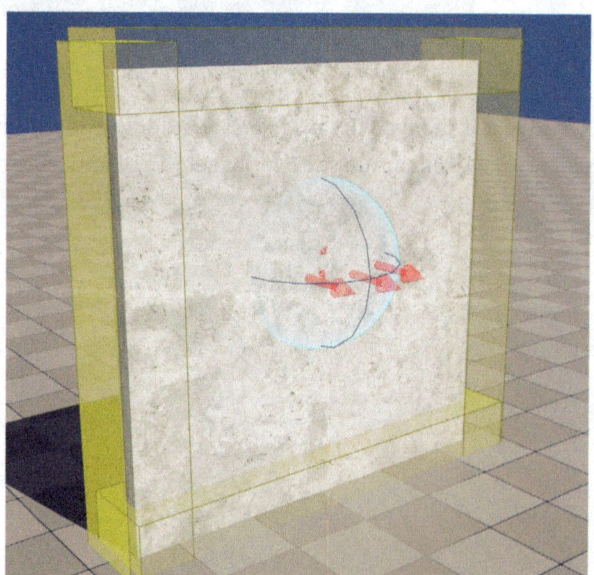

Figure 8.22 - Using the Directional Vector

5. If you have the fragments exploded outwards, you are on the right track. If not, keep repositioning the `FS_MasterField` and re-simulate. Press *Esc* to end the simulation. Save the project.

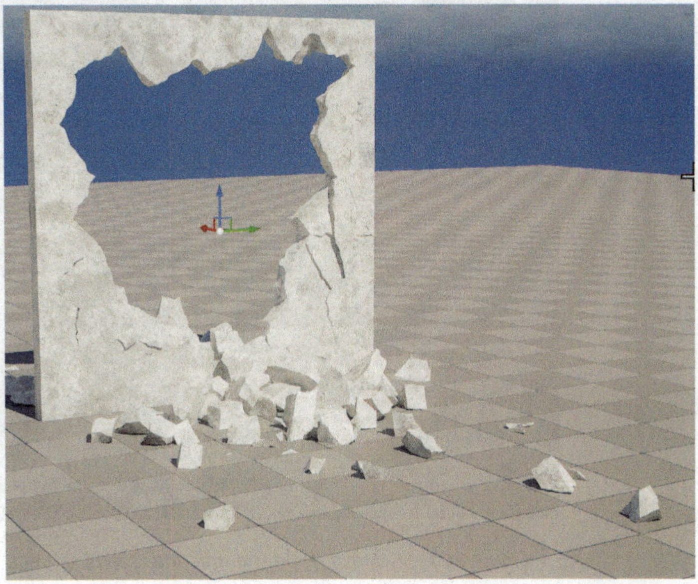

Figure 8.23 - Fragments exploding outward

6. The strength and spread of the explosion are controlled by the size of `FS_MasterField`, along with the **Radial Magnitude** and **Directional Magnitude** values. **Torque Mult** controls how much the fractured pieces rotate as they are pushed outward. Adjust these settings to shape the explosion and achieve the debris movement you want for the shot.
7. To get different results, try switching **Activation Type** to **OnTick**, **Field Falloff Shape** to **Box**, and **Delay** to `0.0` to get a different outcome. Save your project as you go along.

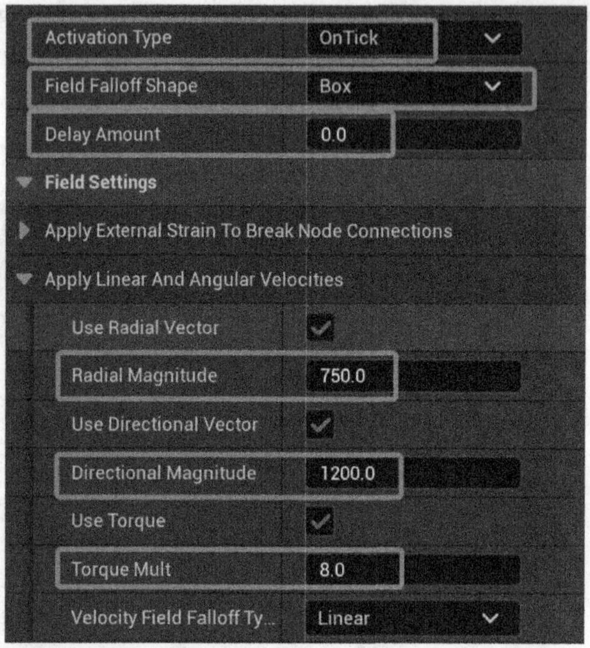

Figure 8.24 - FS_MasterField strength and spread settings

Integrating Niagara Fluids

There are a fair number of settings you can experiment with in Niagara Fluids, but let's stick to the basics for now. We have loads more to learn. Up next, let's add Niagara Fluids particle to create some aftermath smoke. But first, we need to activate some Chaos features:

1. Access the **Project Settings** from the **Edit** menu. In the search window, type `Chaos`, scroll down, and enable **Generate Collision Data**, **Generate Break Data**, and **Generate Tailing Data**. These are all crucial settings for the **Chaos** plugin to communicate with Niagara.

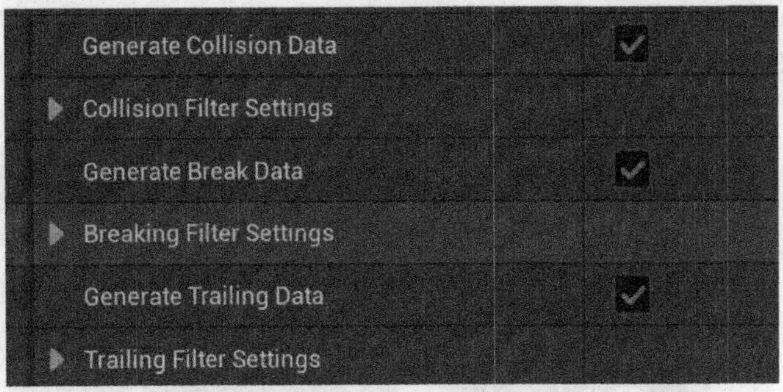

Figure 8.25 - Enabling Chaos features in Project Settings

> **Tip**
>
> To make this section easier to follow, I strongly recommend going through *Chapter 7* first, as it covers Niagara Fluids in detail.

2. Now it's time to create Niagara particles. In the `Niagara_Systems` folder, create a new Niagara System, as we have done many times before, choose the **Minimal** emitter, and rename it as `NF_WallDestruction`. Double-click to open it.
3. In the **Properties** section, change to **GPUCompute Sim** and set **Calculate Bounds Mode** to **Fixed**. We will utilize the GPU to generate the particles.
4. In the **Emitter Update** section, add the **Spawn From Chaos** module. Search for `Chaos` and ensure you enable the **Plugins** option.

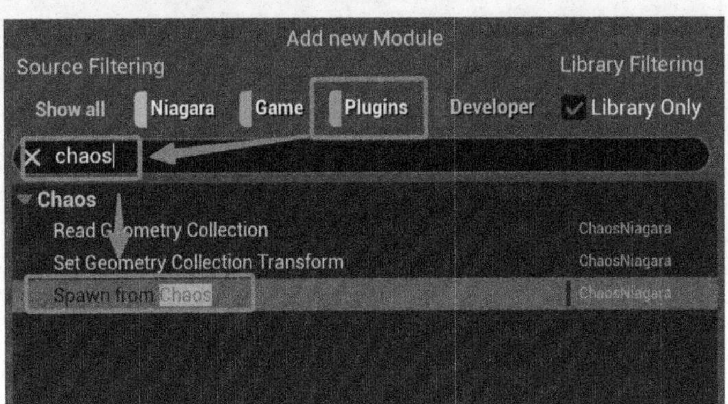

Figure 8.26 - Adding Spawn from Chaos module

5. Using the dropdown arrow for **Spawn from Chaos**, in the **Make** category, choose **Read from new User parameter**. We are converting this parameter into a User Parameter.

This will allow you to change the destruction data setting in the **Details** panel in the main level.

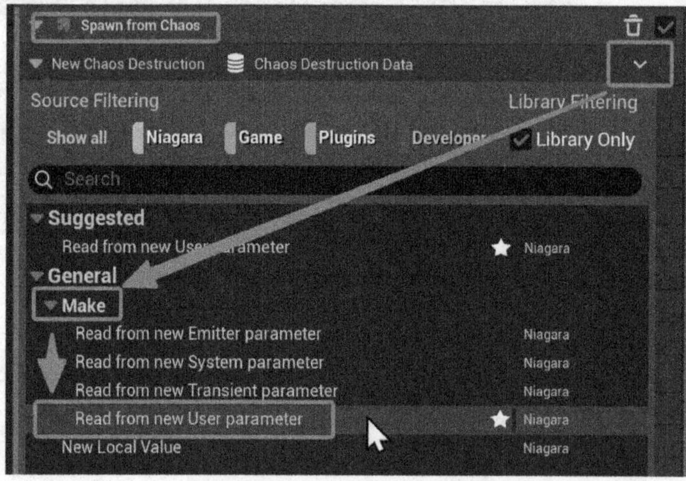

Figure 8.27 - Converting into User Parameter

6. In the **Particle Spawn** section, add the **Apply Chaos Data** module. Convert it into a User Parameter as well.
7. In the **Initial Particle** module, set **Lifetime** to **Random Range Float**, set **Minimum** to `2.0`, and **Maximum** to **5.0.** Change **Color Mode** to **Direct Set** and make a bright red color using **R** = `1`, **G** = `0`, **B** = `0`. We want to ensure the particles are visible during the simulation. We will turn them off at the final stage.
8. Change **Sprite Size Mode** to **Uniform** and leave **Uniform Sprite Size** as `10`.

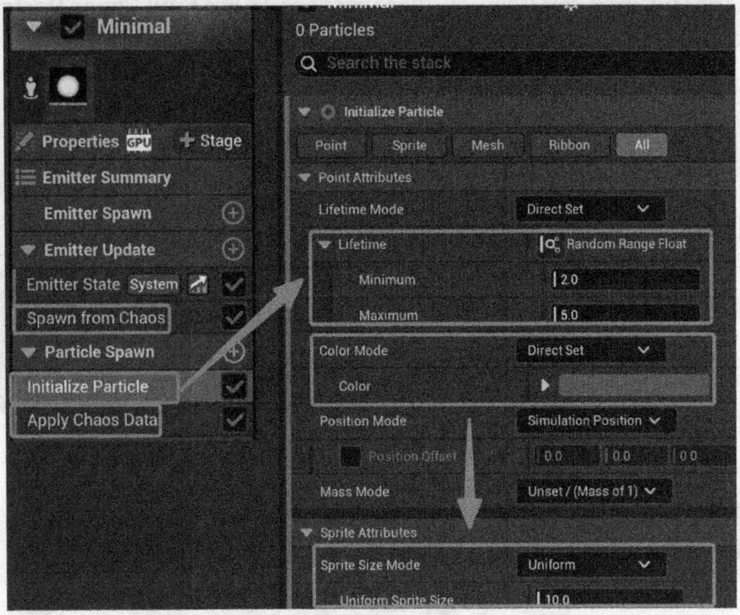

Figure 8.28 - Initialize Particle module settings

9. In the **Particle Update** section, add the **Collision module,** click **Fix issue**, and change **GPU Collision Type** to **GPU Distance Fields.** Then add the **Gravity Force** module. I find that setting **GPU Collision Type** to **GPU Distance Fields** gives a better outcome. A GPU Distance Field in a Niagara **Collision** module uses whole-scene, volumetric voxel data to calculate particle collisions, which provides a cost-effective outcome.

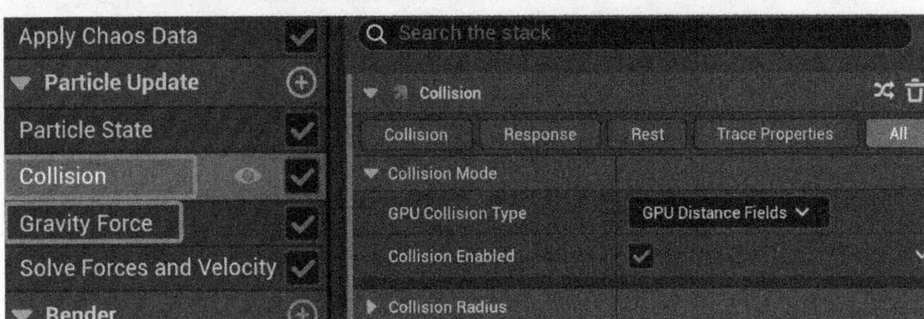

Figure 8.29 - Collision module settings

10. Compile and save, then drag `NF_WallDestruction` into the level. You will not get any particles just yet; there are a few more things we'll have to set up.

11. In the **Outliner**, select `NF_WallDestruction`. In the **New Chaos Destruction Data** section, change **Data Source** to **Trailing Data**, then set **Max Number of Data to Spawn Particles** to `2000`.

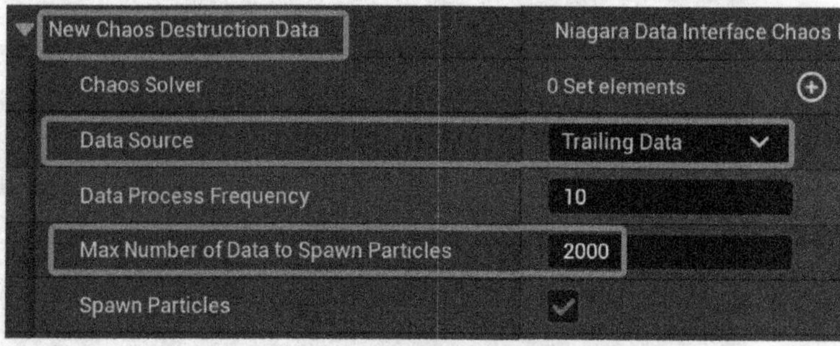

Figure 8.30 - NF_WallDestruction settings

12. Again, in the **Outliner**, select `GC_Wall`**.** In the **Details** panel, scroll down to **Events**, enable **Notify Breaks**, **Notify Collisions**, and **Notify Trailing**.

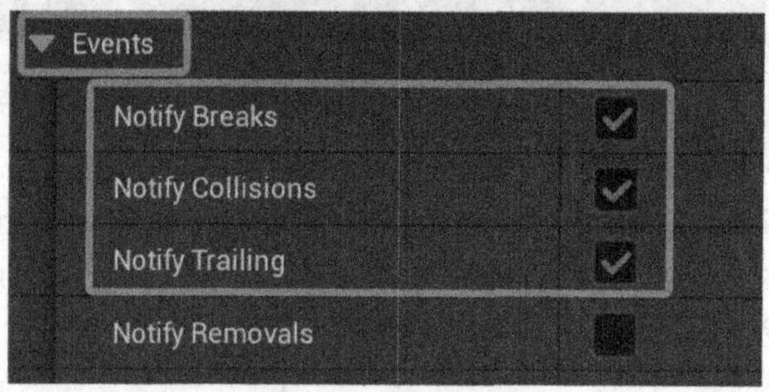

Figure 8.31 - Enabling Notify settings

13. If you have followed along patiently, you should now see particles emitting as the wall explodes when using the *Alt* + *S* keyboard shortcut. Save your project.

Figure 8.32 - Particles emitted with the explosion

Creating the volumetric smoke effect

Now that Chaos is driving Niagara particles, in the next few steps, we will add the **Grid3D_Gas_Master_Emitter** and configure the aftermath smoke. Let's continue:

1. Back in the Niagara Editor, stop the timeline playback to avoid any lag when configuring the properties, then right-click and add the **Grid3D_Gas_Master_Emitter**. Collapse the node and click **Fix issue** if prompted to do so. This is the same workflow we have done in the *Creating low-lying volumetric fog with object collision* recipe in *Chapter 7*. So, I'll speed through the steps you should already be familiar with.
2. Select the **Grid3D_Gas_Master_Emitter**. Then, in the **Sources** tab, disable the **Sphere Source**. Change **Particle Source Type** to **Emitter** and set **Emitter Binding** to the **Minimal** emitter.

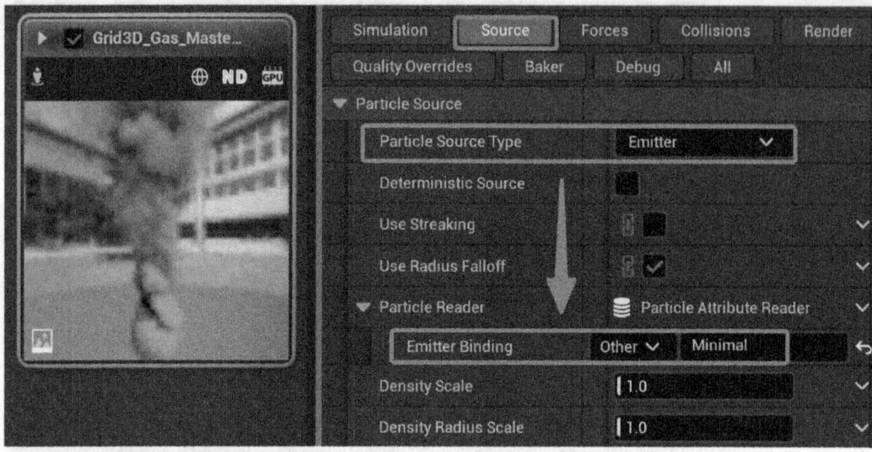

Figure 8.33 - Grid3D_Gas_Master_Emitter Source settings

3. In the **Simulation** tab, set **World Size** to **X** = `1000`, **Y** = `1000`, **Z** = `1000`**.** Back in the main level, use the bounding box as a guide and move `NF_WallDestruction` forward so that the smoke has enough space to expand outward with the wall fragments.
4. Run the simulation to check how much space the effect needs, but try to keep the **Draw Bounds** as small as possible. A larger simulation area can reduce the smoke resolution and slow down the simulation.

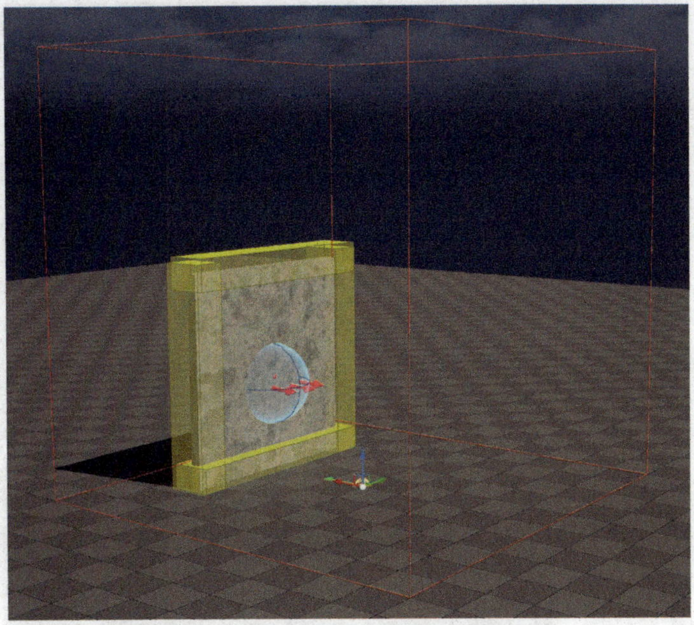

Figure 8.34 - Positioning the bounding box

5. To activate the Smoke, in the **Minimal** emitter's **Particle Update** section, add the **Set Fluid Source Attributes** module. Use the following settings for now:
    - Set **Density** to `0.5`
    - Set **Velocity Scale** to **Random Range Float** and **Minimum** at `0.5` and **Maximum** at `1.0`
    - Set **Divergence** to `1.0`
    - Set **Radius** to **Random Range Float** and **Minimum** to `5.0` and **Maximum** to `7.0`

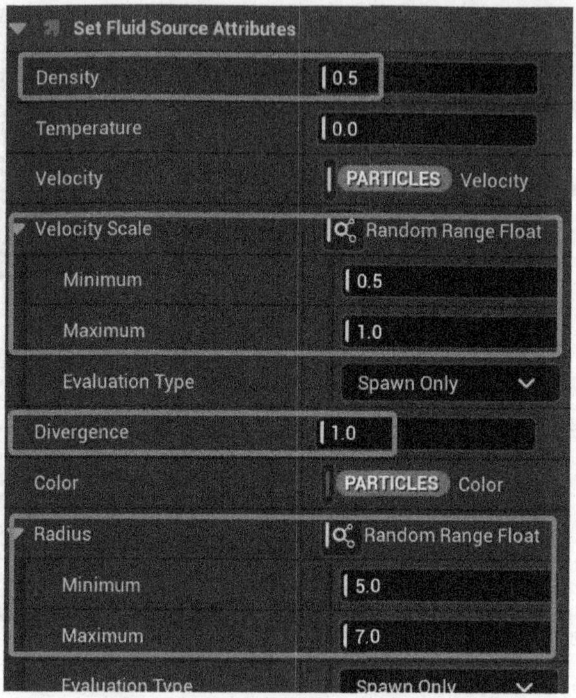

Figure 8.35 - Set Fluid Source Attributes module settings

6. Disable the **Sprite Renderer** and run the simulation (*Alt* + *S*) to test the smoke. If you see smoke emitting from the explosion, pat yourself on the back for a job well done. Save your project.

Now that Chaos Destruction is integrated with Niagara Fluids, the wall explosion is already working. Below are my recommended settings to get a better-looking effect:

- In **Minimal Emitter** settings, change the following:
  - Add **Curl Noise Force** and set **Noise Strength** to `150` and **Noise Frequency** to `40`
  - Add the **Drag** module
- In **Grid3D_Gas_Master_Emitter** settings, change the following:
  - Under the **Simulation** tab:
    - **Resolution Max Axis** = `350~400`
    - **Pressure Solve Iterations** = `12`
    - **Density Buoyancy** = `0`
    - **Dissipation Rate** = `1.5`

- Under the **Forces** tab:
  - Enable **Initial Turbulence**
  - **Turbulence Gain** = 10
  - **Enable Turbulence** = 1
- Under the **Collision** tab:
  - Disable **Z** in **Open Boundary**

> **Note**
>
> Creating a convincing Chaos Destruction shot with Niagara Fluids smoke usually requires some back and forth. You may need to adjust the fracture settings, field strength, debris movement, smoke size, density, and timing several times before the result feels right. Spend some time tweaking these settings and testing the simulation until the destruction and smoke work together for the shot you are trying to create.

You'll find my version of the completed wall destruction Niagara Fluid system, named `NF_WallDestructionDone`, in the `Niagara_Systems` folder for your reference.

Figure 8.36 - Exploding wall with integrated Niagara Fluids smoke

How it works...

In this recipe, we start by learning the basic Chaos Destruction workflow using a simple Sphere before moving on to the wall. When a Static Mesh is converted into a **Geometry Collection**, Unreal Engine treats it as a breakable object that can be fractured into smaller pieces. These pieces are referred to as *bones* in the **Geometry Collection. Fracture Mode** allows us to decide how the object is broken, how many pieces are created, and where extra detail is needed. This is why we added more fracture details to the middle of the wall, where the explosion impact is meant to happen.

The wall does not break just because it has been fractured. It still needs force to activate the destruction. The `FS_MasterField` provides that force, while the `FS_AnchorField` helps hold selected areas in place. In this setup, the center of the wall is allowed to break outward, while the edges remain mostly intact. This gives the destruction a more cinematic shape because the debris is guided instead of simply falling apart everywhere. Settings such as **Damage Threshold**, **Radial Magnitude**, **Directional Magnitude**, and **Torque Mult** help control how easily the wall breaks, how far the fragments travel, and how much they rotate as they move.

Before Niagara can react to the destruction, Chaos needs to generate event data from the simulation:

- **Collision Data** records when fractured pieces hit other surfaces
- **Break Data** records when the **Geometry Collection** breaks apart
- **Trailing Data** tracks fragments as they move after breaking

These event types give Niagara useful information about where particles should appear, when they should spawn, and how they should follow the debris movement.

This is why we enable **Generate Collision** Data, **Generate Break** Data, and **Generate Trailing Data** in the **Project Settings**. We then enable **Notify Breaks, Notify Collisions**, and **Notify Trailing** on the **Geometry Collection** so this specific wall can send those events during simulation. Once these events are available, Niagara can read the Chaos data and use it to spawn smoke from the moving wall fragments.

The Niagara Fluids smoke pass is driven by Chaos event data. By enabling Chaos collision, break, and trailing data, the fractured wall can communicate with Niagara. The **Spawn From Chaos** and **Apply Chaos Data** modules allow the Niagara emitter to spawn particles based on the wall fragments as they move and fall. These particles then become the source for the **Grid3D_Gas_Master_Emitter**, which turns the data into volumetric smoke.

The **Set Fluid Source Attributes** module controls how much smoke is generated and how it behaves inside the fluid simulation. **Density** affects the thickness of the smoke, **Velocity Scale** helps it follow the movement of the debris, **Divergence** adds outward push, and **Radius** controls the size of each smoke source. The **Grid3D_Gas_Master_Emitter** then simulates the final smoke volume, giving the destruction more weight, atmosphere, and impact.

The final result works because Chaos creates the physical break, while Niagara Fluids adds the cinematic smoke layer that sells the force of the impact.

There's more...

Here's a quick way to turn smoke into a fiery explosion. Follow these steps:

1. In the Niagara Editor, select the **Grid3D_Gas_Master_Emitter**, then in the **Render** tab, change **Render Temperature** to **Black Body**.
2. To decrease the brightness of the fire, in the **Source** tab, decrease **Temperature Scale** to `2.0`.
3. In the **Simulation** tab, under **Attributes**, ensure **Temperature** is enabled.

If everything is configured correctly, the smoke can be rendered as fire, producing a more explosive-looking effect, as shown in *Figure 8.37*:

Figure 8.37 - Converting smoke into a fiery explosion

See also

- For more information about **Chaos Destruction**, **Geometry Collections**, **Fracture Mode**, and **Physics Fields**, refer to the Unreal Engine documentation: `https://dev.epicgames.com/documentation/unreal-engine/chaos-destruction-in-unreal-engine`. These resources are useful if you want to understand the core Chaos workflow in more detail and explore how fractured objects can be controlled in cinematic destruction shots.

- For more information about the **type of Fractures**, refer to the Unreal Engine documentation: `https://dev.epicgames.com/documentation/unreal-engine/fracturing-geometry-collections-user-guide#usethefracturetools`.

Caching Chaos Destruction for repeatable cinematic playback

In the previous recipe, we created a wall explosion using Chaos Destruction and enhanced it with Niagara Fluids smoke. The result works well as a destruction effect, but for cinematic production, simply simulating the destruction in real time is not always enough. Chaos simulations can be heavy to play back, and the result may be difficult to scrub, review, time, and render consistently in **Sequencer**.

In this recipe, we will cache the Chaos Destruction simulation so it can be played back more reliably during shot work. **Caching** allows the destruction to behave more like a recorded performance, making it easier to control the timing, review the debris movement, adjust the camera, and prepare the shot for final rendering.

We will also add the cached destruction into **Sequencer**, so the wall break can be timed properly within the shot. This is especially useful when you need the destruction to happen at a specific frame, line up with camera movement, or work together with other effects, such as smoke, dust, sound, or lighting changes.

This workflow helps turn a live physics simulation into a repeatable cinematic element that can be played back consistently every time you review or render the sequence.

Getting ready

This recipe continues directly from the *Exploding a wall with Chaos Destruction and Niagara Fluids smoke* recipe, where we created the wall destruction setup using Chaos Destruction and Niagara Fluids smoke. I strongly recommend completing that recipe first before continuing, as we will use the same level, fractured wall, field setup, and simulation as the starting point for caching the destruction in **Sequencer**.

How to do it...

With the `WallDestruction` level open, follow these steps:

1. In the **Outliner**, select `NF_WallDestruction`. In the **Details** panel, search for `Visibility`, then uncheck **Visible**. This will hide the Niagara Fluids smoke effect temporarily, allowing us to focus only on the Chaos wall destruction.

2. Select the wall and from the top menu, click **Actor | Chaos | Create Chaos Cache**.

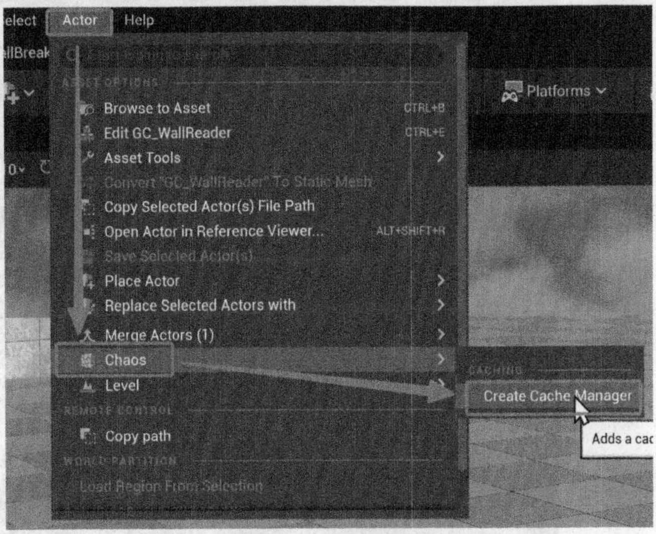

Figure 8.38 - Accessing the Chaos Cache Manager

3. When prompted, save it as **WallChaosCacheCollection** in the `Chaos` folder.
4. The Cache Manager will appear in the **Outliner** as **ChaosCacheManager0**. Select it, then in its **Details** panel, scroll down to the **Caching** section to ensure the **Cache Mode** is set to **RECORD**.

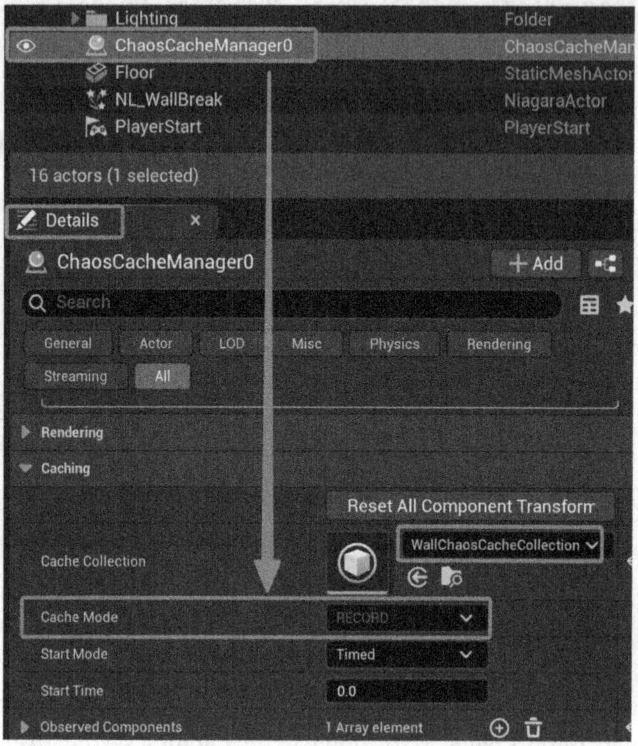

Figure 8.39: Setting Cache Mode to Record

5. All you need to do now is press *Alt* + *S* to simulate the explosion. Once the simulation has been completed, press the *Esc* key to stop the simulation.
6. Back in the **ChaosCacheManager0**'s **Cache Mode**, change from **RECORD** to **Static Pose**. Using the **Start Time**, drag forward and backward to see the cached simulation. How cool!

Figure 8.40 - Testing the recorded cache

7. Next, let's add it to the **Sequencer**. Create a new Level Sequence, rename it as `LS_WallDestruction`.
8. Select **ChaosCacheManager0**, drag it into the **Sequencer**, click the + sign and select **Start Time**.

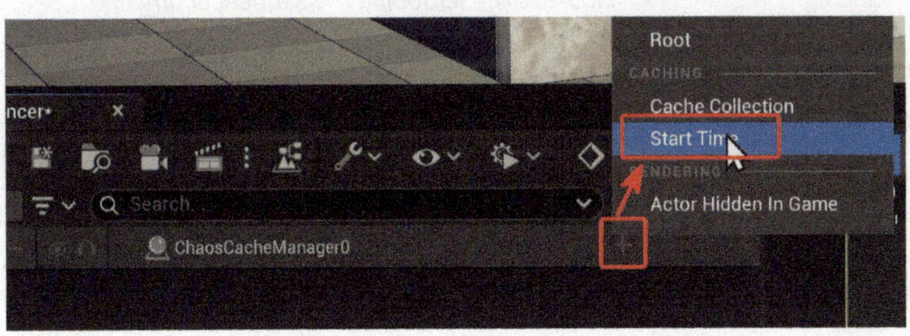

Figure 8.41: Adding the ChaosCacheManager to the Sequencer

9. Make a first keyframe at Frame **0**, then drag the Playhead to, say, 5 seconds and drag **Start Time** until the end of the simulation. You can now scrub back and forth without any lag.

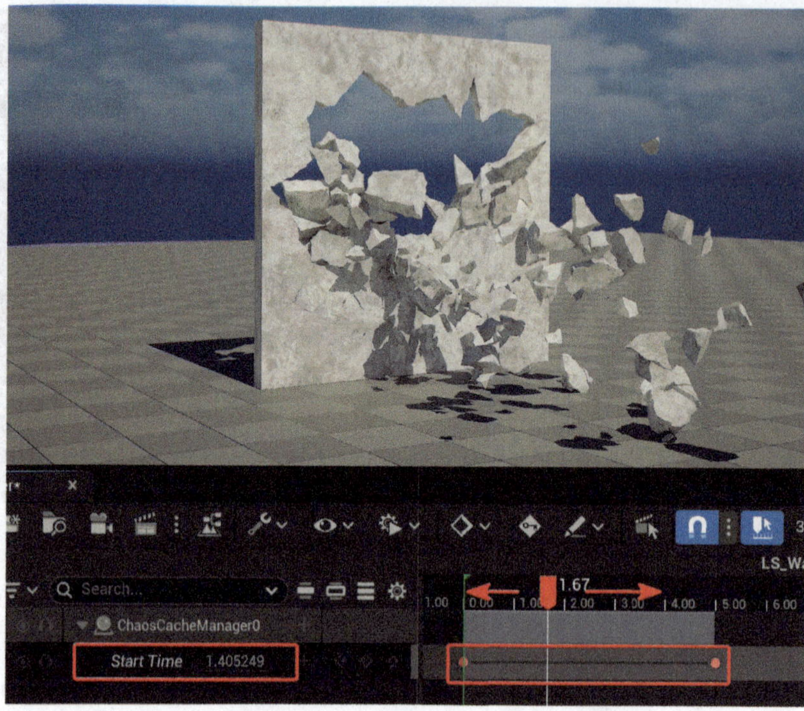

Figure 8.42 - Scrubbing the Sequencer timeline

10. Save your project.

With the Chaos Destruction cached and added to the **Sequencer**, the wall break is now much easier to control as a cinematic shot. You can scrub through the destruction, adjust the camera timing, and even create bullet-time style moments where the debris appears frozen or slowed down in mid-air. This makes the destruction feel less like a live simulation and more like a controlled performance that can be shaped for the final render.

How it works...

Chaos Destruction is a live physics simulation, which means it can be difficult to scrub, review, and time precisely during cinematic work. By creating a **Chaos Cache**, we record the wall destruction simulation and store it as a reusable playback asset. This turns the destruction from a live simulation into something closer to a recorded performance. Once cached, the wall break can be reviewed without having to recalculate physics every time.

The **Chaos Cache Manager** is responsible for recording and playing back the simulation. When the **Cache Mode** is set to **Record**, Unreal Engine captures the movement of the fractured wall pieces during simulation. After recording, switching the cache to **Static Pose** allows you to scrub through the cached result using the **Start Time** value. This makes it much easier to inspect the debris movement, find the best timing, and check the shape of the destruction at different moments.

Adding the **Chaos Cache Manager** to **Sequencer** gives you cinematic control over the destruction timing. By keyframing the **Start Time** value, you can decide when the wall break begins, how quickly it plays, and where it pauses or slows down.

This is useful for timing the destruction with camera movement, lighting, smoke, dust, sound, or other effects. It also allows bullet-time style shots, where debris can appear slowed down, suspended, or frozen in mid-air. Instead of hoping the simulation behaves correctly during every playback, you can shape the cached destruction like any other animated element in the shot.

Creating Chaos Cloth flag/curtain for close-up shots

In this recipe, you will create a simple flag using **Chaos Cloth**. After working with destruction and cached simulations in the previous recipes, we will now move to a softer type of physics simulation: cloth movement. A flag moving in the wind may seem like a small detail, but in a cinematic shot, subtle cloth motion can add realism, atmosphere, and life to the scene.

We will keep the setup simple and practical by using a flag mesh, applying Chaos Cloth, fixing one side of the cloth so it stays attached, and allowing the rest of the mesh to move naturally. This workflow is useful for flags, banners, hanging fabric, curtains, and background set dressing in cinematic environments.

The goal is not to create a complex cloth simulation, but to understand the basic Chaos Cloth workflow and how it can be used to add believable motion to close-up or atmospheric shots.

Getting ready

For this recipe, we will use the **Basic Level Template** that comes with Unreal Engine 5. This keeps the scene simple so we can focus on building, timing, and previewing the effect without extra distractions. Once the effect is working, you can place it into any cinematic scene and trigger it from **Sequencer** at the exact frame needed.

How to do it...

Let's start by creating a new basic level:

1. Go to **File | New Level**. From the pop-up panel, choose the **Basic template**, and click **Create**. Save the Level as `ChaosCloth`.
2. Press the *G* key to hide all the overlay icons. In the **Content Browser**, inside the `Chaos` folder, create another folder named `Cloth`.

3. Press the *1* key on the keyboard to reset the view. We will create the flag shape in **Modeling Mode**.

4. Select the **Chaos | Cloth** folder, then from the top left drop-down, select **Modeling Mode** (or use *Shift* + *5*).

> **Note**
>
> **Modeling Mode** in Unreal Engine allows you to create, edit, and modify simple 3D meshes directly inside the editor without needing to go into a separate 3D application. It includes tools for creating basic shapes, editing geometry, adding subdivisions, sculpting, and preparing meshes for different workflows. In this recipe, we use **Modeling Mode** to quickly create a subdivided rectangle that will become the base mesh for the Chaos Cloth flag.

5. At the bottom of the **Modeling Mode**, for **New Asset Location**, select **Current Folder**. This will create the shape we're making in the `Cloth` folder.

6. Click the **Create** icon and from the shape selection, select **Rectangle**.

Figure 8.43 - Creating a rectangle in Modeling Mode

7. Set **Width** to `100` and **Depth** to `200`. Set both **Width Subdivisions** and **Depth Subdivisions** to `40`. Click anywhere in the Viewport and click on **Accept**.

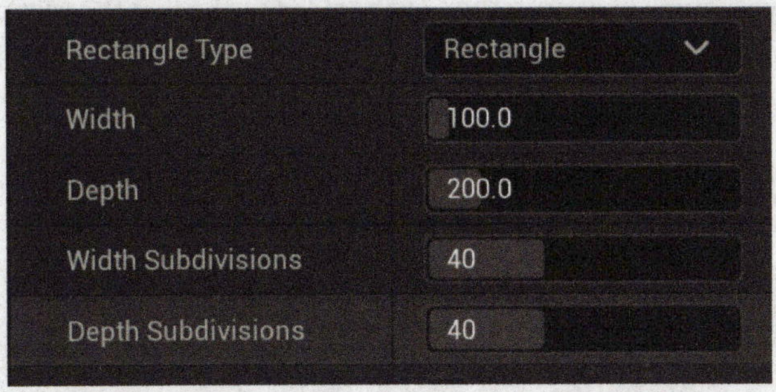

Figure 8.44 - Setting rectangle Width, Depth, and Subdivisions

8. You now have a subdivided rectangle ready to be converted into a cloth. You can confirm this by switching to the **Wireframe** view from the toolbar drop-down.

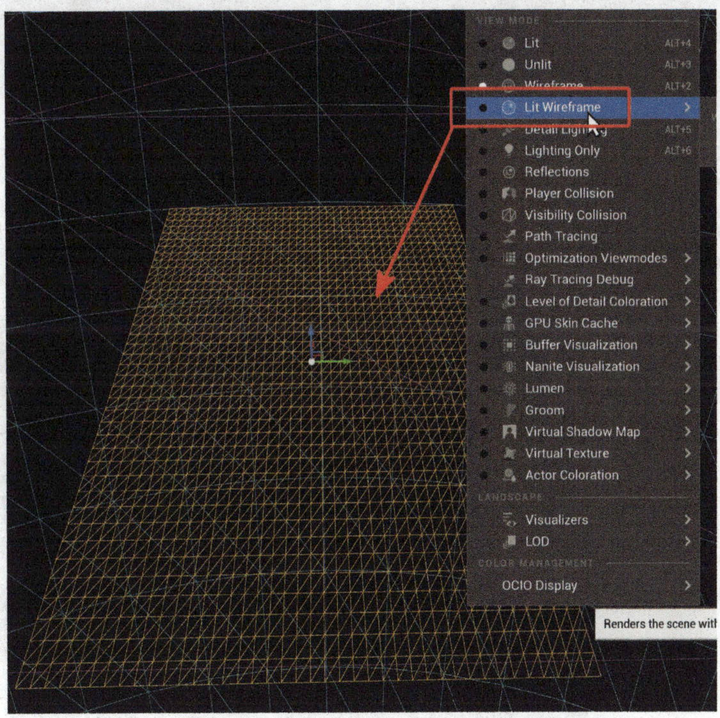

Figure 8.45 - Checking the Rectangle mesh

9. Switch back to the **Selection Mode** and if you're in the **Wireframe** mode, switch back to **Lit view** (or use *Alt* + *4*).

10. Let's have a quick peek into the Cloth folder to check if the rectangle exists. Select the rectangle and rename it to SM_Flag. We will need to convert SM_Flag to a Skeletal Mesh.

11. Right-click on SM_Flag, select **Convert to Skeletal Mesh**. In the pop-up panel, click **Convert**.

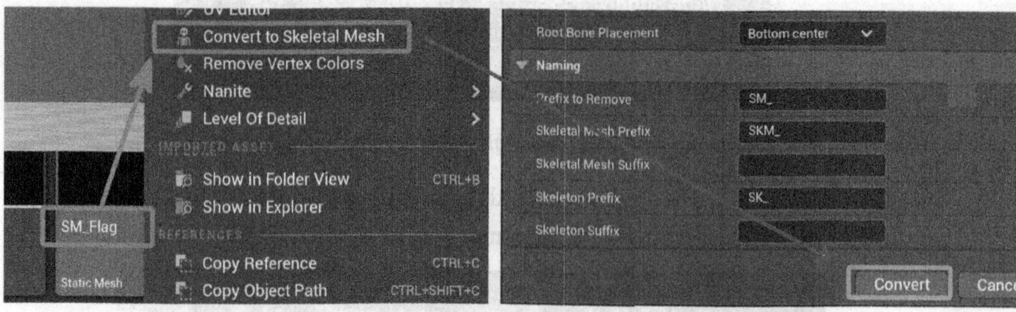

Figure 8.46 - Converting the Rectangle into a Skeletal Mesh

12. You now have two new assets, SKM_Flag and SK_Flag. We're only interested in SKM_Flag. Save the project and double-click on SKM_Flag.

13. In the Skeletal Mesh Editor, look for the **Clothing** panel; if not, you'll find it in **Window** | **Clothing**.

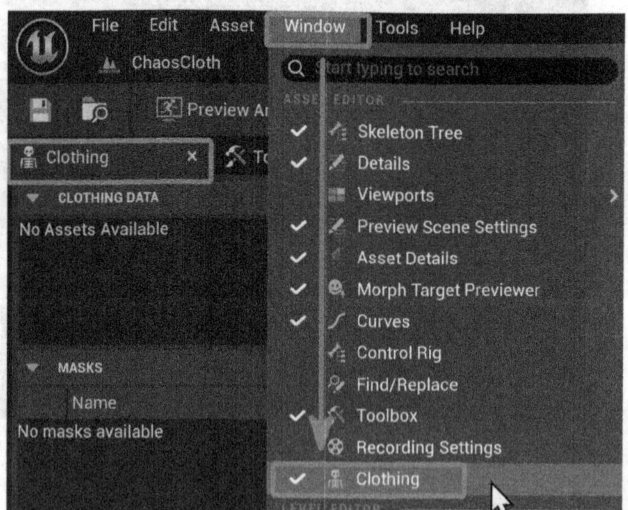

Figure 8.47 - Adding the Clothing panel

14. In the Viewport, right-click on the rectangle and select **Create Clothing Data from Selection** and click **Create.**

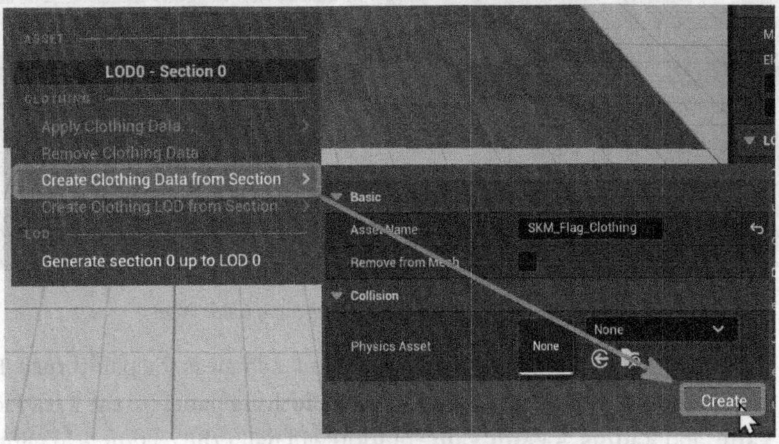

Figure 8.48 - Creating the Clothing Data

15. Repeat the process, this time select **Apply Clothing Data** and choose `SKM_Flag_Clothing_0 - LOD0`.

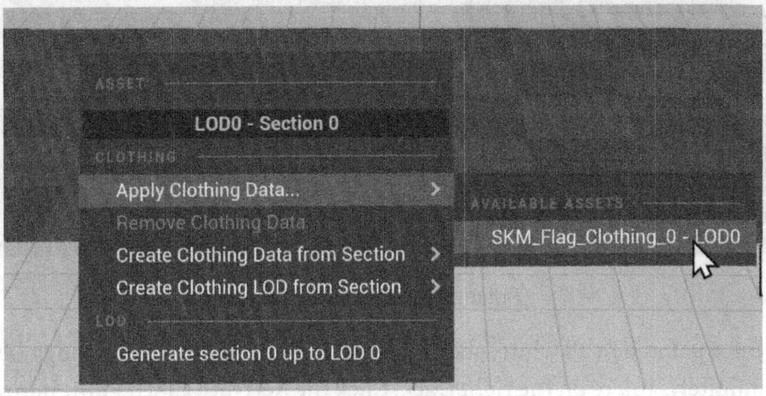

Figure 8.49 - Applying the Clothing Data

16. In the **Clothing** panel, select `SKM_Flag_Clothing_0`, then from the top menu select **Activate Cloth Paint**. Once clicked, it will show **Deactivate Cloth Paint**, and the rectangle will turn *pink*.

Figure 8.50 - Activating Cloth Paint

17. Hover the mouse on the rectangle. The circular shape is the paintbrush. But before going ahead to paint the rectangle, in the **Clothing** panel (to the left), look for **Paint Value** and **Radius**. A **Paint Value** of 1000 will paint the rectangle in white and vice versa. **Radius** will change the brush size.
18. Change **Radius** to `50` and set **Paint Value** to `1000` – yes `1000`! I found that painting at a maximum of 100 will give undesired results. Start painting the rectangle.

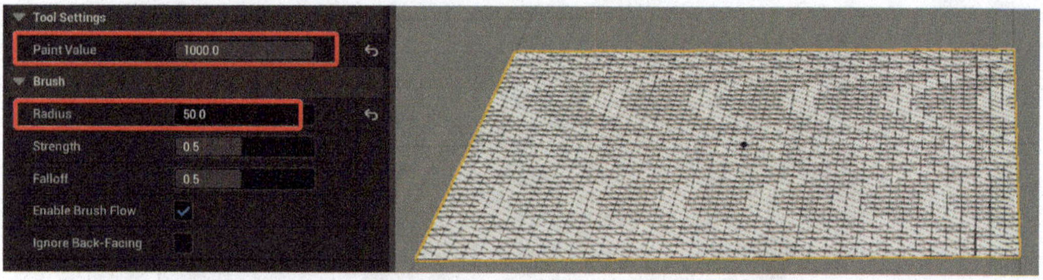

Figure 8.51 - Setting Paint Value and Brush Radius

19. Once painted in all white, click **Deactivate Cloth Paint**; the rectangle should fall infinitely. You're on the right track. Click the **Activate Cloth Paint** button again.
20. This is where you need to decide how the flag will be tethered to the pole. If you are going for the whole left edge, then that edge needs to be painted in *black* (paint value = 0); otherwise, just paint the *left top* and *bottom tip* with black, as shown in *Figure 8.52*.

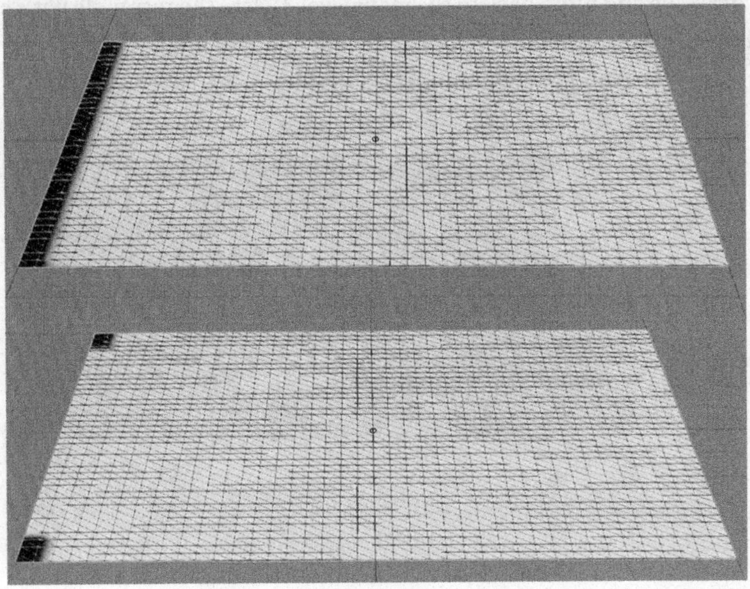

Figure 8.52 - Painting the flag edges with black

21. Now, when you click **Deactivate Cloth Paint,** only the right side of the flag should collapse while the other end stays intact.

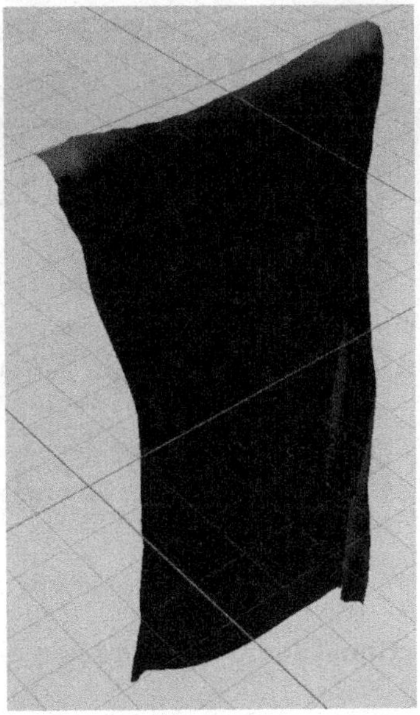

Figure 8.53 - Flag with correct behavior

22. Click **Save** and jump back to the main level. Delete the rectangle if it's still there, then drag `SKM_Flag` into the level. Position and rotate so it is upright and forward-facing. From the `Material` folder, drag `MI_FlagBlack` onto the rectangle.

Figure 8.54 - Assigning the material to the flag

23. Click the **Simulate** button, or press *Alt* + *S*, to test the flag. The flag should collapse naturally while one side remains tethered, showing that the painted fixed area is holding the cloth in place. Let's add wind.

24. From the **Add to Project** menu, search for `wind` and select **Wind Directional Source**.

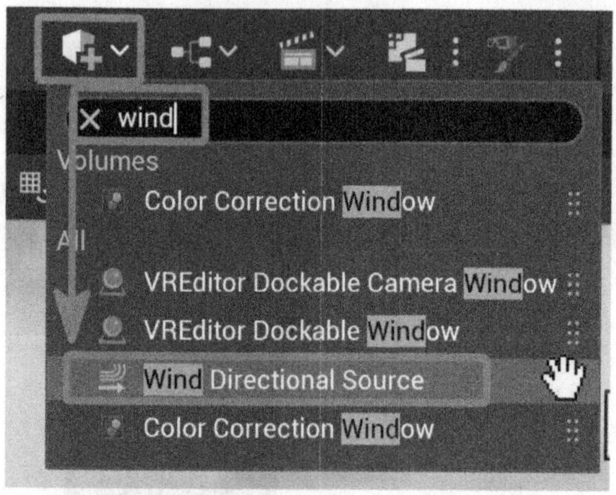

Figure 8.55 - Adding the Wind component

25. Point the **Wind Directional Source**'s *blue arrow* to the right and set its **Strength** and **Speed** to `10.0`.

Figure 8.56 - Setting wind direction, strength, and speed

26. Click **Simulate** or press *Alt + S*. You should now have a realistic wavy flag. Congratulations! For the flagpole, I added a Cylinder from the **Shapes** menu, shaped it to look like a pole, positioned it close to the flag, and used a material from the **Starter Content** (see *Appendix* for details)—easy peasy!

Figure 8.57 - The completed flag (left); examples of various flags (right)

At this stage, you have created a simple Chaos Cloth flag that can move naturally in the scene. Even though this is a basic setup, the same workflow can be adapted for many cinematic cloth elements, such as banners, curtains, hanging fabric, torn cloth, table covers, sails, capes, or background set dressing.

The key idea is to control which parts of the mesh are fixed and which parts are allowed to simulate. Cloth simulation may be subtle, but it can add life, motion, and atmosphere to a shot, especially in close-ups or quiet cinematic moments where small details matter.

If you want to use the flag in a cinematic shot, you can add it to **Sequencer** using the same idea covered in the previous recipe on repeatable playback. This allows you to control when the flag simulation appears in the shot, review the movement with the camera, and prepare it for cinematic rendering. Once the cloth motion works well, treat it like any other shot element and judge the result through the camera.

How it works...

In this recipe, we created a simple flag by starting with a subdivided rectangle mesh. The subdivisions are important because cloth needs enough geometry to bend and deform smoothly. A plane with too few subdivisions will not move like fabric, because there are not enough points for the cloth simulation to solve. By creating a rectangle with many subdivisions, we give Chaos Cloth enough surface detail to create soft folds and waving motion.

The flag mesh is then converted into a **Skeletal Mesh** because the Chaos Cloth workflow needs a mesh format that can support cloth data. Creating and applying **Clothing Data** tells Unreal Engine which part of the mesh should behave as cloth. **Cloth Paint** (using a brush with a white paint value of `1000` and a black paint value of `0`) is then used to control which areas are fixed and which areas are free to simulate. In a flag setup, one side needs to stay attached to the pole, while the rest of the cloth is allowed to move.

The painted fixed area acts like the anchor point of the flag. When the simulation runs, the free part of the cloth reacts to gravity and wind, while the fixed side remains held in place. This is the same core idea used for many cloth setups: some areas are pinned, and other areas are allowed to move. By changing the painted areas, you can create different cloth behaviors, such as hanging curtains, banners, sails, table covers, torn fabric, or background drapery.

The **Wind Directional Source** adds motion to the flag by pushing the cloth in a chosen direction. Adjusting the wind **Strength** and **Speed** changes how active or subtle the fabric movement feels. For cinematic shots, the goal is usually not extreme movement, but believable motion that adds life to the frame. A gently moving flag, curtain, or hanging fabric can make a close-up shot feel more atmospheric and less static.

9

Unlock the Code/Resource Bundle and the PDF Version

Your copy of this book includes the following exclusive benefits:

Complete Code Bundle

Download the full source code for this book's examples and projects.

DRM-Free PDF Version

Download DRM-free PDF and ePub copies of this book.

7-Day Packt Library Access

Get 7-day unlimited access to 8,000+ books and videos. No credit card required.

Available for first-time Packt+ trial users only.

Next-Gen Reader Access

Read this book on Packt Reader with progress sync, dark mode and note-taking.

Follow this guide to unlock them. The process takes only a few minutes and only needs to be completed once.

Unlock this book's free benefits in three easy steps

Step 1

Have your purchase invoice ready for *step 3*. If you have a physical copy, scan it using your phone and save it as a PDF, JPG, or PNG.

For more help on finding your invoice, visit `https://www.packtpub.com/unlock-benefits/help`.

> Note
>
> **Note**: If you bought this book directly from the Packt website, no invoice is required. After *step 2*, you can access your exclusive content right away.

Step 2

Scan the QR code or go to `packtpub.com/unlock`.

On the page that opens (similar to *Figure 9.1* on desktop), search for this book by name and select the correct edition.

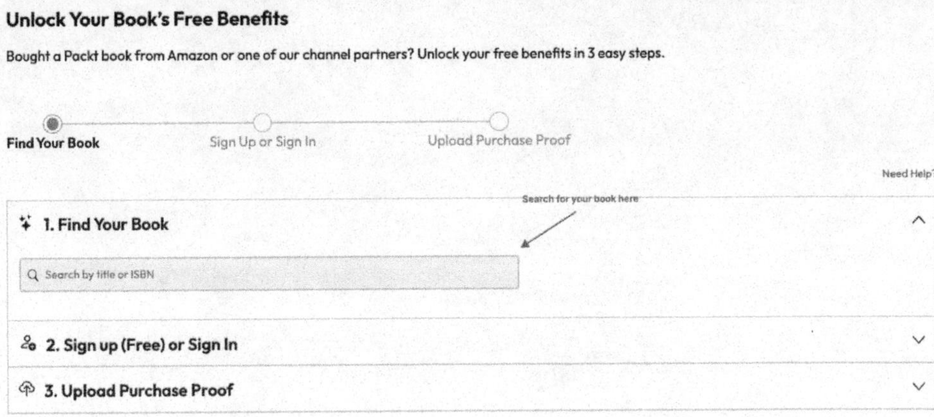

Figure 9.1 - Packt unlock landing page on desktop

Step 3

After selecting the book, sign in to your Packt account or create one for free. Then, upload your invoice (PDF, PNG, or JPG, up to 10 MB). Follow the on-screen instructions to finish the process.

Need help?

If you get stuck and need help, visit `https://www.packtpub.com/unlock-benefits/help` for a detailed FAQ on how to find your invoice and more. This QR code will take you to the help page.

> Note
>
> **Note**: If you are still facing issues, reach out to `customercare@packt.com`.

Appendix

Transferring Starter Content to Newer Unreal Engine Versions

In several recipes in this book, we use Unreal Engine's **Starter Content** for simple materials, meshes, and test assets. These assets are useful because they allow us to focus on the VFX workflow without spending extra time creating or importing custom content.

If you are using Unreal Engine 5.6 or an earlier version, **Starter Content** may already be available when creating a new project. However, in newer Unreal Engine versions, such as 5.7 and beyond, **Starter Content** may not be included in the same way during installation or project creation. Because of this, some of the materials or assets referenced in the book may not appear in your project by default.

This appendix shows a simple way to transfer **Starter Content** from an Unreal Engine 5.6 or earlier project into a newer Unreal Engine project. Once copied, you can continue following the book using the same materials, meshes, and folders used in the recipes.

Getting ready

Before you begin, make sure you have access to an Unreal Engine 5.6 or earlier project that already contains the `Starter Content` folder. You will also need the newer Unreal Engine project where you want to use those assets.

For safety, it is a good idea to close Unreal Engine before copying folders manually and always keep a backup of your project before moving content between versions. Once the **Starter Content** has been transferred, reopen your project and check that the assets appear correctly in the **Content Browser**.

How to do it

1. Close all instances of the Unreal Engine Editor.
2. Open Windows Explorer and browse to `C:\Program Files\Epic Games\UE_5.6`. Then open another window and browse to `C:\Program Files\Epic Games\UE_5.7` (or `5.8`). Arrange them as shown in the following figure:

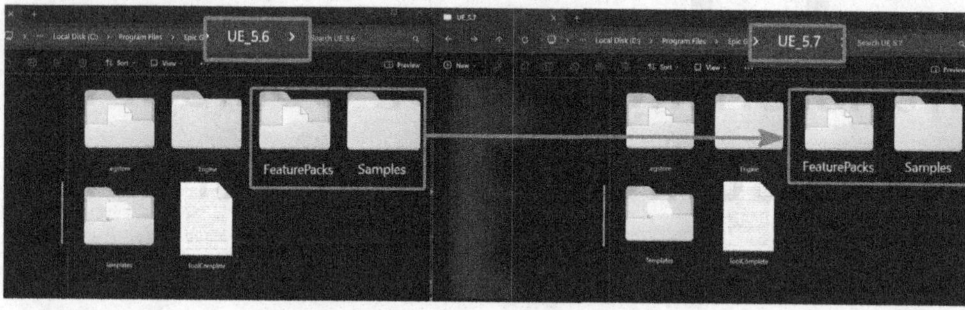

Figure Appendix.1 - Arranging the folders

3. Drag the `FeaturePacks` and `Samples` folders from `UE_5.6` to the `UE_5.7` (or `5.8`) to copy them. On some occasions, `FeaturePacks` may not be available. In that case, just copy the `Samples` folder.
4. Now open your project, and the **Starter Content** will be available in your project.

<packt>

packtpub.com

Subscribe to our online digital library for full access to over 7,000 books and videos, as well as industry leading tools to help you plan your personal development and advance your career. For more information, please visit our website.

Why subscribe?

- Spend less time learning and more time coding with practical eBooks and Videos from over 4,000 industry professionals
- Improve your learning with Skill Plans built especially for you
- Get a free eBook or video every month
- Fully searchable for easy access to vital information
- Copy and paste, print, and bookmark content

At www.packtpub.com, you can also read a collection of free technical articles, sign up for a range of free newsletters, and receive exclusive discounts and offers on Packt books and eBooks.

Other Books You May Enjoy

If you enjoyed this book, you may be interested in these other books by Packt:

Reimagining characters with Unreal Engine MetaHuman Creator, Second Edition

Brian Rossney

ISBN: 9781806024681

- Create your own bespoke character with Metahumans Creator directly in UE5
- Develop custom faces based on real people
- Utilize Blueprints to take control of digital characters
- Retarget animations using the retargeter
- Use DeepMotion and Live Link for complete body and face animation
- Use the Control Rig to refine animations with rough camera blocking
- Set up a Camera for Camera Tracking using an iPhone and a webcam using the Take Recorder
- Export and render your character animation using simple and professional settings for compositing and grading

VFX Made Easy with Houdini, First Edition

Alasgar Hasanov

ISBN: 9781835882917

- Understand Houdini's UI, node-based workflow, and procedural fundamentals
- Build and organize procedural models and flexible assets
- Design particle systems, from emitters and forces to simulation settings
- Create pyro FX, including smoke, fire, and explosions
- Simulate rigid bodies, destruction, and FLIP fluids, such as water and splashes
- Apply materials, textures, and shaders to light and render with Karma
- Improve efficiency with best practices for workflow, optimization, and production

Packt is searching for authors like you

If you're interested in becoming an author for Packt, please visit `authors.packt.com` and apply today. We have worked with thousands of developers and tech professionals, just like you, to help them share their insight with the global tech community. You can make a general application, apply for a specific hot topic that we are recruiting an author for, or submit your own idea.

Share your thoughts

Now that you've finished *Unreal Engine 5 VFX Cookbook*, we'd love to hear your thoughts! Scan the QR code below to go straight to the Amazon review page for this book and share your feedback or leave a review on the site that you purchased it from.

https://packt.link/r/1836209053

Your review is important to us and the tech community and will help us make sure we're delivering excellent quality content.

Index

P

R

S

U

V

W

Made in the USA
Monee, IL
15 September 2026

63035038R00214